AutoCAD® 2000 For Dummies

W9-BEK-536

Sheet

Ten Top AutoCAD 2000 Dialog Boxes

Command	Dialog Box Name	Purpose
ADCenter	DesignCenter	Copy named objects (layers, block definitions, etc.) between drawings; search for drawings
Dimstyle	Dimension Style Manager	Set options for dimensioning; includes preview of the options' effect
DSettings	Drafting Settings	Control snap and grid, tracking, and object snaps
Insert	Insert	Insert a block
LAyer	Layer Properties Manager	Create, set options for layers; use Object Properties toolbar instead for most functions
mText	Mulitline Text Editor	Create and edit multi-line text strings; apply special formatting to characters
PLOT	Plot	Control plot devices, plot settings, layouts, and page setups; preview plots; plot
PROPERTIES	Properties	Set options such as color, layer, linetype, thickness; additional options depend on the type of object selected
UNits	Drawing Units	Manage and change linear and angular unit settings
VPoint	Viewpoint Presets	Change the viewing angle; used for 3-D objects

Ten Top Commands

Command	Key Options	Purpose
OPEN	Preview; Find File	Find and open drawing files
QSAVE	If not named: "Save As"dialog box	Save currently open file to current name, no options
U	None	Undo last command
Real-time Pan and Zoom	Pan, Zoom	Start and control panning and zooming by right-clicking in the drawing area
Line/PLine	From point/To point	Draw line segments as separate objects/ single object
DimLInear	Dimension points	Draw linear dimensions
Move	Press Enter for second point to specify a relative displacement	Move objects in your drawing
COpy	Enter m for multiple copies	Copy objects in your drawing
Erase	Uses all object selection methods	Get rid of stuff in your drawing
Stretch	What gets stretched	Alter the size of the lines in an object; practice this one!

IDG BOOKS WORLDWIDE

...For Dummies®: Bestselling Book Series for Beginners

AutoCAD® 2000 For Dummies®

Cheat Sheet

Ten Top AutoCAD 2000 New Features

Feature	Benefit	Alert
Multiple Design Environment (MDE)	Work on several drawings at once	Now no screen is truly large enough for AutoCAD
Shortcut menus	Lots more right-click menus guide you to available options	Mouse buttons work differently than in AutoCAD Release 14
AutoCAD DesignCenter	Like a dashboard for copying elements from a drawing	Can take time to find just the right elements
In-place block and xref editing	Don't have to go open other documents	Can be too easy to change a drawing that affects many people
Quick Dimensioning (QDIM)	Makes some dimensioning easier	Much more work needed if you have to use regular dimensioning
True linewidth and color control in drawings	No more mapping colors to linewidths	You may still have to work with legacy print/plot setups
Dimension preview	Preview the effect of options	Still a lot of options to think about
Improved Windows printing	Less hassle with printing	Some printers still need special drivers
Layouts for printing	Create multiple printable views of your model	Can spend more time on style than substance
Improved Web integration	Include content in drawings	Is the Web ready for production use?

Ten Handy Toolbar and Status Bar Buttons

Button	ToolTip	Purpose
	Print Preview	Create on-screen preview of drawing printout
	Match Properties	"Paint" properties from one object onto another
	Distance	Measure distance and angle between points
	Named Views	Create and manage named view areas
	Zoom Window	Zoom by specifying the corners of a window
	Zoom Previous	Return to the previous zoom or pan area
	Rectangle	Draw a rectangular polyline
SNAP	Snap Mode	Toggle snap mode on and off; right-click to change snap spacing and other settings
ORTHO	Ortho Mode	Toggle orthographic mode on and off
OSNAP	Object Snap	Toggle running object snap on and off; right-click to change osnap modes and other settings

...For Dummies®: Bestselling Book Series for Beginners

by Mark Middlebrook
and
Bud Smith

IDG Books Worldwide, Inc.
An International Data Group Company

Foster City, CA ◆ Chicago, IL ◆ Indianapolis, IN ◆ New York, NY

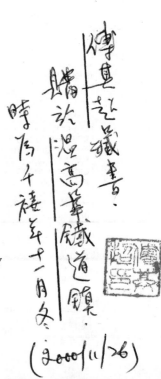

傳真赴藏書、

贈於混高華鐵道鎮、

時為千禧年十一月冬

(2000/11/26)

AutoCAD® 2000 For Dummies®

Published by
IDG Books Worldwide, Inc.
An International Data Group Company
919 E. Hillsdale Blvd.
Suite 400
Foster City, CA 94404
www.idgbooks.com (IDG Books Worldwide Web site)
www.dummies.com (Dummies Press Web site)

Library of Congress Catalog Card No.: 99-63199

ISBN: 0-7645-0558-0

Printed in the United States of America

10 9 8 7 6 5 4 3 2 1

1B/QW/QX/ZZ/IN

Distributed in the United States by IDG Books Worldwide, Inc.

Distributed by CDG Books Canada Inc. for Canada; by Transworld Publishers Limited in the United Kingdom; by IDG Norge Books for Norway; by IDG Sweden Books for Sweden; by IDG Books Australia Publishing Corporation Pty. Ltd. for Australia and New Zealand; by TransQuest Publishers Pte Ltd. for Singapore, Malaysia, Thailand, Indonesia, and Hong Kong; by Gotop Information Inc. for Taiwan; by ICG Muse, Inc. for Japan; by Norma Comunicaciones S.A. for Colombia; by Intersoft for South Africa; by Eyrolles for France; by International Thomson Publishing for Germany, Austria and Switzerland; by Distribuidora Cuspide for Argentina; by Livraria Cultura for Brazil; by Ediciones ZETA S.C.R. Ltda. for Peru; by WS Computer Publishing Corporation, Inc., for the Philippines; by Contemporanea de Ediciones for Venezuela; by Express Computer Distributors for the Caribbean and West Indies; by Micronesia Media Distributor, Inc. for Micronesia; by Grupo Editorial Norma S.A. for Guatemala; by Chips Computadoras S.A. de C.V. for Mexico; by Editorial Norma de Panama S.A. for Panama; by American Bookshops for Finland. Authorized Sales Agent: Anthony Rudkin Associates for the Middle East and North Africa.

For general information on IDG Books Worldwide's books in the U.S., please call our Consumer Customer Service department at 800-762-2974. For reseller information, including discounts and premium sales, please call our Reseller Customer Service department at 800-434-3422.

For information on where to purchase IDG Books Worldwide's books outside the U.S., please contact our International Sales department at 317-596-5530 or fax 317-596-5692.

For consumer information on foreign language translations, please contact our Customer Service department at 1-800-434-3422, fax 317-596-5692, or e-mail rights@idgbooks.com.

For information on licensing foreign or domestic rights, please phone +1-650-655-3109.

For sales inquiries and special prices for bulk quantities, please contact our Sales department at 650-655-3200 or write to the address above.

For information on using IDG Books Worldwide's books in the classroom or for ordering examination copies, please contact our Educational Sales department at 800-434-2086 or fax 317-596-5499.

For press review copies, author interviews, or other publicity information, please contact our Public Relations department at 650-655-3000 or fax 650-655-3299.

For authorization to photocopy items for corporate, personal, or educational use, please contact Copyright Clearance Center, 222 Rosewood Drive, Danvers, MA 01923, or fax 978-750-4470.

is a registered trademark or trademark under exclusive license to IDG Books Worldwide, Inc. from International Data Group, Inc. in the United States and/or other countries.

About the Authors

Mark Middlebrook used to be an engineer but gave it up when he discovered that he couldn't handle a real job. He is now principal of Daedalus Consulting, an independent CAD and computer consulting company in Oakland, California. (In case you wondered, Daedalus was the guy in ancient Greek legend who built the labyrinth on Crete. Mark named his company after Daedalus before he realized that few of his clients would be able to pronounce it and even fewer spell it.) Mark is also a contributing editor for *CADALYST* magazine. *AutoCAD 2000 For Dummies* is his third book on AutoCAD and his second with Bud Smith.

Bud Smith started with computers as a data entry clerk in 1981. He has since worked as a computer programmer, technical writer, computer journalist, and product manager. He is quite at home around computers — even those loaded with programs as complex as AutoCAD. *AutoCAD 2000 For Dummies* is his fourth book about AutoCAD and his twelfth book about computing topics in general. In order to avoid dealing with all the new features in AutoCAD 2000 himself — what he calls the "A2K problem" — he asked Mark Middlebrook to coauthor this version with him.

ABOUT IDG BOOKS WORLDWIDE

Welcome to the world of IDG Books Worldwide.

IDG Books Worldwide, Inc., is a subsidiary of International Data Group, the world's largest publisher of computer-related information and the leading global provider of information services on information technology. IDG was founded more than 30 years ago by Patrick J. McGovern and now employs more than 9,000 people worldwide. IDG publishes more than 290 computer publications in over 75 countries. More than 90 million people read one or more IDG publications each month.

Launched in 1990, IDG Books Worldwide is today the #1 publisher of best-selling computer books in the United States. We are proud to have received eight awards from the Computer Press Association in recognition of editorial excellence and three from Computer Currents' First Annual Readers' Choice Awards. Our best-selling ...For Dummies® series has more than 50 million copies in print with translations in 31 languages. IDG Books Worldwide, through a joint venture with IDG's Hi-Tech Beijing, became the first U.S. publisher to publish a computer book in the People's Republic of China. In record time, IDG Books Worldwide has become the first choice for millions of readers around the world who want to learn how to better manage their businesses.

Our mission is simple: Every one of our books is designed to bring extra value and skill-building instructions to the reader. Our books are written by experts who understand and care about our readers. The knowledge base of our editorial staff comes from years of experience in publishing, education, and journalism — experience we use to produce books to carry us into the new millennium. In short, we care about books, so we attract the best people. We devote special attention to details such as audience, interior design, use of icons, and illustrations. And because we use an efficient process of authoring, editing, and desktop publishing our books electronically, we can spend more time ensuring superior content and less time on the technicalities of making books.

You can count on our commitment to deliver high-quality books at competitive prices on topics you want to read about. At IDG Books Worldwide, we continue in the IDG tradition of delivering quality for more than 30 years. You'll find no better book on a subject than one from IDG Books Worldwide.

IDG BOOKS WORLDWIDE

John Kilcullen
Chairman and CEO
IDG Books Worldwide, Inc.

Steven Berkowitz
President and Publisher
IDG Books Worldwide, Inc.

*Eighth Annual
Computer Press
Awards 1992*

*Ninth Annual
Computer Press
Awards 1993*

*Tenth Annual
Computer Press
Awards 1994*

*Eleventh Annual
Computer Press
Awards 1995*

IDG is the world's leading IT media, research and exposition company. Founded in 1964, IDG had 1997 revenues of $2.05 billion and has more than 9,000 employees worldwide. IDG offers the widest range of media options that reach IT buyers in 75 countries representing 95% of worldwide IT spending. IDG's diverse product and services portfolio spans six key areas including print publishing, online publishing, expositions and conferences, market research, education and training, and global marketing services. More than 90 million people read one or more of IDG's 290 magazines and newspapers, including IDG's leading global brands — Computerworld, PC World, Network World, Macworld and the Channel World family of publications. IDG Books Worldwide is one of the fastest-growing computer book publishers in the world, with more than 700 titles in 36 languages. The "...For Dummies®" series alone has more than 50 million copies in print. IDG offers online users the largest network of technology-specific Web sites around the world through IDG.net (http://www.idg.net), which comprises more than 225 targeted Web sites in 55 countries worldwide. International Data Corporation (IDC) is the world's largest provider of information technology data, analysis and consulting, with research centers in over 41 countries and more than 400 research analysts worldwide. IDG World Expo is a leading producer of more than 168 globally branded conferences and expositions in 35 countries including E3 (Electronic Entertainment Expo), Macworld Expo, ComNet, Windows World Expo, ICE (Internet Commerce Expo), Agenda, DEMO, and Spotlight. IDG's training subsidiary, ExecuTrain, is the world's largest computer training company, with more than 230 locations worldwide and 785 training courses. IDG Marketing Services helps industry-leading IT companies build international brand recognition by developing global integrated marketing programs via IDG's print, online and exposition products worldwide. Further information about the company can be found at www.idg.com.   1/24/99

Dedication

From Bud: This book is for my loving wife, Jacyn, and for the kids, James and Veronica. It's been said that it takes a whole village to raise a child. It also takes a whole family to write a book, and rarely more so than on this one. Thanks, you guys.

From Mark: To Puck and Pretzel, two absolute AutoCAD dummies who never cease to inspire and amuse. It was during walks in the woods with them that I worked out some of the details of these chapters. I'm pretty sure that Puck could learn AutoCAD if only he could figure out how to manipulate a mouse. Pretzel, on the other hand, is too interested in squirrels to bother with mice.

Authors' Acknowledgments

The staff at Dummies Press has helped create something uncommon: a highly approachable and easy to follow book about AutoCAD. As Project Editor, Susan Christophersen has been both patient and persistent. Susan also copyedited the book, introducing to our sometimes tortured, tag-team approach to prose a degree of clarity and correctness that we couldn't have achieved on our own. Ron Morin gave the book a thorough technical edit and pushed us toward consistency and accuracy. Stephen Hayes signed us to the book contract and oversaw the whole process with his usual calm and good humor.

Robert Schutz of Off Broadway Business Systems and Bob McNeel of Robert McNeel & Associates helped Mark learn how to keep the average, beleaguered AutoCAD user in mind. They continue to be great sources of information, friendship, and a good meal.

Publisher's Acknowledgments

We're proud of this book; please register your comments through our IDG Books Worldwide Online Registration Form located at http://my2cents.dummies.com.

Some of the people who helped bring this book to market include the following:

Acquisitions, Editorial, and Media Development

Project Editor: Susan Christophersen
 (Previous Edition: Jennifer Ehrlich)

Acquisitions Editor: Steven Hayes

Technical Editor: Ron Morin

Media Development Manager: Heather Heath Dismore

Editorial Assistants: Jamila Pree, Alison Walthall

Production

Project Coordinator: Tom Missler

Layout and Graphics: Angela F. Hunckler, David, McKelvey, Barry Offringa Brent Savage, Jacque Schneider, Michael A. Sullivan, Brian Torwelle, Dan Whetstine

Proofreaders: Steven Jong, Marianne Santy, Rebecca Senninger

Indexer: Sharon Hilgenberg

Special Help
 Suzanne Thomas

General and Administrative

IDG Books Worldwide, Inc.: John Kilcullen, CEO; Steven Berkowitz, President and Publisher

IDG Books Technology Publishing Group: Richard Swadley, Senior Vice President and Publisher; Walter Bruce III, Vice President and Associate Publisher; Steven Sayre, Associate Publisher; Joseph Wikert, Associate Publisher; Mary Bednarek, Branded Product Development Director; Mary Corder, Editorial Director

IDG Books Consumer Publishing Group: Roland Elgey, Senior Vice President and Publisher; Kathleen A. Welton, Vice President and Publisher; Kevin Thornton, Acquisitions Manager; Kristin A. Cocks, Editorial Director

IDG Books Internet Publishing Group: Brenda McLaughlin, Senior Vice President and Publisher; Diane Graves Steele, Vice President and Associate Publisher; Sofia Marchant, Online Marketing Manager

IDG Books Production for Dummies Press: Michael R. Britton, Vice President of Production; Debbie Stailey, Associate Director of Production; Cindy L. Phipps, Manager of Project Coordination, Production Proofreading, and Indexing; Shelley Lea, Supervisor of Graphics and Design; Debbie J. Gates, Production Systems Specialist; Robert Springer, Supervisor of Proofreading; Laura Carpenter, Production Control Manager; Tony Augsburger, Supervisor of Reprints and Bluelines

Dummies Packaging and Book Design: Patty Page, Manager, Promotions Marketing

◆

The publisher would like to give special thanks to Patrick J. McGovern, without whom this book would not have been possible.

◆

Contents at a Glance

Cartoons at a Glance

By Rich Tennant

page 107

page 9

page 205

page 341

page 357

page 283

Fax: 978-546-7747 • E-mail: the5wave@tiac.net

Table of Contents

· ·

Introduction

● ●

AutoCAD is kind of an amazing thing. It was dreamed up in the early '80s at a time when most people thought that personal computers weren't a big deal, when even someone who liked PCs would hardly dream of pushing them to do something as hard as CAD (which can stand for Computer- Aided Design, Computer-Aided Drafting, or both, depending on whom you talk to). After all, CAD could run only on the most powerful graphical computers of the day. But AutoCAD, to the surprise of many, was a hit from its first day, and it has grown to define a whole new way of creating architectural, mechanical, geographical, and other kinds of drawings.

In its evolution, however, AutoCAD had also grown more complex and some-what difficult to use. AutoCAD Release 2000 finally fixes many problems that had become barriers to efficient use of AutoCAD. AutoCAD 2000 really is easier to use. At the same time, it's packed with features, so there's a lot to learn. (Many of the features in AutoCAD 2000 present easier ways to do exist-ing tasks rather than totally new capabilities. Still, there is indeed a lot to learn.) With this book, you have an excellent chance of creating an attractive, usable, and printable drawing on your first or second try without putting a T-square through your computer screen in frustration.

About This Book

This book is not designed to be read straight through, from cover to cover. It's designed as a reference book so that you can dip in and out of it as you run into new topics. Look for the part that contains the information you want, narrow your search down to a specific chapter, find out what you need to know, and then get back to work. This book is also not designed to be com-pletely comprehensive. Thousands of pages of documentation are required to describe completely how to use AutoCAD, and the resulting proliferation of weighty manuals and third-party books just leaves many people confused. With this book, you're able to get right to work.

How to Use This Book

AutoCAD is bound to leave you wondering what's going on at some point. If you're new to the program, the first time you click an icon and the only response is that a prompt shows up on a command line, you may wonder whether something's wrong with your computer. Slightly more experienced users are likely to trip up on the intricate relationship among setup, drawing, and printing. And sometimes even experts may stumble over the details of paper space, starting to work in 3D, or mastering the completely revamped AutoCAD 2000 Plot dialog box.

Use the table of contents and the index in this book to find the topic that stumps you. Go to that section and read up on the topic. Usually, you find a set of steps, a picture, or a description of how to do the task that's troubling you — and often, you find all three. (How's that for service?) Use that section to get yourself back on track and then close the book and go on.

What's Not in This Book

Unlike many other...*For Dummies* books, this one does tell you to consult the manuals sometimes. AutoCAD is just too big and complicated for a single book to attempt to describe it completely (though some 1,000-page-plus tomes on AutoCAD do try). The manual set is so big that Autodesk doesn't even print all of it; in AutoCAD 2000, several of the manuals are included only in online help, and you have to pay extra for printed versions.

Make no mistake about it: AutoCAD is a beast, a huge program/environment that is an entire world of computing unto itself. So occasionally, this book points you to the manuals for more detailed or advanced information.

This book is also carefully restricted as to which versions of AutoCAD it covers. It covers only AutoCAD 2000, with occasional mention of AutoCAD Release 12, Release 13, and Release 14 — nearly a decade of AutoCAD. This book doesn't talk about the less-capable, lower-cost sibling of AutoCAD, AutoCAD LT, for example, nor AutoCAD-based products such as AutoCAD Architectural Desktop Release 2, except for some general discussion in Chapter 1.

This book focuses on AutoCAD 2000, the newest and easiest-to-use version of the program. This book tells new users how to become productive quickly with AutoCAD 2000; it tells current users who are upgrading from Release 12, Release 13, or Release 14 what's new and how to take advantage of those new features. This book doesn't give a great deal of coverage to higher-end features such as customization, add-on programs that make new features available, and other complicated areas.

Please Don't Read This!

Sprinkled through the book are icons labeled *Technical Stuff.* These icons alert you to discussions of minute detail that are unlikely to concern you unless you're a confirmed AutoCAD techno-nerd. As you slowly advance to expert status, however, you may find yourself going back through the book to read all that technical stuff. (At that point, you may also want to ask your boss for a vacation, because you just may be working a little too hard!)

Who Are — and Aren't — You?

AutoCAD has a large, loyal, and dedicated group of long-time users. This book may not meet the needs of all these long-time members of the AutoCAD faithful. This book is probably not for you if

- ✔ You were using AutoCAD when it still had Versions rather than Releases.

- ✔ You wrote the benchmarks that Autodesk used to test the performance of AutoCAD 2000 while it was being developed.

- ✔ You have lectured at Autodesk University.

- ✔ You founded Autodesk University.

- ✔ You read all those 1,000-page-plus technical tomes about AutoCAD for pleasure.

- ✔ You sent suggestions for changes in AutoCAD 2000 to the AutoCAD Wish List and saw them incorporated in the new release of the program.

- ✔ After your suggestion was incorporated into the program, you sent e-mail to Autodesk explaining how it did it wrong.

If you don't fall into any of these categories, well, this is definitely the book for you.

However, you do need to have some idea of how to use your computer system before tackling AutoCAD — and this book. You need to have a working computer system on which to run AutoCAD and be able to connect it to a monitor, printer, and network, as well as the World Wide Web. If not, pick up *PCs For Dummies,* 6th Edition, by Dan Gookin (from IDG Books Worldwide, Inc.).

You also need to know how to use Windows 98, Windows 95, or Windows NT to copy and delete files, create a subdirectory (the DOS word for it) or folder (the official Windows term), and find a file. You need to know how to use a mouse to select (highlight) or to choose (activate) commands, how to close a window, and how to minimize and maximize windows. If not, run — don't walk — to your nearest bookstore and get IDG Books' *Windows 95 For Dummies,* 2nd Edition, or *Windows 98 For Dummies,* both by Andy Rathbone, or *Windows NT 4 For Dummies* by Andy Rathbone and Sharon Crawford, and try to master some basics before you start with AutoCAD. (At least have those books handy as you start using this book.)

How This Book Is Organized

This book is really well organized. Well, at least it's organized. Well, okay, we drew some circles on the floor, threw scraps of paper with different ideas and topics written on them toward the circles, and organized the book by which scrap landed in which circle.

Seriously, the organization of this book into parts is one of the most important, uh, *parts* of this book. You really can get to know AutoCAD one piece at a time, and each part represents a group of closely related topics. The order of parts also says something about priority; yes, you have our permission to ignore the stuff in later parts until you've mastered most of the stuff in the early ones. This kind of building-block approach can be especially valuable in a program as powerful as AutoCAD.

The following sections describe the parts that the book breaks down into.

Part I: AutoCAD 101

Need to know your way around the AutoCAD screen? Why does AutoCAD even exist, anyway? What are all the different AutoCAD 2000-based products that Autodesk just introduced? Is everything so slooow because it's supposed to be slow, or do I have too wimpy a machine to truly use this wonder of modern-day computing? And why am I doing this stuff in the first place?

Part I answers all these questions — and more. This part also includes what may seem like a great deal of excruciating detail about configuring AutoCAD. But what's even more excruciating is to do your configuration work incorrectly and then feel as though AutoCAD is fighting you every step of the way. With a little setup work done in advance, it won't.

Part II: Let There Be Lines

Now it's time for drawing setup! What could be worse? How about having the printer laugh at you as you make your "witching hour" attempt to print the final version of the drawings due the next day at 9 a.m. (And let us tell you, a

Hewlett-Packard inkjet plotter can slide its ink cartridges back and forth in a rhythm eerily reminiscent of a head-wagging "nyah-nyah nyah-nyah-nyah.") Read this stuff.

This part also contains "real" AutoCAD — drawing two-dimensional lines, circles, rectangles, and so on, all of which become a CAD drawing that represents a real-world design (if you're both lucky and good). After you get these lines and circles, also known as *geometry,* down and find out about the new Object Snap Tracking feature in AutoCAD 2000, you'll undoubtedly want to know how to edit and view your drawing. Or someone else's drawing. Or something. This part has you covered.

Part III: Make Your Drawing Beautiful

AutoCAD has more ways to gussy up a drawing than you could ever think of. And maybe more than you need. First, you need a plot. No, not a plan, a plot — a printout of your drawing. Then add text, dimensions, and hatch patterns to contribute to the appearance of your drawings. This part helps you find your way through the maze of possibilities to a good solution and then tells you how to get the drawing off your screen, out through a printer or plotter, and onto paper where it belongs.

Part IV: Having It Your Way

All right, we admit it: This part is less than perfectly organized. The main relationship between blocks, external references to data, the new DesignCenter in AutoCAD 2000, and 3D is that they're all things you can probably wait to investigate until after you've mastered the basics of making AutoCAD work. They're also powerful features that would be nearly inconceivable in old-style, pencil-and-paper design and drafting. Dip in and out of this part to experiment and do even more neat things with AutoCAD.

Part V: The Part of Tens

Everyone loves lists, unless it's the overdue list at the local library. This part contains pointers to AutoCAD resources, a quick guide to mastery of the AutoCAD command line, and some details on how to use the World Wide Web with AutoCAD. Are the Parts of Ten information-packed nutrition or junk food foisted on the reader by self-indulgent authors? You be the judge.

Part VI: Appendixes

Yes, this book has appendixes, and we'd prefer that you not have them taken out! The appendixes here give you some tips on correctly installing AutoCAD 2000, detailed tables relating paper sizes to drawing scales to AutoCAD settings, and a relentlessly and thoroughly updated glossary of AutoCAD terms.

Icons Used in This Book

Icons, once confined to computer screens, have escaped and are now running amok in the pages of this book. (Yeah, we know that icons started out in print in the first place, but computer people stole them fair and square. Now we writers are getting even.) These icons are like the ones in AutoCAD 2000 except that they're fewer, simpler, easier on the eyes, and used more consistently. (What, us, an attitude problem?) The icons used in this book are described next.

This icon tells you that a pointed insight lies ahead that can save you time and trouble as you use AutoCAD. For example, maybe learning how to type with your nose would help increase your speed in entering commands and moving the mouse at the same time. (And maybe not. . . .)

The Technical Stuff icon points out places where you may find more data than information. Unless you're really ready to find out more about AutoCAD — much more — steer clear of these paragraphs the first time you read a given section of the book.

This icon tells you how to stay out of trouble when living a little close to the edge. Failure to heed its message may have disastrous consequences for you, your drawing, your computer — and maybe even all three.

Remember when Spock put his hand over McCoy's face and implanted a suggestion in his brain that later saved Spock's life? This icon is like that. Helpful reminders of things you already know but that may not be right at the tip of your brain . . . or whatever.

This icon tells you how to do things from the keyboard instead of by using menus, toolbars, or random mouse clicks. The keyboard stuff is usually harder to remember but quicker to use.

This icon points to new stuff in AutoCAD 2000. It's mostly designed for those of you who know AutoCAD pretty well already and just want to find out what's new in this release, but new AutoCAD users starting out their CAD working lives with AutoCAD 2000 may find this stuff interesting, too.

Sometimes we feel the urge to point you to some good information on the Information Superhighway, and this icon lets you know that it's time to grab your wetsuit — you're going surfin'!

A Few Conventions — Just in Case

You probably can figure out for yourself all the information we're about to impart in this section, but just in case you want to save that brain power for AutoCAD, here it is in cold type.

Text you type into the program at the command line, in a dialog box, text box, and so on appears in **boldface type**. Examples of AutoCAD commands and prompts appear in a `special typeface`, as does any other text in the book that echoes a message, a word, or one or more lines of text that actually appear on-screen. (Longer segments also have a shaded background.)

Sidebars also are set off in their own typeface, with a fancy head all their own, and are surrounded by a shaded box, much like this:

This is a sidebar head

And this is how the text in a sidebar appears. Neat, huh? Well, different at least. Hey, two-column text can be pretty nifty all on its own, even without peripheral AutoCAD material to occupy its space! What? You don't buy that? Oh, well, back to our main event, then.

Regarding menus and menu items or commands, if you're told to open a menu or choose a command, you can use any number of methods to do so — pressing a shortcut key combination on the keyboard, clicking the corresponding toolbar button, or clicking the menu or command name with the mouse, highlighting the name by moving over it with the cursor arrow keys, and then pressing Enter — whatever way you're most comfortable with. Sometimes we tell you to do it a certain way because that's how we, as the AutoCAD authorities du jour, think it's done best. But if you already know what we're talking about, feel free to do it your way instead. (And if it doesn't work, of course, you didn't hear this from us.)

Anytime you see a menu name or command name with an underlined letter, such as File, it means that the underlined letter is the Windows shortcut key for that menu name or command. Hold down the Alt key and press the first underlined key to select the menu. Then, continue to hold down the Alt key and press the second underlined key to select the command. (You can let up on the Alt key after you select the menu if you'd like, then press the command's shortcut key to access it. But don't press the Alt key down a second time, or Windows will select a different menu instead of the command you want.) Oh, and often in this book you see phrases such as "choose File⇨Save As from the menu bar." The funny little arrow (⇨) separates the main menu name from the specific command on that menu. In this example, you would open the File menu and choose the Save As command. Again, the underlined letters are the *hot keys* — keys you can press in combination with the Alt key to open menus and activate commands.

AutoCAD has an interesting convention for command-line shortcuts: the shortcut letters appear in capital letters, whereas the rest of the command appears in lowercase. So when you see a sentence like "enter **DimLInear** for a linear dimension," it means "for a linear dimension, enter **DIMLINEAR**, or **DLI** for short, at the command line." Because you will be seeing this convention used AutoCAD's Help files and printed documentation, we used it in this book as well.

Well, that covers the basics. The details — ah, those are yet to come. And believe us when we tell you with the utmost sincerity that you have much to look forward to . . . (cue lightning, thunder, and a low moan from the nether regions of your computer).

Where to Go from Here

If you've read this Introduction, you're probably at least a little bit like us: You like to read. (People who don't like to read usually skip this front matter stuff and scurry to the index to get to exactly, and only, the part they need at that moment.) So take a few more minutes to page through and look for interesting stuff. And pick up a pen and some stick-on notes; the icons and headings in this book are only a start. Personalize your book by circling vital tips, drawing a smiley face if you like a joke, even X-ing out stuff that you disagree with. (And we've hidden plenty of our own opinions in this book, so get those Xs ready.)

Part I

AutoCAD 101

The 5th Wave   By Rich Tennant

It started as a wraparound porch, and then Stuart began learning AutoCAD.

In this part . . .

AutoCAD is more than just another application program, it's a complete environment for design and drafting. So if you're new to AutoCAD, there are several things you need to learn to get off to a good start. These key facts are described in this part of the book.

If you're an experienced AutoCAD user, you'll be most interested in the high points of the new release and a quick look at how to get productive on it fast. All that is here, too. (*Tip:* Look for the 2Kicons for AutoCAD 2000 highlights.)

Chapter 1

Introducing AutoCAD 2000

· ·

In This Chapter

▶ Understanding the AutoCAD advantage

▶ Using AutoCAD and DWG files

▶ Meeting the AutoCAD product family

· ·

*A*utoCAD isn't just another software program. It's actually a drawing environment and a software platform in its own right, although one that's more and more integrated into the Windows environment. AutoCAD, though powerful, is not the easiest program in the world to learn, but it's getting easier with every new release. This book will help close any remaining gap.

In recent years, Autodesk has reduced the number of "flavors" of AutoCAD that it continues to upgrade to two: AutoCAD 2000 and AutoCAD LT 98. The colloquial names for these products are "AutoCAD," or "full AutoCAD," and "LT." These two products continue to be improved and upgraded to new versions. Other versions of AutoCAD for UNIX and Macintosh are stuck on earlier releases — Release 12 for Macintosh, Release 13 for UNIX. These products are basically like a fly with its feet stuck in amber: not dead yet, but not going anywhere, either.

So, Autodesk has committed the future of AutoCAD — and by extension, the future of the company — to Windows. If you're a new user, this will make perfect sense; if you're a long-time AutoCAD user who's upgrading to AutoCAD 2000, most of what you need to learn that's new in this version are Windows-based and Windows-like features that have been added to AutoCAD.

Why AutoCAD?

AutoCAD may seem like a basic fact of life — like gravity or the tendency of the phone to ring as soon as you step into the shower. And AutoCAD has, indeed, been around a long time: since 1982, at the beginning of the PC revolution. It was the very first product of Autodesk, a company founded with a commitment to giving programmers fun things to do. Autodesk initially planned four products for introduction, but AutoCAD was such an instant hit that it quickly became the mainstay of the fledgling company.

AutoCAD is, first and foremost, a program to create printed drawings. The drawings you create with AutoCAD must adhere to standards established long ago for blueprints and other very specific types of drawings that have long been drawn by hand and that, in many cases, are still hand drawn. The up-front investment to use AutoCAD is certainly more expensive than the investment needed to use pencil and paper, and the learning curve is much longer, too; you have to learn to use a computer as well as learn AutoCAD. So why bother?

The key reasons for using AutoCAD rather than pencil and paper are

- ✔ **Exactitude:** When AutoCAD is properly set up (something we discuss extensively in Chapter 4), creating lines, circles, and other shapes of the exactly correct dimensions is easier with AutoCAD than on paper.

- ✔ **Modifiability:** Drawings are much easier to modify on the computer screen than on paper. (Though both traditional and computer-aided drafters are often far too reluctant to consider the possible speed advantages of just giving up on a drawing that's really out of whack and starting over from scratch!)

Figure 1-1 shows a simple building plan on the AutoCAD 2000 screen.

Now that we've established the advantages of computer-aided drafting over pencil and paper for much of the design and drafting work that people want to do, why choose AutoCAD over the competition? Well, AutoCAD is just the starting point of a whole industry of software and hardware products designed to work with AutoCAD. Autodesk has helped this process along immensely by designing a whole series of programming interfaces to AutoCAD that other companies have used to extend the application. (Some of these products are winners, some are dogs, but the point is that Autodesk keeps hacking away at extensibility.) Every new programming interface generates new books, new training courses, new add-ons, and ideas for even more new stuff. As a result, when you compare "whole products" — not just the core program, such as AutoCAD, but all the add-ons, extensions, training courses, books, and so on — AutoCAD doesn't really have much competition.

A note on pricing

Autodesk's software pricing is very high compared to typical "office"-type PC programs, yet quite low compared to prices for some other PC-based and most workstation-based CAD software. Autodesk and its dealers also provide lower prices for volume deals, bundles of products, and network licenses. Contact Autodesk or your dealer for pricing if you're working in an environment that has, or could use, multiple copies of Autodesk products.

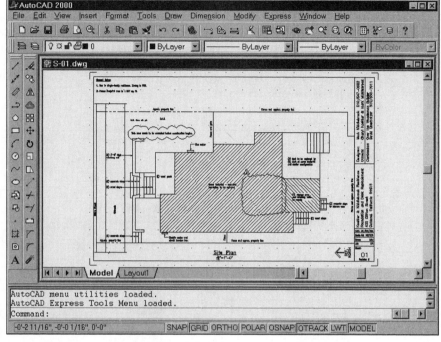

Figure 1-1:
Get ready
to be
ex-site-ed
about the
new look of
AutoCAD
2000.

DWG for Me, See

To take full advantage of AutoCAD in your work environment, you need to be aware of the DWG file format, the file format in which AutoCAD drawings are saved. With almost every release of AutoCAD, the DWG file format is upgraded. Working with AutoCAD is much easier when your coworkers and colleagues in other companies that you exchange drawings with all use the same version of AutoCAD and AutoCAD-related tools. That way, your DWG files, add-on tools, and even the details of your CAD knowledge can be freely mixed and matched among your workgroup and partners.

To reduce the difficulty of sharing files among people with different versions of AutoCAD and encourage people to upgrade, each new version of AutoCAD includes the ability to save a file in earlier versions' form of the DWG file format. For instance, AutoCAD 2000 can save files as Release 14- or Release 13-compatible files. A separate conversion tool allows you to convert AutoCAD 2000 files to Release 12-compatible files. When AutoCAD opens a file from an earlier version of AutoCAD, it reads it in normally, then saves it as an AutoCAD 2000-compatible file unless you specifically "save as" an earlier version of the DWG file format. Figure 1-2 is a conceptual drawing showing how different users must "save as" to meet the needs of the lowest-numbered AutoCAD drawing in their workgroup.

Many programs claim to be *DWG-compatible* — that is, able to convert data to and from AutoCAD's DWG format. The trouble is, achieving this compatibility is a difficult thing to do well, and even a small error in file conversion can have results ranging in severity from annoying to truly disastrous. (With the advent of machines that create parts directly from CAD drawings, you really don't want errors creeping in.) Be wary of trusting your precious DWG files to any kind of file conversion.

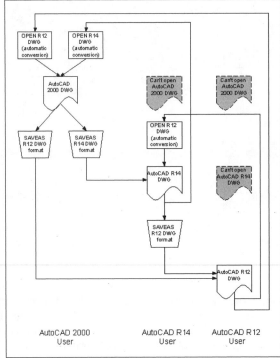

Figure 1-2:
"Save as" in a workgroup with different versions of AutoCAD.

AutoCAD users who are running different versions of AutoCAD have to do extra work to share files. Usually, the people with the lowest-numbered version of AutoCAD have to ask their colleagues to "save as" their version. This greatly increases the pressure on people to upgrade, or not upgrade, together. People on earlier releases are likely to get newer files that they want to use but can't open in their version of AutoCAD; people on later releases are worried that some features will disappear from their drawings when they save the files in an earlier format.

If you're a new user, it's good to know what the "buzz" is around different versions of AutoCAD. Release 12 was basically a DOS release that also had a UNIX version and a Windows add-on; the DOS version was considered a good, solid release. Release 13 included the first "full" Windows version of AutoCAD, as well as DOS and UNIX versions, and is generally considered to be slow and unreliable. Release 14 was the first Windows-only release. It fixed most of the problems of Release 13 and is generally considered another good release. The jury is still out on AutoCAD 2000, but the ability to work with multiple documents simultaneously — previous versions of AutoCAD allowed only one open file at a time(!) — should be enough, all by itself, to make AutoCAD 2000 a winner.

A widely held belief is that even-numbered AutoCAD releases — Release 10, Release 12, Release 14—are good, and odd ones are not as good. From this point of view, calling the latest release AutoCAD 2000 might be seen as a trick to stay on an even number!

If you are new to AutoCAD and are working with seasoned veterans, be aware that they may be very reluctant to upgrade, even from very old versions of AutoCAD. Only about 30–40 percent of existing users upgrade to each new release of AutoCAD. Users of older versions may have work habits, add-on-software, and hardware such as old drawing tablets or pen plotters that they have struggled to integrate into an overall system and that may now all work together in a very efficient way. It may be expensive and a big productivity hit for such people to upgrade. So respect what may seem to be unreasonable stubbornness on your colleagues' part even as you plot and plan to bring them with you into the 21st century.

In general, it's more convenient to have your workgroup or company on the newest possible version of AutoCAD. Each newer version has more features, fewer quirks, and is easier for people who have some experience with Windows to learn than older versions. And your life will be much easier and, frankly, your career will benefit if you can stay up-to-date by working on the latest and greatest version of AutoCAD. However, upgrading is expensive; a new copy of AutoCAD costs $3,750 in the U.S., and upgrading from the previous version costs $500. And even workgroups that say "hang the expense" and upgrade as fast as possible wait until their AutoCAD-based applications and utilities are all upgraded to the new version before they make the move.

Don't be the first one on your block — or, more specifically, in your workgroup or company — to start using AutoCAD 2000. Find out what version of AutoCAD your colleagues are using and get that version; upgrade to AutoCAD 2000 when they do. Unless you're knowledgeable and adventurous, the advantages of having an easier-to-learn program with the latest and greatest features will probably pale beside the difficulties of being "out of synch" with others.

AutoCAD-based applications

Autodesk has expanded AutoCAD into a whole product line of programs with AutoCAD as a base and different, specialized add-ons built on top. As a Release 2000 user, you'll be looking for the AutoCAD 2000-compatible versions of these tools, which can be expected to appear a few months after AutoCAD 2000 itself ships. A brief list of tools that are basically enhanced versions of AutoCAD 2000 includes the following; most of the names are self-explanatory:

- AutoCAD Architectural Desktop Release 2
- AutoCAD Mechanical 2000
- AutoCAD Mechanical Desktop (Mechanical 2000 with additional 3D capabilities)
- AutoCAD Map 2000, MapGuide, and World
- AutoCAD Land Development Desktop, Civil Design, and Survey

To really know your way around the Autodesk product line requires experience you may be lacking. One of the very best ways to get the real insider story on this kind of information is to visit an AutoCAD user group and ask lots and lots of questions. For an up-to-date list, visit *www.autodesk.com/support/resource/usergrps/usergrps.htm*, or follow the User Groups link from the Autodesk home page.

No one needs all the software described in this chapter and many AutoCAD users get by with "plain old" AutoCAD; according to Autodesk, about 50 percent of AutoCAD customers use a third-party application of some sort. However, in sticking with "plain" AutoCAD 2000, you may be missing out on time-saving and productivity-enhancing capabilities that allow you to do better work faster. The trick is to talk to people in your field who you respect and see what tools they use. If they can make a good case for a tool, seriously consider buying it.

Autodesk also makes other tools that work with AutoCAD. Those tools include:

- **AutoCAD LT** — Lower-cost (under $500) version of AutoCAD without 3D or customizability
- **Actrix Technical** — Diagramming product with DWG export capability
- **Autodesk CAD Overlay** — For scanned documents
- **Volo View** — For viewing and marking up DWG files
- **Volo Explorer** — For file sharing
- **3D Studio VIZ** — Lower-end version of 3D Studio

Chapter 2

Le Tour de AutoCAD 2000

*I*t's hard for a recent convert to AutoCAD to appreciate the sense of peace and tranquillity that some long-time users feel when seeing the AutoCAD 2000 screen. If you're new to AutoCAD with AutoCAD 2000, or even if you "joined up" with Release 14 and are now upgrading to the latest release, you've missed the chance to fully appreciate how good AutoCAD 2000 is.

That's because AutoCAD has long, deep roots in the DOS world. For a long time, DOS-based AutoCAD — with ugly screens, clunky dialog boxes, and an odd interaction between the command line, menus, and the mouse — was the only way to go. Even after Windows versions of AutoCAD started to become available more than ten years ago, the DOS version was much faster and the Windows version was pretty funny looking. Because most AutoCAD users care greatly about speed — and very little about the program's appearance — DOS-based AutoCAD lived on well past the time that most PC users had moved to Windows.

The ability to open multiple files simultaneously, new with AutoCAD 2000, is the last major Windows advantage to finally be added to AutoCAD. (And barely. At a pre-launch event, an Autodesk product manager hinted that this feature almost didn't make it into the AutoCAD 2000 release.) The extensive use of right-click menus is a new feature in AutoCAD 2000 and is one way in which AutoCAD has actually moved ahead of many other Windows programs.

The command line is still an odd feature, very un-Windows-like, but Autodesk has improved it further in this release. You can now almost completely avoid typing commands, or use the command line as an accelerator for frequently repeated commands, or, if you're used to it, continue to do a lot of your work there. Those of you who are used to that DOS interface that I just called ugly can find some comfort in the command line.

Like the rest of the book, this chapter is written for someone who has used other Windows programs but has never used AutoCAD before, and also includes pointers and insights for experienced users who are upgrading. If you're new to AutoCAD or new to the Windows version, read this chapter carefully — while running AutoCAD if you can. Try things that are new or seem as though they may be confusing. An hour invested in poking around now can greatly improve your productivity later. And if you still aren't fully used to Windows, check out *Windows 95 For Dummies*, 2nd Edition, by Andy Rathbone; *Windows 98 For Dummies,* by Andy Rathbone, or *Windows NT 4 For Dummies,* by Andy Rathbone and Sharon Crawford (all published by IDG Books Worldwide, Inc.).

If you're experienced with Windows versions of AutoCAD, especially Release 14, most of this chapter is old hat for you. Just scan through it and read the parts marked with the AutoCAD 2000 icon, which indicates something truly new.

Winning with Windows

Finding your way around AutoCAD 2000 can be an odd experience. You recognize from other Windows applications much of the appearance and workings of the program, such as its toolbars and pull-down menus, which you use for entering commands or changing system settings. But other aspects of the program's appearance — and some of the ways in which you work with it — are quite different from nearly any other program.

You can, in many cases, tell the program what to do in at least four ways — the menu bar, the command line, keyboard shortcuts, or right-click menus — none of which is necessarily the best method to use for every task. The experience is much like that of having to act as several different characters in a play; you're likely to forget your lines (whichever "you" you are at the time!) at least every now and then.

Getting AutoCAD installed

One of the most interesting things about past releases of AutoCAD has been getting the program installed correctly. With Windows-specific versions of AutoCAD, this situation has improved considerably. The AutoCAD installation process is easier, is much better integrated with the Windows environment, and is well documented in the AutoCAD 2000 _Installation Guide_ that comes with the product. It describes the installation process, including network installations, hardware locks (for users outside of the U.S. and Canada), the Preferences dialog, and profiles, a new feature as of Release 14 that allows you to customize your AutoCAD setup for multiple users or multiple use scenarios. For example, you could set up seven different profiles and tell AutoCAD to use a different color for the drawing background with each one. Well, maybe you wouldn't want to do that, but you get the picture.

This book assumes that you have AutoCAD installed and running already. If you are having trouble, the _Installation Guide_ is your first resource.

To get started with AutoCAD 2000, focus on using the menus at the top of the screen. These menus enable you to access most of the program's functions and are the easiest-to-remember method of issuing commands. You can safely delay committing to memory the other, faster ways of making AutoCAD do your bidding until after you master these handy little menus.

Touring the menus is a good way to familiarize yourself quickly with the features in AutoCAD 2000. If you're upgrading from Release 14, most of what you see will be familiar, with some welcome additions; if you're upgrading from Release 13 or earlier, be prepared to re-learn much of what you knew. If you're a new AutoCAD user, you'll find more to learn in the AutoCAD menus than in just about any other Windows program you've seen.

The extensive Help system in AutoCAD is another saving grace; expect to spend a great deal of time using it, especially if you don't like referring to printed manuals. Because the AutoCAD Help system is based on Microsoft's widely used Help engine (vrooommm!), you may already know how to use it. If not, what you discover in mastering the AutoCAD 2000 Help system can help you get more out of the Help systems of other Windows programs.

Try looking up something in the Help system for AutoCAD 2000. Then try looking up something in the Help system for Microsoft Windows 95 or NT. You can see that the interface is nearly identical.

Honey, I changed the screen!

The on-screen appearance of AutoCAD is often different for different users' AutoCAD setups. AutoCAD 2000, even more than previous versions, is very easy to *configure* — that is, to modify, change, add to, rebuild, or whatever you want to do to it. (Hey! Maybe you, too, can be an AutoCAD guru, if only you configure it out! Sorry — again.)

The screen shots and descriptions in this chapter refer to the *default* version of AutoCAD — that is, the way the screen looks if you are using the base version of AutoCAD, not a "flavored" version such as Architectural Desktop. Your screen will also look different if you've changed your AutoCAD setup or added third-party programs

that change its appearance. If you have installed the Express tools, described briefly in Chapter 19, you will have an additional menu.

If you are using a "flavored" version of AutoCAD, or if someone has already changed your configuration or added a third-party program to your setup, your screen may look somewhat different from the ones depicted in the figures in this chapter (and in others). But most of what's written herein still applies, and by reading this chapter, you should be able to figure out what's different about your setup — and why.

The Magnificent Seven

The starting screen for AutoCAD 2000 has seven parts, as shown in Figure 2-1. The screen displays all the elements found in other modern Windows programs, plus a few more. Make no mistake about it — this screen is busy! And that's even before you start using it!

But don't worry; for now, you can just ignore that pesky command line and most of those enigmatic icons. (Later, they become key to your productivity.) The most important elements you need to get started are the *title bar* and *menu bar* at the top of the screen, the *status bar* at the bottom, and the *Startup dialog box* and the *drawing area* in the middle. The icons on the *toolbars* and the *command line* are accelerators that help you do your work faster after you master the basics. All the pieces of the screen make sense — really, they do! — and this chapter gets you well on your way to understanding exactly what they all do.

Startup dialog box

Toolbars   Title bar   Menu bar   Drawing area

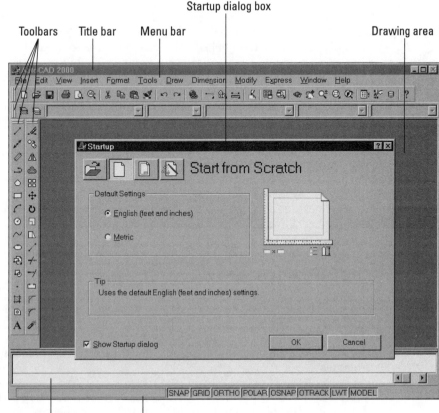

Figure 2-1:
Starting
with seven
parts to the
AutoCAD
screen.

Command line area   Status bar

The title bar — where everybody knows your (drawing's) name

Okay, so the title bar is where you go to order a royal coat of arms on the rocks, right? No, nothing so esoteric, I'm afraid. The title bar is simply the little bar across the top of the screen that shows you the program's name. This is useful when you're running several programs simultaneously in Windows.

Something that's not shown in Figure 2-1 is the title bar for a specific drawing. Because AutoCAD 2000 is the first version of AutoCAD to support multiple drawings open in a single session of AutoCAD, this is a new feature. Every drawing you open has its own menu bar with the drawing's name in it that takes up precious space in the overall AutoCAD window. Just be aware that the Window menu, new in AutoCAD 2000, helps you manage multiple drawing windows at the same time.

If you use the Maximize button on a drawing's window, it expands to fill the whole AutoCAD drawing area, and the drawing's name then appears in the AutoCAD title bar. The drawing's Minimize, Maximize, and Close buttons migrate to the menu bar (below). You can minimize your entire AutoCAD session — that is, reduce its on-screen appearance to a button in the Windows taskbar — by clicking the little button with a flat line in the upper-right corner of the screen. This button is loads of fun; you can have a complex AutoCAD session in progress and then clear it from your screen with a single mouse click. Or you can use the button next to the Minimize button, the one with a rectangle across it, to maximize the AutoCAD window so that it fills the screen — another great trick for multitasking with other programs.

Don't click the X, or Close, button when you actually want to minimize the overall window. The X closes the program — but only after you get a helpful warning message asking if you want to save any files that have changes first. Click Cancel at this point to avoid leaving the program.

Bellying up to the menu bar

The *menu bar* contains the names of all the primary menus in your version of AutoCAD.

The AutoCAD 2000 menu bar looks just like the menu bars in other Windows programs.

Figure 2-2 shows the menu bar for AutoCAD 2000 with the Draw menu open. If you spend a few minutes in AutoCAD 2000 touring the menus, opening dialog boxes, and so on, you quickly notice that AutoCAD 2000 makes considerable use of submenus to expand your range of choices. AutoCAD also contains many dialog boxes. You find more information about using these dialog boxes in the section "Dancing with dialog boxes," later in this chapter.

Getting started in the Startup dialog box

The *Startup dialog box,* shown in Figure 2-3, is the first thing you see when you start AutoCAD without selecting a drawing. The dialog box appears when you start AutoCAD by double-clicking it; a similar dialog box called Open a drawing appears when you are running AutoCAD and then choose File⇨New. (When you start AutoCAD by double-clicking a drawing, or when you choose File⇨Open, neither the Create New Drawing, nor Open dialog box appears.)

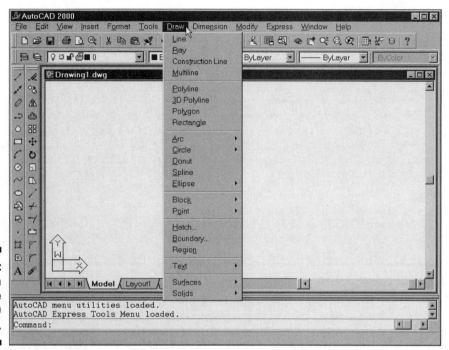

Figure 2-2:
Taking a
look in the
AutoCAD
menus.

Figure 2-3:
A close-up
view of the
Startup
dialog box.

As mentioned in the Introduction, we give the shortcut keys in this book
whenever we mention an AutoCAD or Windows menu name and command
name. The names are given in the right order for you to enter them from the
keyboard. For example, to open a new drawing by using the File menu's New
command, hold down the Alt key and then choose File⊅New. The Create New
Drawing dialog box appears.

Hot-wiring the menu bar

Some standard tips and tricks for Windows are especially useful in AutoCAD. Control-key shortcuts for the most popular functions — CTRL+S to save, CTRL+O to open a file, CTRL+P to print — work the same way in AutoCAD as in Microsoft programs. Use them!

Also worth learning are the Alt-key shortcuts, which are available for all menu choices, not just the most popular ones. To fly around the menus, just press and hold the Alt key and then press the letters on your keyboard that correspond to the underlined letters on the menu bar and in the menu choices. To bring up the aerial view of your drawing, for instance, as described in Chapter 8, just press and hold the Alt key, press V for View, and then press V for Aerial View. If all you glean from this book is to press Ctrl+S to save and Alt+V+V for Aerial View, you've learned more than all-too-many other users.

The purpose of the Startup and Open dialog boxes is to help you create a new drawing that works the way you want — that is, a drawing that fits on the page, with text in proportion to the drawing, and that easily scales to larger or smaller paper. In earlier releases of AutoCAD, you had to do a bunch of separate setup steps before starting, or odds were good that your drawing wouldn't fit well on the paper, that text would be out of proportion to the rest of the drawing and to the paper, and more. With these dialog boxes, you can use a Microsoft Office-style wizard to step through the drawing setup process, use an existing drawing as a template (the recommended option), or start from scratch.

Starting from scratch seems simplest because you don't have to make any other choices before starting to draw. However, if you choose this option, it's easy to end up with a drawing that doesn't print well and is hard to fix. The wizards may therefore seem to be the best choice, but at this writing, they don't work all that well. The easiest way is to use a template that is already set up like the end result that you want. For more details, see Chapter 4.

Drawing on the drawing area

Although the AutoCAD drawing area seems to just sit there, it's actually the program's most important and valuable piece of on-screen real estate. The drawing area is where the images you create in AutoCAD take shape. And the drawing area can actively help you do your work. If you enter the correct configuration settings to set the screen up the way you want, as described in Chapter 3, the drawing area can almost magically take on the dimensions and other characteristics you need to help you create the exact drawing you want. Two important configuration settings help determine the drawing area's effectiveness:

✔ **Limits:** The first key setting is the limits of the drawing you're working on. To draw a football stadium, for example, the limits may be set at about 500 units (yards or meters) in the horizontal direction and 300 units (yards or meters) in the vertical direction. After you set these limits, the drawing area acts as a 500-x-300-unit grid into which you can place objects. (Footballs, hot dog vendors, and rabid fans excepted, of course.)

Looking at Figure 2-4, you can see a simple drawing in the drawing area. This drawing has been maximized using the middle of the three Windows window control buttons in the upper-right corner of the window. (Try saying that three times fast!) As a result, the window control buttons for this drawing have migrated to the upper-right corner of the menu bar, and the drawing's name appears in the AutoCAD title bar.

✔ **Snap setting:** The second important setting for the drawing area is the snap setting, which causes the mouse pointer to gravitate to certain points on-screen. If you're working on your football stadium and set the snap setting to ten units, for example, you can easily draw end lines and sidelines that fall on 10-yard intervals. To draw in the seating area, however, you may want to set snap to a finer setting, such as one unit, or turn off snap altogether so that you can start your line anywhere you want. No matter what changes you make, the point is to make the drawing area help you do your work.

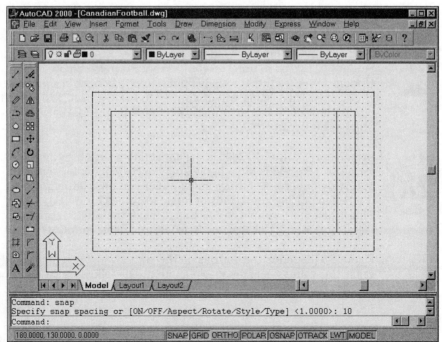

Figure 2-4: Canadian football rules!

As you can see, you can make the drawing area work absolute wonders for your drawings — but only if you set up AutoCAD correctly in the first place. If you don't configure these settings correctly, the drawing area can become really, really mad at you and may even fight back — with potentially devastating results to your drawings. Wrong settings can, for example, turn perfectly acceptable on-screen text into microscopic — and unreadable — ant tracks on paper. But don't freak out just yet: Valuable setup information awaits your discovery in Chapters 4 and 5 of this book.

Looking for Mr. Status Bar

The *status bar,* at the very bottom of the screen, tells you several important bits of information about the drawing you're working on, some of which may not make sense at first glance. These elements include the current *coordinates* of the mouse cursor; whether *snap, grid, ortho,* and *polar tracking* modes are on or off; whether running *object snaps* are on or off; whether running *object snap tracking* is on or off; whether *lineweights* are shown; and whether you're in *model space* or *paper space.* (What all these things mean is explained briefly in the next few paragraphs and in depth through the book.)

Before Release 14, the status bar indicated certain AutoCAD settings. It was frustrating to have the status indicators there and not be able to click them to change them. In AutoCAD Release 14 and AutoCAD 2000, the status bar display also functions as a set of buttons for turning features on and off.

You can maximize the screen space available for AutoCAD and other programs by setting the Windows taskbar to auto-hide. Choose Start➪ Settings➪Taskbar to bring up the Taskbar Properties icon. In the Taskbar Options tab, click the Auto hide option to put a check in the check box. Then click Apply. The taskbar will disappear; to bring it back, just move the mouse pointer down to the area formerly occupied by the taskbar. The taskbar will pop back up, ready to use.

Brand new in AutoCAD 2000 is the capability to reach settings dialog boxes for AutoCAD options by right-clicking the corresponding button. This makes accessing important settings much easier and takes away the need to remember command-line commands or menu locations for quickly changing them. This is just one example of how much easier the proliferation of right-click menus in AutoCAD 2000 makes learning and using AutoCAD.

Figure 2-5 pinpoints the buttons on the status bar. If you're new to the program, these areas bear some explanation. The following list does just that.

Figure 2-5:
The status
bar keeps
you up-to-
date.

| -2.0831, 0.8937, 0.0000 | SNAP | GRID | ORTHO | POLAR | OSNAP | OTRACK | LWT | MODEL |

✔ **Coordinates of the cursor:** The current *cursor coordinates* are extremely important in CAD (computer-aided design or drafting, as you may recall) because they actually relate the drawing to the real-world object or scene the drawing represents. The cursor coordinates aren't the coordinates on-screen or on paper; they're the real-world location of a point on or between objects. In a CAD drawing of a soft drink can, for example, the top of the can should be about 5 inches, or 12.5 centimeters, from the bottom of the can. After you set up AutoCAD correctly for your drawing, the cursor coordinates on the status bar reflect the real-life dimensions of the object or scene you're working on. You can customize the number of digits displayed for the coordinates.

If you're new to AutoCAD, try rolling the cursor around the drawing area to watch the cursor coordinates update. (After that, you can go out and watch the grass grow for even more excitement!)

If the coordinates in the lower-left corner of the screen are grayed out, then coordinate tracking is turned off. Click the coordinates so that they appear in dark lettering that updates when you move the cursor.

✔ **SNAP, GRID, and ORTHO mode buttons:** As described in Chapter 4, you can bring order to the AutoCAD drawing area in three ways: first, by telling it to *snap* the cursor to certain regularly spaced "hot spots," enabling you to more easily draw objects a fixed distance apart; second, by making the drawing area display a *grid* of dots to align objects with; and third, by setting *Ortho* mode, which makes drawing straight horizontal and vertical lines easy. The snap, grid, and ortho buttons appear to be "out" or "raised" if the mode is off, "in" or "recessed" if the mode is on. Right-clicking on the SNAP or GRID button and choosing Settings brings up the Snap and Grid tab of the Drafting Settings dialog box. The default setting for the snap, grid, and ortho modes is "off."

✔ **POLAR tracking mode button:** Polar tracking causes the cursor to "prefer" certain angles when you draw and edit objects. By default, the preferred angles are multiples of 90 degrees, but you can specify other angle increments. Clicking the POLAR button toggles polar tracking on or off. If you right-click the POLAR button and Choose Settings, AutoCAD displays the Polar Tracking tab of the Drafting Settings dialog box, in which you can specify preferred angles and other polar tracking settings. See Chapter 7 for more information about polar tracking. Right-clicking the POLAR button brings up a Settings dialog box for polar mode. The default setting for polar mode is "on."

✔ **Running Object Snap (OSNAP) and Object Snap Tracking (OTRACK) buttons:** A *running object snap* is a setting that causes the cursor to snap to specific locations on objects that you've drawn, such as corners and centers of shapes. This feature is nice to have turned on sometimes and a real pain to have on at other times. (For example, if you're trying to click a point near but not on a corner, and AutoCAD keeps snapping to the corner, you're going to get frustrated.) In AutoCAD 2000, you can easily set the features you want to snap to and then turn the whole set on or off by clicking the OSNAP button. This capability makes using running object snaps much more practical. *Object snap tracking* is a new, AutoCAD 2000 feature in which AutoCAD displays tracking vectors as you draw. More on this in Chapter 7. Right-clicking the OSNAP or OTRACK button and choosing Settings brings up a combined dialog box for setting running object snap and object snap tracking options. The default setting for both running object snap and object snap tracking modes is "on."

✔ **Lineweight (LWT) display mode button:** In AutoCAD 2000, you now have the option of having AutoCAD display the lineweight of your lines — lines appear thicker on-screen if they're thick, thinner on-screen if they're thin. These lineweights also appear on printed drawings by default. However, having this option on makes updating the screen slower, and may make your drawing dense and hard to "read." Turn it off if it bothers you. Right-clicking this button brings up a dialog box for setting lineweight display options. The default setting for lineweight display mode is "off."

✔ **MODEL/PAPER space:** Briefly, *model space* is where you create and modify objects; *paper space* enables you to arrange elements in your drawing for printout. A *layout* is a specific display on your model based on specific paper space settings. (Paper space has been in AutoCAD for several releases, but layouts are a new embellishment of paper space in AutoCAD 2000.) Stick with model space until you master it; then learn paper space to create layouts — multiple views on the objects you've drawn. The MODEL/PAPER button indicates whether you're working in model or paper space. The default setting is "MODEL." Right-clicking this button does *not* bring up a settings dialog; see Chapter 9 for fuller descriptions — in excruciating detail — of these settings.

✔ **Time:** Unlike Release 13 and earlier versions of AutoCAD, the status bar no longer shows you the time, because the Windows 95 taskbar does that instead. (Of course, if you've hidden the taskbar to get more drawing space, you're out of time!)

It's hard to tell whether the appearance of the different status bar button as either raised or depressed means "on" or "off." Depressed, or down, means on; raised, or up, means off. To quickly check, click a button; its mode will change and the new setting will be reflected on the command line — "<Osnap off>", for instance. Click again to restore the previous setting.

Better living with power toolbars

The most important elements in making AutoCAD 2000 do your bidding are the various *toolbars* that enable you to enter commands quickly and control how you draw, what you draw, and maybe even whether you're quick on the draw. The following sections describe how to use toolbars in the default setup that's standard for AutoCAD, how to move the toolbars, and how to customize the toolbars.

All the AutoCAD 2000 toolbars provide *ToolTips,* an indispensable feature that identifies each icon by its function . . . if you lean on it a bit. Simply hold the mouse pointer over an icon — no need to click it — and, like magic, the name of the icon appears in a little yellow box below the icon. The ToolTip feature incorporates yet another component that can be easy to miss: A longer description of the icon's function appears in the status bar, at the very bottom of the screen. (ToolTips work for status mode buttons, but the longer descriptions don't appear.) If the identifying name and the description at the bottom of the screen aren't enough to tell you what the icon does, you can always bring in a little "out-of-town muscle" — in other words, look it up in the Help system, which is described in the section "Fun with F1," later in this chapter.

Figure 2-6 shows the ToolTip, tool description, and help for the Undo icon on the Standard toolbar. The ToolTip identifies the icon, and the tool description in the status bar gives a longer explanation of the icon's function. If AutoCAD were to suddenly talk when you were stuck and say, "Icon help!," it wouldn't be exaggerating much!

Use the AutoCAD 2000 menus as your first stop in getting to know the program. Then begin clicking icons for the functions you use most and right-clicking for option settings. Finally, move on to the command line equivalents for the fastest power use.

Setting the standard in toolbars

AutoCAD ships with toolbars in a default setup:

- Standard toolbar on top, just below the menu bar
- Object Properties toolbar beneath the Standard toolbar
- Draw toolbar (vertical) on the far-left edge of the screen
- Modify toolbar vertically aligned just inside the Draw toolbar

The picture of the AutoCAD screen in Figure 2-1 near the start of this chapter shows the default toolbar setup. Use Figure 2-1 for reference in case you change your toolbar setup and then want to go back to the original.

The Standard toolbar helps you quickly access a number of file management, drawing management, and view functions. Using the Standard toolbar enables you to perform common file operations by clicking the New, Save, and Open icons, fix a mistake by clicking the Undo or Redo icon, and move around in your drawing by clicking the Pan and several useful Zoom icons.

The Object Properties bar actually consists of several different elements lumped together. By using the drop-down lists that appear on the Object Properties bar, you can change the current layer and modify any layer's characteristics, change the colors used to draw objects, and change the linetype used to draw objects. You also can edit two characteristics that are new in AutoCAD 2000, lineweights and plot styles. Not only can you change the *current* settings for all of these properties (that is, the properties AutoCAD applies to objects as you draw them), you can also select existing objects and change *their* properties with these drop-down lists. Although all these capabilities are highly desirable, the ways in which their functions differ can be highly confusing. The capability to change layers quickly, however, is well worth the price of admission by itself. (See the sidebar "Looking at layers" for a somewhat technical description of AutoCAD layers.)

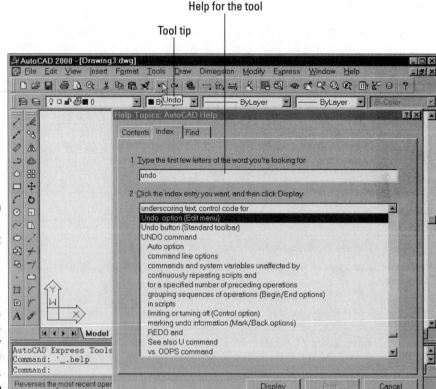

Figure 2-6:
You can get help from the ToolTip, tool description, and the Windows Help system for every AutoCAD icon.

Tool description

The Draw toolbar roughly matches the functions available in the AutoCAD Draw menu. The Draw toolbar may be the one you use most when starting a new drawing; it pulls together frequently used drawing functions into a single place. It gives you quick access to several kinds of lines, basic shapes, hatching, and text. If a drawing function that you use frequently isn't already on the Draw toolbar, consider adding it by using the customization capability described later in this chapter.

Like the Draw toolbar, the Modify toolbar is patterned after its namesake menu, in this case the Modify menu. This setup is different than add-on toolbars for earlier releases or the toolbars in Release 13, which had less correspondence between the toolbars and the menus. In use, the Modify toolbar is the kissing cousin of the Draw toolbar and may be the toolbar you use most frequently when you edit an existing drawing. The Erase icon is right at the top, followed by different options for creating new geometry from existing parts of the drawing and for adjusting lines and shapes that you have already added to the drawing. As with the Draw toolbar, consider customizing the Modify toolbar if a modification function that you use frequently isn't there.

The default toolbar setup is intended to expose as many of the frequently used commands in AutoCAD as possible in a convenient and easy-to-access yet unobtrusive format. Although you can move and even customize the toolbars, you may not want to; part of the value of the toolbars is that you become accustomed to clicking key icons quickly and without conscious effort. If you move the toolbars and their icons around, your "muscle memory" of where your most-used icons are must be retrained each time.

Try moving each of the toolbars around and then moving each back to where it started. We found the toolbars pretty easy to move, with the exception of the command line, which can float (good), but is harder than the others to get back into place (bad).

The icons in the default setup of the AutoCAD 2000 toolbars reflect some of the new and changed functions in AutoCAD. For example, new features that have been given icons in the Standard toolbar are the 3D Orbit capability (for fast 3D display; see Chapter 15) and AutoCAD DesignCenter icon, for quick access to this new feature (see Chapter 14), and dbConnect, for quick database access. The Object Properties bar embodies new capabilities such as the ability to change displayed and printed lineweights.

Toolbars on the move

You can easily move the toolbars around the screen — just grab a corner and drag. As you drag the toolbar, it changes shape to reflect how it would appear if you were to let it go right then and there — a nice feature, but one that takes a little getting used to.

Looking at layers

In AutoCAD, a drawing consists of one or more *layers.* Layers are similar to those clear sheets of mylar (not plastic, *The Graduate* notwithstanding) that you place on top of one another to build up a complete drawing. (You may remember something like this from a textbook about human anatomy, with the skeleton on one sheet, the muscles on the next sheet that you laid over the skeleton, and so on until you built up a complete picture of the human body. That is, if your mom didn't remove some of the more grown-up sections.)

Layers are the most important organizational tool for your drawing, and knowing which layer you're currently working in is vitally important. The Object Properties bar lists the layer name after several icons that tell you things about the current layer. The initial layer in a drawing that hasn't yet had layers added to it is named *0* (zero).

Actually, moving toolbars around may be a little easier in concept than in practice. Toolbars don't really have easy-to-grab borders, as do windows and dialog boxes — just little strips around the edges that you can grab with the mouse if you try hard. You may need a little practice to find just the right spot on the edge to click and drag.

You can move toolbars into either a *docked* or a *floating* position. When you move a toolbar right up against any edge of the drawing area, it docks; the toolbar seems to become part of the border that AutoCAD puts around the drawing, and the drawing area gets redrawn to exclude the area where the docked toolbar is. All the toolbars are docked in the AutoCAD default startup configuration, so if you weren't reading this paragraph, you might think that the toolbars are stuck in place.

AutoCAD also allows *floating toolbars* — toolbars that "float" over the program window. A floating toolbar is any toolbar not pushed up into a docked position against the edge of the screen. Instead of disappearing behind whatever window you clicked most recently, it continues to be visible, or to "float" in front of the drawing area. Floating toolbars and dialog boxes can be more of a pain than a pleasure; they constantly get in the way as one tries to draw or pan and zoom around a drawing. But if you like this sort of thing, AutoCAD is more than ready to accommodate you. Figure 2-7 shows the AutoCAD window with the toolbars rearranged and the Draw and Modify toolbars floating, as they were in Release 13.

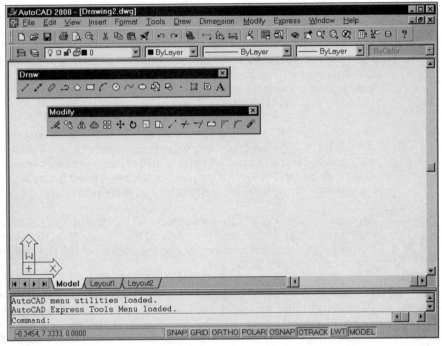

Figure 2-7:
Toolbars
moooove
until the
cows come
home.

Knowing a couple of tricks about floating toolbars is useful: When a toolbar floats, a title appears on it, which makes it take up a little more screen space. And some toolbars dock well only in certain places; for example, the Standard toolbar is too long to dock well on the sides of the AutoCAD window, unless you have a really big screen, and the Object Properties toolbar's pull-down menus work well only if the toolbar is kept horizontal; you can't dock it vertically on the left or right edge of the AutoCAD windows and still use the menus. Here are a few tips:

- ✔ Undo doesn't work for moved toolbars. Make sure that you take a moment to notice where a toolbar is before you grab it, in case you want to move it back to where it started.

- ✔ Hold down the Control key while floating a toolbar to keep it from docking.

- ✔ Drag the bottom edge of a toolbar to change it to vertical.

- ✔ Drag the side of a toolbar to change it to horizontal.

- ✔ The toolbars in Windows can be dragged and dropped, too, as can the Windows Taskbar. Try resizing the taskbar (the one at the bottom of the screen with the Start menu in it). Then try moving it to different locations on the screen. This drag-and-drop capability is just one of the ways in which AutoCAD 2000 is consistent with newer versions of Windows.

Toolbars to the nth degree

Though most people are likely to take the four toolbars in the default setup as a given, 24 toolbars are actually available in AutoCAD, and turning each of them on and off is pretty easy. Choose View⇨Toolbars. The Toolbars dialog box appears (see Figure 2-8). With the Toolbars dialog box, you can turn toolbars on and off, select from among named groups of turned-on toolbars, change the button size, and toggle ToolTips on and off.

No one set of toolbars is right for everyone, so start out by just using the default set. As you become more expert, experiment with all the toolbars until you know which ones work for you. Basically, the more time you spend using a given type of AutoCAD function, the more good it may do you to have the corresponding toolbar turned on while you work.

An even quicker way to turn toolbars on and off in AutoCAD 2000 is to right-click any toolbar and choose the name of the toolbar from the cursor menu that appears. The Customize choice at the bottom of the right-click menu opens the Toolbars dialog box.

The AutoCAD screen gets pretty crowded when you start turning on toolbars. Consider getting a fast video card that supports high resolutions and a big monitor to display results on. (If you display at high resolution on a medium-sized monitor, everything is small; you can get eyestrain trying to find details and read text.)

To make program menu and label text appear larger on your screen, right-click the desktop; a menu appears. Choose Properties. Within the dialog box that appears, choose the Settings tab and then change Font size from Small Fonts to Large Fonts. Text will appear larger.

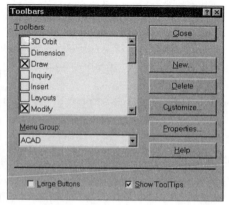

Figure 2-8:
The
Toolbars
dialog box
lets you turn
on and drop
in toolbars.

Custom toolbars

The (nearly) final frontier of setting up the AutoCAD toolbars to meet your needs is the capability to customize them. We don't describe this procedure in detail; we just want you to know that it can be done. If you want to modify the toolbars so that they have just the icons you want on them, click the Customize button in the Toolbars dialog box. The Customize Toolbars dialog box appears. You can move icons among toolbars until you have the configuration just the way you want it.

Do try to get to a stable state for your AutoCAD display window so that your subconscious can start clicking the icons you need without troubling your overburdened conscious mind.

The actual final frontier is that the icon population, like everything else in AutoCAD, is extensible. You can create custom icons and assign them to any function you want. This capability is covered in the online AutoCAD 2000 *Customization Guide*. Even if you never go to this extreme yourself, you may well find yourself getting new toolbars with custom icons as part of add-on applications that you buy for AutoCAD.

Who are we and why are we here? Like many other capabilities in AutoCAD, being able to customize icons can help make you forget what your purpose is. Are you using AutoCAD to do design and drafting or some other kind of real work, or has AutoCAD become an end in itself? Don't get so caught up in the fine points of AutoCAD customization that the amount of time you spend doing it outweighs any possible benefits.

Commanding the command line

The *command line* is a unique feature of AutoCAD and is probably the hardest for new users to get used to. Windows users who thought that they had escaped the dreaded DOS command line may be especially surprised to find a command line still lurking smack dab at the heart of AutoCAD. Yet the command line is actually a very handy tool for increasing speed and productivity in AutoCAD. Figure 2-9 shows the command line as it appears after you first open AutoCAD, skulking away down at the bottom of the screen, hoping you don't notice it below that big, open drawing area.

If you have an 800 x 600 screen or larger and like to use the command line, you can make the command line taller. If you have the Windows 95 taskbar hidden, you can make the command line six lines rather than its normal three without obscuring any of the icons in the default toolbar set. To make the command line bigger, just rest the mouse over the top edge of the command line; it turns into a vertical, two-headed arrow. Click the mouse button and hold, and then drag the top edge of the command line upward. (The command line area will allow you to resize it only to display full lines of text; you can't resize it to, for instance, two-and-a-half lines high.)

Figure 2-9:
The
AutoCAD
2000
command
line.

```
Regenerating model.
AutoCAD menu utilities loaded.
Command:                                                                    ◄  ►
-0.5728, 1.7137, 0.0000          SNAP GRID ORTHO POLAR OSNAP OTRACK LWT MODEL
```

If you don't like to use the command line, you can minimize it. Just drag the top edge of the command line window downward until it's down to a single line.

What is it? Why is it here?

The command line dates back to a long-ago time in the mists of computer history, when computer screens that used graphics were still relatively new. CAD users used just one main, text-only screen for communicating with the program; a second, graphics-only screen showed the results of the commands they entered. The fairly recent adoption of graphical screens, *graphical user interfaces* (or *GUIs*), and direct manipulation of on-screen elements by using a mouse might seem to have relegated the AutoCAD command line to the status of a lost relic from the "good ol' days" of computerdom. Yet even today, the command line, when mastered, can have a strongly positive effect on productivity.

The command line is especially challenging if your main experience in using PCs is with Windows rather than DOS. (DOS users actually have a rare advantage here.) The difference between the AutoCAD command line and the hated DOS command line that most Windows users try to avoid is that the AutoCAD command line need not be your main vehicle for interacting with AutoCAD. You can instead use the menu bar and icons to find and enter most of your commands, and use the command line primarily as an accelerator to quickly enter those commands you use most.

Even if you decide to use the menus and toolbars to enter most of your commands, you need to be aware of the command line as the AutoCAD way of prompting you for additional information. For example, you can start the circle command by clicking the Circle icon on the Draw toolbar, but AutoCAD is going to prompt you at the command line for the parameters you need to supply before AutoCAD can draw the circle. You'll usually use the mouse to specify those parameters, but if you aren't watching the command line prompts, you won't always know what AutoCAD wants from you and you might miss out on helpful options. So even if you don't want to type commands at the command line, keep an eye on it at all times!

By using the command line, you can quickly instruct AutoCAD to perform functions via your keyboard that otherwise require opening several menus and navigating your way through one or more dialog boxes. And, unfortunately, you must use the command line to carry out some functions that you can't perform in any other way. (Drat!) If you treat it as a productivity tool and an adjunct to the menus whenever possible, however, the command line actually helps you more than it frustrates you. (Well, most of you, anyway.)

Using the command line

AutoCAD actually makes finding out how to use the command line fairly easy. After you choose a command from the menus, for example, AutoCAD echoes that command on the command line preceding the command with an underscore character and sometimes with an apostrophe: **'_dsettings**, for example, is how the AutoCAD command line displays the command to open the Drafting Settings dialog box. The apostrophe allows the command to run *transparently* (that is, while a drawing or editing command is in progress), and the underscore allows the menu choice to work in foreign-language versions of AutoCAD.

Watch the command line as you use the menus and dialog boxes and memorize those commands that you use most — or write 'em down if you're a card-carrying member of the MTV generation (short attention span and all that, you know. . .). Then enter the command directly from the command line whenever you need to use that function swiftly.

In recent releases of AutoCAD, along with making the strongest possible commitment to Windows, Autodesk has actually improved the command line. You can now use the arrow keys to move up in the list of commands that you have previously entered; each time you press the up-arrow key, another previously entered command appears. When the command you want is in your sights, edit it if needed and then press Return to execute it (so to speak). This function, similar to the DOSKEY program that helps users manage DOS commands, should further improve command-line productivity.

New with AutoCAD 2000, you can right-click the command line to bring up the six most recent commands and other useful options. Try it!

You can bring up a large text window with command line contents in it. (You can also panic really inexperienced AutoCAD users by pulling this trick on their screens when they're not looking!) Just press F2 at any time and a large text window will appear, as shown in Figure 2-10; press F2 again and it will vanish. (The "magic key" used to be F1, but Autodesk finally yielded to Microsoft's insistence that F1 means "help.")

Unlike in DOS versions of AutoCAD, you can scroll up and down in the text window through all the commands you've entered during your entire current session — not just the last several that are all the DOS crowd can access this way. Just press F2 again to return the command line to its previous size and position.

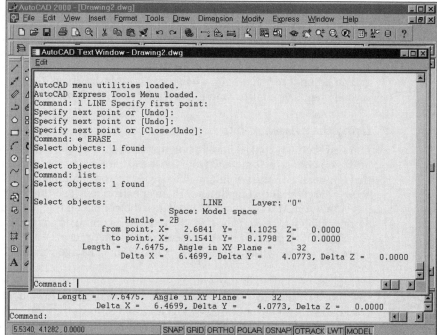

Figure 2-10:
The
command
line that ate
Detroit.

When you scroll up to choose a previous command from the AutoCAD command line, only commands that you typed are available, not commands that you generated by making menu choices or changing settings in a dialog box. And when you do press Enter to choose a command, you then must press the down-arrow key if you want to get back to the bottom of the "stack" of commands; in DOSKEY and some similar utilities, you drop back to the bottom of the stack as soon as you enter a command.

The way AutoCAD handles the command stack is the same as the way Windows NT does it, so if you ever upgrade to Windows NT, you'll know what to do.

A Bright Light and a Dim Bulb

One of the biggest difficulties in using AutoCAD is the tradeoff between ease-of-use features, such as toolbars, and the ever-present need for more screen space. Two optional AutoCAD features take up a great deal of screen space but differ radically in the value they offer you. One of these screen hogs is not strictly necessary but is highly useful; the other is clumsy and hard to use, but it's a real necessity for running some older programs.

Taking the aerial view

The *aerial view* is a feature idea borrowed from third-party utilities and included as a built-in feature of AutoCAD 2000. The aerial view is flexible and powerful — but unfortunately, like a toolbar, it takes up valuable space in the drawing area. And like a floating toolbar, it floats on top of everything; if you open a dialog box, the aerial view (which is also sort of like a dialog box) pops up right on top of it — plop! But the aerial view is helpful when you're first investigating the Pan and Zoom features and otherwise navigating your way into and out of complicated drawings. Figure 2-11 shows the Aerial View window.

The aerial view hasn't changed much since Release 13, but the need for it is reduced. Like Release 14, AutoCAD 2000 supports an improved real-time pan and zoom feature that provides instant feedback and may, in many cases, be more convenient than the aerial view. Additionally, AutoCAD 2000 supports Microsoft's IntelliMouse, a two-button mouse with a wheel that you can use for zooming. But for large drawings — whether large in extent or just in drawing complexity and file size — real-time pan and zoom may not be enough. Having the aerial view in your bag of tricks to use with big drawings is a real plus.

Because aerial view takes up so much screen space, you'll probably want to turn it on and off frequently. In AutoCAD 2000, the button with the airplane-shaped icon about two-thirds of the way across the Standard toolbar that was found in Release 14 to turn aerial view on and off has been removed. You can restore it to its rightful place by choosing View⇨Toolbars; choose Customize, then find the airplane icon in the Standard category. Drag it onto the Standard toolbar. You can also quickly turn aerial view on and off by choosing View⇨Aerial View (Alt+V+V). Or from the command line, enter DSVIEWER or AV to make the Aerial View come and go.

Snapping to the side-screen menu

Figure 2-12 shows the *side-screen menu,* or *screen menu* for short. The side-screen menu has largely served its purpose and is on the way out. It may hang on for a while, however, because some people are used to it and because many older third-party programs placed their options in this menu.

Digitizing's demise

Another command input interface that's waned in popularity is the *digitizer,* which is a combination of mouse and tracing tablet. A healthy debate continues between those who love and hate digitizers, but for most users, they're on the way out, too. (Digitizers are great for tracing paper drawings and for freehand sketching, but as a way to drive AutoCAD itself, they're not worth the trouble to buy, hook up, learn, and use.)

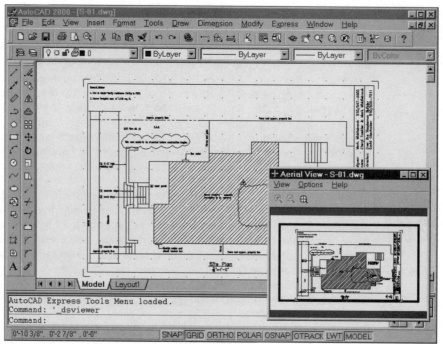

Figure 2-11:
The aerial
view is a
pan-acea
for larger
drawings.

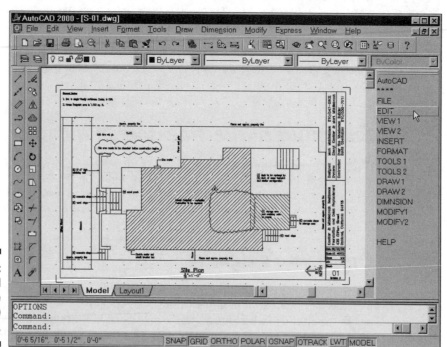

Figure 2-12:
Here's a real
side
(-screen)
splitter.

Menus versus the command line

Some experienced AutoCAD users — especially those who are long-time DOS users — think that menus, icons, and so on are for wimps. New users, on the other hand, may want to get rid of that seemingly annoying command line altogether. But each feature actually has a useful purpose all its own.

For starting out in AutoCAD and for parts of the program that you use occasionally (for some people, that's the whole darn program), menus and other parts of the graphical user interface are great. You can just mouse around on-screen

until you locate the exact command, icon, or dialog box you need.

To get fully up-to-speed in AutoCAD, however, you really do need to use the keyboard to enter your most common commands. (Unless, of course, your typing speed makes a dead tortoise look swift in comparison.) So, a good tactic is to memorize any commands you use frequently that aren't represented by an icon in the toolbars displayed on-screen and then use the command line to enter them without navigating your way through the menus.

With the new support that AutoCAD 2000 has for scanned objects (such as old paper drawings and freehand sketches), the need to trace the outlines by hand to bring them into AutoCAD may fade fast.

The AutoCAD dialog boxes, Help files, and documentation refer to the side-screen menu as the "screen menu." This name is kind of dumb, because all the AutoCAD menus are on the screen; so just think "side-screen menu" and you'll have no problems.

If you do need the side-screen menu, it's always available. Just choose Tools⇨Options to see the Options dialog box. Click the Display tab and then click the Display screen menu option. (If you like ancient history, you may be interested to know that the initial choices on the screen menu are the same as the menu choices from an AutoCAD release many years back. If you're *really* interested in ancient history, you're probably running that release right now!)

What Really Makes AutoCAD Tick?

In reading about and using AutoCAD, you encounter two topics frequently: *system variables,* which are very old, and *dialog boxes,* which in their current, highly usable forms are relatively new. System variables and dialog boxes are closely related, because they both affect the settings that control the way AutoCAD works. Understanding them and how they work together can dramatically speed your ascent to proficiency in AutoCAD.

Setting system variables

System variables are settings that AutoCAD checks before it decides how to do something. If you set the system variable SAVETIME to 10, for example, AutoCAD automatically saves your drawing file every ten minutes; if you set SAVETIME to 60, the time between saves is one hour. Hundreds of system variables control the operations of AutoCAD.

Of these hundreds of system variables in AutoCAD, almost 70 system variables control dimensioning alone. (*Dimensioning* is the process of labeling objects with their lengths, angles, or special notes. Different professions have very different standards for how dimensions on their drawings should look. Using dimensions is described in detail in Chapter 11.)

To change the name of a system variable, just type its name at the AutoCAD command prompt. The capability to change a system variable directly is very powerful, and knowing the names and appropriate range of settings for the system variables that you use regularly is worth the time and effort. But expecting you to remember literally hundreds of variables, how they work, and how they interact with one another is just too much — even for all you "power users" out there. This is where dialog boxes come in.

To see all the system variables in AutoCAD as shown in Figure 2-13, type **SETvar ?** at the AutoCAD command prompt. If you want to learn more about what each one does, look up "system variables, listed" in the AutoCAD online help.

Sometimes, watching AutoCAD work as you use it is like having X-ray vision into the workings of the program. Even as you use a modern-looking program with menus, dialog boxes, and icons, you can watch AutoCAD turn your mouse clicks into typed commands and system variable settings on the AutoCAD command line. At startup, you can even watch the program load its menus file and then display the menus. Watching AutoCAD work can be hours of fun if you're kind of strange and don't have any real work to do. But, more seriously, every one of the operations you see represents another area where third-party developers can — and most likely will — customize the look, feel, and function of AutoCAD.

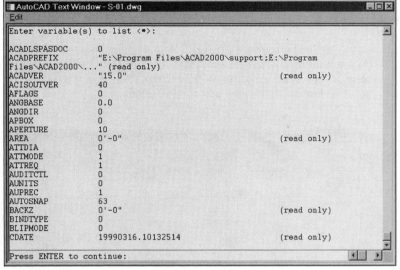

```
AutoCAD Text Window - S-01.dwg                                    _ □ ×
Edit
Enter variable(s) to list <*>:                                        ▲

ACADLSPASDOC         0
ACADPREFIX          "E:\Program Files\ACAD2000\support;E:\Program
Files\ACAD2000\..." (read only)
ACADVER             "15.0"                              (read only)
ACISOUTVER          40
AFLAGS              0
ANGBASE             0.0
ANGDIR              0
APBOX               0
APERTURE            10
AREA                0'-0"                               (read only)
ATTDIA              0
ATTMODE             1
ATTREQ              1
AUDITCTL            0
AUNITS              0
AUPREC              1
AUTOSNAP            63
BACKZ               0'-0"                               (read only)
BINDTYPE            0
BLIPMODE            0
CDATE               19990316.10132514                  (read only)      ▼
Press ENTER to continue:                              ◄│ │►
```

Figure 2-13: The first few dozen system variables in AutoCAD.

Dancing with dialog boxes

The AutoCAD dialog boxes are an easy way to control collections of related system variables, much like a dashboard controls a car's functions. By using dialog boxes, you can handle all the related settings that may otherwise be confusing if you changed them directly through system variables.

The best single example of the power inherent in using dialog boxes to set system variables can be demonstrated through the set of dialog boxes that enable you to manage dimensions. Because you can specify so many different elements about each dimension, AutoCAD enables you to create *dimension styles,* which are named groups of dimension settings that you can choose from a list. The Dimension Style Manager dialog box, as shown in Figure 2-14, controls dimension styles.

To access this dialog box, choose Format⇨Dimension Style or type **Dimstyle** on the command line and press Enter. The Modify button on the right side of the Dimension Style Manager dialog box opens the Modify Dimension Style dialog box, which contains a series of tabbed pages giving you control over the dimensioning system variables.

Fun with F1

AutoCAD 2000 features a powerful Help system, shown in Figure 2-15, based on the Windows Help system. AutoCAD 2000 Help includes a searchable database of topics, information on how to use Help, a quick tour of AutoCAD, and an overview of what's new in AutoCAD 2000.

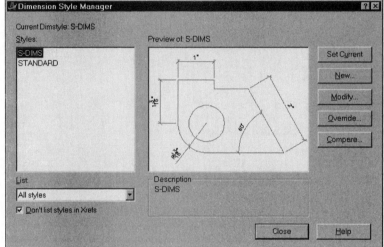

Figure 2-14:
Setting your
dimensions
with style(s).

 AutoCAD 2000 includes a full documentation set, accessible through the Help system. Click the Index tab in Help to see the documents available, which include a *How To* guide, an alphabetical *Command Reference*, a *Visual Basic for Applications and ActiveX Automation* guide for programmers, and a guide to the *AutoCAD Express Tools* — the tools formerly known as Bonus tools in Release 14.

 AutoCAD 2000 even goes beyond the bounds of the AutoCAD program and Windows 95 to give you help. You can install a CD-ROM called *AutoCAD Learning Assistance* that comes with AutoCAD. You choose AutoCAD Learning Assistance from the AutoCAD 2000 Help menu, but it actually runs as a separate program. Also available from the Help menu is a Connect to Internet option. It links you to an Autodesk Web site with frequently updated help information about AutoCAD 2000. For more information on both options, keep reading.

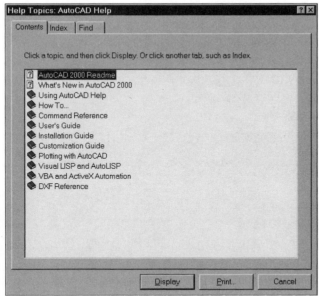

Figure 2-15:
Your
AutoCAD
SOS.

Extra-sensitive Help

No, *extra-sensitive Help* isn't some kind of new, improved psychotherapy. It's just another term for *context-sensitive Help,* which is probably the most useful kind of help in AutoCAD 2000. You access context-sensitive Help in AutoCAD in two ways: by pressing F1 or by clicking the Help button in a dialog box. And if you're in the middle of entering a command, you can access Help by pressing the F1 key. Help then appears for that command.

If you've used Release 13 for Windows or Release 14, the Help system in AutoCAD 2000 isn't much of a shock to you; it's very much like Release 13, with just a few changes in buttons and the "look" of individual Help panels. (Plus, as one would hope, some updated content!) But if you've never used a Windows version of AutoCAD before, you're in for a treat. The Help system is a major asset of Windows versions of AutoCAD.

If you simply hold the mouse cursor over the Circle icon in the Draw floating toolbar and then press F1, for example, the Help screen titled "Contents" appears. But if you click the Circle icon, a command appears on the command line. If you press F1 to choose Help at this point, a specific Help screen for the CIRCLE command appears. Figure 2-16 shows AutoCAD Help for the CIRCLE command.

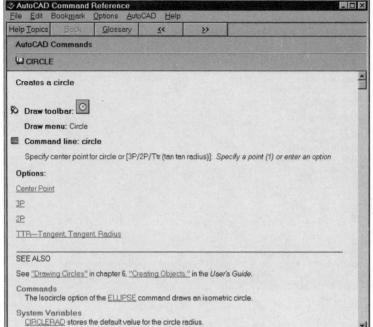

Figure 2-16:
Get Help
going
around in
circles.

It's not unreasonable to think that, if AutoCAD knows enough to put up the ToolTip for CIRCLE when the cursor is over the Circle icon, it should know enough to get Help for circles if you press F1 at that point. But no luck; maybe next release!

Help yourself?

You can even annotate Help and put bookmarks in it. (No, don't go trying to shove a paper bookmark into your screen; these are electronic bookmarks.) Bookmarks are probably worthwhile only if you make a real project out of creating them and then distribute the resulting bulked-up Help file to all the other AutoCAD users in your organization. Then, of course, you must be prepared to redo them — that's the bookmarks, not the other AutoCAD users! — the next time you get a good idea about what should be bookmarked. Check out the Bookmark entry in the AutoCAD Help system if you really want

(and think you need) instructions on how to use bookmarks; because most of you are unlikely to use bookmarks in the normal course of human events, they're not covered any further in this book.

AutoCAD Help, accessed through the F1 key or Help⇨AutoCAD Help Topics, is context-sensitive: If you access it in the middle of executing a command, Help for that specific command appears first. (You can then navigate to anyplace else in the Help system.)

F1 also works when you have a dialog box open. Alternatively, you can access Help for dialog boxes by pressing the Help button in a dialog box. This Help feature is otherwise identical to Help for other parts of AutoCAD.

A quicker but abbreviated version of dialog box help is available if you click the little question mark in the dialog box's title bar (next to the X that closes the dialog box), and then click an area in the dialog box that you're confused about. AutoCAD displays a short description of what that part of the dialog box is for.

Though linked, Help runs as a separate task from AutoCAD itself. Any time you use Help in AutoCAD 2000, you can keep Help open in the background and return directly to the main AutoCAD screen by pressing the Alt+Tab key combination to cycle through your currently running tasks.

A typical Help screen contains several live areas, which enable you to move around in the Help system, as well as dead areas, which just kinda lie there and contain information. (If the latter start to decompose a bit, don't worry; no one can smell anything in cyberspace, anyway!) The live areas of the Help screen include the following elements (refer to Figure 2-18, shown later in the chapter, for a look at some of them):

✔ **Menu bar:** Each Help window has its own menu bar that you can use to control Help in general. The most important function here is probably the Print Topic option on the File menu.

✔ **Toolbar:** Help even has its own toolbar for use in navigating through the Help system by using the following buttons:

- The Contents and Index buttons open the Help window to the Contents or Index tab, respectively. You can then click the Display button in the Search window to move to a secondary topic.

- The Back button returns you to previously viewed Help screens visited during the current session. Back is something you're likely to use often, because it keeps you from feeling lost in Help.

- The Print button prints the current Help screen.

- The << button takes you to the topic just before the current topic in some kind of order that we can't quite figure out.

- The >> button takes you to the topic just after the current topic in the same unknown order as for the << button.

✔ **Solid green underlined text:** Text underlined in solid green is linked to other topics related to the one described in the current Help screen. Clicking this text opens a new window that gives you additional information.

Finding happiness in Help

You can access the same Help screens a couple of other ways. Pressing F1 whenever you're not in the middle of any specific command or choosing Help➪AutoCAD Help topics opens the Help Topics dialog box with the tab that you used most recently (Contents, Index, or Find) selected. The Index tab enables you to find help for AutoCAD menu items, for commands, or for system variables. This feature is pretty useful, and just clicking around in it is a good way to get familiar with some basics of AutoCAD.

Clicking the Find tab within Help opens a dialog box containing a long, scrolling list of topics. Unfortunately, this dialog box contains literally hundreds of topics, and finding the one you need can be very difficult unless you already know the command name, menu name, or system variable name you want. (The first time you use this dialog box, you have to tell AutoCAD how to set it up. We recommend that you choose Maximize Search Capabilities rather than Minimize Database Size, because if you need help, you really need it.)

After you're in the Find tab of the Help dialog box, just follow the steps labeled 1, 2, 3 in order to locate the topic that you're interested in and display help about it. Figure 2-17 shows a Find search already in progress.

The What's New in AutoCAD 2000 feature of AutoCAD Help is pretty useful for becoming familiar with new features of the program. You can access this feature by choosing Help➪What's New. Then select from the topics listed. Each topic describes the feature and provides a link to one or more relevant areas in the online documentation. Figure 2-18 shows the What's New page for the topic, Heads-Up Design Environment.

And if that's not enough help . . .

The AutoCAD Learning Assistance tutorials are intended to help get users up to speed in many areas. To access the tutorials, choose Help➪Learning Assistance. Then set aside some time to go through all of the tutorials (they're pretty self-explanatory). Unless you already know AutoCAD well, the tutorials are a worthwhile investment of your time.

The Help system in AutoCAD 2000 also contains the entire AutoCAD 2000 documentation set online. That's thousands of pages of manuals, all readable and searchable while you run AutoCAD. Don't read the manuals online for long, however; use the online version for searching and jumping around. Your AutoCAD 2000 package comes with a big, fat, printed *User's Guide*, organized by topic. It's great for reading on the bus, in bed, or in those other places you

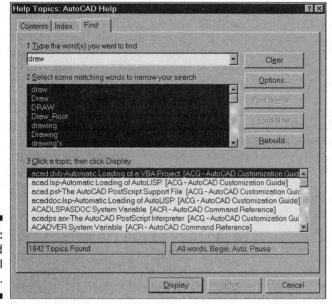

Figure 2-17:
Search and
ye shall
Find.

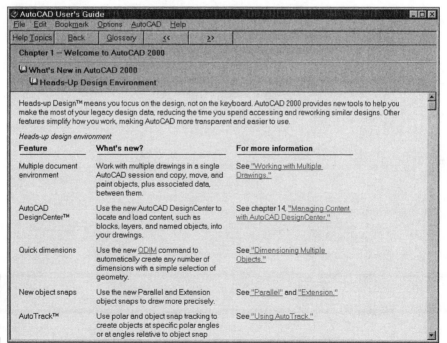

Figure 2-18:
Getting a
toolbar tour.

like to read. If you need to read big sections of the other manuals, buy the printed versions from Autodesk. (You can share one copy of the printed manuals for each group of users to save money while still making reference easier.) By reading from paper instead of from a glowing, flickering screen, your eyes are much less likely to feel like hard-boiled eggs halfway through a section. (Better yet, start by grabbing this book!)

The Help menu in AutoCAD also includes Support Assistance and Autodesk on the Web options. These are places you can look for more information and help on specific questions.

The Help system, like AutoCAD itself, can be kind of intimidating. If you use it on an as-needed basis to search for specific topics you're wondering about, you'll get comfortable with it without getting lost in it.

Chapter 3

Taking Control of AutoCAD

● ●

In This Chapter

▶ How AutoCAD works

▶ How AutoCAD looks

▶ How AutoCAD draws

● ●

*Y*ou can customize a ton of features in AutoCAD, but there are a few key AutoCAD settings that you must set correctly before you can even start doing full-speed, productive work. Even working through examples is hard unless you have a few of the program's configuration options set up correctly. So use this chapter to fix up AutoCAD and make it look sharp and act cool — just the way you want it to.

AutoCAD was one of the first PC graphics programs available, so its developers had to make some best guesses in deciding how things should work in the program. They tried hard, but in several cases, they guessed wrong — that is, they guessed one way, and the people who developed the Macintosh did it a different way. Because the decisions made for the Macintosh became the basis for how things are done in Windows, we now have a program that works one way, AutoCAD, running in a software environment that works a different way, Windows. Starting with Release 12 and continuing to a greater degree with Releases 13 and 14, AutoCAD opened the door for you to configure many aspects of the program to the point that it can now work like a standard Windows program. Many, but, alas, not all. So . . . follow the instructions in the remainder of this chapter to make AutoCAD work as it should.

If AutoCAD 2000 is your first AutoCAD experience and you have experience with Windows, you probably want AutoCAD to work like other Windows programs. But if you're upgrading from an earlier version of AutoCAD, you may be tempted to set or retain various options so that they work like old-style AutoCAD, not like Windows.

The authors are actually of two minds on this. One of us — an old Macintosh hand who values consistency in a computer's operations — says: "Make the change! If you do, your work in AutoCAD, the Windows environment, and other Windows programs will be easier." The other author, a long-time AutoCAD user, says: "The existing settings work more consistently within AutoCAD; consider sticking with them." On balance, new users should change the settings; existing users should do whatever feels more comfortable to them. The rest of this chapter is focused on making the change and moving to a Windows-like environment within AutoCAD.

Making AutoCAD Work with You

If you're experienced in working with a graphical user environment such as Windows, Macintosh, or even a typical DOS drawing program, using the mouse has probably become second nature to you. You simply click a command, an object, or almost anything else on-screen to *select* (or highlight) it; you can then click something else to select that item instead. To select two items, click the first, press and hold the Ctrl key, and then click the second. (Ditto for the third, fourth, and so on.)

It's not my (de)fault

Your copy of AutoCAD is currently set up as it is for many reasons. Autodesk can change the default settings created at installation for different versions of AutoCAD and for different releases. The AutoCAD dealer, CAD manager, or other person who set up your system may have changed some things around. A third-party program you're using also may change certain default settings. Finally, if you or anyone else has used your version of AutoCAD at all, it's more than likely that a few settings have been changed.

This book tells you how to modify the default AutoCAD settings that come with AutoCAD 2000. If some of the settings are already set correctly on your system because someone already reconfigured your program to the correct settings, that's one less thing for you to worry about.

More important than "what" to do, this book tells you "why" to do it — what the settings mean, so that you can understand when they should be set different ways. After you understand these settings and what they control — no mean feat, because AutoCAD is one of the most configurable programs around — you can always change them again if you need to. Also, you can use someone else's system that's set up differently and know how to change the settings to fit your workstyle. (And change them back when you're done to the other person's weird way of working! The Technical Stuff paragraph on AutoCAD profiles in the next section describes the most reliable way of doing so.)

But not in AutoCAD! AutoCAD works exactly the opposite of every major operating environment or graphics program known to man, woman, child, or computer nerd. But never fear! This chapter helps you fix whatever you can and work around what you can't. Left to its own devices, AutoCAD can seem to be working against you. But with a little effort, you can get AutoCAD on your side and get it to work.

Making AutoCAD work like other programs

Using a graphical interface such as Windows can be likened to driving a car: After you know how to do it, you don't think about the details any longer. But to make AutoCAD work right, you must explicitly specify to the program certain details that may, to you, seem obvious. (Ah, but not to AutoCAD! At least not until you set them. . . .) You must, therefore, correctly configure the following settings, called *selection settings,* to make AutoCAD work more intuitively. (This section describes what the settings are; how to set them is described on following pages.) You need to know about the following settings:

✔ **Noun/verb selection:** AutoCAD's long-time, built-in mode of interaction calls for you to enter a command and then choose the objects to which the command applies. In Windows, you normally select objects first and then specify the command. AutoCAD calls the Windows method Noun/Verb Selection.

Some advanced AutoCAD commands do not work on objects that you've already selected, even if Noun/Verb Selection is turned on. These commands ignore your current selection after you enter the command and ask you to make a new selection.

✔ **Use Shift to add to selection:** In other programs, clicking different items changes the current selection; you must press and hold the Shift key to add additional items to the selection. AutoCAD, on the other hand, adds items to the current selection when you click each subsequent item; if you hold Shift down, the item you click is actually deselected and removed from the current selection set. (Hmmm. Maybe the programmer working on this feature got the Shift scared out of him? Naaaaahhhh.) This crazy feature, of course, drives non-AutoCAD veterans nuts! To make the Shift key work as it does in Windows, turn on this option.

✔ **Press and drag:** To create a selection window in AutoCAD, you click one place in the drawing area, let go of the mouse button, and then click again somewhere else. In doing so, you establish the two corners of the selection window; this procedure is called "picking" the corners of the window. But in Windows, you click the spot where you want one corner, hold down the mouse button, and drag to the other corner. To enable this click-drag-release style of windowing that the rest of the world is used to, turn on the Press and Drag option.

✔ **Implied windowing:** With the Implied Windowing option on, AutoCAD enables you to use selection windows in two different ways: If you drag from left to right, everything inside the window is selected; if you drag from right to left, everything inside and crossing — that is, partly in and partly out of — the window is selected. This feature takes practice to use effectively but is well worth the trouble. On the other hand, if you don't turn this feature on — well, believe me, you don't want to know what it takes to establish a selection window if you leave this option turned off. So leave this feature on.

✔ **Object Grouping:** Although the Object Grouping selection setting is not a "fix-it" item, as are the previous four settings, it's a neat feature, so be sure to enable Object Grouping. In Release 13, AutoCAD added the capability to create named groups of objects and select them by typing in the name (if you're upgrading to AutoCAD 2000 from Release 12 or earlier, this feature is new to you). You can lump together all the executives' desks in a building, for example, and name them Executive Desks. (Then, if you're paid late for the drawing, you can specify that all objects in the Executive Desks group be made out of particle board. Heh, heh, heh. . . .)

If you're using someone else's computer to run AutoCAD, you should set up your own AutoCAD *profile* before making the kinds of configuration changes described in this chapter — especially if the computer's owner has a short temper! You should also set up a profile on your own machine if others are going to be running "your" copy of AutoCAD. No one likes to come back to his or her computer to find that AutoCAD suddenly is acting differently.

Why is AutoCAD so weird?

As is true of so many other questionable practices in computing, the odd style of AutoCAD user interaction is an effort to maintain *backward compatibility* — the same commands and working style — with earlier versions of the program. Or in other words: "Gee, we did a really bad job of interface design in the previous ten versions; better not change anything now, or our users may be upset."

In its defense, the AutoCAD default mode of operation is fast, and it works well after you get used to it. But anytime you work in another program or even on the Windows desktop, you get un-used to it. So unless you work almost exclusively in AutoCAD, or unless you're able to "mode switch" seamlessly between the AutoCAD way of working on the one hand and everything else in Windows on the other, you want AutoCAD to work the same way as other programs.

Setting up your own AutoCAD user profile is easy. Choose Tools⇨Options to display the Options dialog box, then choose the Profiles tab. Choose the Add to List button and type a name and optional description for your profile. After you choose the Apply & Close button, AutoCAD creates your new profile and adds it to the list of Available profiles. Choose your profile and pick the Set Current button to use your profile. Now you can change configuration settings to your heart's content without annoying Mr. or Ms. Grumpy.

Before you exit AutoCAD, open the Options dialog box again, choose the original profile, and then the Set Current button to restore the computer owner's original settings. Look up "profiles (of drawing environment settings), creating and saving" in the AutoCAD online help for more information.

Hands-on: Making AutoCAD 2000 work like Windows

If you want to make AutoCAD work like Windows instead of driving you nuts, you need to change the previously described settings. To set the selection settings from the AutoCAD Object Selection Settings dialog box, follow these easy steps:

1. **Choose Tools⇨Options, or type** OPtions.

   The Options window appears. Choose the Selection tab; the Options dialog box's Selection tab appears (see Figure 3-1).

   AutoCAD versions from Release 13 on use the word *object* to refer to a single, selectable element in the drawing; previous releases used the word *entity* to mean the same thing. Despite its science-fictional implications, entity was one term in previous versions that we liked. Oh, well. (AutoCAD veterans are likely to continue to use the word *entity*, both out of habit and to show how veteran they are. Also, *entity* is used in a cool way in Neal Stephenson's *Snow Crash* (Bantam Spectra, 1993). If you haven't read it already, stop what you're doing and go do so, just for fun.)

2. **Click the Noun/Verb Selection check box to turn on this setting (if currently off).**

   The setting is on if a check mark appears in the check box, as shown in Figure 3-1. (In this figure, for example, Use Shift to add to selection and Press and drag are turned off.)

3. **Turn on Use Shift to add to selection.**

4. **Turn on Press and drag.**

5. **Turn on Implied windowing.**

6. **Turn on Object Grouping.**

7. **Leave Associative Hatch alone for now.**

   We look at Associative Hatch more closely in Chapter 12.

8. **Click the OK button to accept the changes and close the dialog box.**

Selection modes   Grips options

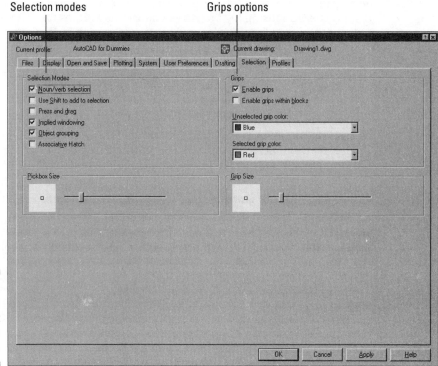

Figure 3-1:
Select the
best
Selection
settings.

In case you want or need to know whether anyone's changed your settings, or in case you ever want to go back to Ground Zero, the default settings are Noun/Verb Selection, Implied Windowing, and Object Grouping on and Use Shift to Add and Press and Drag off, as shown previously in Figure 3-1.

Setting selection settings from the command line

You're likely to change these selection settings only infrequently, so using the menus to set them is probably your best bet. When you want to change your settings a year from now, you're far more likely to remember how to do so from the menus if you did it that way in the first place. But if you're a real keyboard fan, just follow these steps to set selection settings from the command line:

1. **At the command line, type** PICKFIRST 1 **and then press Enter to turn on Noun/Verb Selection.**

2. **Type** PICKADD 0 **and press Enter to turn on Use Shift to add to selection.**

   (And don't ask us why, but 0 means *on* for the Use Shift to Add option, but it means *off* for all the other options. That means, of course, that if

Macintosh user's gloat note

If you're a longtime Mac user, you're no doubt feeling smug right now. And you're right: Everything described here as "how Windows works" and "the right way to do things" was first popularized by the Macintosh and such programs as MacWrite and MacPaint, starting waaaay back in 1984. But this book addresses Windows users because that's where the action is in CAD these days. (Sorry to be the one to say this, but I was an Apple employee for seven years — and no, I didn't break any mirrors in 1990 just before I was hired at Apple.)

Maybe the next generation of the PowerPC chip will change things, and the next release of AutoCAD will come out for the Macintosh first — or at least second. Until then, any Mac users reading this book must settle for feeling slightly superior whenever user interface considerations are mentioned . . . and also hope for a bargain on a Windows PC to run AutoCAD 2000 on.

you want to turn off any of these options by using the command line, type the appropriate command and a 0 rather than a 1 — except for PICKADD, in which case . . . well, you get the idea.)

Actually, you *can* ask us: the reason "PICKADD 0" turns off the Use Shift to add option is that it's actually turning *off* AutoCAD's internal system variable, "use pick to add" or PICKADD. Doing this has the effect of turning on Use Shift to add to selection. The negative of a negative is a positive. . . .

   3. **Type** PICKDRAG 1 **and press Enter to turn on Press and drag.**

   4. **Type** PICKAUTO 1 **and press Enter to turn on Implied windowing.**

   5. **Type** PICKSTYLE 1 **and press Enter to turn on Object grouping.**

Making it work the AutoCAD way

If you want AutoCAD to work the way it always has, AutoCAD 2000 lets you do that, too. If you're familiar enough with AutoCAD to want the old settings, you're probably aware of how to change them, too. Follow the preceding instructions to bring up the Object Selection Settings dialog, but make the settings almost opposite:

   ✔ Noun/Verb Selection off

   ✔ Use Shift to Add off

   ✔ Press and Drag off

Don't stay completely in the Stone Age; turn Implied Windowing and Object Grouping on and learn to use them, as described in Chapter 7.

To use the command line for setting these options, enter these commands:

```
PICKFIRST 1
PICKADD 1
PICKDRAG 0
PICKAUTO 1
PICKSTYLE 1
```

(Those last two commands turn implied windowing and object grouping on; if you really have to have them off, enter **0** instead.)

Getting saved

You know all those little things in life you wish you'd done way back when you had the chance, such as filling out your taxes before midnight on April 15; getting your brakes fixed before that nasty little accident; backing up your hard disk before it crashes forever? Well, setting the *save interval* is another one of those little things.

Saving your files more frequently is especially important in AutoCAD 2000. Why? Because of the Multiple Document Environment — that is, because you can have several files open at a time.

Uh, why is that? Because it's hard to remember exactly what work you lost because of a crash when you're working on one file at a time. But with AutoCAD 2000, you can work on multiple files simultaneously. That means that you can be *completely* befuddled about what you were trying to do in each of the open documents since the various times when you last saved each of them. Save early and often — with AutoCAD 2000, this is true now more than ever.

AutoCAD saves your drawing whenever a designated number of minutes has passed since your last save. If you save your drawing yourself before the automatic save kicks in, the save timer starts over again from the point of your save.

Here's the quick version for setting this option: To change the save interval by using the menus in AutoCAD 2000, choose <u>T</u>ools⇨Optio<u>n</u>s⇨Open and Save tab. Check the Automatic save check box, and enter any number of minutes between saves that suits your fancy; we suggest 10 minutes. (If you choose just a few minutes, your data will be safer, but you'll have to wait while the save happens; if you choose too many minutes, you may lose a lot of work when a problem occurs.) Click OK to accept the change.

To change the save interval by using the command line, type **SAVETIME** at the command line and press Enter. However you enter the SAVETIME command, the completed sequence appears on the command line as follows:

```
Command: SAVETIME
New value for SAVETIME <120>: 10
```

AutoCAD offers a default value for many options on the command line. If you simply press Enter at the prompt rather than type something, AutoCAD uses the default. The default value appears on the command line in angle brackets (< >). The <120> in the preceding line, for example, means that 120 minutes is the default value here.

If you try to enter SAVETIME 10, AutoCAD treats the spacebar as a return character. (This arrangement is a time-saver for AutoCAD power users, because the spacebar is easier to find than the Enter key.) It then gives you the prompt for the number of minutes, accepts 10 as the response, and completes the command. So entering the command as SAVETIME 10 ends up working, but the visual feedback you get is a little confusing at first.

After you enter the SAVETIME command, AutoCAD prompts you for the save interval and then automatically saves the drawing anytime you wait longer than that interval between saves. Ten minutes is usually a good choice, but any interval you choose will work. AutoCAD saves the drawing in the Windows Temp directory (C:\Windows\Temp on one of the systems we tested on; D:\Temp on another) under a name invented by AutoCAD that ends in the characters .SV$.

You can change the directory in which temporary files are saved by choosing Tools⇨Options to bring up the Options dialog box and then choosing the Files tab. Click the Temporary Drawing File Location option and double-click the path shown. A Browse for Folder dialog box will appear; use it to select the new folder for temporary files to be saved in.

Getting a grip

Grips are little handles that show up on an object after you select it. Grips enable you to grab an object and manipulate it. Grips are cool. Having grips turned on is a Good Thing.

Like so many other features in AutoCAD (sigh), grips don't always work exactly as you'd expect them to. Chapter 8 discusses grip editing in detail. For now, however, you just need to know how to turn them on. You can do this by following these steps:

1. **Choose Tools⇨Options.**

   The Options window appears.

2. **Click the Selection tab or type** ddGRips **on the command line and press Enter to go straight to the Selection tab.**

   The Selection tab opens with the Grips area on the right side, as shown on the right side of Figure 3-1, which appeared previously.

3. **Click the Enable grips check box to turn on this feature (if it's not already on).**

4. **Click the Enable grips within blocks check box to turn off this feature (if it's not already off).**

   You can turn this option back on later if you need to grab grips on objects within a block. (See Chapter 13 for more about playing with blocks.) An empty check box means that the feature is turned off, as shown in Figure 3-1.

If you want, you can also change the Grip Colors in the Grips dialog box. Grip colors help identify whether a grip is on and ready for selection (blue) or on and already chosen as a handle (red). Unselected grips are also called cool grips and should be kept in a background color such as the default blue. Selected grips are called hot grips and should be flagged with an attention-getting color such as the default red. Click the pull-down menu beneath either of the Grip Colors icons, Unselected or Selected, to change colors; choose More to open the Select Color dialog box and select from a wide range of colors. The Grip Size, too, can be changed by moving the slider near the bottom of the Grips dialog box from left (minimum) to right (maximum). The example window to the left of the size bar shows you the size increases or decreases of the grips as you change this option.

You can also use the command line to enable and turn off grips — especially if you're an experienced AutoCAD for DOS user who is sometimes inflicted with "GUI fatigue" and you need to go back to the old-style AutoCAD user interface as a remedy. The following steps describe the keyboard commands you use to turn grips on and grips-in-blocks off:

1. **At the command line, type** GRIPS 1 **and then press Enter.**

   This command turns on grips. To turn them off, you use a 0 rather than a 1.

2. **Type** GRIPBLOCK 0 **and then press Enter.**

   This command turns off grips within blocks; to turn them back on, you use a 1 with the command rather than a 0.

Making AutoCAD Quicker on the Draw

You can spend the rest of your career fine-tuning how AutoCAD draws — if you really want to, that is. You don't want to, of course, or you'd be reading *AutoCAD Disassembled: Vol. XXIII* rather than this book. But you do need to know how to set a couple of drawing-related settings to do much of anything. This section tackles those particular settings, providing you with just enough info to get you started, and the book harps on them again later as necessary.

Turning on running object snaps

In most drawings, different objects touch each other, usually at specific points such as the endpoint of a line, the center of a circle, or the intersection of two existing objects. Drawing becomes much easier if these points act as *hot spots* for the mouse pointer. That is, the mouse pointer is pulled toward specific kinds of points, which enables you to more easily draw objects so that they align correctly with each other. *Object snaps* give you the flexibility to control which points on each object draw the cursor to them.

There are even two types of object snaps. A *single* object snap lasts for just one mouse click. You turn it on by holding down the Shift key and right-clicking the mouse to make the AutoCAD cursor menu appear. Then choose the object snap you want from the cursor menu; for instance, the Midpoint object snap. Pick a point on an object such as a line — no matter where you pick on the object, AutoCAD "snaps" the cursor to its midpoint ("ten-hut!").

If you have a three-button mouse and used previous versions of AutoCAD, you might be surprised — and annoyed — to discover that pressing the middle mouse button in AutoCAD 2000 doesn't display the cursor object snap menu. The middle button instead enables real-time panning when you press and hold it down. If this change annoys you too much, set the new MBUTTONPAN system variable to 0 in order to restore the old behavior.

Cosmetic surgery via third-party applications

Third-party applications can make a big difference in the appearance of AutoCAD; they can add menus and dialog boxes and set customization defaults in specific ways, which may be matters of substance or merely of style. If you use a third-party application, some of the information in this book may not apply directly to your working environment. If so, look for visible differences in the interface of your version of AutoCAD and adjust around them as needed.

A *running* object snap is similar, but it lasts longer. You can turn on any number of running object snaps simultaneously. All the running object snaps that you select stay on until you turn them off, either one at a time or by turning off the running object snaps feature. (To turn running object snaps on and off, click the word OSNAP in the status bar.) You can still use single object snaps whether or not running object snaps are on.

Don't feel bad if you become confused over the difference between the *snap grid* and *object snaps*, or between *single* object snaps and *running* object snaps. Because they all have *snap* in their names, the distinction can sometimes seem a little tricky. (Kinda like if you're cooking and you ask your significant other for the thyme; if he or she says "5:30" instead of handing you a jar of spice, it's really your own fault.) The snap grid makes objects snap to points a predefined distance apart in the drawing area, whereas object snaps force points that you select to snap to certain locations on other objects. But don't worry: The more you use AutoCAD, the less often these terms confuse you.

Okay, back to the subject. If you're a new user, listen up, because object snaps are really important. If you don't use object snaps, you can draw lines that *look* as though they connect but really don't. As you build up your drawing, these nasty little unconnected lines can cause you more and more problems — and they show you up as a novice if someone has to come in and fix your drawing later. What's more, that glitch is just in two-dimensional (2D) drawings. In three-dimensional (3D) drawings, unconnected objects that look as though they're touching from one point of view may actually be inches, meters, or even miles apart when viewed from a different angle.

This discrepancy becomes evident because, without the benefit of object snaps, lines can all too easily fail to connect. So use your object snaps to avoid this unfortunate problem; they enable you to draw connecting lines quickly and accurately, making such lines much harder for you to mess up, even if you try.

Important object snaps available in AutoCAD include snaps to the endpoint of a line, the midpoint of a line, the intersection of two objects, and the center of a circle. Using object snaps all the time takes a little self-discipline until you get good at using them, so try out the steps in the following section a few times and then use them in your own work whenever possible, until the steps become second nature.

Using the Osnap Settings dialog box

The most comprehensive way to manage object snaps is by using the Osnap Settings dialog box. Open this dialog box often and use it to control exactly which object snaps are on. Follow the steps below to control object snap settings.

1. **Choose Tools⇨Drafting Settings.**

   The Drafting Settings menu will appear.

2. **Click the Object Snap tab or type** OSnap **on the command line and press Enter.**

   The Object Snap area of the Drafting Settings dialog box opens.

3. **Click the different settings check boxes to set the ones you want and clear the ones you don't want.**

   A good initial working set is to have the Endpoint, Center, Intersection, and Extension options turned on, as shown in Figure 3-2.

To change these settings, you can also right-click the OSNAP button in the status bar and choose Settings.

You can use the Clear All button to clear all the current object snap settings and then just click the ones that you want to set. (You can also choose Select All, but it's less likely that you'll want to set all or nearly all object snaps.) Even if this method takes more mouse clicks in some cases, starting from a clean slate may be quicker than thinking about which snaps are already set when you first open the dialog box and which of those snaps need to be turned off.

After you've set a group of object snaps, you can turn them on and off easily. (This is a valuable capability, especially in busy drawings in which you might snap to the wrong kind of object snap.) Just click the OSNAP button in the Status bar at the bottom of the screen or press the F3 key. The group of running object snaps that you've selected toggles on and off. (If no running object snaps have been selected, AutoCAD brings up the Osnap Settings dialog to let you set some.)

Turning on AutoSnap

AutoSnap is a new feature of AutoCAD as of Release 14, and a good one. It can change the cursor shape, show a label with the snap name, and even draw the AutoCAD drawing cursor into any snap point that you've set with running object snaps. AutoSnap is like running object snaps on steroids.

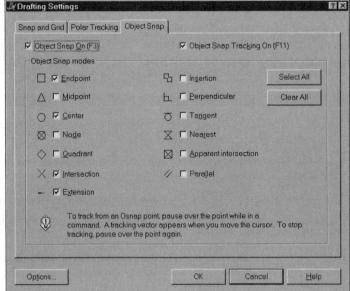

Figure 3-2:
Snap to it
with running
object
snaps.

AutoSnap is one of those things you have to see to believe and to try to find out whether you like. I'm just going to tell you how to set it up and recommend that you get to know this feature well. After you know how to use both running object snaps and AutoSnap, see whether you agree with us that this feature is worth the price of admission.

Using the Osnap Settings dialog box for AutoSnap

The most comprehensive way to manage AutoSnap is by using the Drafting tab in the Options dialog box. Use this dialog box to control exactly which AutoSnap settings are on.

1. **Choose Tools➪Options or type** OPtions **on the command line and press Enter.**

2. **Choose the Drafting tab.**

   The Drafting tab of the Options dialog box opens, as shown in Figure 3-3.

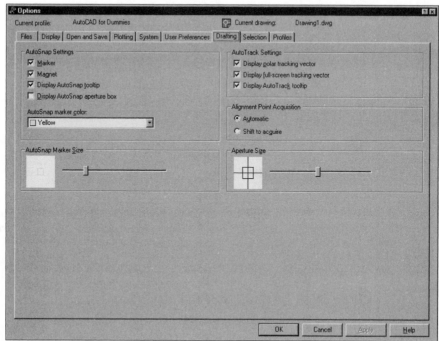

Figure 3-3:
You really
auto try
AutoSnap.

3. Click Marker to turn the Marker on or off.

The Marker is a special shape displayed when the drawing cursor moves over a running object snap point.

4. Click Magnet to turn the Magnet on or off.

The Magnet is the feature that pulls your drawing cursor toward the snap point.

The Magnet feature can be wonderful or irritating, depending on what you're trying to do, so be ready to turn this one on and off a lot.

5. Click Display AutoSnap ToolTip to turn the AutoSnap ToolTip on or off.

The AutoSnap ToolTip is a label, like a Windows ToolTip, that shows the name of the snap location.

6. Click Display AutoSnap aperture box to turn the aperture box in the drawing cursor on or off.

The object snap aperture box is displayed (or not) as a box around the point of the drawing cursor.

7. **Use the AutoSnap marker color pull-down menu and the AutoSnap Marker Size slider to change the marker color and size.**

   These options control the display of the Marker that appears when the drawing cursor moves over a running object snap point.

   You should keep the marker color one consistent color so that you get used to it. Yellow is a good color unless you already use a lot of yellow in your drawings or you use a white drawing background, in which case you'll want to change the color.

8. **Click OK.**

   Your changes take effect.

The AutoSnap feature is an excellent example of the ongoing integration of AutoCAD with the Windows user interface and of the benefits that can accrue when everything falls into place. If we weren't so tasteful in our jokes, we'd say it's a Win-Win situation for everyone.

Getting the layered look

Layers are the most important tool you have in AutoCAD for organizing your drawings. Imagine for just a moment how your body would look if it didn't have a skeleton. (*That* vision should wake you up!) Well, that's exactly what your AutoCAD drawing is like without layers: a pulsating, jumbled mass that can't do very much. Putting different elements of your drawing on different layers, such as text on one layer and dimensions on another, is an important factor in creating perfect AutoCAD drawings.

Layer decisions are even more important in AutoCAD 2000 because of the addition of new features that can be assigned to layers: lineweight and plot style. You can also easily specify whether or not a layer should be plotted. All these decisions are easier to manage if you 1) separate your drawing elements logically into layers and 2) use project, workgroup, office, company, and professional standards in your layer management decisions.

You needn't make all your layer decisions up front, however, because AutoCAD enables you to add a layer or rename an existing layer at any point in the drawing cycle. (Deleting a layer, however, is harder work.) I suggest that you always create at least a couple of additional layers as you start drawing, however, so that you aren't forced to stick everything in layer 0 and thus end up with a spineless blob of a drawing, like that hapless body without its skeleton. (Blecchh!)

Layers also interact with the AutoCAD drawing updates, called screen refreshes and REGENs, or screen regenerations. A screen refresh occurs quickly and occasionally as you make changes to the drawing; but when too many changes, or certain types of changes, occur, AutoCAD launches a more thorough and time-consuming screen update called a REGEN. The criteria that force a REGEN, and the resulting delay in your work, are too complicated to explain here, but luckily, fewer REGENs occur in the most recent releases of AutoCAD than in previous releases.

As you create new data, it goes on the layer that is designated "current." (Initially, layer 0 is the current layer.) You can make the data on a layer invisible by turning off that layer; you can prevent data on a layer from being updated during a REGEN by freezing it. You can modify or erase data on any layer that's not turned off or frozen.

These possibilities may seem like much ado about nothing if you're new to AutoCAD. But as a drawing gets more complex, seeing what you're doing becomes increasingly more difficult, and a REGEN of the drawing takes increasingly longer when you make certain kinds of changes. The capability to create and control layers is the single best tool you have to battle this visual complexity and slowness. It also allows you to plot the drawing different ways — for instance, with and without text showing, or with and without the furniture in a room being displayed.

AutoCAD enables you to specify different colors and linetypes for different objects. You can use this capability to distinguish and organize different types of objects. But the best way to use colors and, in many cases, linetypes is to group objects that need to be the same color and linetype on the same layer. By default, objects inherit the color and linetype — and lineweight and plot style — of the layer they're on. This feature makes it easy to modify the color — or other properties — of a bunch of related objects. You just change the color of the layer and then all the objects on that layer immediately inherit the new color.

Layer usage — that is, what exactly goes on each layer — and *layer names* are a big deal in AutoCAD, because drawings from different people don't work well together without a consistent layer usage and naming scheme. If your workplace uses a set of standard layer names, find out what it is and then use it. Otherwise, you need to figure out your own approach and stick with that. Dimensions in your drawings, for example, usually are placed on their own separate layer, and you should always assign that layer a consistent name, such as DIMENSIONS. This way, you can easily add elements of one drawing to another. If you need to share drawings with others, you need only to rename your layers to match their layer names and then get back to work.

The American Institute of Architects has published guidelines for layer use in the architectural and building engineering professions. Check with the AIA for a copy at www.aia.org.

Unfortunately, making mistakes in creating and using layers is far too easy to do, so you need to just keep on practicing until you finally get it right. By following the steps in this section, you can actually create and name a layer and then modify it to use a specific color and linetype. If you're in a hurry to create many layers, you can go ahead and do all the creating and naming first and then make all your color and linetype assignments afterward.

Creating and modifying layers with the Layer Properties Manager dialog box

Using the Layer Properties Manager dialog box is your best bet to create, edit, and manage layers. It's a little hard to use, however, so make sure that you follow these steps carefully:

1. **Choose Format⇨Layer or type** LAyer **on the command line and press Enter.**

   The Layer Properties Manager dialog box appears, as shown in Figure 3-4. Learning what all the icons represent can take a while. But don't worry; we explain what all the icons mean, and the AutoCAD tool tips help as well.

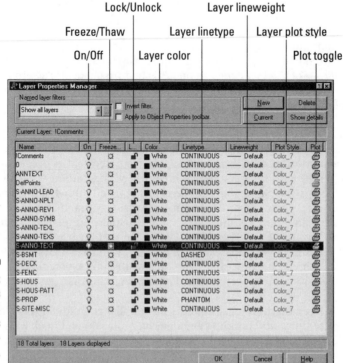

Figure 3-4: Layers revealed! Layer icons with callouts.

You can also open the Layer Properties Manager dialog box from the Object Properties toolbar by clicking the Layers icon, the second icon from the far left end of the bar — the icon displays three stacked planes (geometric planes, not airplanes).

2. **Click the <u>N</u>ew button to create a new layer.**

3. **Type the new layer's name in the text entry box of the new layer, under the column heading Name.**

   The new layer name appears in the Layer Name list. If, for example, you type **Geometry**, Geometry appears in the list as the name of your new layer.

   The headings at the top of the Layer Name list further describe your layer. The default state for this new layer is On, the Color is White, and the Linetype is Continuous. Now, however, you can modify these settings in the layer.

4. **Repeat to create additional layers.**

   A good starting set of layer names (in addition to 0, of course) may be Geometry, Text, Dimensions, and Underground.

   The next few steps apply to any layer. Just use the icon for the layer you want.

   You can create multiple new layers quickly by typing commas between the names.

   If you intend to share this drawing with others, find out what layer names the other people use and adopt those names.

   The AutoCAD 2000 DesignCenter makes it easy to steal — we mean, re-use — layer definitions from existing drawings, and for other people to re-use yours. This means it's easier to do layers right — but also more important to do them right, so that good work gets propagated and not mistakes. See Chapter 14 for more.

5. **Click the On/Off lightbulb to keep a layer off after you return to your drawing; click it again to turn the layer back on.**

   If a layer is off, your drawing doesn't display or print it.

   If you click the layer off, the little lightbulb for that layer goes dim.

6. **Click the Freeze/Thaw button to freeze the selected layer after you return to your drawing; click it again to unfreeze, or thaw, the layer.**

   If you freeze a layer, your drawing doesn't display it. Unlike with the Off setting, if you update the drawing in a way that causes a regeneration, AutoCAD doesn't regenerate the frozen layer. Because each layer takes time to regenerate, freezing layers saves REGEN time. And if you create a print or plot of the drawing, AutoCAD doesn't print the frozen layer.

   If you click the Freeze button, the little sun for that icon goes dim.

7. **Click the Lock icon to lock the selected layer; click it again to unlock the drawing.**

   Locking a layer prevents you from modifying the objects on it. You can create new objects on a locked layer, however, and you can display, regenerate, and print the layer.

   If you click the Lock button, the lock icon changes to show the hasp closed rather than open.

8. **Click the Color button to change the color you want to use on the layer.**

   The Select Color dialog box appears. Choose the color you want to use by clicking it in this dialog box. Objects drawn on this layer will be displayed in the color you choose here. The nine Standard Colors listed at the top of the dialog box are the most transferable from one system to another. If you're using a white background in the drawing area, objects drawn in the color named White appear black on-screen.

   If you change the color of a layer, the name of the new color appears under the Color heading in the Layer Name list.

   Consider using shades of gray instead of colors; grays are a more subtle indicator, and they can more clearly indicate relative depth than different colors can. They also print accurately on a noncolor printer and photocopy well on a noncolor copier.

9. **Click the Linetype name to bring up the Select Linetype dialog box and change the linetype.**

   Choose the linetype you want to use from the Loaded linetypes list in the dialog box. Objects drawn on this layer will be displayed in the linetype you choose here. If the linetype you need doesn't appear on this list, you must load it. Click the Load button and choose a linetype to load from the list that appears.

   If you change the linetype, the name of the changed linetype appears under the Linetype heading in the list of layers.

10. **Click the Lineweight to bring up the Lineweight dialog box and change the lineweight.**

    A scrolling list of lineweights and their display widths (shown by the visible line width) and plotted widths (shown as a measurement, in millimeters) appears. Choose the lineweight you want from the dialog box.

11. **Click the Plot Style to bring up the Plot Style manager and change the plot style.**

    You can change the plot style only if you are using named rather than color-dependent plotting styles. For more on this complex topic, see Chapter 9.

12. **Click the Plot icon to turn plotting of the layer on or off.**

    Layers that are on or thawed and therefore eligible to be plotted can still be prevented from plotting with the Plot option.

13. **Click a layer's name to select it and then click the Current button to designate the layer as the Current Layer — that is, the one you'll draw on after you return to your drawing.**

    The name of the Current Layer appears next to the Current button. Any new objects you create on your drawing are put onto the current layer, but you can edit objects on any layer that's on and not frozen or locked.

14. **Click OK to exit the Layer Properties Manager dialog box after you finish creating layers.**

    Figure 3-5 shows the Layer & Linetype Properties dialog box with a bunch of new layers in it. The !Comments layer is the current layer, A-ANNO-NPLT is turned off, and S-ANNO-TEXT is selected for possible editing.

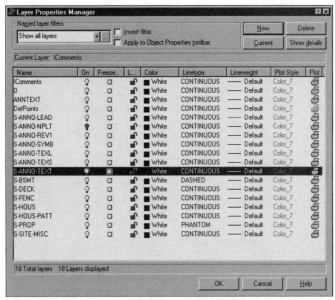

Figure 3-5:
In control of your layers.

As you create new layers, AutoCAD adds them to the existing list in the order in which you create them. You can sort the layers by any layer option simply by clicking that option's name across the top of the layer list. That's right; even a stray mouse click on the name of one of the options re-sorts the list, in ascending order. To sort them in descending order, just click the column name again. (No, you can't un-sort them!)

This fact is important to keep in mind, because this surprise re-sorting may make you think that some of your layers have disappeared when actually they've only been scrolled off the part of the layer list that is visible on-screen. And we don't want you to, uh, "resort" to doing anything drastic if this event occurs. Ouch — sorry. For example, if you want to sort the list of layers by name, click the word Name; by color, click the word Color. The list re-sorts to fit.

To work more quickly, create all your layers first by using the New command. Then change the settings by clicking the settings for the layer you want. You can make the same change to multiple layers by selecting more than one layer name before choosing the setting — as in Windows Explorer, hold down the Ctrl key or Shift key while selecting names. The Layer Properties Manager dialog box immediately updates all the highlighted layers with their new settings.

AutoCAD 2000 adds to the cool feature that lets you manage layer properties from the Object Properties toolbar. Just click the layers pull-down list to open it and then click layer properties to change them! You can change the On/Off, Freeze/Thaw, and Lock/Unlock properties. As of AutoCAD 2000, you also can change the plottability and color of a layer. To change the layer name or linetype you still have to go to the Layer Properties Manager dialog box.

Chapter 4

Setup Comedy

· ·

· ·

*W*ell, you've heard of standup comedy, so why not setup comedy? (Okay, it should be situp comedy; so sue us.) Unfortunately, AutoCAD setup can become a comedy of errors if not performed correctly.

AutoCAD does a great deal for you. But the pleasure it provides is not without an occasional jolt of pain. People who most often feel that pain haven't set up their drawings correctly. Although not fatal, this affliction can cause you to hate any and all of the following: yourself, your boss, your client, and, above all, AutoCAD. The remedy is uncomplicated: Know the steps to set up your drawing correctly. Doing right by your setup saves you trouble down the road.

The main thing that's new in setup for AutoCAD 2000 is the AutoCAD DesignCenter. DesignCenter allows you to copy all sorts of elements from existing drawings, saving you time and effort. See Chapter 14 for more on DesignCenter.

In AutoCAD 2000, AutoCAD provides setup help in the form of wizards and templates. The templates are fine if you know how to use them. However, the wizards don't set up your drawing well. To find out how to use the wizards and templates appropriately, see the section "Start Me Up?," near the end of this chapter.

You need to set up AutoCAD correctly, partly because AutoCAD is so flexible and partly because, well, you're doing *CAD* — computer-aided drafting (or design). In this context, the following three key reasons help explain why AutoCAD drawing setup is important:

- **Smart Paper:** The one thing that can do the most to make using AutoCAD fun is to work on a drawing correctly set up so that your screen acts like paper, only smarter. When drawing on real paper, you constantly have to translate between units on the paper and the real-life units of the object you're drawing. But when drawing in AutoCAD, you can draw directly in real-life units — feet and inches, meters, or whatever you use. AutoCAD can then calculate distances and dimensions for you and add them to the drawing. You can make the mouse pointer snap directly to "hot spots" on-screen, and a visible, resizable grid gives you a better sense for the scale of your drawing. This smart paper function, however, works well only if you tell AutoCAD how you set up your specific drawing. AutoCAD can't really do its job until you tell it how to work.

- **Dumb Paper:** Creating a great drawing on-screen that doesn't fit well on paper is all too easy. After you finish creating your drawing on the smart paper AutoCAD provides on-screen, you must print it on the dumb paper used for thousands of years. Then you must deal with the fact that people use certain standard paper sizes and drawing scales. (Most people also like everything to fit neatly on one sheet of paper.) If you set up AutoCAD correctly, good printing results automatically; if not, printing time can become one colossal hassle.

- **It Ain't Easy:** AutoCAD provides setup wizards and templates for you, but they don't work well unless you understand them. This particular deficiency, though improved in AutoCAD 2000, is still one of the weakest areas in AutoCAD. You must figure out on your own how to make the program work right. If you just plunge in without carefully setting it up, your drawing and printing efforts are likely to wind up a real mess. You may, in fact, end up with a virtually unprintable drawing (and probably mutter a few unprintable words in the process, too).

Fortunately, although the steps to performing your setup correctly are overly complex, you can master them with a little attention and practice. If you're somewhat familiar with AutoCAD, skip to the end of this chapter and use the section "Seven Not-So-Deadly Steps to Setup" — as well as Appendix A — to help you in your setup work. If you're new, read through this chapter once and then use the setup section and Appendix A for reference.

While you're working in AutoCAD, always keep in mind what your final output looks like on real paper. Even your first printed drawings should look just like hand-drawn ones — only better.

AutoCAD and Paper

In other Windows programs, you can squeeze content onto paper using any scaling factor you want. You've probably printed an Excel spreadsheet or Web page at some odd scaling factor such as 82 percent of full size because that's what it took to make it just barely fit on a single sheet of paper while keeping the text as large as possible.

The difference is that in drafting, your printout needs to be to a specific scaling factor, such as ½" = 1', in order to be useful and

understandable to others. But the AutoCAD screen does not automatically enforce any one scaling factor or paper size. If you just start drawing stuff on the AutoCAD screen to fit your immediate needs, it's unlikely that the final result will fit neatly on a piece of paper at a desirable scale.

This chapter tells you how to start your drawing in such a way that you will like how it ends up. With practice, this kind of approach will become second nature.

So, You're Really in a Hurry?

Tying together all the elements necessary for an acceptable drawing — the size of the actual objects you're drawing, the size of the paper you print on, and other important quantities, such as the grid display and snap grid you use — is not an easy task. (See the section "Making Your Screen Smart," later in this chapter, for details on grid and snap.)

Understanding all the pieces that contribute to the "look" of your drawing when you print it out and the "feel" of AutoCAD as you use it to create different kinds of drawings is important. However, you may already know how these different elements work, and you just need a quick guide to setting up AutoCAD correctly. Or you may be in a really big hurry and don't have time to understand it all just yet. If so, you've come to the right place.

Use Tables 4-1 and 4-2 to determine the correct settings for the major setup options in AutoCAD. (These tables are examples for some smaller sheet sizes that you're likely to use for check plots; for more comprehensive information, go to Appendix A.) Then go to Table 4-5 at the end of this chapter to find the AutoCAD options and commands that control these settings. In between, you can page through more detailed explanations of the key AutoCAD setup options. Come back to these sections when you want or need to know more.

Under *Limits* in Table 4-1, Table 4-2, or in Appendix A, find the area that comfortably encloses the size of the object(s) you want to draw as well as dimensions and text that you add outside the object(s). (Doing a quick pencil sketch of the drawing, title block, and any large areas of text might help clarify your thinking at this point.) Then coordinate that area with the *Paper Size* you plan to use and the *Drawing Scale* at which you want to present the draw-ing on the printout. Taking all these elements into account should result in a single set of figures that you can use to set up your drawing. How to use the numbers in these tables is explained in more detail in the rest of this chapter and in Appendix A.

Printing in AutoCAD 2000 benefits from the use of *layouts*, a new term for dif-ferent printable views on your document. See Chapter 9 for details.

Table 4-1	Picking Limits — Architectural Units, Horizontal Orientation				
Paper Size	Drawing Scale	Limits	Grid	Snap	Linetype &Dimension Scale
8½"x11"	¼" = 1'	44' x 34'	4'	1'	48
8½"x11"	¼" = 1'	22' x 17'	2'	1'	24
8½"x11"	1" = 1'	11' x 8½'	1'	6"	12
11"x17"	¼" = 1'	68' x 44'	4'	1'	48
11"x17"	½" = 1'	34' x 22'	2'	1'	24
11"x17"	1" = 1'	17' x 11'	1'	6"	12

Table 4-2	Picking Limits — Mechanical and Other Units, Horizontal Orientation				
Paper Size	Drawing Scale	Limits	Grid	Snap	Linetype & Dimension Scale
8½"x11"	1 = 100	1100 x 800	100	10	100
8½"x11"	1 = 20	220 x 170	20	2	20
8½"x11"	1=10	110 x 80	10	1	10
11"x17"	1 = 100		100	10	100
11"x17"	1 = 20		20	2	20
11"x17"	1 = 10		10	1	10

The number in the Linetype & Dimension Scale column is actually the *drawing scale factor* for the drawing — that is, the conversion factor between any measurement in the drawing and the real-world object it represents. If the Linetype and Dimension Scale, or drawing scale factor, is 96, for example, then a 2"-long element in your drawing represents a 192"-, or 16'-, long object in the real world.

If your dash-dot linetypes come out with the dashes and gaps seeming too large, cut the linetype scale in half.

Don't just use one of the wizards in the AutoCAD Startup dialog box and then start drawing. Your drawing is likely to be at a nonstandard scale and, therefore, difficult for others to comprehend. If you later try to change these settings, you may have to make complicated adjustments to AutoCAD and your drawing to make your drawing easy to modify and print.

If you're really in a hurry, find an existing drawing that's already at the correct scale and intended to print on the paper size you plan to use. Make a copy of that drawing and then modify the copy to create the drawing you want.

Drawing Scale Basics

The single most important item in AutoCAD setup is setting up your drawing so that it prints correctly. That means that the drawing fits nicely on the chosen paper size, leaving room for the *title block* (an area that describes drawing facts, such as the drafter's name and company name). The drawing can't be so large that it spills over onto another sheet nor so small as to leave the paper dominated by white space. Text and dimensions must be large enough to be readable but not so large as to overshadow the drawing itself.

The key element in making your drawing fit onto the paper is the drawing scale. The drawing scale is a ratio that converts the actual dimensions of the object you're representing into the dimensions that fit best on paper. However, don't use just any scale; use a recognized, easy-to-remember scale, such as 1" = 1' or ⅛" = 1'. (Anyone who has done much drafting recognizes the value of the metric system, even if it can't be used in his or her work.) The size of the paper you're drawing on, combined with the scale you're using, determines the maximum size of a real-world object that you can fit onto the paper.

Table 4-3 shows the maximum object size that can fit on a number of different paper sizes at several popular drawing scales. To use the table, determine the dimensions of a rectangle that can enclose the object you're drawing. Then find the paper size and units (English or metric) that you want to use and look under *Largest Object* to find the corresponding rectangle that is just large enough to hold your object. Read across to see the drawing scale to use.

Table 4-3	Drawing Scales, Horizontal Orientation, A-Size Paper			
Paper Size	*Drawing Scale (English units)*	*Largest Object*	*Drawing Scale (Metric units)*	*Largest Object*
8½"x11"	1" = 1'	11' x 8½'	1 = 10 mm	2.79 x 2.16 m
	½" = 1'	22' x 17'	1 = 20 mm	5.59 x 4.32 m
	¼" = 1'	44' x 34'	1 = 100 mm	27.94 x 21.59 m
	⅛" = 1'	88' x 68'	1 = 200 mm	55.88 x 43.18 m
	1⁄16" = 1'	176' x 136'	1 = 1000 mm	279.40 x 215.9 m
11"x17"	1" = 1'	17' x 11'	1 = 10 mm	4.32 x 2.79 m
	½" = 1'	34' x 22'	1 = 20 mm	8.64 x 5.59 m
	¼" = 1'	68' x 44'	1 = 100 mm	43.18 x 27.94 m
	⅛" = 1'	136' x 88'	1 = 200 mm	86.36 x 55.88 m
	1⁄16" = 1'	272' x 176'	1 = 1000 mm	431.8 x 279.4 m

The table doesn't set aside room on the paper for a title block, because the size and placement of title blocks can vary widely, so choose a scale that leaves enough room on the paper for your title block. If none of the entries in the table is close to what you need, don't worry; more-complete tables that include additional information can be found in Appendix A.

In most cases, the largest area available for your drawing will be slightly smaller than what's shown in Table 4-3 because of the small margin required by most plotters and printers. For example, a Hewlett-Packard LaserJet III has a printable area of about 7.9" x 10.5" on an 8.5" x 11" ANSI A size (letter size) sheet. If you know the printable areas for your printers and plotters, you can create a table similar to Table 4-3 using the calculation technique described in the next paragraph.

To calculate your own drawing areas and required scales, compare the horizontal and vertical dimensions of the real-world area you're depicting to the horizontal and vertical dimensions of the sheet you'll be printing on — or, better yet, to its printable area.

If you know the sheet size and drawing scale factor, you can calculate the available drawing area easily. Simply multiply each of the sheet's dimensions (X and Y) by the drawing scale factor. For example, if you choose an 11" x 17" sheet and a drawing scale factor of 96 (corresponding to a plot scale of ⅛" = 1'), then you multiply 17 times 96 and 11 times 96 to get an available drawing area of 1,632" x 1,056" (or 136' x 88'). If your sheet size is in inches but your drawing scale is in millimeters, then you need to multiply by an

A few thoughts on paper

You may already know what you need to about the paper sizes used in your profession and in your office's printers and plotters; but if not, here are a few important facts. The standard paper sizes are lettered A, B, C, D, and E. Their sizes, using ANSI standards prevalent in the U.S., are as follows:

- *A* = 8½" x 11" (standard letter-size paper in the U.S.)

- *B* = 11" x 17"

- *C* = 17" x 22"

- *D* = 22" x 34"

- *E* = 34" x 44"

ANSI sizes are different from both architectural and ISO international standards — see Appendix A for more information. An architectural D sheet is 24" x 36", for example. Make adjustments as needed for your actual paper sizes.

Knowing the following relationships makes using the tables later in this chapter — as well as switching among ANSI paper sizes — easier for you:

- *C* paper is double the length and width of *A* paper.

- *D* paper is double the length and width of *B* paper.

- *E* paper is double the length and width of *C* paper.

Because printing to a large printer, such as an E-sized inkjet printer, is expensive and time-consuming, you may often find yourself sending *check prints* to a standard office printer as a test. (The words *print* and *plot* are now used more or less interchangeably; *plotting* is often used to refer to any printing that creates a large format, such as D or E.)

To maintain correct proportions and layout, you can make check prints for C or E paper on standard A paper (for example, 8½" x 11" copier paper) and check prints for D paper on standard B legal paper. Reading some of the lettering may be hard if printing this small, but such a printout preserves the correct proportions of your drawing.

An 11" x 17" laser or inkjet printer makes a great, economical CAD output device, especially for the small office. You can do reduced-size plots for checking in-house, and have a service bureau do the final, full-size plots. (Bill the full-size plots to your client!) Most 11" x 17" printers will print on 8½" x 11" paper as well, so one device can serve both your CAD and general printing needs.

additional 25.4 to convert from inches to millimeters. For example, with an 11" x 17" sheet and a scale of 1 = 200 mm (drawing scale factor = 200), you multiply 17 times 200 times 25.4 and 11 times 200 times 25.4 to get 86,360 x 55,880 mm (or 86.36 x 55.88 m).

Conversely, if you know the sheet size and real-world size of what you're going to draw and you want to find out the largest plot scale you can use, you have to divide rather than multiply. Divide the needed real-world drawing area dimensions (X and Y) by the sheet's dimensions (X and Y). Take the larger number — X or Y will control — and round up to the nearest "real" drawing scale factor (that is, one that's commonly used in your industry). For example, suppose you want to draw a 60' x 40' (= 720" x 480") floor plan and print it on 11" x 17" paper. You divide 720 by 17 and 480 by 11 to get 28.24 and 43.64, respectively. The larger number, 43.64, corresponds in this example to the short dimension of the house and the paper. The nearest larger common architectural drawing scale factor is 48 (corresponding to ¼" = 1'), which leaves a little bit of room for the plotting margin and title block.

Taking Your Measurements

The type of units used for measuring distances and angles may well be something that you can set and then forget about for the duration of a project, if not longer. (For example, if all your work is on building plans, you may rarely need to change units.) But getting them right whenever you do set them is important. You may also need to change the precision with which AutoCAD displays units and the direction in which AutoCAD measures angles. The program provides a handy dialog box for changing units, and you can make changes from the command line as well.

Choosing your units

The *units* used within a drawing are the same units of measurement the real world uses. You draw an eight-foot-high line, for example, to indicate the height of a wall and an eight-inch-high line to indicate the cutout for a doggie door (for a Dachshund, naturally). The on-screen line may actually be only two inches long, but AutoCAD indicates that it is eight feet long if that's how you set up your drawing. This way of working is easy and natural when you understand that your drawing is printed at a scale factor. (It's a lot easier and more natural if you're working in metric units, which scale much more smoothly than feet and inches.)

For units, you choose a *type* of unit — Scientific, Decimal, Engineering, Architectural, and Fractional — and a *precision* of measurement. Engineering and Architectural units are in feet and inches; Engineering units represent partial inches using decimals, and Architectural units represent them using fractions. AutoCAD's other unit types — Decimal, Fractional, and Scientific — are called "unitless" because AutoCAD doesn't know or care what the base unit is. If you configure a drawing to use Decimal units, for example, each drawing unit could represent a micron, millimeter, inch, foot, meter, kilometer, mile, parsec, the length of the king's forearm, or any other unit of measurement that you deem convenient. It's up to you to decide.

You can choose and change the type of units you use in your drawing by changing settings in the Drawing Units dialog box. To access this dialog box to choose units (and control how angles are measured), follow these steps:

1. **Choose Format⇨Units from the menu bar; or type** UNits **at the command line and press Enter.**

   The Drawing Units dialog box appears, as shown in Figure 4-1.

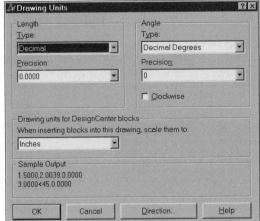

Figure 4-1:
The
Drawing
Units dialog
box.

2. **Choose from the Units area the unit option you want for your drawing.**

   Choose a unit type from the pull-down menu. As you select from among the five different options, the appearance of the text in the Precision drop-down list box changes to reflect exactly how AutoCAD displays that choice on-screen:

Architectural:	0'-0 1/16"
Decimal:	0.0000
Engineering:	0'-0.0000"
Fractional:	0 1/16
Scientific:	0.0000E+01

   In this release, AutoCAD uses drop-down lists rather than radio buttons for choosing unit types. AutoCAD also allows you to choose a unit for blocks that you insert, as described in Chapter 13. Units include not only feet, inches, and meters but also microns, astronomical units, light years, and parsecs. Whether you're a nanomechanical engineer or doing GIS work for StarFleet, AutoCAD 2000 is ready for you!

   Choose the type of unit representation that is appropriate for your own work. Engineering and Architectural units are displayed in feet and inches; the other types of units aren't tied to any particular unit of measurement. You decide whether each unit represents a millimeter, centimeter, meter, inch, foot, or something else. Decimal units usually are a good choice for metric drawings.

AutoCAD can "think" in inches! If you're using Engineering or Architectural units (feet and inches), AutoCAD understands any coordinate you enter as a number of inches. Be able to swiftly find the ' (apostrophe) character on your keyboard so that you can quickly specify feet if that's what you mean.

3. **From the Precision list box, choose the degree of precision you want when AutoCAD displays coordinates and linear measurements.**

   For Architectural and Fractional units, the choices are fractions, such as 0, ½, ¼, and so on. (Figure 4-2 shows many of the precision choices for Architectural units.) For the other three types of units, the choices offered represent the number of decimal places you can use.

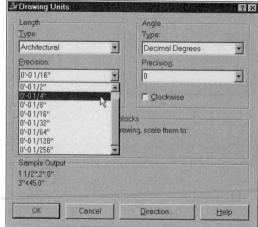

Figure 4-2:
Precision choices for Architectural units.

The precision setting controls how precisely AutoCAD displays coordinates, distances, and some dialog prompts. In particular, the Coordinates box on the status bar displays the current cursor coordinates using the current precision. A grosser — that is, less precise — precision setting makes the numbers displayed in the status bar more readable and less "jumpy." So be gross for now; you can always act a little less gross later.

4. **Click OK to exit the dialog box and lock in your unit choices.**

The linear and angular precision settings affect only AutoCAD's *display* of coordinates, distances, and angles. AutoCAD always uses maximum precision to store the objects that you draw.

If you really like using the command line, you can set units with the -UNITS command, which asks you a series of questions corresponding to the dialog box settings.

See the Sample Output area at the bottom of the dialog box for an example of what your units of length and angular units will look like when displayed.

Calculatin' all the angles

In AutoCAD, you also specify *angular units* — the way in which angles are measured, such as a circle having 360 degrees — and the direction in which to draw them. If you use decimal degrees, want to use a precision of one degree (no fractions of a degree), treat a horizontal line pointing to the right as an angle of zero degrees (as in architecture), and measure angles counter-clockwise (as in architecture), you need make no changes here. Otherwise, fire away.

In AutoCAD, you can specify the units in which AutoCAD measures angles. You choose a *type* of angular unit — *Decimal Degrees* (the most common), *Deg/Min/Sec* (useful if you're planning a sea voyage), *Grads, Radians,* and *Surveyor* — and a *precision* of measurement. You can also choose the *direction* in which angles are measured. If you set these options now but change your mind after you start your drawing, you can change angular units, precision, and direction later without causing much trouble for your drawing.

The easiest way to set and change angular units and direction is by using the Units Control dialog box. To use the dialog box to control how angles are measured, follow these steps:

1. **Choose Format⇨Units from the menu bar; or type** UNits **at the command line and press Enter.**

   The Drawing Units dialog box appears. (Refer to Figure 4-1, shown previously.)

   To enter the same keyboard command again, press Enter at the command line. This works even if the command was entered the first time by your making a menu choice.

2. **Choose from the Angles area of the dialog box the angular units you want to use in your drawing.**

   Choose the angle type you want from the pull-down menu. As you select different options, the appearance of the text in the Precision drop-down list box changes to reflect how AutoCAD displays that choice, as follows:

   Decimal Degrees: 0

   Deg/Min/Sec: 0d

Grads:	0g
Radians:	0r
Surveyor's Units:	N 0d E

The default choice is Decimal Degrees. You should, however, choose whichever angular unit you need.

3. **From the Precision drop-down list box, choose the degree of precision you want when AutoCAD displays angular measurements.**

   For Decimal Degrees, Grads, and Radians, the choices are the number of decimal places you can use.

   For Deg/Min/Sec and Surveyor units, the choices are whole degrees; degrees and minutes; degrees, minutes, and seconds; and degrees, minutes, and seconds plus additional decimal places of precision for the seconds (see Figure 4-3). For these kinds of units, be able to find the ' (apostrophe) and " (quotes) characters swiftly on your keyboard so that you can quickly specify minutes and seconds.

4. **Click to set the Clockwise check box if you need to change the direction of measurement.**

   Architects and others tend to use a counterclockwise measurement so that angles are measured "from the ground up"; it's rare to use clockwise.

5. **To change the base direction from which AutoCAD measures angles, click the Direction button below the Precision drop-down list.**

   The Direction Control dialog box appears, as shown in Figure 4-4.

6. **Choose the Angle 0 Direction you want: East, North, West, South, or Other.**

   If you choose Other, click the button below Other — it shows a little cursor pointer on it — and then pick an angle on-screen or type in the Angle you want.

   The Angle 0 Direction is the direction that AutoCAD uses as 0 for angular measurements. East is to the right on-screen, North is up, West is left, and South is down. Architects, for example, tend to use East as the Angle 0 Direction; that way, flat things are at 0 degrees and straight up is 90 degrees, which fits architectural usage. A few others tend to use North as the Angle 0 Direction, which fits compass measurement, a generally well-understood usage.

7. **Click OK to exit the dialog box and activate your choices.**

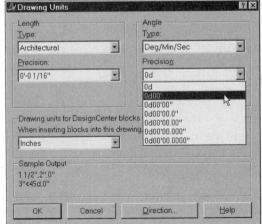

Figure 4-3:
Precision
choices for
degreed
units.

Figure 4-4:
The
Direction
Control
dialog box.

As with linear units, you can change angular units with the -UNITS command.

Setting Some Limits!

Your second chore in making AutoCAD really perform for you (after setting your drawing's units of measurement, as described in the preceding sections) is to communicate to AutoCAD how you want it to behave by setting some more of the famous AutoCAD system variables. When the system variables are set correctly, they help you create a drawing that prints comfortably onto the paper you're using, at the correct scale.

One important setup step is to set the *limits* of your drawing correctly. The limits define the size and shape of a rectangular box into which your drawing goes. This rectangular box should represent the dimensions of the paper you plan to print to, adjusted by the drawing scale you're using. That way, you can work in AutoCAD in units that fit the real-world object or area that you're drawing. Equally important is the fact that anything you draw within the limits, when they're correctly set, automatically fits on the paper at print time.

To know what to set the limits to, use Table 4-3 or Appendix A. Then follow the instructions in this section to set the limits.

Don't just set the limits to something "reasonable," such as a box that encloses the object you're drawing; you may not be able to get external elements such as dimensions, text, and the title block arranged correctly for successful printing.

Notice that you can start the LIMITS command from a menu choice but that all the action takes place on the command line; in spite of the importance of the topic, AutoCAD has no dialog box for setting limits, although the Plot Preview dialog box may prove useful for checking limits and paper size. So just follow these steps to set your drawing limits:

1. **Choose Format⇨Drawing Limits from the menu bar to start the LIMITS command; or type LIMITS on the command line and press Enter.**

   The LIMITS command appears on the command line, and the command line displays the following at the bottom of the screen:

   ```
   Command: '_limits
   Reset Model space limits:
   Specify lower left corner or [ON/OFF] <0'-0",0'-0">:
   ```

   The value at the end of the last line of the prompt is the default value for the lower-left corner of the drawing limits; it appears according to the units and precision that you selected in the Drawing Units dialog box — for example, 0'- 0" if you selected Architectural units with precision to the nearest inch.

2. **Type the lower-left corner of the limits you want to use and press Enter.**

   The usual value to enter at this point is **0,0**. (That is, type a zero, a comma, and then another zero, with no spaces.) Or you can just press Enter to accept the default value. You can adjust the limits later if you want.

   AutoCAD now prompts you for the upper-right corner of the limits:

   ```
   Specify upper right corner <1'-0",0'-9">:
   ```

3. **Type the upper-right corner of the limits you want to use and press Enter.**

   Use the Limits column in Table 4-1, Table 4-2, or Appendix A to decide on an upper-right limit that works for your drawing size, scale factor, and paper size.

   For horizontally oriented A, C, or E paper, if you know the width you want, divide it by 1.3 to get the correct proportional height to fit the paper; if you know the height you want, multiply it by 1.3 to get the height. For B or D paper, divide the known width by 1.55, or multiply the known height by 1.55, to get the other dimension.

   For vertically oriented A, C, or E paper, if you know the width you want, multiply it by 1.3 to get the correct proportional height; if you know the height, divide it by 1.3 to get the width. For vertically oriented B or D paper, multiply the width by 1.55, or divide the height by 1.55, to get the other dimension.

   Multiply the width by 1.55 or divide the height by 1.55, to get the other dimension.

   If you're using Architectural or Engineering units and you want to enter measurements in feet and not inches, you must add the foot designator after the number, such as **6'**; otherwise, AutoCAD assumes that you mean inches.

AutoCAD displays the on-screen grid (described in the next section of this chapter) only within the limits. Thus, after you change limits, AutoCAD redraws the grid — if you have it turned on — in order to indicate the area within the new limits. You might need to use ZOOM All in order to see all of the new area. ZOOM All zooms out to include the entire limits or all objects in your drawing — whichever area is larger. Limits also provide a convenient area to plot.

Making Your Screen Smart

So just what does it mean for a computer screen to be smart? No, not knowing how to tie its shoelaces or spell *cat*. Basically, a smart computer screen helps you do what you want. Now you can set up a *grid* to show you where you are within the limits and a *snap interval* that creates "hot spots" in the drawing area that are easier to draw to.

The *grid* is simply a set of visible, evenly spaced dots that give some orientation as to how you place objects in your drawing in relation to one another on-screen.

The *snap interval* attracts the mouse cursor to invisible hot spots a certain distance apart on-screen, enabling you to easily align objects a predetermined distance apart. For example, if you're designing a soccer field, having a snap interval of one meter may make good sense.

If you're using both the on-screen grid and the snap interval, you'll usually want to use spacings that relate them to each other. The snap interval should be an even fraction of the grid distance (½, ¼, or ½ of the grid distance, for English (feet and inches) units; or one or more *orders of magnitude,* that is, multiples of 10, for metric units). In this way, the grid serves as a visual reminder of the snap interval.

Technically savvy people love to say "order of magnitude," a term that simply means "a factor of ten." A dollar is an order of magnitude more valuable than a dime and is two orders of magnitude less valuable than a hundred-dollar bill. Now you can toss around the phrase *order of magnitude,* too. (Your friends may accuse you of having an odor of magnitude!)

You nearly always want a grid in your drawing because it's so useful in orienting objects to one another. (You can turn it on and off by clicking the GRID button in the status bar or by pressing the function key F7.) You may not always want to use a snap interval, however, because some drawings, such as a contour map, don't contain objects that align on specific points. (However, if you're designing a building, not having a snap interval that works may be a bad sign. You may get a thumbs up from the client but a thumbs down from the general contractor who has to build the thing.)

You can set your grid to work in one of two ways: to help with your drawing or to help you remain aware of how objects will relate to your printout. For a grid that helps with your drawing, set the grid points a logical number of measurement units apart. Grid points, for example, may be 30 feet (10 yards) apart on a drawing of a football field. A grid that helps with your printout is different; you space this kind of grid so that a grid square represents a one-inch square on your final printout.

In either case, set the snap interval at the same value or any even division of it: One-half, one-fourth, and one-twelfth work well for architecture; one-half and one-tenth work well for mechanical drawings and for other disciplines. Good starting points for grid and snap intervals for specific drawings are provided in Tables 4-1 and 4-2, which appear earlier in this chapter, and in Appendix A.

Setting grid and snap intervals in the Drawing Aids dialog box

If you're just finding out about grid spacing and snap intervals, use the Drafting Settings dialog box at first. By using the dialog box, you can quickly note and adjust the relationship between the grid and snap intervals. You're likely to want to change these settings often, however; if you do, you may also want to know how to use the command line to set them, as described in the next section.

To set the grid and the snap intervals by using the Drawing Aids dialog box, follow these steps:

1. **Choose Tools⇨Drafting Settings from the menu bar; type dSEttingsMODES on the command line and press Enter; or right-click the Snap or Grid button in the status bar and choose Settings.**

   The Drafting Settings dialog box appears (see Figure 4-5) with the Snap and Grid tab selected.

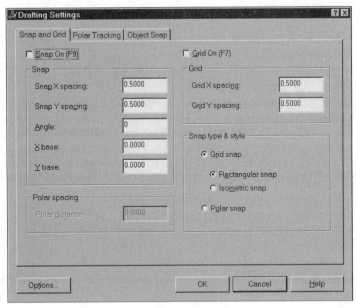

Figure 4-5:
Get your
Drafting
Settings
here!

The Snap and Grid tab has four parts, but we concern ourselves only with the Snap and Grid sections for now. Some of the other settings are nerd stuff that you can probably live a long time without ever needing to think twice about; still others are covered later in this book.

2. **Click the On check box in the Snap section (or press F9) to turn on Snap.**

This action creates default snaps half a unit apart.

3. **Enter the X̲ Spacing for the snap interval in the accompanying text box.**

Use Table 4-1, Table 4-2, or Appendix A to select a snap spacing that works best for your drawing, or just enter a value that makes sense to you; any value that's an even fraction of the grid spacing works.

The Y spacing automatically changes to equal the X spacing. Don't change it; having them the same creates a square snap grid, which is just what you want for now.

4. **Click the On check box in the Gri̲d section to turn on Grid.**

Clicking this box creates a grid with grid points spaced half a unit apart.

5. **Enter the X S̲pacing for the grid in the accompanying text box.**

Use Table 4-1, Table 4-2, or Appendix A to select a grid spacing that maps to one plotted inch, based on your drawing size, scale factor, and paper size. Or just enter a value that makes sense to you in relation to the size of the objects you're drawing and your screen area; you probably want to have at least a 10 x 10 grid to start.

The Y spacing automatically changes to equal the X spacing. Don't change it; having the X and Y spacing equal creates a square grid, which is just what you want for now. (Maybe later you'll want a different X value in your grid, but this setting is fine 'til then.)

X measures horizontal distance; Y measures vertical distance. The AutoCAD drawing area normally shows an X and Y icon in case you forget. Legend has it that the mathematician René Descartes devised this scheme after watching a fly walk on a patterned ceiling. (This story, would be better if he had thought it up while watching horses graze in a field, but to tell that story you'd have to put Descartes before the horse.)

The array of snap points is sometimes referred to as the *snap grid.* This term makes sense because the snap points do form a grid, but it's easy to get confused between the snap grid and the other grid. What to call that one? The *visible grid* is a good name because its purpose is to be seen (but not heard — or plotted). So if you use the term *snap grid* for your snaps, call the other grid the *visible grid.*

Setting grid and snap intervals from the command line

If you need to change the visible grid and the snap grid often — for example, if you switch frequently between detail work on a small part of your drawing and large-scale work on the whole thing simultaneously — knowing how to change grid and snap settings from the command line is definitely worth the effort. Follow these steps to use the command line to change these settings:

1. **Type** GRID **at the command line and press Enter.**

   The following prompt appears:

   ```
   Specify grid spacing(X) or [ON/OFF/Snap/Aspect] <0'-0 1/2">:
   ```

2. **Type the value for the grid spacing at the prompt and press Enter.**

   Use the suggested values from Table 4-1, Table 4-2, or the more complete list in Appendix A.

   When you press Enter, the grid appears.

   If you're using Architectural or Engineering units, indicate feet by entering an apostrophe after the number, unless you're sure that you want a grid spacing in inches. (Fine for a light switch, but maybe not so good for the Los Angeles Coliseum seismic retrofit!)

3. **Type** SNap **at the command line and press Enter.**

   The following prompt appears:

   ```
   Specify snap spacing or [ON/OFF/Aspect/Rotate/Style/Type]
           <0'-0 1/2">:
   ```

   The other SNAP command options — Aspect, Rotate, Style, and Type — are nerd material; look up "snap grid" in the AutoCAD online help for more information.

4. **Type the value for the snap spacing at the prompt and then press Enter.**

   Use the suggested values from Table 4-1 or Table 4-2, or use the more-complete list in Appendix A.

   After you press Enter, your cursor begins to snap to invisible "hot spots" that are separated by the snap distance.

   Use an even division of the grid spacing for your snap setting. Values of ½, ¼, and ⅛ of the grid spacing work well, for example, if you're using feet and inches; values of ½ and ⅒ of the grid spacing work well if you're using metric units or miles.

You can quickly turn on or off the grid and snap spacings by entering the commands **GRID ON**, **GRID OFF**, **SNap ON**, and **SNap OFF** at the command line.

You can also click the SNAP button in the status bar to toggle snap on and off; the same goes for the GRID button and the grid setting.

Be aware that in order to use snap effectively, you need to make the snap setting smaller as you zoom in and work on more detailed areas, and larger as you zoom back out. You are likely to find yourself changing the snap setting fairly frequently. The grid setting, on the other hand, can usually remain constant even as you work at different zoom settings.

Press F7 to toggle the grid on and off; press F9 to toggle snap mode on and off.

Scaling, Scaling, over the Bounding Main . . .

Even though you know from the tables earlier in this chapter what scale your drawing is in, AutoCAD doesn't know the scale until you tell it. This situation is fine as long as you're just drawing shapes, but you're likely to want to use different *linetypes* (patterns that make some lines look different from others) and to want to add *dimensions* (measurements that show the size of the things you're drawing).

To help AutoCAD handle these additional elements correctly, you need to tell it your *drawing scale factor* — how much it should magnify or shrink the appearance of linetypes and dimension elements in your drawing. If AutoCAD doesn't know what scale factor to use, dimensions can come out very tiny or very large, and dash-dot linetype patterns can look waaaay too big or too small.

The scale factor that controls dash-dot linetypes is found in a system variable called LTSCALE (as in LineType SCALE). The scaling factor that control dimensions is found in a system variable called DIMSCALE. Chapter 2 offers more information on system variables.

You can start the LTSCALE command from a menu choice, but you can finish it only from the command line. You can also set the linetype scale in the Linetype Manager dialog (click the Show details button) or the Properties window. You can set DIMSCALE through the Dimension Style Manager dialog box. You can change either of these settings at any time.

To set the linetype scale from the command line, follow these steps:

1. **Type** LTScale **on the command line and press Enter.**

   AutoCAD responds with a prompt, asking you for the scale factor. The value at the end of the prompt is the current linetype scale setting, as in the following example:

   ```
   New scale factor <1.0000>:
   ```

2. **Type the value you want for the linetype scale on the command line and press Enter.**

   This value is the scaling factor for linetypes that's appropriate for your drawing, as listed in Tables 4-1 and 4-2 and Appendix A. (You may want to use a somewhat smaller factor, such as half the scaling factor in the drawing; experiment with the dash-dot linetypes that you customarily use.)

To change the dimension scale, you use the Dimension Style Manager dialog box. Dimensions are described in detail in Chapter 11, but you should get in the habit of setting the dimension scale during drawing setup, as shown in the following example:

1. **Choose Format⇨Dimension Style from the menu bar, or Enter Dimstyle at the command line.**

   The Dimension Style Manager dialog box appears. New drawings contain just the default dimension style named Standard.

2. **Choose the New button to create a new dimension style that's a copy of Standard.**

   The Create New Dimension Style dialog box appears.

   Although you can modify the default Standard style, we suggest that you leave the Standard style as is and create your own dimension style(s) for the settings that you'll actually use. This approach ensures that you can use the default Standard style as a reference. More important, it avoids a potential problem in which your dimensions change the way they look if the current drawing gets inserted into another drawing.

3. **Enter a New Style Name that makes sense to you and click Continue.**

   The New Dimension Style dialog box appears.

4. **Click the Fit tab.**

   The Fit tab options appear, including an area called Scale for Dimension Features.

5. **In the Scale for Dimension Features area, make sure that the radio button next to the "Use overall scale of" setting is selected.**

6. **In the text box next to "Use overall scale of," type the drawing scale factor for the current drawing.**

7. **Click OK to close the New Dimension Style dialog box.**

The Dimension Style Manager dialog box reappears.

8. **Choose your new dimension style from the Styles list and then click the Set Current button.**

Your new dimension style, with the appropriate dimension scale factor, becomes the current dimension style that AutoCAD uses for future dimensions.

9. **Click the Close button.**

The Dimension Style Manager dialog box closes.

Make a couple of check prints of your drawing at an early stage — before you draw many objects — to make sure that everything works out the way you expect. Include dimensions, text, a couple of different linetypes, and graphics to test all the key elements of your drawing. Chapter 9 has more details.

Start Me Up?

The Startup dialog box (shown in Figure 4-6) comes up every time you start AutoCAD by choosing AutoCAD 2000 from the Windows Start menu or double-clicking on an AutoCAD 2000 program icon. The dialog box is shown with the Start from Scratch option selected. A very similar dialog box called Create New Drawing (only the Open a Drawing button is missing) comes up whenever you choose File⇨New in AutoCAD. (To get the same reaction as when you click the Open a Drawing button, choose File⇨Open.) These two dialog boxes are new as of AutoCAD Release 14 and are an attempt to ease the all-too-difficult process of setting up an AutoCAD drawing. In AutoCAD 2000 they are neither new nor, unfortunately, much improved.

Figure 4-6:
Do get me
started.

The Startup dialog box looks kind of funny — more like a little application than a dialog box. The banner across the top of the dialog box changes, depending on which button you click. But it is indeed a dialog box, one that you see quite often as you use AutoCAD.

The Start up dialog box can be a big help or a big hindrance, depending on how you use it. Its options vary greatly in their usefulness.

(Starting from) scratch where it itches

Eleanor Roosevelt was famous for advising people to "scratch where it itches." That's kind of what you're doing when you use the Start from Scratch option — that is, you do whatever you want, without any help from anyone. AutoCAD just comes up with a blank document.

This blank document is set up with the drawing area representing an area 12 units wide by 9 high and a drawing scale factor of 1. The dimensions 12" x 9" correspond to an A size architectural sheet, which almost no one uses — not even most architects. In addition, this size is inconveniently just a bit larger than normal, ANSI A size — 8½" x 11", turned on its side.

Thus, if you choose the Start from Scratch option, immediately use the setup options in the preceding sections to set limits, scale factors, grid, and snap. Then you'll be in great shape.

Using a template of doom

Using a template is actually a great idea. A *template* is simply a drawing whose name ends in the letters DWT, which you use as the starting point for another drawing. When you create a new drawing from a template, AutoCAD makes a copy of the template and opens the copy in a new drawing editor window. The first time you save, you're prompted for a new filename to save to; the original template file stays unchanged.

So templates serve as body parts, and you're Dr. Frankenstein — you make a copy of the original and then modify it to suit your evil purposes. Sounds like fun, huh?

Well, templates are fun. Using the correct template can save you hours of time and much needless worry because all the options are already set correctly for you. You know the drawing will print correctly; you just have to worry about getting the geometry and text right.

The only problem with templates is finding the right one to use. Fortunately, the Select a Template list in the Create New Drawing dialog box displays both a preview and a short description for each template.

Here are the steps for creating a new drawing from a template drawing:

1. **Close AutoCAD and restart it by double-clicking the AutoCAD icon or by choosing AutoCAD from the Start menu.**

   The Startup dialog box appears.

   You can accomplish the same thing by choosing File⇨New from within AutoCAD. If so, the dialog box that appears is the same except that it's called Create New Drawing and doesn't have a button labeled Open a Drawing.

2. **Click the Use a Template button.**

   • *Select a Template* presents a list of templates that come with AutoCAD. (Many of the templates have two versions — one for color-dependent plot styles and another for named plot styles. See Chapter 9 for information about plot styles. Consider using named plot styles if you're not sure.)

   • *Preview* shows a small thumbnail sketch of what the currently highlighted template looks like.

   • *Template Description* gives a brief description of what the template contains.

3. **Highlight the template name you want to look at in the scrolling list.**

   The Preview and Template Description change to reflect the highlighted template.

4. **Click OK or double-click the template name to open the template you choose.**

   A new drawing with no name appears. (The template you opened remains unchanged.)

5. **Save the file under a new name.**

   Take the time to save the drawing to the appropriate name and location now so that you can worry about getting your drawing right.

6. **Make needed changes.**

   For most of the templates that come with AutoCAD, you need to consider changing the units, limits, grid and snap settings, linetype scale, and dimension scale. See the section "Seven Not-So-Deadly Steps to Setup," later in this chapter.

7. Consider saving the file as a template.

If you'll need other drawings in the future similar to the current one, consider saving your modified template as a template in its own right. See the section "Creating Terrific Templates," later in this chapter.

Find or create templates for the main types of drawings that you do. Perfect them over time. You'll save yourself hours of setup hassles and the quality of your work will go up. Encourage others to do the same, and share templates. Instructions on how to set up templates appear later in this chapter.

Using a (not-so?) wonderful wizard

One of the most promising features in AutoCAD Release 14 was the Setup Wizards in the Startup dialog box. Given how hard it can be to set up an AutoCAD drawing so that everything fits and prints successfully, the wizards seemed very promising indeed.

Unfortunately, the wizards didn't do everything you need in Release 14, and they're not much improved in AutoCAD 2000.

To use a wizard, just click the Use a Wizard button in the Startup dialog box or the Create New Drawing dialog box. Then choose Quick Setup or Advanced Setup. (Figure 4-7 shows the choice between the two.) The appropriate wizard starts.

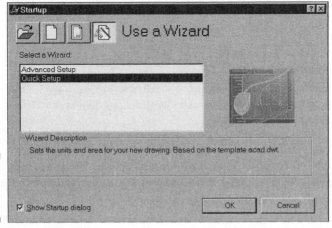

Figure 4-7:
Choose a
wizard.

The good news is, the wizards set up several parameters for you:

✔ **Quick Setup Wizard:** Sets up units and prompts you for the drawing area to represent

✔ **Advanced Setup Wizard:** Adds angular units, title block, and paper space layout questions

The bad news is, neither wizard ever asks you the paper size or the drawing scale. This omission might be okay if the wizards assumed some standard paper size and then calculated an appropriate drawing scale. But instead, the wizards invent a drawing scale that doesn't fit any standard.

Unfortunately, a drawing with a nonstandard drawing scale is almost useless. Trying to fix the drawing scale is more trouble than just following the steps in this chapter to set up your drawing.

Hopefully, the setup wizards will be improved in a future release of AutoCAD. Until then, you're best off avoiding them and advising others to do so, too.

Getting a drawing open

Opening an existing drawing is something you do every day. AutoCAD 2000 makes finding the drawing you need easier than in previous releases.

You can use one of two dialog boxes to find files:

✔ The Select File dialog box enables you to choose a file whose name and location you know.

✔ The Locate button takes you straight to a file whose name you know, as long as it's the AutoCAD library search path. Don't have a library card, you say? No problem. AutoCAD's library search path comprises the folder in which you started AutoCAD, the Support File Search Path folders listed on the Files tab in the Options dialog box, and the AutoCAD program executable folder.

✔ The Browse/Search dialog box enables you to do more speculative searching — to find a file whose location you don't know or to preview many files to see whether one that meets your needs is available. You reach the Browse/Search dialog box by choosing the Find File option within the Select File dialog box.

The AutoCAD library search path is a useful concept to understand, because AutoCAD uses it when searching for other kinds of files, such as xrefs, fonts, and AutoLISP programs. "The folder in which you start AutoCAD" — or, more succinctly, the AutoCAD startup folder — is the first place that AutoCAD looks when it performs a library search. If you start AutoCAD 2000 with a shortcut icon, then the AutoCAD startup folder is specified in the Start in folder on the Shortcut tab of the shortcut's properties. If you start AutoCAD 2000 by double-clicking a DWG file in Explorer, then the AutoCAD startup folder is the folder in which the DWG file lives.

When AutoCAD does a library search, it's supposed to include the current drawing's folder in the search as well — after the startup folder but before the Support File Search Path. The Select File dialog box's Locate button doesn't look in this additional folder. Maybe Select File lost some of its library borrowing privileges?

The shortcut for creating a new drawing is Ctrl+N; for opening an existing drawing, the shortcut is Ctrl+O.

Getting a select-ed file

To select a file to open from the Startup dialog box, click the Open a Drawing button in the Startup dialog box. A short list of recent files appears. If this list doesn't go back far enough to include the file you want, click the Browse button to open the Select File dialog box, shown in Figure 4-8. If you want to open a file and you're not in the Startup dialog box, simply choose File⇨Open from the AutoCAD menu bar to open the same Select File dialog box.

List/Details buttons

Preview box

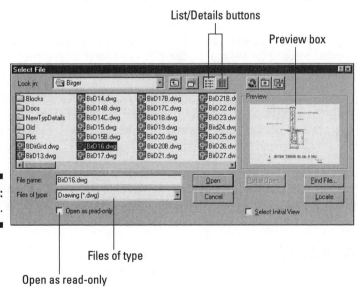

Figure 4-8:
Select a file.

Files of type

Open as read-only

The Select File dialog box is a standard Windows "Open File" dialog box, with some special features. Try clicking all the different buttons and options now so that you know what capabilities are available when you need them. Include the Browse/Search dialog box and its Browse and Search tabs, described in the following list, in your experimenting.

Some of the standard and special features of the Select File dialog box that are of special interest to AutoCAD users include:

- ✓ **List/Details:** This pair of buttons enables you to toggle between a view of filenames only and a view of filename, type, size, modification date, and more. In the Details view, you can sort by a different column, such as modification date, just by clicking the column heading. Click again to reverse the sort order.

- ✓ **Preview:** This preview window is larger than the ones in the Startup or Create New Drawing dialog boxes but smaller than the largest preview available in the Find File dialog box. It shows a preview of any Release 13, Release 14, or AutoCAD 2000 drawing file you've highlighted.

- ✓ **Files of type:** You can choose drawing (DWG) files, interchange format (DXF) files, or template (DWT) files.

- ✓ **Open as read-only:** Click this check box to open a file as read-only. When in doubt, use this option, especially if you're opening someone else's drawing!

Use these options to help find the file you need. But if you can't find the right file with the Select File dialog box, the Browse/Search dialog box offers even more powerful searching options.

Partial Open is a new feature in Release 2000 for your use in opening just part of a large file that might otherwise take a long time to load. If someone asks you to work on a file that takes forever to load, ask that person to show you how to use Partial Open. (That'll show 'em!)

To find a file located in one of the AutoCAD library search path folders quickly without navigating through multiple folders, enter its exact name in the File name area, then click the Locate button. AutoCAD will open to the folder that contains the file.

Browsing for a file

To use the Browse tab of the Browse/Search dialog box, click the Find File button in the Select File dialog box. The Browse/Search dialog box, as shown in Figure 4-9, appears, with the Browse tab at the front. (If you have previously used the Search option, the Search tab may be chosen. Click the Browse tab to bring it to the forefront.)

Browse lets you see files by previews. Most of the features of the Browse tab are either standard features of Windows dialog boxes or the same as in the Select File dialog box. The coolest parts of the Browse dialog box are the resizable previews and the network connection options:

- ✔ **Size:** This option lets you change the size of previews and includes the capability to specify the largest preview area of any file searching mechanism in AutoCAD. Figure 4-9 shows the Browse tab with this largest option selected.

- ✔ **Network:** This option brings up another dialog box that enables you to specify network drives to search on. It even has an option that automatically reconnects you to the drive each time you start up — a real time-saver when you're using a drive on an ongoing basis, such as when you join a new project.

If the Browse tab isn't enough to help you track down that file, it's time to go to your last resort: the Search tab.

The Network dialog box is the standard Windows 95/Windows NT 4.0 Map Network Drive dialog box, which you may see used outside of AutoCAD.

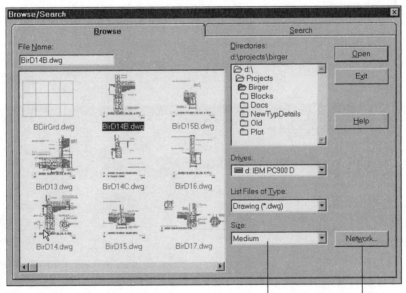

Figure 4-9: Browse for a file.

Size drop-down list

Network dialog box

Searching for a file

To use the Search tab of the Browse/Search dialog box, click the Find File button in the Select File dialog box. The Browse/Search dialog box appears, with the Browse tab at the front. Click the Search tab to bring it to the front. The Search tab is shown in Figure 4-10.

Search gives you some options regarding the search pattern or location, but the main options that Search has that the regular Select File dialog box doesn't have are a *filter,* for finding files by date, and a different kind of display. We give the date filter a thumbs up and the file display a thumbs down:

- ✔ **Date Filter:** The date filter enables you to specify an after or before date and time, based on when the drawing was last saved.

- ✔ **File display:** The display of files shows preview images of the drawings in a size that's too small to see much but that sometimes doesn't leave enough room to see the entire pathname and filename. You may have to scroll horizontally and vertically to see everything.

If you frequently have a hard time finding the files you need, consider creating some kind of record of files you've worked on. If you were to print an A-size view of each file on which you did significant work; write the filename, date, and a couple of notes on the printout; and stick that page in a file by chronological order, you'd be better able to find files than 90 percent of your coworkers.

File list   Date and time

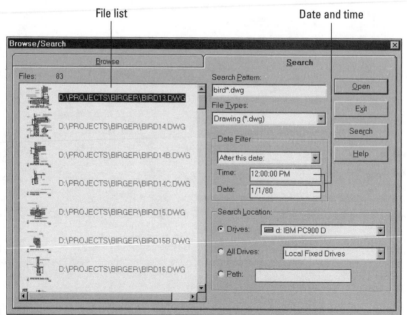

Figure 4-10:
Search
for a file.

Creating Terrific Templates

We bet you didn't notice this fact, but every drawing you create in AutoCAD is based on a *template* — a file that AutoCAD uses as the base for the initial drawing — whether or not you choose the Use a Template option in the Start Up or Create a New Drawing dialog boxes. Templates enable you to create special files for use as "masters" or starting points for new drawings. (Templates are an upgraded replacement for *prototypes,* a previously existing feature.) Templates have a special filename extension, DWT, and short descriptions that display in the Create New Drawing dialog box.

After you finish the initial setup work on a new drawing, but before you set up a lot of details, consider saving that drawing as a template. Eventually, you'll have a template for each paper size and scale factor combination that you use. You may also want to include a basic set of layers and a suitably scaled title block in each template.

After you save your drawing as a template, save it again under its regular name in the folder you want. Then you can go back to working on the drawing.

You can initiate the save process from either the menus or the command line. In either case, you use the Save As dialog box to save your work. Follow these steps to save your drawing as a template:

1. **Choose File⇨Save As from the menu bar; or type** SAVEAS **at the command line and press Enter.**

   The Save Drawing As dialog box appears, as shown in Figure 4-11.

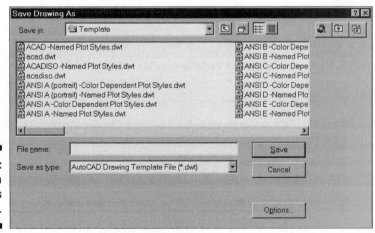

Figure 4-11:
Saving a
drawing as
a template.

2. **From the Save as type pull-down menu, choose Drawing Template File (*.dwt).**

3. **Navigate to the folder where you want to store the drawing.**

   The AutoCAD 2000 default folder for template drawings is \Program Files\Acad2000\Template. Save your templates there if you want them to appear in the Create New Drawing dialog box's Select a Template list. You can save your templates in other folders, but then when you want to use them later, you'll have to click the Browse button in the Create New Drawing dialog box and navigate to a different folder.

4. **Enter a name for the drawing template in the File name text box.**

   A name such as ESIZ48SC.DWT may seem cryptic at first glance, but a name that includes the paper size (ESIZ, or E size) and scaling factor (48SC) actually may help you find the template you need later.

   Because AutoCAD 2000 runs only on Windows 95, Windows 98, and Windows NT, all of which support long filenames, you may be tempted to use a long filename for your AutoCAD 2000 files. That's fine, because AutoCAD 2000 drawings can be opened only by people who are also running 32-bit versions of Windows, which support long filenames. But if you save the file for use by AutoCAD Release 12 or earlier, be sure to give it a filename using the DOS 8.3 pattern (an eight-character filename followed by a three-character extension, such as BUDSMITH.DWG).

5. **Click the Save button to save your drawing template.**

   The drawing is saved as a template. A dialog box for the template description appears.

6. **Enter the template file description and measurement units (English or Metric).**

   Enter the key info now; you can't do it later unless you save the template to a different name.

7. **Click OK to save the file.**

8. **To save your drawing as a regular drawing, choose File⇨Save As from the menu bar; or type SAVEAS at the command line and press Enter.**

   The Save Drawing As dialog box appears again.

9. **From the Save as type pull-down menu, choose AutoCAD 2000 Drawing (*.dwg).**

10. **Navigate to the folder where you want to store the drawing.**

    Use a different folder than the one with your template drawings.

11. **Enter the name of the drawing in the File name text box.**

12. **Click the Save button to save your drawing.**

    The file is saved. Now, when you save it in the future, the regular file, not the template file, gets updated.

Following Seven Not-So-Deadly Steps to Setup

Of the hundreds of commands available to you in AutoCAD, you really need concern yourself with only seven commands for setting up your drawing correctly. Use Table 4-5 to find both menu-driven and command line versions of these seven basic steps to setup.

Table 4-5	Seven Serviceable Setup Steps	
Step	*Menus/Dialog Boxes*	*Command Line*
Units & Angles	Format⇨Units; or UNITS command	-UNITS command
Limits	Format⇨Drawing Limits	LIMITS command
Grid	Tools⇨Drafting Settings; or dSEttings command	GRID command
Snap	Tools⇨Drafting Settings; or dSEttings command	SNAP command
Linetype scale	Format⇨Linetype; or LINETYPE command	LTSCALE command
Dimension scale	Format⇨Dimension Style, Modify button, Fit tab; or Dimstyle command	DIMSCALE command
Save template drawing	File⇨SaveAs; or SAVEAS command	SAVEAS command

Using the DIMSCALE system variable is dangerous because it creates an "override" of the current dimension style's setting. Avoid using DIMSCALE unless you're sure of what you're doing. Instead, use the Dimension Style Manager dialog box procedure described earlier in this chapter.

After you know the basic steps of setup, you can get off to a much better start on your AutoCAD drawings. Just keep in mind the following tips:

✔ Saving your drawing as a template requires no special procedures; just save it with the extension DWT and save it someplace away from your regular drawings.

✔ For the linetype scale and dimension scale, use the values that you find in Table 4-1 or Table 4-2, appearing earlier in the chapter, or in the more complete list in Appendix A.

Part II
Let There Be Lines

The 5th Wave   By Rich Tennant

GUS & LILY'S
DOG GROOMING
NOW USING
CAD SOFTWARE

In this part . . .

Setting up the program correctly makes AutoCAD work better, but all the setup in the world doesn't get your drawing done. Points, lines, circles, and other elements of geometry make up the heart of your drawing. AutoCAD offers many different drawing tools and many ways to use them to draw objects precisely. After you draw your lines, you usually must add more geometry and go back and make a few changes in your work. And in the process, you probably need to zoom in and out and pan all around to see how the entire drawing is coming together, a process that you can drive from the right-click menu in AutoCAD 2000. Editing and viewing your work are important elements of the drawing process; this part covers it all.

Chapter 5

Ready, Set, Draw!

You're never off the hook entirely when it comes to AutoCAD setup, so this chapter starts out with a quick look at the minimal amount of setup you need to create a simple drawing in AutoCAD. Then it's off to the races with some of the more meaty aspects of CAD: drawing from the command line using different kinds of coordinates, undoing what you draw, controlling the appearance of the objects you draw on-screen, and organizing your objects.

Basic drawing is one of the least-changed aspects of AutoCAD in AutoCAD 2000, but a big change in AutoCAD 2000 is that you should be doing *less drawing*. Use AutoCAD DesignCenter (see Chapter 14) and the improved intranet and Internet file access (see Chapter 20) of AutoCAD to reuse as much existing drawing content as possible. Then draw the things that are truly new in your drawing.

Making Setup a Snap

The easiest way to set up your drawing correctly is to use an existing drawing that's as similar as possible to the one you're going to create. This fact helps explain why so many drawings look so much alike and why offices often insist upon strict standards concerning the drawings created on a project. You can actually waste far more time perfecting an AutoCAD drawing — or trying to rescue a problematic one — than you would creating a hand-drawn one. So, using a copycat approach — that is, starting with an existing drawing to use as a template for your new one, as described in Chapter 4 — often is a good idea.

But many times you may just need to start from scratch to fit the specific needs of your drawing or to avoid inheriting junk that *your* ever-so-special drawing simply doesn't need. This section therefore helps you quickly set up a couple of key settings. For the complete story on AutoCAD and drawing setup, see Chapters 3 and 4.

Setting selection settings . . . selecting set- . . . er, whatever

In case you skipped over Chapter 3 too quickly, we remind you here to make sure that the AutoCAD selection settings are the way you want them. Set your selection settings as described in this section to make AutoCAD behave like a standard Windows application. You need to set your selection settings only once — AutoCAD stores these settings globally, rather than in each drawing.

To set your selection settings to Windows style, follow these steps:

1. **Choose Tools⇨Options, or type** OPtions.

   The Options window appears.

2. **Choose the Selection tab.**

   The Options dialog box's Selection tab appears.

3. **In the Selection Modes area, click the following check boxes as needed to turn on the first five selection settings:**

   - Noun/Verb Selection
   - Use Shift to Add to Selection
   - Press and Drag
   - Implied Windowing
   - Object Grouping

   Leave the final setting, Associative Hatch, turned off. This setting is misleadingly named. It doesn't turn the AutoCAD associative hatching feature on and off. Rather, it controls whether selecting a hatch object also selects the boundary with which the hatch object is associated.

4. **Click OK to exit the dialog box and put your settings into effect in your drawings.**

Note: If you're an experienced AutoCAD user and you don't want to change to the more modern way of operating, be aware that the balance of this book assumes that you use the Windows-style settings. You may need to be flexible in interpreting the detailed instructions in some of these procedures if you still use the old AutoCAD-style settings. See Chapter 3 for more information on keeping the old-style settings.

Getting a grip on your drawing

AutoCAD *grips* (little handles that show up on objects after you select the objects) are different from grips found in other drawing packages, but they're also powerful and flexible. You can easily turn the grips feature on and off from the Selection tab of the Options dialog box that you used in the preceding section. Alternatively, you can do it from the command line by following these steps:

1. **To turn on grips, simply type** GRIPS 1 **on the command line and press Enter.**

2. **To turn off grips, type** GRIPS 0 **on the command line and press Enter.**

As with the selection settings, AutoCAD stores the grip settings globally, rather than in each drawing. After you turn the grips feature on (or off), it remains on (or off) for all drawings until you change it again.

Zooming in on the results

After your other settings, such as limits, grid, and snap — see Chapter 4 — are, well, *set,* you can use the ZOOM command to zoom in on the drawing so that your screen displays the entire limits, as indicated by the grid dots. (*Zooming* just gives you a closer-up or farther-away view of your drawing.)

Whether you create a new drawing or open an existing one for editing, you usually want to start by zooming to the drawing limits so that you can see the entire working area. You then will want to zoom in when doing detail work, and zoom back out to show the full limits at various times during your work so that you can examine your entire drawing at one time. Two commands give you a view of the drawing limits: The first command zooms out so that the limits area fills your drawing window; the second command zooms out an additional 10 percent to give you a little working room around the edges of the drawing area. With both commands, you start by typing **ZOOM** on the command line, but that similarity shouldn't confuse you at all if you simply follow these steps:

1. **Type** ZOOM **on the command line and press Enter.**

2. **To show the full drawing limits on-screen, type** All **at the prompt and press Enter.**

   AutoCAD zooms the drawing so that the full limits area, as indicated by the grid dots, is visible. The AutoCAD command prompt reappears.

In fact, ZOOM All zooms to the larger of the limits or the extents — *extents* being an imaginary rectangle that just surrounds all of the objects in your drawing. If you accidentally put any objects outside the limits area, you'll see those objects now, and you can figure out whether to move them into the limits area or erase them.

3. **Type** ZOOM **on the command line a second time and press Enter.**

   Rather than retype ZOOM, you can simply press Enter to repeat the previous command, which was Zoom.

4. **At the prompt, type** .9X **to give yourself a little working space, and press Enter again.**

It's good practice to ZOOM All and then save before you close a drawing. You can do the additional ZOOM .9X step as well if you like to have the little margin. By zooming to a view that shows the full limits, or a little bit more, at the end of a drawing session, you'll be ready to go the next time you open the drawing.

The following example shows the command line with these commands entered:

```
Command: ZOOM
[All/Center/Dynamic/Extents/Previous/Scale/Window] <real
        time>: All
Regenerating drawing.
Command: ZOOM
[All/Center/Dynamic/Extents/Left/Previous/Scale/Window)] <real
time>: .9X
```

In AutoCAD 2000, right-clicking the mouse no longer simulates pressing Enter in most cases (as it did in previous AutoCAD versions). If you prefer the old "right click = Enter" behavior, you can change the settings in the Options dialog box. To do so, choose Tools➪Options, then choose the User Preferences tab. Click the Right-Click Customization button and follow the on-screen instructions to change the right-click actions. Be warned, though, that doing this will limit your access to the right-click menus that are a key feature of AutoCAD 2000.

If you're an experienced AutoCAD user, you'll notice that the command line looks different in AutoCAD 2000. After you enter a command, AutoCAD now responds with a line listing the current settings, if any. It then prompts you for your entry. It lists the default choice in <angle brackets> and puts other options, if any, in [square brackets]. (The command-line entry for ZOOM, shown previously, gives an example of how square brackets are used in AutoCAD 2000.) These are minor changes but make the command line easier to understand and use.

Drawing with AutoCAD

The rudest shock for the novice user of AutoCAD is the level of complexity involved in using AutoCAD as opposed to using most other drawing programs. (Well, actually, the rudest shock is probably the price — ten times what a standard drawing program costs; the *second* rudest shock is the additional complexity.) The difficult setup procedures and numerous methods of controlling what's happening on-screen in AutoCAD can be quite daunting without help. At no point is the program's complexity more apparent than when you're simply trying to draw something — *anything!* — on-screen. But the power of AutoCAD makes the price and initial learning curve worthwhile. (The additional power of add-on programs for specific needs, available from Autodesk and other companies, is what makes AutoCAD invaluable.)

In AutoCAD, you can draw either by using the mouse or by entering commands, coordinates, and distances from the command line. Each drawing option offers its own special advantages. But to really make AutoCAD sing, you want to use a combination of the two methods. The command line is good for entering commands that you use often and for specifying numerical coordinates and distances. The mouse is good for picking commands that you use less often from the Draw toolbar and menu, for specifying coordinates and distances with respect to existing objects, and for placing text, dimensions, and annotations.

Drawing on command

Whenever AutoCAD users talk about using the command line to "enter geometry," they mean something quite different from merely using the command line to enter commands. You can enter commands from the command line any time if you want; in fact, how you enter commands in AutoCAD is just a matter of deciding which of the following methods is fastest for you to use and easiest for you to remember:

- ✔ Use the mouse to choose the command from a menu.
- ✔ Use Windows keyboard shortcuts to choose the command from a menu.
- ✔ Use the mouse to click a toolbar button to launch the command.
- ✔ Use the keyboard to enter the command from the command line.

Entering geometry from the command line, on the other hand, means using the command line to specify the actual coordinates of points on your drawing. This method enables you to draw complicated shapes, with great accuracy, without picking up the mouse. (Unless you become really, really confused in placing your points on-screen, in which case your drawing is likely to wind up looking like mouse droppings.)

Experienced AutoCAD users can work faster than novices, especially when creating a new drawing, because they are quite accustomed to using the command line to quickly enter coordinates for their drawing. Entering drawing coordinates from the command line effectively, in the efficient manner of these AutoCAD experts, requires that you master the following different ways to enter keyboard coordinates:

✔ Absolute entry of X,Y coordinates

✔ Relative entry of X,Y coordinates

✔ Relative entry of polar coordinates

X,Y coordinates are two-dimensional coordinates defined by the Cartesian coordinate system. A specific point, called the *origin,* is defined as being 0,0. Other points are defined by moving first in an *X,* or right/left, direction, and then in a *Y,* or up/down, direction.

The grid you define shows some of the points in the X,Y map, and the snap grid you define — if you turn on the snap grid — tells you which points in the X,Y map you can select with a single click of the mouse.

The following sections further define the two types of X,Y coordinates as well as the third type of coordinates — polar coordinates.

If you're new to AutoCAD or just not yet familiar with all the different types of coordinate entry, try doing the following examples yourself; knowing all the different ways to enter geometry is a good way to improve your productivity with AutoCAD.

You can use the instructions in this section to practice or to do real work — but if you're doing real work, you should *always* draw objects on a properly defined and set-up layer. If you're working in a new drawing without any layers other than 0, see the section later in this chapter on layers before doing "real" drawing.

Absolute coordinates

Absolute coordinates are an unvarying description of a point's location. For relative coordinates and polar coordinates, described later, you need to enter a special symbol with the numbers to specify the coordinate type; but with absolute coordinates, you just enter the numbers, separated by a comma. If the lower-left corner of your drawing is 0,0, for example, the absolute coordinates 2,1 take you 2 units to the right of the lower-left corner and 1 unit above the corner. No matter where on-screen you're working at a given time, the absolute coordinates 2,1 describe that same location. If you try to draw a line from 2,1 to 2,1, it doesn't go anywhere; it starts and ends at the same point.

If you're working in architectural or engineering units, the default unit of entry is *inches*, not feet. (If you're not careful, you could end up designing a very finely detailed scale model of that office tower you've been commissioned to build!) To specify feet, you must enter the symbol for feet after the number, for instance: 6' for 6 feet. You can enter a dash to separate feet from inches, as architects often do: 6'-6" is 6 feet, 6 inches. Both the dash and the inch mark are optional when you're entering coordinates and distances: AutoCAD understands 6'6"and 6'6 as the same as 6'-6". If you're typing a coordinate or distance that contains fractional inches, you *must* enter a dash — not a space — between the whole number of inches and the fraction: 6'6-1/2 (or 6'-6-1/2) represents 6 feet, 6½ inches. If all of this dashing about confuses you, enter partial inches using decimals instead: 6'6.5 is the same as 6'6-1/2 to AutoCAD, whether you're working in architectural or engineering units.

Actually, we weren't being completely truthful when we said that absolute coordinates are unvarying. Absolute coordinates are defined with respect to the 0,0 point of the current *User Coordinate System* (UCS). AutoCAD allows you to define different UCSs, each of which can have a different 0,0 point. The UCS feature is especially useful for 3D AutoCAD work, and we discuss it briefly in Chapter 15. Throughout this book, you'll use only the default UCS — called the *World Coordinate System*, or WCS — so you won't need to worry about absolute coordinates becoming less than absolute (which would be absolutely confusing!).

The following example displays the commands you would enter on the command line to draw a three-unit-wide square starting at 2,4 by using absolute coordinates:

```
Command: LINE
Specify first point: 2,4
Specify next point or [Undo]: 5,4
Specify next point or [Undo]: 5,7
Specify next point or [Undo]: 2,7
Specify next point or [Undo]: C
```

Rather than enter point coordinates such as 2,4 from the keyboard, you can enter them by clicking at the appropriate point on-screen with the mouse. However, you must have the snap grid set up correctly or you'll pick a point near but not exactly on 2,4.

You can always complete a line command for a triangle, square, or other shape by typing **C**, for *close*, at the command prompt. The C closes the shape.

In case you've forgotten or haven't read our advice in Chapter 3, do *not* use spaces on the command line, such as between point coordinates, because AutoCAD interprets them as Enters. A definite no-no!

Figure 5-1 shows the screen with a square drawn on it by entering absolute coordinates.

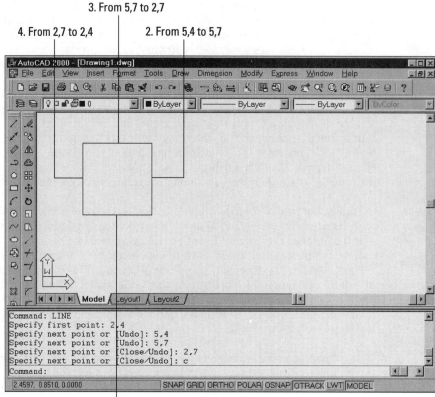

3. From 5,7 to 2,7

4. From 2,7 to 2,4   2. From 5,4 to 5,7

1. From 2,4 to 5,4

Figure 5-1:
Drawing a
square from
the com-
mand line
with
absolute
coordinates.

Relative coordinates

Relative coordinates describe where a point is in relation to the previous
point you specified. A set of relative coordinates is designated by preceding
the coordinates with the @ symbol. You need to type the @ symbol only once;
it applies to both the X and Y coordinates that appear after it.

If the first point you specify is **0,0**, for example, you can move to 2,1 from the
command line two ways: by entering the absolute coordinates **2,1** or by
entering the relative coordinates **@2,1**. Now if, at this point (pun intended),
you enter the absolute coordinates **2,1** again, you don't go anywhere new;
but if you enter the relative coordinates **@2,1**, you move right two units and
up one again.

The relative coordinates described here use the X and Y displacement from
the previous point; for relative coordinates that use an angle and a displacement, see the next section.

The following example displays the commands you would enter on the command line to draw a four-unit-wide, two-unit-high rectangle starting at 4,4 by using relative coordinates:

```
Command: LINE
Specify first point: 4,4
Specify next point or [Undo]: @4,0
Specify next point or [Undo]: @0,2
Specify next point or [Undo]: @-4,0
Specify next point or [Undo]: C
```

You can always complete a line command for a triangle, square, or other shape by typing **C**, for *close*, on the command line. The C closes the shape. (Sorry to repeat this note from the previous page, but as we mention elsewhere, plenty of people use this book as a reference and therefore miss some of the context.)

Figure 5-2 shows the screen with a rectangle drawn on it by using relative coordinate commands.

3. From 8,6 to @-4,0

4. From 4,6 to 4,4

2. From 8,4 to 0,2

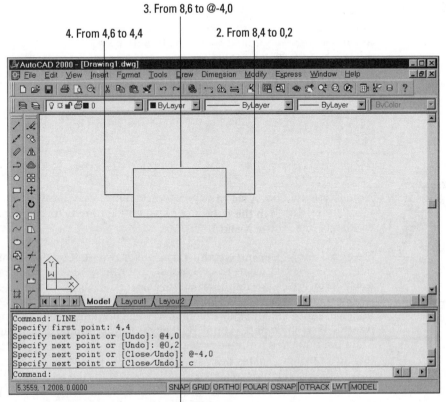

Figure 5-2: Drawing a rectangle from the command line with relative coordinates.

1. From 4,4 to @4,0

Polar coordinates

Polar coordinates are always relative, because they describe the angle and distance of one point from the previous point. The angles you enter for polar coordinates depend on the angle direction you specify; the default in AutoCAD assumes that an angle to the right is 0 degrees, an angle straight up is 90 degrees, an angle to the left is 180 degrees, and an angle straight down is 270 degrees. This default setting represents the most commonly used angle directions.

To change the angle direction to something different, such as designating straight up as 0 degrees, type **UNits** on the command line and press Enter to open the Drawing Units dialog box. Then click the Direction button in the dialog box. Chapter 4 contains more detail on changing angle measurement this way.

The odd thing about polar coordinates is that, although they specify a point relative to the last point you entered, the *angle* you enter is absolute. No matter the direction of the last line segment you draw, the polar coordinates angle is always with respect to the zero angle direction that you specified in the Drawing Units dialog box.

You specify a polar coordinate on the command line by using the @ symbol to indicate relative coordinates and the less-than symbol (<) to indicate an angle. The following example displays the commands necessary to draw an equilateral triangle, three units on a side, starting from the coordinates 5,5 and using polar coordinates:

```
Command: LINE
Specify first point: 3,3
Specify next point or [Undo]: @3<0
Specify next point or [Undo]: @3<120
Specify next point or [Undo]: C
```

As mentioned in previous examples, you can always complete a line command for a triangle, square, or other shape by typing **C**, for *close*, on the command line. The C closes the shape.

Figure 5-3 shows the screen with a triangle drawn on it by using polar coordinate commands. Drawing the second side of the triangle demonstrates why polar coordinates are so important, because entering the uppermost vertex of the triangle exactly using absolute or relative X,Y coordinates requires a bunch of those algebra and trigonometry calculations that you probably haven't used since high school. By using polar coordinates, you can enter the exact point needed for the drawing and preserve the precision of the objects in your drawing.

3. From approx 4.5,5.6 to 3,3   2. From 6,3 to @3<120

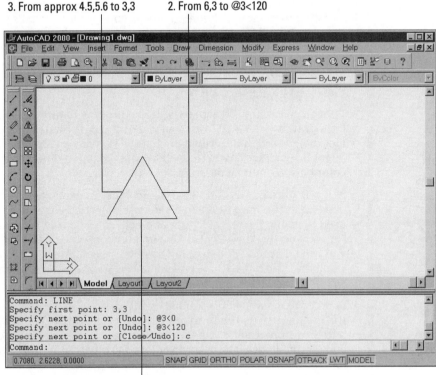

Figure 5-3:
Drawing a
triangle
from the
command
line with
polar coor-
dinates.

1. From 3,3 to @3,0

Getting the look right

Wanting different objects in your drawing to look different is a pretty natural desire. A different look — different colors, lineweights, linetypes, or line widths — can communicate important information about the characteristics of the object being drawn, about what other objects it may be like, or even about the relative depth of objects within a drawing. (That is, which *real-world* objects are above or in front of one another; the drawn objects are, of course, all flat and only as far from your nose as the screen or paper. Maybe we've been spending too long looking at a screen ourselves. . . .)

The most commonly used ways that AutoCAD enables you to make objects look different from one another are through changes to the *color* of an object or to the *linetype* of an object:

  ✔ *Linetype* describes the pattern of dashes, dots, and empty spaces in a line. For example, you might use a dashed linetype to indicate objects that are below the ground, or a special sequence of dashes and dots to indicate a boundary between two countries.

✔ *Color* is also used to differentiate objects, but more for on-screen differentiation than for any differentiation on the printout. That's mainly because most CAD drawings are either printed in black and white in the first place or are eventually copied using a monochrome device such as a black-and-white photocopier or a blueline machine. So in most cases, plan to use color mainly to communicate nice-to-have information rather than must-have information.

Though color often "disappears" in the process of printing or reproducing a drawing, AutoCAD offers another way to distinguish lines. In the Plot dialog box, as described in Chapter 12, you can assign colors to different linewidths. This setting allows lines that are differentiated by color on-screen to be differentiated by thickness on the plot.

A new feature in AutoCAD 2000 is the ability to explicitly assign *lineweights*, or line widths, to layers and objects. Lineweights can be used to mimic the use of lighter and heavier pencils in manual drafting. Not only do the lineweights show up in the printed or plotted drawing, you can tell AutoCAD to display them on-screen. AutoCAD 2000 lets you explicitly specify what on-screen lineweights will be used to represent which printed lineweights, as described later in this chapter.

In order to maintain compatibility with existing drawings, many offices will continue to use color to represent plotted line width for some time into the future. Check with your colleagues before specifying on-screen and plotted linewidths or using colors as colors rather than as a stand-in for linewidths.

Users of AutoCAD assign linetype, color, and lineweight distinctions according to conventions that make them valuable. Linetypes most often indicate different types of objects; color, as often as not, indicates the layer that an object is on. (Color is then translated into lineweight at printing time, if you are still using color to stand in for line width.) Sometimes the linetype, the color, and the layer mean exactly the same thing; you may draw all the trees in your drawing in dashed lines, in green, on the Foliage layer. But you can also use layers to subdivide a category; you may subdivide the foliage into Trees, Bushes, and Grass layers, for example, all of which are green and all drawn with the same linetype.

You can also specify linetypes, colors, and lineweights for each individual object you create, which at first seems like a good idea because it gives you a great deal of control. But this practice can quickly become cumbersome if you must assign separate linetypes, colors, and lineweights for each type of object, as well as remember *why* you made all the decisions for each object. Sometimes, however, you simply find it necessary to be that specific, and if that's the case, AutoCAD quite handily supports this capability; just make sure that you use it as sparingly as you can. (Or you may need a whole 'nother computer just to keep track of what all the colors, linetypes, and lineweights for all your different objects mean.)

Using colors as colors?

In previous releases of AutoCAD, color was used to indicate what lineweight to use in printing out each object. With AutoCAD 2000, you can actually use colors to indicate colors. This makes much more realistic representations possible. However, it also means that you lose a lot of information if your printer, plotter, or photocopier doesn't reproduce color.

We recommend that you begin using color as color as soon as reasonably possible. Getting there may take a while, though. Your whole office, and possibly also relevant colleagues outside your office, should be on AutoCAD 2000 so that you can all edit the color information in one anothers' drawings. Also, you should be ready to print and photocopy the majority of your drawings in color. Though getting to this point may be time-consuming and difficult, it will make your drawings better at communicating your intent and representing the reality they'll someday be converted into.

 Many professions and projects have developed detailed standards for how to use linetypes, lineweights, and layers. Linetypes and lineweights help the users of your drawings distinguish different kinds of objects. Layers are especially important when you share drawings with others who are currently working on the project or who may later want to reuse your work. Determine what standards, if any, exist for your profession and follow them relentlessly; doing so makes it possible for you and others to reuse your current work in later work that you do. Not following standards can cost you and others hours and hours of work, or even cause you to ruin existing drawings when you edit them.

Using that layered look

In the following example, you create two layers with different linetypes and colors, and then draw objects on these layers. The objects in this example are the outline of a swimming pool and the fence around it (but you can plug your own layer names into these basic steps at any point to create your own drawings). You use the Layer Properties Manager dialog box in this example.

 In AutoCAD 2000, you use the Layer Properties Manager dialog box for this procedure; it replaces the Release 14 Layer tab of the Layer & Linetype Properties dialog box, and the Layer Control dialog box of Release 12 and Release 13.

Follow these steps as a guide to creating layers for different linetypes and colors:

1. **Choose Format⇨Layer from the menu bar; or type** LAyer **at the command line and press Enter.**

   The Layer Properties Manager dialog box appears, as shown in Figure 5-4. A new drawing has only one layer, Layer 0. You need to add the layers you need for your drawing.

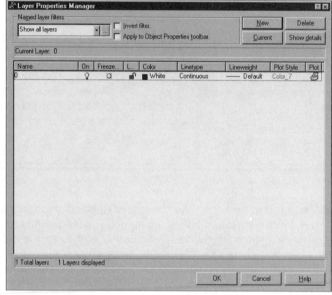

Figure 5-4:
The Layer
Properties
Manager
dialog box
with only
Layer 0
defined.

2. **Click the New button to create a new layer.**

   A new layer appears. It's given the name Layer1, but the name is selected so that you can easily type a new name to replace it.

3. **Type a name, Concrete in this example, as the name for the new layer.**

   In AutoCAD 2000, unlike in Release 14, AutoCAD no longer automatically converts the layer name to an initial capital letter followed by lowercase letters. You can enter layer names in any combination of lowercase and uppercase that suits your fancy. Be aware that uppercase letters are wider than lowercase letters, so layer names written completely in uppercase are much wider, which means that they often get truncated in the Object Properties toolbar's layer drop-down list. In addition, uppercase layer names look like they're SHOUTING at you, which is not what you need at the end of a long, hard day in front of the AutoCAD screen. Use layer names with initial caps instead.

4. **On the same line as the new layer, click the color block or color name,** White, **of the new layer.**

   The Select Color dialog box appears, as shown in Figure 5-5.

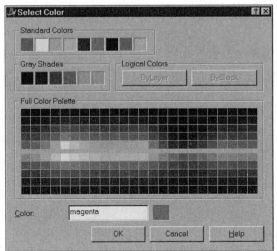

Figure 5-5:
The Select
Color dialog
box with the
color
magenta
selected in
the
Standard
Colors list.

5. **Click a color to select it as the color for this layer and then click OK.**

   For the Concrete example, click dark gray (color 8), the eighth color
   from the left in the Standard Colors list.

   The colors available on your system may be different from those on
   ours, so the exact appearance of your Select Color dialog box also may
   be different than that shown in the figure. But that's okay; just pick any
   of the Standard Colors that you want from the list on your system.

   The Layer Properties Manager dialog box reappears. In the Name list,
   the Color for the Concrete layer changes to 8, which is the color number
   for dark gray. (This number also appears in the Color text box at the
   bottom of the Select Color dialog box after you select the color.)

6. **On the same line as the new layer, click the Linetype name of the new
   layer.**

   In this case, the Linetype name is Continuous.

   The Select Linetype dialog box appears, as shown in Figure 5-6.

   If you already loaded the linetypes you need for your drawing, the Select
   Linetype dialog box displays them in the Loaded linetypes list. If not,
   click the Load button to open the Load or Reload Linetypes dialog box.
   By default, AutoCAD displays linetypes from the standard AutoCAD 2000
   linetype definition file, Acad.lin, which is located in your Support
   folder — \Program Files\Acad2000\Support in a normal AutoCAD
   installation. Load the linetype named Border by selecting its name and
   clicking the OK button. You can also load the linetype Divide2 at this
   time, because you can use that linetype to indicate the fence around the
   swimming pool.

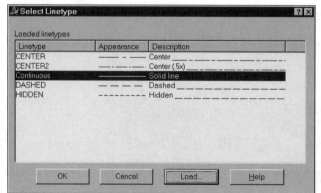

Figure 5-6:
The Select
Linetype
dialog box.

Remember that AutoCAD is now highly Windows compliant, and many tricks that work in other Windows dialog boxes work in AutoCAD. For instance, to sort your linetypes in ascending alphabetical order, click the column header Linetype in the Select Linetype dialog box. To change the order to Descending, click the column header again. You can also click Description to sort by description, but clicking Appearance doesn't do anything. (Yes, we think Autodesk should use one of those little Tower of Hanoi icons to indicate which direction the list is sorted in.)

7. **Click Border in the Loaded linetypes list to highlight and select it as the linetype for the Concrete layer and then click OK.**

   After you click OK, the Select Linetype dialog box disappears, returning you to the Layer Properties Manager dialog box. In the Name list, the Linetype for the Concrete layer changes to Border, the linetype you just selected.

8. **On the same line as the new layer, click the lineweight of the new layer.**

   The Lineweight dialog box appears.

9. **Choose the line width you want from the scrolling list; click OK.**

   For the example, we use .30mm, a moderately thick line, for the Concrete layer.

   For more information on the two remaining choices, see Chapter 9 for Plot Style and see Chapter 3 for Plot.

10. **Repeat Steps 2 through 9 to create another layer called Fence with the standard color cyan (light blue), the linetype Divide2, and lineweight 0.00mm (which tells AutoCAD to use the thinnest possible lineweight on the screen and on the plot).**

    The Layer Properties Manager dialog box reappears with your two new layers set up.

11. **Select your new Concrete layer and choose the Current button to make it the current layer.**

    The current layer is the one on which AutoCAD places objects that you draw.

12. **Click OK to accept the new layer settings.**

    Notice that the Layer drop-down list on the Object Properties toolbar now displays `Concrete` as the current layer.

13. **Draw the outline of the pool using commands such as LINE or PLINE (see Chapter 6 for details).**

    The objects you draw appear dark gray and with the Border linetype, because they inherit these properties from the Concrete layer.

14. **Open the Layer Properties Manager dialog box again, set the Fence layer current using the procedure described in Step 11, choose OK to close the dialog box, and then draw the fence around the pool.**

    The objects you draw appear cyan and with the Divide2 linetype, because they inherit these properties from the Fence layer.

After you've created layers, you can set any one of them to be the current layer by making sure that no objects are selected and then choosing the layer name from the Layer drop-down list on the Object Properties toolbar. See the following section for details.

Objective properties

In Release 13 and previous versions of AutoCAD, you used the Object Creation Modes dialog box to change colors, linetypes, and other settings. If you're an experienced AutoCAD user, you probably have typed DDEMODES from the command line many times to bring up this dialog box. But now you don't have to bring up this dialog box anymore; it's gone! In Release 14, most of the functions of the Object Creation Modes dialog box were moved into the Object Properties toolbar, where they're much more readily available. AutoCAD 2000 adds the Lineweight and Plot Style options to the Object Properties toolbar.

In AutoCAD 2000, you can use the Object Properties toolbar in two ways: to change the *current* properties — those that get applied to objects that you draw subsequently — and to change the properties of existing objects. In both cases, the properties you can change are layer, color, linetype, lineweight, and plot style. Each property has its own drop-down list on the Object Properties toolbar, as shown in Figure 5-7. (You've heard of *MTV Unplugged?* Well, we have Object Properties undocked!)

Make object's layer current button

Layer control pull-down menu

Layers button

Plot style control pull-down menu

Linetype control pull-down menu

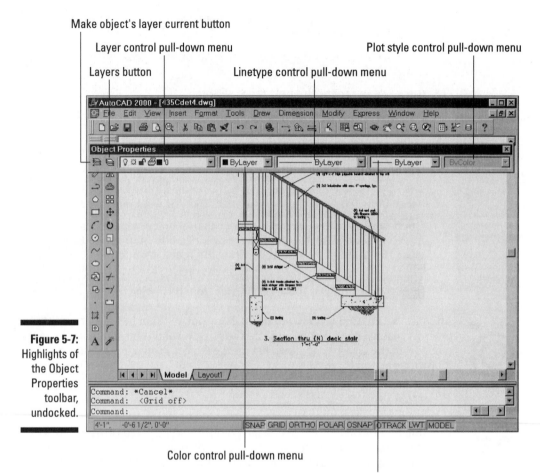

Figure 5-7:
Highlights of
the Object
Properties
toolbar,
undocked.

Color control pull-down menu

Lineweight control pull-down menu

If you haven't selected any objects, the Object Properties toolbar drop-down lists display the current properties — those properties that get applied to new objects when you draw them. You change any of the current properties by dropping down the appropriate list and choosing a different setting. If you have selected objects, the Object Properties toolbar lists change to display the properties that those objects have in common. If you choose a different setting from one of the lists while objects are selected, AutoCAD changes the properties of those objects — it doesn't change the current settings that get applied to new objects.

ByLayer is the default setting for colors, linetypes, lineweights, and plot styles. The ByLayer setting enables you to automatically use the color, linetype, or lineweight defined for a layer on objects on that layer. If an object has ByLayer assigned as its color, for example, and is on a layer assigned the color green, that object is shown in green. If you later change the layer's color to, say, red, all objects on the layer that are assigned ByLayer as their color property instantly become red as well.

In some cases, you will want to set specific colors or other properties for specific objects. Although it's best in most cases to use ByLayer to allow the layer to determine an object's properties, it's the exception that proves the rule, and sometimes you will need to set property values specifically for an object. To change an object's color and linetype, follow these steps:

1. **Open or create a drawing with at least one object.**

   If you're just getting started with AutoCAD, you can use one of the drawings in the AutoCAD Samples folder.

2. **Select an object.**

3. **In the Object Properties toolbar, click the Color Control pull-down menu in the middle of the toolbar.**

   The Color Control menu appears, as shown in Figure 5-8. It contains the standard colors plus any additional colors you have selected in this drawing.

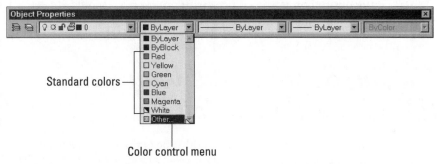

Figure 5-8:
The Color Control pull-down menu.

4. **Click the color that you want to use for your object.**

   The pull-down menu pulls back up and the color you selected is applied to the selected object.

   To bring up the Select Color dialog box from the Color Control pull-down menu and choose a different color than those already on the list, choose Other, the last item in the list.

5. **Click the Linetype Control pull-down menu.**

   The Linetype Control menu appears, as shown in Figure 5-9. It contains all the linetypes you have loaded for use in the current drawing plus ByLayer, which assigns the linetype of the current layer, and ByBlock, which is for use with block definitions and which you should avoid — at least until you read about blocks in Chapter 13.

Figure 5-9:
The
Linetype
Control
drop-down
list.

6. Click the linetype that you want to use for your object.

The linetype of the selected object changes. Experiment with different linetypes to see how they look when used on a real object.

If you don't have enough linetypes to experiment with, choose Other from the Linetype Control drop-down list to load additional linetypes into the current drawing.

In many offices, overriding the default ByLayer properties with different colors, linetypes, lineweights, and plot styles is a CAD no-no. In most cases, you should control objects' properties by putting them on layers that have the desired properties. Check with others in your office to see what the local rules and regulations are.

Making Repairs: The Way You UNDO the Things You Do

One of the biggest problems in drafting is the sheer ease involved in thoroughly messing up an otherwise great drawing just by mismeasuring something or drawing an errant line or two. In a paper-and-pencil drawing, fixing such a mistake may require so much erasing and redrawing as to make the mistake irreparable. But with AutoCAD, you can fix most mistakes. (Not all, mind you, but hey, you can't have everything!)

The mistakes that you *can* fix in AutoCAD are mostly errors of *commission;* that is, you commit an act you shouldn't have. You may, for example, draw a square in the middle of a complex drawing and then realize — ackkkk! — you should have drawn a circle instead. Well, no problem. Mistakes such as these are easy to fix in AutoCAD; these types of mistakes, in fact, are what the undo capability was designed for. (Da da da da ta-daaa!)

But before we discuss this modern wonder of CAD, we must take time to mention the horror of (pause for effect) the mistakes you *can't* fix easily in AutoCAD! (Cue thunder and lightning.) These mistakes are mostly errors of *omission;* in other words, you neglect to perform a setup step or you set a mode setting incorrectly, and as a result, your drawing becomes very testy when you or others attempt to work with it. If you complete a complicated drawing but neglect to set limits correctly, for example, you may find that creating a usable, single-sheet printout of your drawing that looks at all fetching becomes very, very hard. You may need to rearrange the elements in your drawing considerably or even perform complicated manipulations in paper space (described in Chapter 9) just to get a decent-looking printout.

To help you repair either kind of error, AutoCAD provides a powerful undo/redo feature. Unlike the undo capabilities of many other programs, the AutoCAD UNDO command does — or undoes — almost anything you want, up to and including the following feats of design derring-do:

- ✔ Undo goes back a nearly unlimited number of steps, all the way back to the beginning of the current drawing session.
- ✔ Undo is not affected by saves; you can save your drawing and still undo actions performed before the save.
- ✔ Undo affects almost all commands. The undo capabilities of some programs affect only specific commands; AutoCAD undoes not only items you actually draw but also mode settings, layer creation, and more.
- ✔ The UNDO command offers several different options for handling groups of commands or erasing several commands simultaneously.

This section describes the most useful features of the AutoCAD undo capability, those you need 99 percent of the time. For more details and information on other, less frequently useful features, especially should an emergency arise, look up "UNDO command" in the AutoCAD 2000 on-line Help facility.

The AutoCAD undo capability does not work for all AutoCAD commands and does not reverse changes made to all system variables. Among the important commands AutoCAD can't undo are the following:

- ✔ Adding a new plotter or printer configuration.
- ✔ NEW or OPEN, used to create or access drawings.
- ✔ QSAVE, SAVE, and SAVEAS, used to save drawings to disk, as well as commands such as DXFOUT and WMFOUT that export versions of the drawing to other file formats on the disk.
- ✔ PLOT, used to plot a drawing. (Because creating an UNDO command that makes the printer pick up a sheet of paper and erase it would be pretty difficult!)

If you're using the UNDO command to fix a complicated or long-ago mistake, consider saving your drawing to a different name before starting the undo process. You may want to save some parts of your work but not others, and having an additional copy of the messed-up drawing can help you do so.

AutoCAD provides two kinds of UNDO commands for reversing a single step. The more common command is *U*, short for UNDO (well, what did you expect — Unicorn?), and the less commonly used command is *OOPS* (for obvious reasons).

Typing **U**, as described in this chapter, undoes a single step; typing out **UNDO** at the command line brings up several options, which you will rarely need. Experiment with the UNDO command if you do need more than one-step-at-a-time undo capabilities.

OOPS reverses the last ERASE command, even if you used a bunch of other commands in between the time you used ERASE and the time you realize you didn't really want to erase those objects. Just enter **OOPS** at the command line after you accidentally use ERASE to . . . uh, well, erase something, or some things. OOPS instantly reverses the effect of that ERASE. (This command also works if you simply change your mind, rather than make an out-and-out mistake.) Be careful, though — OOPS works only for the last ERASE. You can't use OOPS again to get back the second-to-last set of objects that you erased! Maybe AutoCAD needs a TWOOPS command?

You can start the ERASE command by typing **Erase** at the command line or by clicking on the Erase button, the button that looks like a pencil with an eraser at the top of the Modify toolbar.

The UNDO command, however, does much more. The simplest way to use the undo capability is to just keep undoing your previous actions, one U at a time, until you work your way back to your mistake. To UNDO and REDO a command sequence a single step at a time, follow these steps:

1. **Use the U single-step undo command.**

   You can run the U command in any of the following ways:

   - Choose <u>E</u>dit⇨<u>U</u>ndo from the menu bar.

   - Press Ctrl+Z.

   - Type **U** at the command line and press Enter.

   - On the Standard toolbar, click the button that displays a curved arrow pointing to the left.

   - Right-click in the drawing area and choose Undo from the cursor menu.

The UNDO capability works even across saves of your drawing. It does not, however, work after you close your drawing and then reopen it. Think twice, therefore, before you close any drawing; you may later wish you had undone something in it first — but by then it's too late.

2. **Think carefully now, before doing anything else, about whether you really wanted to perform an UNDO operation.**

   This warning is a *very important* one: The AutoCAD REDO capability redoes only the *last* step that you undo; unlike the UNDO command (or that annoying Energizer bunny), REDO does *not* just keep on going. In AutoCAD, as in life, you really don't want to undo much without thinking about it first. Otherwise, you can all too easily just keep undoing and undoing — and then realize too late that you've gone too far and undone valuable, even irreplaceable, work. Also, it is far too easy to undo one action, replace it with another, and only then realize that you didn't really want to undo the first action at all. Too late! If you enter another command after using UNDO, REDO doesn't work. Not even a little. So after each individual UNDO you perform, think — THINK, as those old IBM signs used to say — about what you've just (un)done and make sure that you're truly glad you got rid of it, whatever it was, before you lose the capability to replace it.

3. **If you need to, redo the step by performing a REDO operation.**

   Your choices include the following actions:

   - Choose Edit⇨Redo from the menu bar.

   - Type **REDO** at the command line and press Enter.

   - On the Standard toolbar, click the button that displays a curved arrow pointing to the right.

   - Right click in the drawing area and choose Redo from the cursor menu.

   You can redo only *one action.*

   Do not try to type **R** at the command line to redo a command. REDO does not work like UNDO in using its initial as the command to activate it. *R,* in fact, is the abbreviation for the REDRAW command, not REDO. If you enter **R** at the command line, not only must you wait while AutoCAD redraws the screen, you will also discover that the REDO command doesn't work anymore because you executed another command after the UNDO. (If you think that this scenario seems like paying twice for one mistake, you're not alone.)

4. **Use one the single-step U command (described in Step 1) again if you want to continue undoing.**

   Continue to choose Edit⇨Undo, press Ctrl+Z, enter **U** at the command line, or click the Standard toolbar button with the arrow curved to the left. Continue to consider, after each UNDO step, whether you're sure that you haven't already undone too much.

The best way to get to know the UNDO capability in AutoCAD is to experiment with it. Create a test drawing with different layers and other settings and create some geometry on-screen. Then use UNDO to back up through your actions, watching what happens as you do so. Read the command line after each undo — AutoCAD tells you which command it's undoing. Experimenting helps you use UNDO intelligently and not overdo it when you really need it — and not overdo UNDO when you really need to REDO.

Chapter 6

Tooling Around in Your Drawing

*T*he main purpose of AutoCAD, of course, is to support computer-aided drafting (what a concept!). And the most important activity in drafting is drawing *geometry* — shapes such as lines, circles, rectangles, and so on. Dimensions, text, and other important parts of the drawing — neat as they are — don't matter much unless the underlying geometry is right.

AutoCAD offers a powerful range of drawing tools. The drawing tool lineup isn't changed much in AutoCAD 2000; it wasn't changed in Release 14, either. What has changed since Release 13 is that the toolbars — the *flyouts* that enabled you to access suboptions — in the Draw toolbar are gone. (Maybe the AutoCAD programming team went to a *San Francisco Giants* game and decided to "sacrifice flyouts." Sorry. . . .) Instead, you start the command from the Draw toolbar and then use the new AutoCAD 2000 right-click menus that offer options relevant to the current command. Alternatively, you can enter options at the command line, as in previous AutoCAD versions.

Many of the choices on the AutoCAD 2000 Draw menu open submenus containing several variations on each drawing command. (A *submenu* is a secondary menu that is available as an additional choice only after you choose a menu item by highlighting it. We just want to make sure that you know that a submenu isn't what the crew of a submarine uses to decide on dinner.)

In this chapter, you find out how to get the most out of the AutoCAD drawing tools. You also discover — in detail — how to get what you want out of the AutoCAD user interface, whether you use the menus, the toolbars, or the command line. The tips and tricks you find in this chapter, in fact, help you navigate through all of AutoCAD.

Introducing the AutoCAD Drawing Tools

For descriptive purposes, this chapter divides the drawing tools into the following three groups:

- ✔ Lines
- ✔ Points and polygons
- ✔ Curves

Third-party add-on packages that run with AutoCAD often add extra drawing tools to the mix; see the documentation that comes with the add-on program for information on such tools.

With AutoCAD 2000, Autodesk continues its push to make AutoCAD easier for third-party developers to customize. Autodesk also offers an increasing number of specialized versions of AutoCAD (such as Architectural Desktop), some of which compete with products from those same third-party developers. Use this chapter to learn the core tools that come with all versions of AutoCAD; then use the documentation that comes with your specialized version or add-on program to learn the additional capabilities it has. (You might well need some extra training in the add-on application, because many of them are powerful but complicated.)

Using the command line — or at least watching the command line for prompts — is unavoidable when drawing. You can start drawing commands from the Draw menu, which gives you submenus from which to choose options, but this method is slow. You also can use the Draw toolbar, but it simply types the initial command on the command line for you; you then must respond to prompts that display on the command line. You can respond by typing at the command line or, in many cases, by selecting options from the right-click menu, which changes to reflect the current command's options. The examples in this chapter just cut right to the chase and show you how to do things from the command line. You can start the commands any way you like, and you can use the right-click menus rather than the keyboard to respond to prompts.

Table 6-1 offers an overview of most of the drawing tools native to AutoCAD, without the 3D-related commands. It describes the tools' major options and shows you how to access them from either the command line, the Draw menu, or the Draw toolbar. Use the table for an initial survey of what's available and as a quick refresher course if you're working along and suddenly find yourself at a loss for the command to access the tool you need. (Oh, and don't worry just yet if not all the terms on the table are familiar to you; they all become clear as you read through the chapter and use the commands. Trust us.)

Table 6-1		AutoCAD Drawing Tools and Commands		
Tool Entry	*Command*	*Major Options*	*Toolbar Button*	*Draw Menu*
Line	Line	Start, end points	Line	Line
Ray	RAY	Start point, point through which ray passes	None	Ray
Construction line	XLine	Two points on line	Construction line	Construction line
Multiline	MLine	Justification, scale, style	Multiline	Multiline
Polyline	PLine	Vertices	Polyline	Polyline
3D Polyline	3dPoly	Vertices		3D Polyline
Polygon	POLygon	Number of sides, inscribed/ circumscribed	Polygon	Polygon
Rectangle	RECtang	Two corners	Rectangle	Rectangle
Arc	Arc	Various methods of definition	Arc	Arc; submenu for definition methods
Circle	Circle	Three points, two points, tangent	Circle	Circle; submenu for definition methods
Donut	DOnut	Inside, outside diameters	None	Donut
Spline	SPLine	Convert polyline or create new	Spline	Spline
Ellipse	ELlipse	Arc, center, axis	Ellipse	Ellipse; submenu for definition methods
Point	POint	Point style	Point	Point; submenu for definition methods

Flyouts and secondary menus

A flyout is not something sticky that you hang up on hot days to catch bugs and then toss out after it's full of the nasty beasties. A feature of some AutoCAD 2000 toolbar buttons, a *flyout* is an additional row or column of buttons that appears, or *flies out,* after you click a particular button. In AutoCAD, a button with a flyout toolbar lurking underneath always displays a tiny, difficult-to-see, black triangle in its bottom-right corner; see whether you can find the four buttons with flyouts on the Standard toolbar, for example.

Back in Release 14, flyouts were removed from all the Draw toolbar buttons. If you want to avoid the command line by *choosing* suboptions instead of *typing* them, you need to use the Draw menu instead. Figure 6-1 shows the Draw menu with options for an arc.

Figure 6-1:
The Draw
menu and
arc options.

In AutoCAD 2000, many functions are available by right-clicking at the right time and place. For drawing tools, you might make the mistake one of the authors made and try right-clicking in the command area during a command to see the options. Don't do that! Right-click in the drawing area instead. The needed options will magically appear.

To use a submenu, simply highlight the menu item you're interested in. (Any menu item with a submenu has a little right-pointing triangle next to it.) The submenu then appears next to the item. Drag the mouse straight across into the submenu; if you miss and drag the mouse up or down too far before you reach the submenu, the submenu disappears.

Commands versus the (ooey!) GUI

So what's your best course: to enter drawing commands from the command line or to choose them from the menus or toolbars in the graphical user interface — or the *GUI*, as those of us fond of sticky treats like to call it? Choosing from the Draw menu is slow, especially if you must locate command options on a secondary menu. Using the toolbar buttons just starts the command and doesn't let you specify options; you usually need to finish the command at the command line or with the right-click menu. We recommend that you memorize the command line entries for the drawing commands you use most. Start other commands from the Draw toolbar, and use the new AutoCAD 2000 right-click menus or the command line to specify options and respond to command-line prompts.

So, as we've told you we've-forgotten-how-many times before (and will keep telling you until you commit it firmly to memory), use the command line for frequently used options and use the menus and toolbars for less frequently used ones!

This chapter is filled with "Keyboard" icons to point out paragraphs that tell you how to create shapes from the command line. Go through and try them all. Getting a feel for working from the command line now puts you on the road to much faster work in AutoCAD later.

Toeing the Lines

You can create a rough drawing of just about anything by using only straight lines, so they're worth tackling first. The following two line commands are the most important ones you use in AutoCAD:

- ✔ Lines
- ✔ Polylines

The following additional line commands are also available in AutoCAD:

- ✔ Rays
- ✔ Infinite lines
- ✔ Multilines
- ✔ Sketches

The sections that follow describe each of these line-related commands.

AutoCAD uses the terms xline or "construction line" to describe a line with no beginning or endpoint, but we use "infinite line" instead because it's infinitely more descriptive.

Lines (lines, everywhere a line . . .)

A *line* in AutoCAD is actually a series of one or more connected line segments. Each *segment*, or piece of a line with endpoints, is a separate object. This construction doesn't seem like a big deal until you try to move or otherwise edit a multi-segment line and find that you must select each and every piece of it. To avoid such a hassle, use polylines, described later in this chapter, rather than lines when you want the connected segments to be a single object.

Your first few attempts to draw a line in AutoCAD can be very confusing, because AutoCAD keeps prompting you for additional points. A *point* in AutoCAD can be either an endpoint, which marks the end of an object such as a line, a point you use to define an object, such as a point on the diameter of a circle, or a true *point* that you draw with the AutoCAD POINT command, a single object that's not a part of anything else. CAD programs compose many objects in multiple connected line segments, so AutoCAD just keeps asking you for more points until you tell it to stop by pressing Enter or the spacebar.

Unlike a lot of AutoCAD drawing commands, LINE doesn't offer a bunch of potentially confusing options. There's a Close option to create a closed polygon and an Undo option to remove the most recent segment that you drew.

Like all drawing commands, LINE puts the line segment objects that it draws on the current layer, and uses the current color, linetype, lineweight, and plots style properties. Thus you should make sure that you've set these properties correctly before you start drawing. See Chapter 5 for information on setting the current properties with the Object Properties toolbar.

Creating a line

The three different ways to tell AutoCAD to create a line are as follows:

- ✔ Type **Line** on the command line and press Enter.
- ✔ Click the Line button on the Draw toolbar.
- ✔ Choose Draw➪Line from the menu bar.

Line example

The following example shows all the commands you need to enter on the command line to create a square made up of individual line segments:

```
Command: LINE
Specify first point: 2,2
Specify next point or [Undo]: 5,5
Specify next point or [Undo]: 5,8
Specify next point or [Close/Undo]: 2,8
Specify next point or [Close/Undo]: C
```

Rather than type C to choose the Close option, you can right-click in the drawing area and choose Close from the cursor menu.

In the examples in this chapter, we use typed coordinates to make the examples easy for us to describe and for you to duplicate on your computer. In real life, you'll often pick points on the screen with the mouse.

Ortho mode is an important AutoCAD mode that affects lines and polylines. If ortho mode is on, you can draw lines only straight up, straight down, directly left, or directly right — and in no other direction. You can turn ortho mode on and off in the middle of a line command by clicking the word ORTHO in the status bar; by pressing the function key F8; or by preceding the ortho command with an apostrophe, as in **'ORTHO ON**. Entering the command **'ORTHO OFF** turns off ortho mode and enables you to draw lines in any direction. (The apostrophe makes the command *transparent,* meaning that you can enter it in the middle of another command.)

Of course, unless your mouse stops working, you're probably not going to go to the trouble of typing 'ORTHO ON when you can pick the ORTHO status bar button instead. But if your mouse stops working, you probably won't be doing much of anything in AutoCAD! Anyway, we're pointing out the "transparent apostrophe" here because many other AutoCAD commands are transparent in the same way. For example, you can type 'Zoom to zoom in the middle of a drawing or editing command. Most toolbar and menu items work by generating a command-line entry, and that entry includes the prepended apostrophe for transparent commands automatically. (*Prepended* means "stuck to the front of," for those of you who weren't English majors.)

Polylines (wanna crackerline?)

A *polyline,* in its simplest form, is just like a line — that is, a series of connected line segments. Polylines, however, can include arcs as well as line segments. But no matter how many line segments and arcs it encompasses, a polyline (as a whole) is still one object. Plus, polylines offer options that regular lines lack: You can control the width of each segment or even specify a *halfwidth* that causes the polyline to taper along its length. (But *never* call your boss a halfwidth, even if he or she tapers along his or her length.)

After you create a polyline, you can adjust its segments by grip editing any of the vertex points (see Chapter 7 for details on grip editing). For more complicated polyline editing tasks, you can use the PEDIT command to edit it, or you can convert the polyline to a collection of line and arc segments by using the EXPLODE command — although you lose the width defined for each segment when you explode a polyline.

Creating a Polyline

The three different ways to tell AutoCAD to create a polyline are as described in the following list:

- ✔ Type **PLine** on the command line and press Enter.
- ✔ Click the Polyline button on the Draw toolbar.
- ✔ Choose Draw➪Polyline from the menu bar.

Polyline example

The following example shows the commands you enter on the command line to create a polyline with a straight segment, an arc, and another straight segment:

```
Command: PLINE
Specify start point: 3,2
Current line-width is 0.0000
Specify next point or [Arc/Close/Halfwidth/Length/Undo/Width]:
        3,6
rc/Close/Halfwidth/Length/Undo/Width/<Endpoint of line>: A
Specify endpoint of arc or [Angle/CEnter/CLose/Direction/
        Halfwidth/Line/Radius/Second pt/Undo/Width]: 4,6
Specify endpoint of arc or [Angle/CEnter/CLose/Direction/
        Halfwidth/Line/Radius/Second pt/Undo/Width]: L
Specify next point or [Arc/Close/Halfwidth/Length/Undo/Width]:
        4,2
Specify next point or [Arc/Close/Halfwidth/Length/Undo/Width]:
<Enter>
```

Figure 6-2 shows the polyline — a single object — created by these commands.

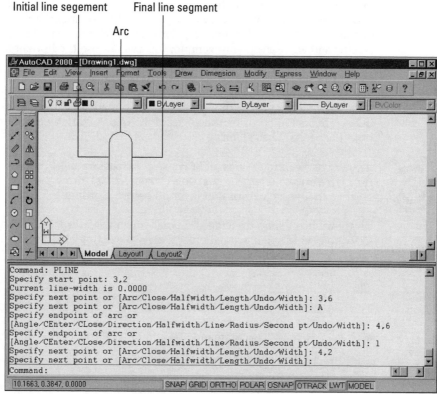

Figure 6-2:
A polyline
with two
line
segments
connected
by an arc.

Rays and infinite lines
(Buck Rogers, watch out!)

You can use both *rays* and *infinite lines,* also known as *xlines,* mainly as guides to construction as you create your drawing because no real-world object that you represent in a drawing can contain a true ray or infinite line. (Nothing in real life goes on forever, although some things — we hope not this book — may seem to!) Even if you want to depict a ray or infinite line in your drawing, you simply use a line segment with one or two arrowheads to get the idea across.

Rays are easy to draw; you just define a starting point and then a second point through which the ray passes. AutoCAD then keeps prompting you for more of these second points, or *through points,* so that you can draw as many rays as you want that start at the same point as the first one. You can't, however, enter an angle to specify how many angular units to offset the current ray from the previous one, which would be fun.

Infinite lines are more complex. For an infinite line, you can specify a *from* and a *to* point, as though you were drawing a line segment, but the XLINE command includes several options for drawing a series of infinite lines rapidly and accurately. For example, you can choose the horizontal, vertical, or angle option and then draw infinite lines by picking single points through which the lines pass. Figure 6-3 shows horizontal and vertical infinite lines and a ray extending down and to the left from their point of intersection. Rays and infinite lines both plot only to the outside edges of the drawing as defined by its limits (or by the edges of the outermost objects, if one or more objects lie outside the limits).

If you're using infinite lines and rays as construction lines (such as tempo-rary or reference lines that you don't want to plot), draw them on a separate layer so that you can turn that layer off before plotting.

The new object snap tracking and polar tracking features make it easier to draw objects at specific locations relative to existing objects without making construction lines first. See Chapter 7 for details.

Creating a ray

The two different ways to tell AutoCAD to create a ray are as follows:

- ✔ Type **RAY** on the command line and press Enter.
- ✔ Choose <u>D</u>raw⇨<u>R</u>ay from the menu bar.

In AutoCAD 2000, rays are one of several commands that are no longer avail-able from a button in the toolbar. If you want to draw rays fast, use the command line or the Windows shortcut for rays, Alt+D, R.

Ray example

The following example shows the commands you enter at the command line to create a ray from point 3,6 through point 7,8, and on into infinity:

```
Command: RAY
Specify start point: 3,6
Specify through point: 7,8
Specify through point: <Enter>
```

Creating an infinite line

The way to tell AutoCAD to create an infinite line is to do one of the following:

- ✔ Type **XLine** on the command line and press Enter.
- ✔ Choose <u>D</u>raw⇨Construction Line from the menu.
- ✔ Click the Construction Line button on the Draw toolbar.

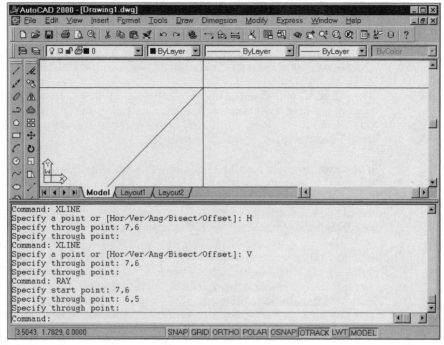

Infinite line example

The following example shows the commands you enter on the command line
to create a horizontal and a vertical infinite line through point 7,6:

```
Command: XLINE
Specify a point or [Hor/Ver/Ang/Bisect/Offset]: V
Specify through point: 7,6
Specify through point: <Enter>
Command: XLINE
Specify a point or [Hor/Ver/Ang/Bisect/Offset]: H
Specify through point: 7,6
Specify through point: <Enter>
```

Multilines (lines aplenty)

Multilines are specialized types of lines that consist of several parallel lines —
up to 16 — that behave as one object. You can use the default style multiline,
which includes two parallel line elements, or you can create your own,
adding additional elements as you choose. Your own multilines can vary in
the presence or absence of *joints* that appear at each corner and in the style
of *end cap* that appears at the beginning and end of the multiline. Multilines

that cross each other can create patterns to represent specific elements. Multilines are useful in architectural drawings and in other kinds of drawings that make heavy use of parallel, straight lines. For example, in an architectural floor plan, you may be able to save time by drawing walls (which usually consist of two or more parallel lines) using multilines.

The AutoCAD multiline feature was full of design flaws, limitations, and bugs when it debuted in Release 13. Unfortunately, it hasn't improved much since then. If you want to use multilines, be prepared to spend some time experimenting and struggling with this feature.

If you want to use a multiline style other than the standard, two-line style, you must load or define it in advance. And if you want to modify the standard style before using it, you must also do so in advance. Use the MLSTYLE command on the command line to load and modify multiline styles. This command opens the Multiline Styles dialog box.

If you're going to use multilines very much, you'll probably have to grapple with this not-very-intuitive dialog box. We show you how to draw a simple, two-line multiline using the default Standard multiline style. Choose the Help button in the Multiline Styles dialog box to learn more about modifying and creating your own multiline styles. You can draw multilines, in either the standard style or a new style you define, by using one of the following options:

- ✔ **Justification (Top, Zero, Bottom):** Specifies whether the points you pick indicate the top line of the multilines, a spot in the middle (zero) of the lines, or the bottom line.
- ✔ **Scale:** Determines the distance between lines.

Creating a multiline

You can tell AutoCAD to create a multiline by using an already loaded multiline style or the standard default style in the following three ways:

- ✔ Type **MLine** on the command line and press Enter.
- ✔ Click the Multiline button on the Draw toolbar.
- ✔ Choose Draw⇨Multiline from the menu bar.

Multiline example

The following example shows the commands you can enter on the command line to create a simple two-line multiline that's centered on the points you pick (that is, Zero justification), with the two lines 0.25 units apart:

```
Command: MLINE
Current settings: Justification = Top, Scale = 1.00, Style =
       STANDARD
Specify start point or [Justification/Scale/STyle]:  J
Enter justification type [Top/Zero/Bottom] <top>:  Z
Current settings: Justification = Zero, Scale = 1.00, Style =
       STANDARD
Specify start point or [Justification/Scale/STyle]:  S
Enter mline scale <1.00>:  .25
Current settings: Justification = Zero, Scale = 0.25, Style =
       STANDARD
Specify start point or [Justification/Scale/STyle]: 2,2
Specify next point: 5,9
Specify next point: 7,11
Specify next point: <Enter>
```

Scoring Points . . . and Polygons

An AutoCAD *point* is a special kind of object used for marking a location, as well as for object snapping to that location later (see Chapter 7 for more about object snaps). The AutoCAD RECTANGLE and POLYGON commands are shortcuts for drawing closed shapes with polylines.

The following sections describe each type of object and how to create it.

Points (game, set, and match!)

We discussed not covering points in this book, but we didn't want you saying that *AutoCAD 2000 For Dummies* is pointless.

Although simple in real life (and in other drawing programs), *points* in AutoCAD are complex because they have so many display options. Luckily, you can change the point style and size at any — forgive us — point, allowing you to hem and haw about how you want points to look right up until the last second.

You can use points not only to represent small objects but also as object snap locations — think of them as "construction points." For example, when you're laying out a new building, you might draw point objects at some of the engineering survey points, and then snap to those points as you sketch the building's shape with the polyline command. You use the NODe object snap mode to snap to AutoCAD point objects.

You can specify how a point is drawn, as well as its size, by using either commands entered on the command line or the Point Style dialog box. The command line commands, PDMODE and PDSIZE, are complex and use arbitrary and hard-to-remember values. (The default for PDMODE is 0, which displays as a one-pixel dot.) Unless you plan on using points frequently and really love the keyboard, we suggest that you use the dialog box instead.

DDPTYPE is the command that opens the Point Style dialog box (see Figure 6-4). You can access it from the menus by choosing Format⇨Point Style. The first line in the dialog box shows the actual point styles available. The second, third, and fourth lines add surrounding shapes to the point — a circle (second line), square (third line), or circle-in-square (fourth line).

You also can specify the Point Size in the Point Style dialog box. You can specify the point size as a percentage of the screen size, which means that when AutoCAD regenerates the drawing, it redraws all point objects at that percentage (for example, 5%) of the current drawing area. In other words, if you zoom way in and enter REGEN, AutoCAD redraws point objects so that they're 5% of the current zoomed-in screen, which makes them much smaller than they used to be with respect to the other drawing objects. The other Point Size option, Set Size in Absolute Units, leaves points the same size no matter where you zoom or when AutoCAD regenerates the drawing. (The only danger there is if you have a large drawing area and specify a small Point Size in absolute units, you might — ba-dum-bump — miss the point.)

Figure 6-4:
The Point Style dialog box with the point size set relative to the drawing zoom.

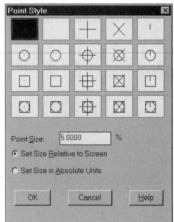

After you specify the point style, actually placing the point on-screen is easy; the following sections show you how to do this task.

Creating a point

You can create a point by using any of the following methods:

- ✔ Type **POint** on the command line and press Enter.
- ✔ Click the Point button on the Draw toolbar.
- ✔ Choose Draw⇨Point from the menu bar (with submenu).

Point example

The following example shows you the commands to enter on the command line to create a point:

```
Command: POint
Current point modes: PDMODE=0 PDSIZE=0.0000
Specify a point: 2,2
```

To draw more points, just press the Enter key to repeat the POINT command and pick another location on the screen. Repeat as required: Enter, pick, Enter, pick, Enter pick . . . by now you should've gotten the point.

Rectangles (oh, what a tangled wreck . . .)

The RECTANG command is a fairly recent addition to AutoCAD, first appearing in Release 12. (Yes, that fact may seem surprising to those of you who have been drawing rectangles in MacDraw since 1984, or in other personal computer drawing programs since roughly the same time, but it's true.) Rectangles are really rather simple to create, which is nice; just pick a corner, move the mouse, and pick another corner. And you don't need to hold down the mouse cursor and drag it anywhere to create a rectangle, either — just click in one corner, move the mouse to the opposite corner, and click there, too.

Rectangles and polygons in AutoCAD are really just polylines that are specified in a way that's appropriate to the shape you're creating. You'll notice this when you grip edit a rectangle or polygon: only the selected vertex moves. AutoCAD doesn't make the entire rectangle or polygon larger or smaller.

Unlike in other drawing programs, you don't click and drag the mouse to draw lines or create rectangles in AutoCAD; instead, after choosing the appropriate command for the object you want to draw, you click and release the mouse at the point on-screen where you want the drawing to begin, and then you do so again at the second point, where you want it to end.

If you chose the Press and Drag option in the Object Selection Settings dialog box at the time you set up AutoCAD (see Chapter 3) — because you wanted AutoCAD to function like other programs when drawing objects — forget it; that setup choice affects how you *select* objects, but not how you *draw* them. You still do a full mouse click for the starting point and then another, separate mouse click for the ending point. Try it and you'll see what we mean.

Creating a rectangle

You can tell AutoCAD to create a rectangle by using the following methods:

- ✔ Type **RECtang** on the command line and press Enter.
- ✔ Click the Rectangle button on the Draw toolbar.
- ✔ Choose Draw⇨Rectangle from the menu bar.

Rectangle example

The following example shows you the commands to enter on the command line to create a rectangle:

```
Command: RECTANG
Specify first corner point or [Chamfer/Elevation/Fillet/
        Thickness/Width]: 4,7
Specify other corner point: 7,4
```

If you really want to eliminate clean-up work at the end of the drawing process and dramatically reduce your odds of creating an unprintable drawing (and then saying unprintable things), start your work by making a rough drawing that contains nothing but rectangles to represent the drawing's major parts. Put the rectangles on their own layer so that you can hide or get rid of it later. Set the correct limits and so on, but don't worry about actually drawing anything; just put rectangles of about the right size anywhere that geometry or text are to go. Print the result to see how it looks. You can quickly get a good idea of the final look of your drawing by using this method.

Polygons (so next time, lock the cage. . .)

Moving from rectangles to *polygons* is much like moving from the very simple to the almost too complex for words — except maybe a few we can't print here. Creating a triangle, a pentagon, or another polygonal shape in AutoCAD can readily be considered a minor feat of engineering in and of itself. The process involved in creating a polygon is exact, however, and relates well to what "real" drafters do. But if all your previous drawing experience is with a drawing package rather than with a drafting board, drawing AutoCAD polygons can seem like a real pain.

To create a polygon, follow these steps:

1. **Type POLygon on the command line and press Enter.**

   AutoCAD prompts you for the number of sides you want on your polygon.

2. **Type at the prompt the number of sides you want for your polygon; then press Enter.**

   If you want to draw a triangle, for example, you type **3** at this prompt. AutoCAD then prompts you to specify either the center of the polygon (the default) or E for the edge of the polygon.

3. **Specify at the prompt whether you want to draw an edge of a polygon or specify the center point of the polygon.**

   You need to type **E** at this prompt and press Enter to specify that you want to draw an edge, and then continue on with Step 4. If you want to use the center point of the polygon, skip to the unnumbered paragraph immediately before Step 6.

   Now here's where you can really get in trouble, so follow along closely.

4. **At the prompt, pick a point — or enter the coordinates of a point — that will serve as the first endpoint of one side of the polygon you want to create.**

   AutoCAD automatically generates an image of a polygon with the specified number of sides — a triangle, square, pentagon, or whatever. As you move the cursor around on the screen, AutoCAD resizes the image dynamically to guide you in choosing the second point. The polygon is actually generated according to the coordinates you enter in the following step.

5. **At the prompt, pick the coordinates for the second endpoint of the edge of your polygon, or type them in and then press Enter.**

   After you specify the second endpoint of the edge, you're done. Whatever shape you're creating is exactly *equilateral* (all sides the same length), so that second endpoint had better be in the right spot; otherwise, you can easily create a pentagon that looks as if its base is horizontal but is really tilted slightly right or left. If you want a *nonequilateral* shape, such as a right triangle, you must edit your equilateral triangle — or draw a polyline — to get it.

   Creating a polygon by specifying its number of sides and what circle it surrounds or is circumscribed by is relatively easy. The circle is used to define either the distance from the polygon's center to the middle of each side — a *circumscribed polygon* — or to each *vertex*, or corner — an *inscribed polygon*. After entering the number of sides for your polygon, as described in Step 2, you click a point on-screen or enter coordinates for the center of the polygon at the following prompt *instead* of entering an E to specify a polygon edge (as described in Step 3, if you're on edge — as you may actually be at this point).

6. **To specify using the center point of the polygon for your drawing, type the coordinates for the center of the polygon, or pick the center point by clicking in the drawing area with the mouse, and then press Enter.**

   Now you must tell AutoCAD whether the polygon is *inscribed in* a circle or *circumscribed around* a circle; inscribed within a circle is the default setting.

7. **At the prompt, type C if you want the polygon circumscribed around a circle, and then press Enter; if you want the polygon inscribed in a circle, either type I at the prompt and then press Enter, or just press Enter.**

   Finally, you must enter the radius of the circle, either by entering a number from the keyboard or by clicking a point on-screen. If you use the keyboard to enter a number at the command line, a polygon of the right size and with a horizontal base appears. If you pick a point, the polygon's exact alignment depends on the point you pick. Again, if you use this latter method, you can easily end up with a slightly misaligned shape.

8. **At the prompt, type the value you want for the radius of the circle and press Enter.**

   AutoCAD draws the polygon.

If you want to turn your equilateral polygon into a nonequilateral one, you must grab the offending corner and drag it to the right spot on-screen to make the shape you want. You can find more information about this particular task in Chapter 7.

Use POLYGON with 4 sides and the Circumscribed option to draw a rectangle centered on a point.

Creating a polygon

You can tell AutoCAD to create a polygon by using any of the following methods:

- ✔ Type **POLygon** on the command line and press Enter.
- ✔ Click the Polygon button on the Draw toolbar.
- ✔ Choose <u>D</u>raw⇨<u>P</u>olygon from the menu bar.

Polygon examples

The following example shows you the commands to enter at the command line to create an inscribed polygon by specifying its bounding circle:

```
Command: POLygon
POLYGON Enter number of sides <3>: 3 (or Enter)
Specify center of polygon or [Edge]: 4,8
Enter an option [Inscribed in circle/Circumscribed about
          circle] <I>: I
Radius of circle: 2
```

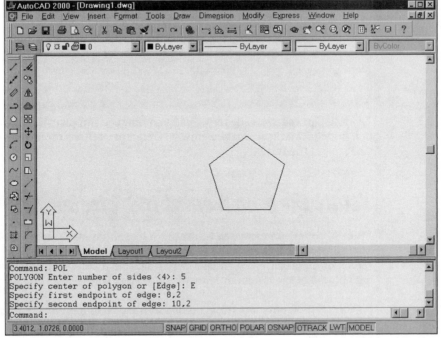

Figure 6-5:
Creating a
pentagon by
specifying
one side at
the
command
line.

The following example shows you the commands to enter on the command line to create a polygon using the Edge option, as shown in Figure 6-5:

```
Command: POLygon
POLYGON Enter number of sides <3>: 5
Specify center of polygon or [Edge]: E
Specify first endpoint of edge: 7,3
Specify second endpoint of edge: 9,3
```

(Throwing) Curves

AutoCAD features a strong selection of curved objects for your drawing needs, as well as many ways to define them. Because you're provided with so many ways to create curves, and because getting them to the right spot requires a fair amount of thought, you may want to consider drawing all your curved objects at one time for a while, especially if you're an inexperienced AutoCAD user, until you get good at creating and placing them. The important curve-shaped objects for most AutoCAD users are as follows:

✔ Circles

✔ Arcs

Other curved objects available in AutoCAD that are not as important to most users as circles and arcs are the following:

- Ellipses
- Splines
- Donuts

The following sections describe each command. You probably need to practice drawing all these shapes, however, except perhaps circles, if you really want to get them right.

(Will they go 'round in) circles . . .

AutoCAD offers an easy way to draw circles, and it also offers . . . *other* ways. The easy way is to define the center point of the circle and then to define the radius or diameter. You can also define a circle by entering one of the following options of the command (for those "other" ways):

- **3P:** Represents any three points on the circumference
- **2P:** Represents the endpoints of a diameter of the circle
- **TTR:** Represents two tangents and a radius

Any of these commands can be useful for getting just the right circle into just the right spot on-screen, but you may find yourself doing what we sometimes do, which is creating the circle you want by using the center point/radius method and then moving it to just the right spot, as described in Chapter 7.

Creating a circle

You can tell AutoCAD to create a circle by using any of the following methods:

- Type **Circle** on the command line and press Enter.
- Click the Circle button on the Draw toolbar.
- Choose <u>D</u>raw⇨<u>C</u>ircle from the menu bar (with submenus).

Circle example

The following example shows you the commands to enter on the command line to create a circle from a center point and radius:

```
Command: CIRCLE
Specify center point for circle or [3P/2P/Ttr (tan tan
          radius)]: 7,7
Specify radius of circle or [Diameter]: 2
```

You can also type **D** and then enter the diameter, if that's more convenient. If you already know the diameter and it's a number that's hard to divide in your head by 2, then entering D and the diameter is probably a time-saver.

Arcs (the 'erald angels sing . . .)

Arcs in AutoCAD are, quite simply, pieces of circles. Or, they're big boats you use to ride out a deluge — noah more arc jokes, we promise. By the time you finish finding out about all the many ways to define arcs, you just may end up drawing a circle where you want an arc and then using correction fluid to cover over everything but the desired arc on your printout. (If you *really* get frustrated, you may find yourself putting correction fluid on the screen instead!)

As with circles, AutoCAD offers you an easy way to define arcs. Just specify three points on-screen to define the arc, easy as one-two-three. These points tell AutoCAD where to start the arc, how much to curve it, and where to end it.

Sounds pretty easy, right? So where's the problem? Well, the trouble is that you often must specify arcs more exactly than is possible by using this method. AutoCAD helps you specify such arcs, true, but the procedure ain't easy.

You can start your arc by specifying the center of the arc or the start point. If you choose the Center option, AutoCAD prompts you for the center point first and the start point second. AutoCAD defines arcs counter-clockwise, so pick a start point in a clockwise direction from the end point. After you specify the center and start point, AutoCAD presents several options you can choose, including the following:

- ✔ **Angle:** This option specifies the included angle that the arc sweeps out. A 180-degree angle, for example, is a semicircle.

- ✔ **Length of chord:** This option specifies the length of an imaginary straight line connecting the endpoints of the arc. If you know the exact length, select Length of chord as the option you want.

- ✔ **Endpoint:** This option specifies where the arc ends. It's the default option and is often the easiest to use.

If you specify the start point as the first option, you then can choose among the following three command line options as well:

- ✔ **Center:** This option takes you back to the preceding options: Enter Angle, Length of chord, or Endpoint.

- ✔ **End:** This option specifies the endpoint of the arc. You then need to define the angle the arc covers, its direction, its radius, or its center point.

 ✔ **Second point:** This is the default option. The second point you choose is not the endpoint; instead, it's a point on the arc that, along with the start and endpoints, defines the arc's curvature — that is, how much it curves. After you enter the second point, you must enter an endpoint to complete the arc.

Creating an arc

You can tell AutoCAD to create an arc by using any of the following methods:

 ✔ Type **Arc** on the command line and press Enter.

 ✔ Click the Arc button on the Draw toolbar.

 ✔ Choose <u>D</u>raw⇨<u>A</u>rc from the menu bar (with submenus for different ways to define the arc).

Arc examples

The following example shows you the commands to enter on the command line to create an arc by specifying three points on the arc:

```
Command: ARC
Specify start point of arc or [CEnter]: 1,1
Specify second point of arc or [CEnter,ENd]: 2,2
Specify end point of arc: 3,1
```

The following example shows the commands to enter on the command line to create an arc starting from the center and specifying an angle, as shown in Figure 6-6:

```
Command: ARC
Specify start point of arc or [CEnter]: CE
Specify center point of arc: 5,3
Specify start point of arc: 7,3
Specify end point of arc or [Angle/chord Length]: Angle
Specify included angle: 95
```

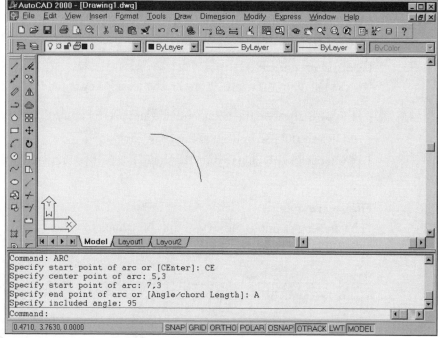

Figure 6-6:
Drawing an arc by specifying its center, its start point, and an angle.

Ellipses (S. Grant?)

An *ellipse*, like an arc, is complex to draw. An ellipse is like a warped circle with a *major* (long) axis and a *minor* (short) axis to determine its length, width, and degree of curvature. After you start to draw an ellipse, AutoCAD presents the following options at the prompts on the command line:

- **Arc:** This option generates an elliptical arc rather than a full ellipse. You define an elliptical arc just as you do a full ellipse. The following methods for creating an ellipse apply to either.

- **Center:** This option requires that you define the center of the ellipse and then the endpoint of an axis. You can then either enter the distance of the other axis or specify that a rotation around the major axis defines the ellipse. If you choose the latter, you can enter (or drag the ellipse to) a specific rotation for the second axis that, in turn, completely defines the ellipse.

- **Isocircle:** This option creates an *isometric circle* — something you're unlikely to use; look up "isometric circles" in the AutoCAD online help if you need details.

- **Axis endpoint 1:** This option requires that you define one axis by entering its end points and the other by entering a distance or rotation.

These options are confusing to master by reading; try creating an ellipse to get a feel for drawing one. If you need to draw an ellipse, you're likely to specify it by using one of these methods.

Creating an ellipse

You can tell AutoCAD to create an ellipse by using any of the following methods:

✔ Type **ELlipse** on the command line and press Enter.

✔ Click the Ellipse button on the Draw toolbar.

✔ Choose <u>D</u>raw⇨<u>E</u>llipse from the menu bar (with submenu for definition methods).

Ellipse example

The following example shows you the commands to enter on the command line to create an ellipse:

```
Command: ELLIPSE
Specify axis endpoint of ellipse or [Arc/Center]: 4,4
Specify other endpoint of axis: 8,4
Specify distance to other axis or [Rotation]: .25
```

You can create elliptical arcs (as opposed to the circular arcs that the AutoCAD ARC command draws) by using the Arc option of the ELLIPSE command — it's perfect for drawing those cannonball trajectories! Alternatively, you can draw a full ellipse and use the TRIM or BREAK command to cut a piece out of it.

Donuts: The circles with a difference

Creating a *donut* (hold the coffee, please) is a simple way to define a single object that consists of two concentric circles with the space between them filled. But watch out; drawing a donut is likely to draw some cops, too! (Sorry. . . .) You probably won't need to draw donuts often, but when you do need to draw them, the DONUT command offers an efficient way to do so.

When you start the DONUT command, AutoCAD prompts you for the inside diameter and the outside diameter — the size of the hole and the size of the donut, as measured across their widest points. After you've entered these values, AutoCAD prompts you for the center point of the donut. But one donut is rarely enough, so AutoCAD keeps prompting you for additional center points until you press Enter (the AutoCAD equivalent of saying, "no, really, I'm full now!").

You can create a filled circle with the DONUT command; specify an inside diameter of zero. Try this one for yourself!

Splines: The sketchy, sinuous curves

Most people use CAD programs for precision drawing tasks: straight lines, carefully defined curves, precisely specified points, and so on. AutoCAD is not the program to reach for when you want to free your inner artist — unless perhaps your inner artist is Mondrian. Nonetheless, even in meticulously created CAD drawings, you sometimes need to add freeform curves. The AutoCAD spline object is just the thing for the job.

In fact, you can use AutoCAD splines in two ways. One way is the freeform, sketchy, not-too-precise approach that we describe here. You just eyeball the location and shape of the curve and don't worry too much about getting it "just so." But beneath their easy-going, informal exterior, AutoCAD splines are really highly precise, mathematically defined entities called NURBS curves (Non-Uniform Rational B-Spline curves). Mathematicians and some mechanical and industrial designers care a lot about the precise characteristics of the curves they work with. For those people, the AutoCAD SPLINE and SPLINEDIT commands include a number of advanced options. Look up "spline curves (NURBS curves)" in the AutoCAD online help for more information.

Creating a spline

You can start the SPLINE command by using any of the following methods:

- Type **SPLine** on the command line and press Enter.
- Click the Spline button on the Draw toolbar.
- Choose Draw⇨Spline from the menu bar.

Drawing splines is fairly straightforward, as long as you ignore the advanced options. The following example shows you the basic procedure and Figure 6-7 shows some examples:

Spline example

```
Command: SPLine
Specify first point or [Object]: 1,1
Specify next point: 2,2
Specify next point or [Close/Fit tolerance] <start tangent>:
      3,1
Specify next point or [Close/Fit tolerance] <start tangent>:
      4,1.5
Specify next point or [Close/Fit tolerance] <start tangent>:
      5,1
Specify next point or [Close/Fit tolerance] <start tangent>:
      <Enter>
Specify start tangent: <Enter>
Specify end tangent: <Enter>
```

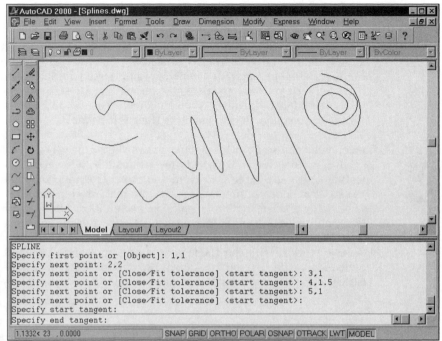

Figure 6-7:
A slew of
splines.

The "Specify start tangent" and "Specify end tangent" prompts at the end of the SPLINE command allow you to control the curvature of the start and end points of the spline. In most cases, simply pressing Enter at both prompts to accept the default tangents works fine.

After you've drawn a spline, you can grip edit it in order to adjust its shape. See Chapter 7 for information about grip editing. If you need finer control over spline editing, look up the SPLINEDIT command in the AutoCAD online help.

Chapter 7

Edit It

● ●

In This Chapter

▶ Snapping to objects

▶ Selecting objects

▶ Editing by command

▶ Editing by direct manipulation

▶ Using grips to edit objects

▶ Editing commands unveiled

● ●

*T*his chapter describes working with existing objects in AutoCAD. The two preceding chapters discuss how to draw in AutoCAD and use the AutoCAD drawing tools. In this chapter, we describe two ways you work with existing objects: One way is to use existing objects as a reference point for adding more geometry; another way is to modify existing objects. In your actual work, you move back and forth among creating brand-new geometry, adding other related geometry to it, and modifying what you've created, which means that you use the information in this group of three chapters interchangeably as well.

Editing may be the function that's most difficult to master in AutoCAD. Editing in any version of AutoCAD is really different from the editing you do in other programs — and some of the AutoCAD commands are inconsistent with one another. Users who have a historical perspective of AutoCAD updates over the last several years, however, recognize that editing in AutoCAD has come a long way since the program's early days; for most of your work, you can now use editing techniques that are similar to, if some-what more complicated than, those of many other programs. As for those folks who may not be as familiar with AutoCAD (the rest of you) — well, you may find yourself checking this book, your AutoCAD books and manuals, and other sources every now and then for guidance. The good news is that the AutoCAD tools, once mastered, are powerful.

AutoCAD 2000 includes new features that make editing easier for most people. Object snaps have been enhanced and AutoTracking added. Together these features create construction lines for you "on the fly" and add text tips so that you can easily add new geometry that's related to, but not necessarily connected to, existing geometry. Another new editing feature is QuickSelect, which makes selecting similar objects for later editing easier. These new features are covered in this chapter, along with the existing features they're most closely related to.

This chapter covers AutoCAD editing commands, as well as features and techniques such as object snaps that you need to know in order to do precision editing. The same precision features and techniques — object snaps, AutoTracking, and direct distance entry — also apply to drawing new objects, so much of what you learn in this chapter is relevant to the material in Chapter 6 as well.

After you successfully scale the learning curve for AutoCAD editing, you can do almost anything you want with your drawings — much more so than is possible in other, less powerful programs. So stick with AutoCAD until it all starts to make sense.

Snapping to Attention

One of the main features of any CAD program is the capability to *snap to objects*. No, this feature doesn't refer to something you do with your fingers; *object snap* is the capability to make newly created objects align correctly with existing ones. For example, you often want a new object to join the end, center, corner, or other particular point of an existing object. When the program helps you find and connect with such a point, that's object snapping.

AutoCAD 2000 has new capabilities for two snap-related features that are explained in the next sections: *running object snap* and *AutoSnap*. Neither of these features is new but they both have new options (and intricacies) in AutoCAD 2000. Though each has a substantial learning curve, these features work both separately and together to make creating accurate drawings quick and easy.

Single object snaps

Single point (or *override*) object snaps enable you to quickly connect the next point on the object you're drawing to any of several particular points on a nearby object. Object snaps are most easily accessed by the object snap shortcut menu, shown in Figure 7-1. To bring up the object snap shortcut menu, hold down the Shift key while right-clicking your mouse.

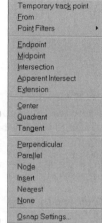

Figure 7-1:
Hold down
Shift while
right-click-
ing to see
this menu.

The object snap shortcut menu lists more than a dozen possible snap points for different kinds of objects; choosing the right one for the kind of snap point and the kind of object you want to connect with is up to you. Among the most useful snap points are the *endpoint* or *midpoint* of a line or arc; the *center* of or *tangent* to an arc or circle (not a rectangle or square!); and the *perpendicular* to or from a line, circle, or arc.

 For a complete description of snap points, press F1 in AutoCAD to bring up the Help system; choose Help topics and enter the topic **Object Snap Shortcut Menu**.

 If you haven't used object snaps before, take some time to experiment with them; they are one of the keys to editing and drawing with precision. They also can save you a great deal of time and are the key to running object snaps and AutoSnap as well.

The object snap shortcut menu, like so much else in AutoCAD, is customizable; see the AutoCAD 2000 online *Customization Guide* for more information.

Trying object snaps

To get a feel for using object snaps, try the following example, which simply draws a circle centered on one side of a rectangle.

1. **Type** RECtangle **at the command line and press Enter.**

2. **Click any two points to draw the rectangle.**

   A rectangle appears on your screen.

3. **Type** Circle **at the command line and press Enter.**

4. **Hold down the Shift key and press the right mouse button.**

   The object snap shortcut menu appears.

5. **Choose <u>M</u>idpoint from the menu.**

   The shortcut menu disappears.

6. **Move the cursor over any side of the rectangle.**

   As soon as the cursor approaches a line, a yellow triangle appears at the midpoint of that line, indicating that AutoCAD wants to snap to that point.

7. **Click anywhere on the line to place the center of the circle at the mid-point of the side of the rectangle.**

8. **Hold down the Shift key and press the right mouse button.**

   The object snap shortcut menu appears again. Figure 7-2 shows the screen at this point in the exercise.

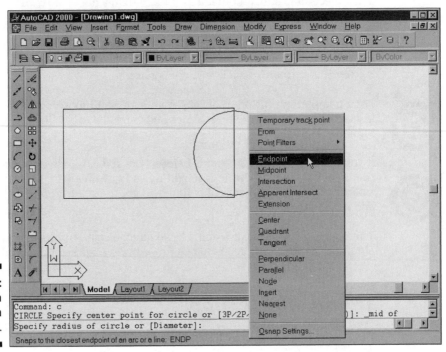

Figure 7-2:
Aligning a circle with a rectangle.

9. **Choose Endpoint from the menu.**

    The menu disappears.

10. **Move the cursor over the same side of the rectangle again and click.**

    As soon as the box around the cursor approaches the side, a yellow box appears at the endpoint of the side that is nearest the cursor. When you click, the circle is completed, with its center on the midpoint of a side and its radius at the endpoint. The circle command is complete.

You may think that ten steps seem like quite a few to create a simple construction, and they are. But the good news is that objects entered this way are exactly where you need them to be. Also, after you get some practice, you execute these steps rapidly without thinking about them. After you build up some experience with object snaps, they become a fast way to enter geometry precisely.

You can use the Object Snap toolbar as an alternative to the object snap shortcut menu as a way of entering single point object snaps. To see the toolbar, right-click on any toolbar and turn on Object Snap.

If the object snap you're using permits multiple possible destinations, use the Tab key to cycle among them. For example, if you're connecting to a tangent point of a circle, you have two tangent points to choose from; AutoCAD displays the closest one for you. Press Tab to see the other. This behavior also applies when you have turned on running object snaps, which gives you multiple possible connection points, as explained in the next section.

Running object snaps

If you use object snaps even a little bit, you're likely to find yourself wishing that you could have them on all the time. Although bringing up the object snap shortcut menu is relatively easy, doing so constantly still gets tiresome.

The good news is that you can have object snaps on all the time by using *running object snaps*. With running object snaps, you simply turn on one or more object snaps, and they stay on. The Osnap Settings dialog box for turning running object snaps on and off is shown in Figure 7-3. To bring up this dialog box, choose Tools⇨Drafting Settings from the menu, type **OSnap** at the command line, or simply right-click the status bar OSNAP button and choose Settings.

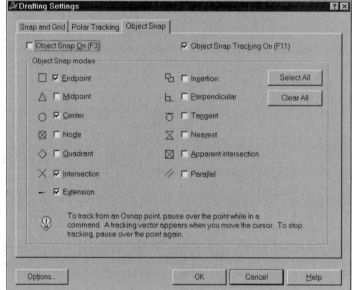

Figure 7-3:
The Drafting
Settings
dialog box.

Running object snaps are often a good thing, but at times you need to get back quickly the capability to draw to a point near, but not on, an object snap point. So the *really* good news is that AutoCAD has a quick way to turn running object snaps on and off. Just set your running object snaps with the Osnap Settings dialog box and then click the OSNAP button in the status bar to turn them on and off as needed. (If no running object snaps are set, clicking the OSNAP button first brings up the Drafting Settings dialog box and then turns on running object snap.) The F3 key also turns object snap on and off.

Try turning on all running object snaps and then turning them on and off as needed. Then leave the ones that are more trouble than they're worth to you turned off. If you're really having trouble picking your intended points in a crowded drawing, try using a single object snap (as described in the previous section) instead.

Try using running object snaps to draw. Create a figure with several kinds of objects and then use running object snaps to add geometry that connects with and depends on those shapes. This way, you can start your way up the learning curve at a time when you don't have to concentrate on getting the details of a drawing right.

Entering the command OSnap brings up the Object Snap tab of the Drafting Settings dialog box instead of prompting you to type running object snap modes at the command line (as previous versions of AutoCAD did). To drive running object snaps from the command line, type **-OSNAP**.

Extending Your Reach

Three new features in AutoCAD 2000 add new ways to create new geometry that's related to existing geometry. These features, from the easiest to learn and use to the hardest, are direct distance entry, polar tracking, and object snap tracking.

Directing your distance

Direct distance entry is a way to locate points using a combination of the mouse and the command line. Basically, it's a more efficient way of entering polar coordinates (see Chapter 5). First, you start a drawing or editing command and pick or type the first point required by the command. Then, to enter the next point, you don't enter its coordinates, nor do you enter a distance and an angle. Instead, you *indicate* the angle by moving the mouse pointer in the desired direction; then you *enter* the length of the line.

Direct distance entry works well when you want to put your next point either

- A specified distance in the direction of an existing snap point
- A specified distance in a set angular direction

Follow these steps to try direct distance entry:

1. **Right-click the OSNAP button to bring up the shortcut menu and choose Settings.**

   The Object Snap tab of the Drafting Settings dialog box appears.

2. **Click the Clear All button to turn off any currently running abject snaps, and then click to turn on the Endpoint object snap; also, make sure that Object Snap On is checked and then click OK to close the Drafting Settings dialog box.**

3. **Enter** Line 1,1 2,2 **and press Enter to complete the LINE command.**

   The line segment appears.

4. **Enter** Line 2,1 **(don't press Enter yet.)**

5. **Move the cursor to either end of the first line segment.**

   An AutoSnap box will appear to show that you are about to snap to the endpoint of the line segment.

6. **Enter** 3 **and press Enter.**

   A line segment will be drawn through the endpoint for a total line segment length of 3.

7. **Press Enter once more to end the Line command.**

Direct distance entry also works with polar tracking to allow you to easily draw line segments of the length you enter in specific directions, as described in the next section.

The Polar Express

Polar tracking is like the snap grid described in Chapter 4. However, rather than make the cursor snap to certain points on the screen, polar tracking makes the cursor snap to certain *angles*. You can then use direct distance entry to specify the length of the line that goes at the specified angle.

Polar tracking is a refinement on Ortho mode, which makes the cursor snap to 90 degree angles. If you haven't used Ortho mode before, click the ORTHO button in the status bar to turn it on. Then try drawing some lines. You'll notice that the cursor snaps to 90-degree angles. With polar tracking, you enter the angular settings that you want to snap to, and then use them.

In a further refinement on polar tracking, you can use it to generate temporary construction lines for you using points you *acquire* for selection purposes. This is called *object snap tracking*. An acquired point is used to create temporary construction lines that AutoCAD will snap to using its standard object snap settings and polar tracking. The acquired point is not used directly to create or snap to geometry.

Why is this technical stuff? Because you have to think a lot when you're first getting started with this business of acquiring points and using polar tracking with temporary construction lines. You have to develop a feel for what kind of polar tracking setup is useful in the drawings you create, and for how AutoCAD is going to generate temporary construction lines so that you can plan to use them in your drawing tasks. After you "get it," these capabilities can be tremendously useful. Until then, though, they can be kind of confusing.

Follow these steps to generate a measured near-triangle using polar tracking:

1. **In the status bar, click the buttons to turn off the SNAP, GRID, and ORTHO buttons; turn on POLAR, OSNAP, and OTRACK.**

2. **Right-click the POLAR button and choose Settings.**

   The Drafting Settings dialog box will appear with the Polar Tracking tab selected.

3. **Click the check box or press the F10 key to turn Polar Tracking On.**

4. **Use the pull-down menu to choose an Increment angle of 30 degrees.**

5. **Choose the radio button for the Track using all polar angle settings option.**

6. **Click OK to exit.**

7. **At the command line, enter the** Line **command.**

8. **Click in the middle of the screen.**

9. **Move the mouse around until AutoCAD generates a temporary construction line at a 120-degree angle.**

10. **Type** 2.9 Enter.

    A line segment 2.9 units long at 120-degrees to the original point will be drawn.

11. **Move the mouse around to the right of the new endpoint until AutoCAD generates a horizontal temporary construction line.**

12. **Type** 3 Enter.

    A horizontal line segment 3 units long will be drawn.

13. **Move the cursor to the original starting point but** *do not click.*

    AutoCAD will "acquire" the original starting point and generate temporary construction lines through it.

14. **Move the cursor straight beneath the original starting point.**

    AutoCAD will track along a vertical temporary construction line, as shown in Figure 7-4.

15. **Type** .1 Enter.

    AutoCAD will draw a line segment 0.1 units directly beneath the original starting point.

16. **Type** Close.

    AutoCAD will complete the figure.

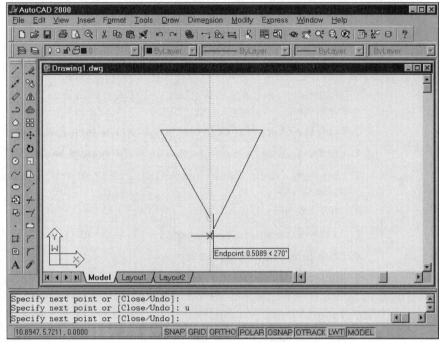

Figure 7-4:
Using polar tracking and object snap tracking.

As in this example, object snap tracking and polar tracking can be used to generate shapes for which you know distances, displacements, and angular relationships but not the specific X,Y coordinates of the elements involved. With practice, you can use these new capabilities to generate complex geometry quickly but accurately without having to precalculate the angles and lengths involved.

Using the Selective Service

Before you can edit something, you must *select* it. Selecting is the process of telling the computer which object(s) the program is to operate on. The usual reason for selecting an object is so that you can somehow modify it. You may even want to get rid of it entirely. You may also select an item so that you can find out something about it or its properties. For all these reasons, understanding how the selection process works is an important first step in mastering AutoCAD editing.

This section discusses all the different ways that AutoCAD selects objects. Taking the time to discover and experiment with these different methods is really worth the effort, because much of the power of AutoCAD is unavailable to you if you don't know how to select objects correctly. So try to follow closely through this section, and practice any tasks that may at first seem confusing to you. Your work becomes better and faster as a result.

Working with selection settings

AutoCAD includes several configuration settings that affect how object selection works. Enter **OPtions** at the command line to display the Options dialog box, and then choose the Selection tab. Figure 7-5 shows the selection settings that we recommend and describe in detail in Chapter 3. The settings in the Selection Modes area of this dialog box affect the creation of a *selection set*, which is what AutoCAD calls a group of selected objects.

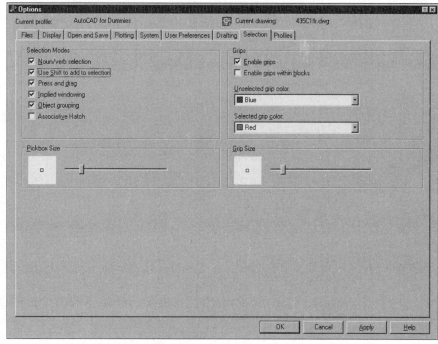

Figure 7-5:
The Selection tab of the Options dialog box with Windows-like settings turned on.

Picking objects one at a time

One way to select objects is to pick (by clicking) them one at a time. The Use Shift to Add option of the Object Selection Settings dialog box, which controls the setting of the PICKADD system variable, controls this option.

If the Use Shift to Add option is off, you build up a selection set cumulatively, by clicking objects one at a time or by using one of the other selection options in AutoCAD, as described later in this chapter. In most programs, you can select only one item at a time when using this method; if you select one object and then another, the first object is deselected and the second one selected. Only the object you select last remains selected. But in AutoCAD, with Use Shift to Add turned off, *all* the objects you select, one at a time, remain selected and are added to the set, no matter how many objects you highlight. Whatever command you choose next affects every selected object.

With the Use Shift to Add option turned on, however, things get almost back to normal. If you click one object and then another, only the second object stays selected. You must click an object, *press and hold the Shift key*, and *then* click another object to build up the selection set. As you select more objects with the Shift key held down, you add selections to the set. Be careful, however: With a few of the less frequently used AutoCAD commands, that old, Shiftless style still applies, even with this option turned on. For those commands, pressing Shift is a waste of effort.

By default — that is, with the Use Shift to Add option turned *off* — you can use the Shift key to *remove* objects from a selection set. Although this default AutoCAD behavior is different from the way most other Windows programs work, it can be quite useful when you're selecting objects in a crowded drawing. You lose this advantage when you turn on the Use Shift to Add option, but you gain more consistency between AutoCAD and other Windows programs.

The most confusing difference between selected objects in AutoCAD and those in other programs involves *grips* (which are described in detail in the section "Grip editing," later in this chapter). In most other programs, only selected objects display grips, or *handles*, at certain points surrounding the objects. In AutoCAD, however, a selected object retains its grips even *after* you deselect it. To the new user, the object probably looks as though it's still selected. In AutoCAD, the only clue you can trust to indicate whether you've actually selected an object — and that it is still selected — is the dotted appearance that the object acquires. The currently selected object in Figure 7-6, for example, displays the dotted linetype to indicate that it is still selected.

Previously selected object (retains grips)

Unselected object

Currently selected object (has grips)

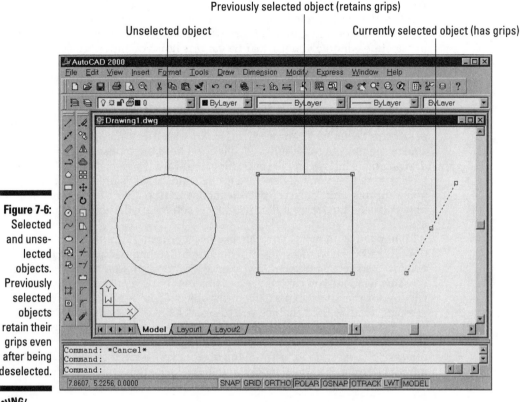

Figure 7-6:
Selected
and unse-
lected
objects.
Previously
selected
objects
retain their
grips even
after being
deselected.

Never assume that an object is currently selected just because it displays
grips. Objects retain grips even when no longer selected.

To unselect all currently selected objects but leave their grips turned on,
press the Esc key. To remove grips from all objects, press the Esc key once
more.

How much is that object in the window?

The Implied Windowing option in the Object Selection Settings dialog box
(backed up by the PICKAUTO system variable) enables a powerful AutoCAD
feature called, appropriately enough, *implied windowing.* Leaving out the history lesson, this feature enables you to use two different types of *selection
windows* easily — although one type does take a bit of getting used to. (A
selection window, by the way, is simply an imaginary rectangle that you specify on the screen by indicating its corners.)

With the Implied Windowing option on, you can use either a *bounding window*, the kind of selection window most other programs use, or a special type of selection window called a *crossing window*. You determine which type of selection window you use just by varying how you move the mouse.

In most graphics programs, you can select a group of objects by dragging the mouse to create a window around those objects. Everything that's *totally inside* the window is then selected; everything that is only partly in the window or that's entirely outside the window isn't selected. To use this kind of selection window in AutoCAD, just start with the mouse pointer on the *left* side of the objects to be selected, click and hold the mouse button to begin drawing the window, and drag the mouse toward the *right* side of the screen, making sure that you fully enclose in the window that's created every object you want to select. Then release the mouse button. Every object that is now fully enclosed by the bounding window is selected; other objects are not.

With implied windowing, you can also use a crossing window for object selection. Just like the window described in the preceding paragraph, a crossing window also selects objects as you drag a window around them. But with a crossing window, you can also select objects that are only *partially* in the window, or that overlap partially other objects you don't want to select. A crossing window thus enables you to select large objects that may not be entirely visible on-screen just by capturing a piece of them within your selection window. This saves you a lot of panning and zooming that you would otherwise need to do to bring all the objects you wanted to select completely into the current drawing window, and makes selecting only the objects you want easier.

To use a crossing window in AutoCAD, just start the mouse pointer on the *right* side of the objects to be selected, click and hold the mouse button to begin drawing the window, and then drag your mouse to the *left* side to create the window, making sure that you enclose at least part of any object you want to select within the window. Then release the mouse button. Every object that is fully enclosed by the window or that is partly enclosed by the window is now selected.

Try drawing a bunch of objects and then selecting different groups of them by using a combination of crossing windows, bounding windows, the Shift key, and mouse clicks. This exercise is great practice for making you a faster AutoCAD user.

To sum up: To create a *bounding window* in which to select objects that are fully within the window, drag the mouse *from the left side* of the objects *to the right*. To create a *crossing window* in which to select objects that are fully or partially within the window, drag the mouse *from the right side* of the objects *to the left*. These two types of selection windows are distinguished *only* by the direction in which you drag the mouse on-screen.

Figures 7-7 and 7-8 show a bounding window and a crossing window, respectively, in action.

If the Press and Drag option in the Object Selection Settings dialog box (also controlled by the PICKDRAG system variable) is turned on (an X appears in its check box), you create any selection window by pressing the mouse button down at the starting corner of the window, dragging the mouse to its destination, and releasing the mouse button at the ending corner of the window, as described in the preceding paragraphs.

If the Press and Drag setting is turned off (its check box is empty), you create any selection window by clicking and releasing the mouse button in the starting corner of the window, thereby "picking" the first point and moving the mouse to its destination *without* pressing the button, and then clicking and releasing the mouse button again to "pick" the ending corner of the window.

Creating a selection window, as you've no doubt figured out by now, is much like drawing an object; the difference is that, to draw an object, you must first enter a drawing command on the command line and then choose a command from the Draw menu or click a drawing button on a toolbar. Creating a selection window requires no such preliminaries — just click and mouse away!

Figure 7-7:
A bounding
selection
window,
created by
dragging the
mouse from
left to right
across the
screen,
selects only
objects
completely
within the
window.

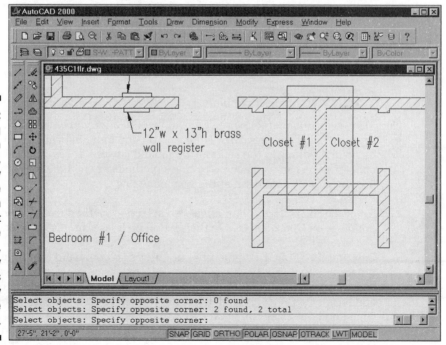

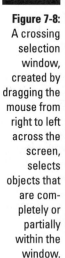

Figure 7-8:
A crossing
selection
window,
created by
dragging the
mouse from
right to left
across the
screen,
selects
objects that
are com-
pletely or
partially
within the
window.

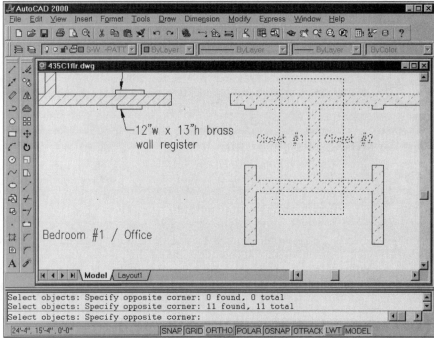

Selecting objects with the SELECT command

Many selection methods aren't available until after you enter a command — a process called *command-first editing*. (You find more information about command-first editing in the section "Command performances," later in this chapter.) You can gain access to these methods at any time, though, by entering the SELECT command at the command line.

AutoCAD 2000 offers a new, advanced selection method called Quick Select. For more on Quick Select, see the section on it later in this chapter.

Entering the SELECT command — or entering a command that operates on objects without first having selected objects — enables you to use a very wide range of methods to select objects. After you finish selecting objects and terminate the command, however, the selection highlights disappear. "So what good does that do?" you may wonder after you've run the SELECT command and nothing happens to the objects. Never fear; the selection you made is now stored as the previous selection set, and you can specify this selection later by typing **Previous** at the command line. The previously selected objects are then selected — and highlighted — again.

Although selecting objects from the command line has a bewildering number of options, the following are the most important ones:

- ✔ **Mouse clicks:** Though it's not listed as an option, just click objects with the mouse to add them to the selection set.

- ✔ **Window:** This option enables you to use a bounding window (as described in the preceding section) to add objects to the selection set.

- ✔ **Crossing:** This option enables you to use a crossing window (as described in the preceding section) to add objects to the selection set.

- ✔ **Group:** If you previously defined a named group of objects, this option enables you to add the group to the selection by entering the group's name at the command line.

- ✔ **Polygon:** This option enables you to use a polygon, instead of a window, to enclose a group of objects. A *window polygon*, or *WPolygon*, selects all the objects surrounded by the polygon you create; a *crossing polygon*, or *CPolygon*, selects all objects surrounded by or crossing the polygon boundary.

- ✔ **Fence:** This option is the most fun. A *fence* is basically a *crossing polyline*. To use it, you just draw a polyline around the screen, through all the objects you want to select, clicking the mouse after every line segment; you thereby select every object the polyline touches. Neat, huh?

- ✔ **ALL:** This option just selects everything — even objects on layers that are turned off and therefore not visible on the drawing screen. However, objects on layers that are frozen or locked are not selected. If you really want to select all the objects in your drawing, turn on all layers before using ALL!

You can use these options in combination or separately.

If AutoCAD is prompting you to select objects and you can't remember all the selection options, enter **?** at the command prompt to see a list of these options. AutoCAD sees the question mark as erroneous input, but then decides to be helpful by showing you a complete list of its selection options.

To use the SELECT command from the command line, start by typing **SELECT** at the command prompt and then pressing Enter. Then type the appropriate designation for any option you want to use (the uppercase letters that appear in the option name on the prompt). To see the options for the SELECT command, enter **?**, and the options appear on the command line as follows:

```
Command: select
Select objects: ?
Window/Last/Crossing/BOX/ALL/Fence/WPolygon/CPolygon/Group/Add
        /Remove/Multiple/Previous/Undo/AUto/Single
Select objects:
```

The important options that aren't available except when you are prompted to select objects are ALL, to select all objects, WPolygon and CPolygon, to create bounding and crossing polygons, and Fence, to draw a polyline through objects you want to select.

When you use the SELECT command or an editing command in command-first mode, AutoCAD keeps prompting you to select objects so that you can build up a selection set in stages. When you're finished selecting objects, press Enter at the select objects prompt to signal that you're finished selecting.

Getting Editing

AutoCAD uses two styles of editing: *command-first editing* and *selection-first editing*. We don't know about you, but we need a review of how these editing styles work.

With *command-first editing*, you enter a command and then click the objects on which the command works. You're unlikely to be familiar with this style of editing for graphics work unless you're a long-time user of AutoCAD. But command-first editing is common in nongraphical environments such as DOS. Whenever you type **DEL *.*** in DOS, you're issuing a command — **DEL**, for *del*ete — and then choosing the objects on which the command works — ***.***, meaning all the files in the current directory. Command-first editing is the default style of editing in AutoCAD.

In *selection-first editing*, you perform the same steps — in the same order — as you do in Windows-based applications, on the Macintosh, or when using a typical word processor, drawing program, and so on: You select the object first and then choose the command. To delete a line of text in a word processor, for example, you highlight (select) the line and then press the Del (Delete) key. The text you highlight is the object you select, and pressing the Del key is the command. Notice that whether you want to delete, underline, or copy the text, the first act is the same: You highlight the text to select it.

For the first decade of its life (all through the 1980s and into the 1990s), AutoCAD was a command-driven, command-first program. Starting with Release 12, the selection-first style of editing has been gradually integrated throughout the program — but it doesn't yet work in some circumstances. AutoCAD Release 12 also marked the debut of *direct manipulation*. Direct manipulation is a refinement of selection-first editing in which you perform common editing operations by using the mouse to actually grab the selected object and perform an action on it, such as moving all or part of it to a different place in the drawing.

A quick look at Quick Select

Quick Select is a new capability in AutoCAD 2000 that allows you to make sophisticated selection choices.

To bring up the Quick Select dialog box, choose Tools⇨Quick Select. The Quick Select dialog box, as shown in the figure, appears.

The Quick Select dialog box allows you to select by various properties — color, layer, linetype, and more — and to select objects with properties that either do or don't equal specified values. You can then include or exclude the specified objects from a new selection set, or append them to the current one. You can even click the Select Objects icon to take a "field trip" into your drawing and add or delete objects from the selection set manually.

Keep this capability in mind as your AutoCAD skills increase, and be ready to use it when editing very complex drawings.

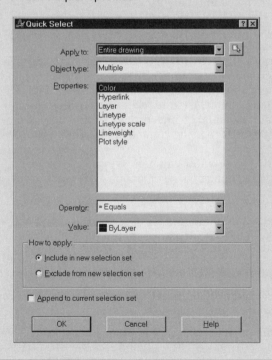

AutoCAD supports direct manipulation through a powerful but somewhat complicated technique called *grip editing*. Grips, as you may well know by now, are handles that appear on an object when you select it; you can use the grips to stretch, move, copy, rotate, or otherwise edit the object. The complications arise from the fact that you can do so many things with an object after you select it. (Look for more information on grips in the section "Grip editing," later in this chapter.)

Command performances

As we explain in the preceding section, command-first editing is the venerable (no, *not* out-moded . . . at least, not totally) practice of first entering an editing command and then selecting what the command works on. Command-first editing is always available in AutoCAD; unlike selection-first editing, command-first editing can't be turned off.

You're usually better off getting in the habit of using one or the other style of editing most of the time. Command-first editing may actually be a good choice for you if you spend most of your time in AutoCAD, because AutoCAD implements this editing style more consistently throughout the program; command-first editing *always* works. Selection-first editing, on the other hand, is more natural for most people and is the style other programs use, so it's the best choice for many users.

Even if you try to stick with selection-first editing, however, you do need to use command-first editing occasionally. (Command-first editing may, in fact, be your choice if you're an experienced AutoCAD user who doesn't want to switch back and forth from one style to another.) Certain commands stubbornly ignore your previous selection and ask you for a new one. In this case, you need to tell AutoCAD to recover the previous selection by typing **Previous** at the command line, or you need to make a new selection — which means you're back to using command-first editing after all.

The following steps show you how to perform command-first editing by using the CHAMFER command (which chops off a corner or intersection and replaces it with a line segment across the gap):

1. **Use the LINE command, as described in Chapter 6, to create two lines that intersect — or that would intersect if extended far enough.**

2. **Type CHAmfer at the command line and press Enter, or click the Chamfer button from the Modify floating toolbar.**

3. **Type D and press Enter to specify chamfer Distances; enter a first and a second chamfer distance.**

   The first chamfer distance is what gets cut away from the first line that you pick (in Step 5). The second chamfer distance is what gets cut away from the second line that you pick (in Step 6). If you specify 0 for both chamfer distances, AutoCAD will extend or trim the lines so that they form a clean corner, with no gap or overhang.

4. **Right-click anywhere in the drawing window and choose Repeat CHAMFER to run the command again.**

5. **Select the first line to be chamfered by clicking the line.**

   If you select the lines to be chamfered *before* you start the CHAMFER command, AutoCAD ignores the selection and you can't restore it.

6. Select the second line to be chamfered by clicking the line.

AutoCAD chamfers the lines, as shown by the example on the right in Figure 7-9.

The CHAMFER command is flexible and offers a number of options. It can add a chamfer line without trimming the existing lines back, and it can chamfer all the vertices of a polyline in one fell swoop. Look up "CHAMFER command" in the AutoCAD online help if you want information on these more advanced options.

Being manipulative

In spite of the ubiquitous nature of command-first editing, selection-first editing and direct manipulation are the preferred ways to edit in AutoCAD for most users. These related methods are closer to how most programs already work now anyway — and (mark our words!) how all programs will eventually work in the future. Most of this chapter concentrates on these types of editing and simply lumps both selection-first editing and its direct manipulation offspring together under the term "direct manipulation" (to avoid being wordy, of course).

Two lines that almost intersect   Similar lines chamfered

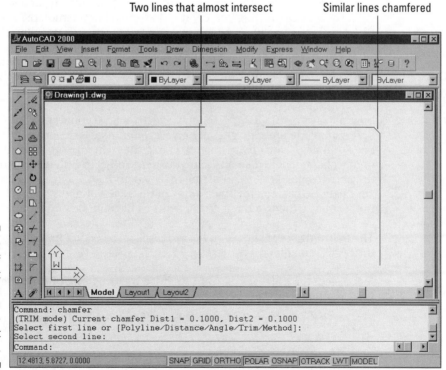

Figure 7-9:
Two sets of almost intersecting lines, with the right-hand set chamfered.

Using direct manipulation to edit, however, may actually require more preparation and forethought than using command-first editing. This additional effort is due partly to the inconsistencies inherent in the way AutoCAD works and partly to the complexity involved in using direct manipulation for such an exacting application as AutoCAD.

Make sure that the Noun/Verb Selection and Enable Grips settings on the Selection tab of the Options dialog are turned on. Direct manipulation doesn't work unless these settings are turned on. See the "Working with selection settings" section earlier in this chapter.

Creating your selection first also may require extra work. To use way-cool selection techniques such as FENCE with direct manipulation, you must enter a drawing command or type the SELECT command on the command line (and press Enter, of course) and then choose the Fence option at the prompt. After you make your selection and press Enter to exit the SELECT command, however, your selection disappears; but you can resurrect the selection for use with a subsequent command by entering P for the Previous option at the command line (it's alive — it's alive!). With some commands, however, not even this roundabout method works; so experiment to discover which of the commands you use demand that you make a selection only *after* the command is entered.

Another difficulty of direct manipulation is that it's hard to use for exacting work such as CAD. You really need to set distances, offsets, and so on exactly right so that the drawing you create can be used as a template for construction or manufacturing. You can't just drag a tangent line up somewhere next to a circle, for example; the tangent must touch the circle at one, and only one, point. And in this sort of work, a two-inch square simply *cannot* be $1\frac{63}{64}$ inches on one side and 2 inches on another. Such a glaring disparity just is not acceptable!

Your allies in getting your geometry exactly where you want it in selection-first editing are the *snap grid* and *object snaps*. As described in Chapter 4, the snap grid helps you create objects of just the right size. As described earlier in this chapter, object snaps help you create objects with just the right relationship to one another. Adjusting the snap grid and using the correct object snaps are extra steps that take some of the ease out of direct manipulation, but if you use them enough, these features become second nature to you.

The following steps show you how to perform selection-first editing, using the ERASE command as an example:

1. **Select the objects you want to erase by using one of the following methods:**

   • Press and hold the Shift key as you click each object.

- Use a bounding window (drag the mouse from left to right) to enclose the objects.

- Use a crossing window (drag the mouse from right to left) to enclose or connect with the objects.

- Type **SELECT** at the command line, press Enter, and at the following prompt choose an option such as ALL, Fence, WPolygon, or CPolygon.

2. **Type** Erase **at the command line or click the Erase button on the Modify floating toolbar.**

   If you used any of the first three methods in Step 1 to select your objects, AutoCAD erases the objects immediately.

3. **If you selected your objects in Step 1 by using the SELECT command, enter** Previous **at the command line and press Enter one more time to complete the ERASE command.**

Figure 7-10 shows several objects selected by using the fence option just before using the ERASE command to erase them. (Zap!)

The Fence option of the SELECT command ignores whether you turned on the Press and Drag selection option; you must define the fence line by clicking and releasing at each *vertex,* or fence point.

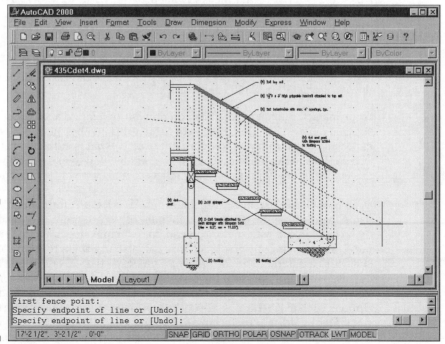

Figure 7-10:
Fence line running through (and thereby selecting) objects to be erased.

Grip editing

Grip editing is familiar to almost anyone who has ever edited graphics on a computer — unless your only graphics experience is with a version of AutoCAD that came out prior to Release 12. If you're an experienced user only of AutoCAD Release 11 or earlier, you've probably never seen grips. And even if you're an experienced user of other graphics programs, you've never seen grips in quite the way AutoCAD uses them. Either way, some explanation is in order.

Grips, as explained earlier in this chapter, are little handles that appear on an object after you select it. You use these handles in many programs for direct manipulation of the object. *Direct manipulation*, as used here, involves the following operations: To move an object, you grab the object's middle grip and drag that grip; to stretch an object, you grab a corner, or edge grip, and drag that grip; to move a copy of the object, you hold down the Shift key while dragging the middle of the object. Even the little frames around the graphics you import into a word processing program are likely to work this way.

Can't get a grip? If you don't see grips when you select objects, then someone turned off the grip feature on your computer. Open the Options dialog box, choose the Selection tab, and turn on the Enable Grips setting.

AutoCAD grips are a little different from those of other programs in the way that grips behave. As in other drawing programs, AutoCAD displays grips on a selected object. But unlike the well-adjusted grips in those other programs, AutoCAD grips *don't go away* after the object they enclose no longer is selected. In fact, they seem to hang around *forever* (much like that annoying *Twilight Zone* theme music that keeps running over and over again through your mind after you've heard it one time too many — do-do-do-do, do-do-do-do, do-do — arrrrrggghhh!).

Grips, in fact, remain visible both on *previously selected* and on *currently selected* objects. The persistence of these grips can become really confusing, especially if you're trying to figure out exactly what is currently selected on-screen. This persistence does, however, enable you to use the grips as targets for future editing chores, such as to make one object touch another.

Despite their persistence problem, AutoCAD grips *are*, for sophisticated users, better than the grips found in most other programs, because you can do so much more with them. You can, for example, use AutoCAD grips to move, stretch, or copy an object. You can also use them to rotate an object, scale it to a different size, or *mirror* an object — that is, create one or more copies. In conjunction with the snap grid, object snaps, and the cursor location display, you can use grips for some pretty complex editing chores. Options such as Ortho also affect the workings of grip editing in interesting ways. Finally, grips actually act as *temporary object snaps* themselves, which is why grips remain on an object even after it's deselected — you may want to snap to that "leftover" grip.

AutoCAD grips are also better — but correspondingly more complicated — than grips in other programs in that AutoCAD grips come in three varieties: hot, warm, and cold. (We could compare these types to the grip a person may have on a significant other, but that would just be causing trouble.) A *hot grip* is the grip that you use to actually perform an action, such as stretching an object. A *warm grip* is any grip on a selected object that isn't a hot grip (nothing's happening to its object at the moment). A *cold grip* is a grip on an unselected object that acts only as a snap target. Cold grips and warm grips both appear as empty, not-filled-in squares; their default color on-screen is blue. Hot grips, on the other hand, appear on-screen as red, filled-in squares.

What all these grip capabilities really mean to the beginning user, however, is that effectively using grips in AutoCAD requires a fair amount of practice. What can help you the most in finding out how to use grips is simply your determination to do so. If you set your mind to use grips as much and as frequently as possible in your drawings, the little buggers slowly — but surely — yield their secrets to you.

Make sure that the Press and Drag and Use Shift to Add object selection settings are turned on in the Object Selection Settings dialog box before you start these steps! See Chapter 3 for details.

The following steps show you all the different operations in which you can use grips:

1. **Click an object on-screen to give it grips (if you don't already have an object selected).**

   Warm grips appear at various points on the object.

   Cold grips and warm grips both are empty squares; their default color is blue. They are identical except that warm grips appear on selected objects, cold ones on unselected objects.

2. **Click one of the grips of your selected object to make it hot.**

   The blue, empty square turns to a red, filled-in square. This grip is now hot.

   Grip editing options now appear on the command line. The first option to appear is STRETCH.

3. **Press the spacebar (or press Enter) to cycle through the grip editing options on the command line.**

   The displayed grip editing option changes as you press the spacebar or Enter. The options that appear are, in order, STRETCH, MOVE, ROTATE, SCALE, and MIRROR. The appearance of your selected object changes as you display each option. Choosing STRETCH, for example, causes a stretched version of the object to appear on-screen.

If all that cycling through grip editing options makes you dizzy, there's an alternative. After you've selected a grip to make it hot, right-click anywhere in the drawing area to display a cursor menu containing all the grip editing options.

4. **Keep pressing the spacebar (or Enter) until STRETCH (or the option you want) reappears as the grip editing option.**

5. **Drag the hot grip in the direction in which you want to stretch (or otherwise manipulate) your object.**

Figure 7-11 shows a line being "stretched" by its midpoint — which is a fast way to move the line. The dotted line shows what the new location of the line will be after you complete the line command by pressing Enter.

You can experiment with all the grip editing options to find out exactly how they affect a selected object, including using all the options that are available while holding down the Shift key (see the following tip).

If you want to see what a grip editing option does to your object without actually changing it, press and hold the Shift key while dragging the object's grip. Holding down the Shift key during grip editing causes the grip editing action to affect a *copy* of the object rather than the original; the original object remains in place, unchanged. (We guess you can consider this one a Grip Tip.)

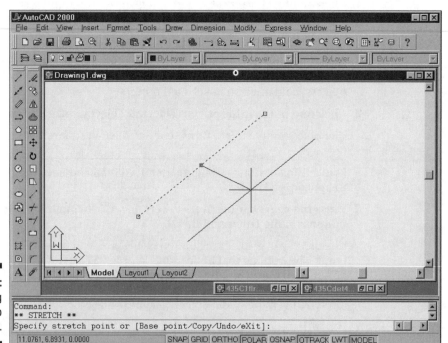

Figure 7-11:
Stretching
the hot grip
of an object.

Using Even More Editing Commands

AutoCAD offers many more editing commands than CHAMFER and ERASE — the two that we've covered so far in this chapter. In fact, a great deal of the power of AutoCAD comes from the flexibility and precision of its editing commands. We can't cover every editing command and option in this book, but we can list the most important ones and demonstrate a couple of them. With this information, you'll be able to get going with the more common editing commands and figure out many of the others. Turn to Chapter 9 of the AutoCAD 2000 *User's Guide* (printed or online) when you're ready to learn about other editing commands and options.

We recommend that, to simplify your life, you learn and use grip editing first and then use editing commands as a turbocharger in cases in which you need to do a lot of editing or need to perform a specific operation that's harder to do with direct manipulation. This gives you the best of both the editing worlds offered by AutoCAD.

Here are the most common editing commands, grouped together conceptually and listed using the convention of capitalizing the letters that work as a command-line shortcut:

- **Erase.** Command for deleting objects; covered previously in this chapter.

- **COpy and Move; Stretch.** Commands that relocate an object, a copy of an object, or parts of an object by a displacement (that is, by a distance). COPY and MOVE work on whole objects. STRETCH can make objects longer or shorter, as well as move entire objects.

- **TRim and EXtend; Fillet and CHAmfer; BReak.** Commands that modify objects by cutting them up or adding to them. TRIM and EXTEND use one object as a "knife" or a "barrier" to cut or lengthen other objects. FILLET is similar to CHAMFER (covered previously in this chapter), except that it can draw rounded corners. BREAK chops a piece out of a line or other object.

- **ARray, Offset.** Commands that copy an object in a structured way. ARRAY can create rectangular arrays (like the squares on a checkerboard) and polar arrays (like the triangles on a Chinese checkerboard). OFFSET copies lines, polylines, and curves to create parallel arrangements of these objects.

- **MIrror, SCale.** Commands that use a similar set of prompts to reflect or resize an object.

- **PEdit.** Powerful editing of polylines, for cases in which grip editing — the easiest way to adjust the vertices of a polyline — doesn't quite make the grade. Examples of good uses for PEDIT include adding or deleting vertices from a polyline.

Following are examples of the MOVE and STRETCH commands that demonstrate the general sequence of AutoCAD editing — select object(s), operate on object(s), stop or repeat. Experiment with the editing commands as you work and gradually build the ones you need into your repertoire.

All the commands listed previously and more are available on the Modify toolbar. Use the Modify toolbar to experiment with editing commands; learn to use the command line for commands that you use frequently.

Base points and displacements

COPY, MOVE, and STRETCH are three of the most useful AutoCAD editing commands. These commands require that you specify how far and in what direction you want the objects copied, moved, or stretched. After you've selected the objects to be edited and started the command, AutoCAD prompts you for two pieces of information:

```
Specify base point or displacement:
Specify second point of displacement or <use first point as
displacement>:
```

These prompts are a not very clear way of saying that there are two possible ways for you to specify how far and in what direction you want the objects copied, moved, or stretched. The most common way — the base point way — is to pick or type the coordinates of two points that define a *displacement vector.* AutoCAD calls these points the *base point* and the *second point.* Imagine an arrow pointing from the base point to the second point — that arrow defines how far and in what direction the objects get copied, moved, or stretched. The other way — the displacement way — to specify how far and in what direction is to type an X,Y pair of numbers that represents a distance rather than a point. This distance is the absolute displacement that you want to copy, move, or stretch the objects.

So how does AutoCAD know whether your response to the first prompt is a base point or a displacement? It depends on how you respond to the second prompt. (Is that confusing, or what?!) If you pick or type the coordinates of a point at the second prompt, AutoCAD says to itself, "Aha — displacement vector!" and moves the objects according to the imaginary arrow pointing from the base point to the second point. If you instead press Enter at the second prompt (without having typed anything), AutoCAD says "Aha — displacement distance," and uses the X,Y pair of numbers that you typed at the first prompt as an absolute displacement distance.

What makes this displacement business even more confusing is that AutoCAD lets you pick a point at the first prompt and press Enter at the second prompt. AutoCAD still says "Aha — displacement distance," but now it treats the coordinates of the point you picked as an absolute distance. For example, if during the MOVE command you pick the point whose coordinates are 14.5,24.2, and press Enter at the second prompt, AutoCAD moves the objects 14.5 units in the X direction and 24.2 units in the Y direction. If the point you picked has relatively large coordinates, the objects can get moved way outside the normal drawing area as defined by the limits. The objects fly off into space, which you probably won't notice at first because you're zoomed into part of your normal drawing area — it just looks to you like the objects have vanished! In short, be careful when you press Enter during the COPY, MOVE, and STRETCH commands. Press Enter in response to the second prompt only if you want your response to the first prompt to be used as an absolute displacement. If you make a mistake, use the UNDO command — described in Chapter 5 — to back up and try again. Also, you can use ZOOM Extents to look for objects that have flown off into space.

A Move-ing example

Moving objects is one of the more common tasks you perform. Although you can move objects with grip editing, the MOVE command is sometimes a more direct route to the same goal. This example demonstrates selection-first editing with the MOVE command using the base point method of indicating how far and in what direction.

1. **Select some objects.**

2. **Start the MOVE command by any of the following methods:**

    • Type **Move** at the command line and press Enter.

    • Choose the Move button (the four-headed arrow) from the Modify toolbar.

    • Choose Modify⇨Move.

    AutoCAD will prompt you for the base point or displacement.

3. **Pick a base point on the screen.**

    This point serves as the tail end of your imaginary arrow indicating how far and in what direction you want the objects moved. After you pick a base point, it's fairly easy to see what's going on because AutoCAD displays a temporary image of the object that moves around as you move the cursor. Figure 7-12 shows what the screen looks like at this stage of the proceedings.

You may want to pick a base point somewhere on or near the object(s) that you're moving. You can use an object snap mode to choose a point exactly on one of the objects.

4. Pick a second point on the screen.

The second point serves as the arrow end of your imaginary displacement arrow. After you pick the second point, AutoCAD moves the objects.

Don't press Enter at this step! If you do, AutoCAD will treat the first point you picked as an absolute displacement, and the objects will fly off in an unpredictable fashion.

You may want to use an object snap mode to pick a second point exactly on another object in the drawing. Alternatively, you can type a relative or polar coordinate, as described in Chapter 5. For example, if you type **@6,2**, AutoCAD moves the objects 6 units to the right and 2 units up. If you type **@3<45**, AutoCAD moves the objects 3 units at an angle of 45 degrees.

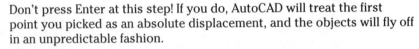

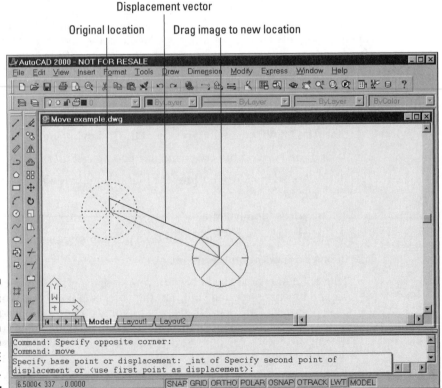

Figure 7-12: Dragging objects in the middle of the MOVE command.

The COPY command works almost identically to the MOVE command, except of course that AutoCAD leaves the selected objects in place and "moves" new copies of them to the new location. In addition, the COPY command includes a Multiple option for making multiple copies of the same set of objects.

Down the home Stretch

The STRETCH command is superficially similar to COPY and MOVE; it has the same inscrutable base point and displacement prompts, and it shifts objects — or parts of objects — to other locations in the drawing. But there are important differences that often confound new AutoCAD users to the point where they give up trying to learn to use STRETCH. That's a mistake, because STRETCH is one of the most valuable commands in the AutoCAD editing tool-box. Here are the things you need to know in order to make STRETCH your friend:

- To use STRETCH effectively, you must select objects using a crossing window (or crossing polygon), as described previously in this chapter.

- STRETCH operates on the defining points of objects — endpoints of a line, vertices of a polyline, center of a circle, and so on — according to the following rule: If a defining point is within the crossing window that you specify, then AutoCAD moves the defining point and updates the object accordingly. For example, if your crossing window surrounds one endpoint of a line but not the other endpoint, then the STRETCH command moves the first endpoint and redraws the line in the new position dictated by the first endpoint's new location. It's as though you have a rubber-band tacked to the wall with two pins and you move one of the pins.

- STRETCH can make lines longer or shorter, depending on your crossing window and displacement vector. In other words, the STRETCH command really combines stretching and compressing.

- You usually want to turn ORTHO on before stretching. Otherwise, you'll end up stretching objects in strange directions.

- In AutoCAD 2000, STRETCH is one of those commands that works only in command-first editing mode. If you select objects and then start the STRETCH command, it not only ignores your selection but also issues an error message! You have to restart the command and then select objects using a crossing window.

This last characteristic appears to be a bug in AutoCAD 2000. AutoCAD Release 14 allowed selection-first editing with the STRETCH command. Autodesk might fix this problem in an update to AutoCAD 2000.

The following set of steps shows you how to STRETCH lines:

1. **Draw some lines in an arrangement similar to the dashed lines shown in Figure 7-13.**

   You don't need to draw the small dotted rectangle in Figure 7-13 — it represents the crossing window that you'll specify in Step 3.

   Start your stretching with simple objects. You can work up to more complicated objects — polylines, circles, arcs, and so on — after you've limbered up with lines.

2. **Start the STRETCH command by any of the following methods:**

   • Type **Stretch** at the command line and press Enter.

   • Choose the Stretch button (the rectangle whose bottom-right corner is getting moved to the right) from the Modify toolbar.

   • Choose <u>M</u>odify➪Stret<u>ch</u>.

   AutoCAD will prompt you to select objects by specifying a crossing window or crossing polygon.

3. **Specify a crossing window that encloses some, but not all, endpoints of the lines.**

   Figure 7-13 shows a sample crossing window that completely encloses the single, short horizontal line and the two very short vertical lines. This crossing window cuts through the four longer horizontal lines, enclosing only one endpoint of each.

   You specify a crossing window by picking a point and then dragging your mouse to the *left.*

4. **Press Enter to end object selection.**

5. **Pick a base point on the screen.**

   This step is just like Step 3 in the preceding example for the MOVE command. After you pick a base point, AutoCAD displays a temporary image of the objects that updates as you move the cursor.

   You may want to pick a base point somewhere on or near the object(s) that you're stretching.

6. **Toggle ortho mode on and then off by clicking the ORTHO button on the status bar; try moving the cursor around first with ortho mode on and then with it off in order to see the difference.**

   Figure 7-13 shows what the screen looks like as you move the cursor around with ortho off.

7. Toggle ortho mode on and then pick a second point on the screen.

This step is just like Step 4 in the preceding example for the MOVE command. After you pick the second point, AutoCAD stretches the objects. Notice that the STRETCH command moved the three short lines — because the crossing window contained both endpoints of all three lines. STRETCH lengthened or shorted the four longer horizontal lines — because the crossing window enclosed only one endpoint of each.

The STRETCH command takes some practice, but it's worth the effort. Draw some additional kinds of objects and practice stretching with different crossing window locations as well as different base points and second points. Also try stretching using an absolute displacement distance, as described previously in the "Base points and displacements" section of this chapter: type an **X,Y** displacement at the first prompt, and then press Enter at the second prompt.

With COPY, MOVE, and STRETCH under your belt, you'll be well on your way to efficient AutoCAD editing. For more information on other editing commands, refer to Chapter 9 of the AutoCAD 2000 *User's Guide*.

Displacement vector

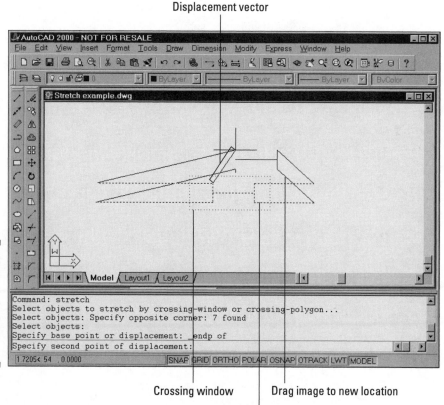

Figure 7-13:
Dragging objects in the middle of the STRETCH command.

Crossing window   Drag image to new location

Original location

Chapter 8

A Zoom with a View

*O*ne of the advantages of CAD over manual drawing is its capability to give you different ways to view your drawing. You can zoom in close, zoom out to a great distance, and pan around. In AutoCAD, you have several different ways to zoom and pan, which are explained in some detail in this chapter.

Keeping the appearance of the screen in synch with the actual drawing file — having the screen reflect changes as you make them — is the biggest single challenge to the performance of AutoCAD. User frustration over having to wait for redraws of the screen and for full regenerations (REGENs) of the screen image from the drawing database has pushed plenty of AutoCAD-related hardware sales over the years.

 In Release 14, the AutoCAD graphics pipeline was redesigned, and AutoCAD 2000 is claimed to have even faster display performance than Release 14. Both of these Windows-based releases are said to perform roughly as fast as the previous speed champ, the DOS-based Release 12. (Which was slow on its own, but quite fast with any of a number of commercially available display drivers.)

AutoCAD 2000 also performs "just-in-time" loading of the different parts of the program. Only a core group of commands and capabilities loads into memory at startup; other commands (for example, the ACIS kernel, used for solid modeling) aren't loaded until needed. The good news is that just-in-time loading means that AutoCAD 2000 loads faster and starts off using less memory; the downside is that you may wait while using certain commands for the first time in a session and may experience a simultaneous decrease in available memory.

In addition to the performance improvements in AutoCAD 2000, you can do certain things to help yourself even more. This chapter describes some of your options for getting more performance out of AutoCAD.

Degenerating and Regenerating

From the AutoCAD point of view, each drawing has two parts. The important part is the DWG (drawing) file, a highly precise database of objects that is stored on disk. AutoCAD uses high precision numbers to describe the location of each object. The less important part is the part that you interact with — the on-screen display of the drawing. For displaying your drawing on-screen, AutoCAD uses less precise integer numbers that are easy to calculate but less accurate than the numbers used in the DWG file. Why would AutoCAD be so stupid as to use less precise numbers for display purposes? Because it can manipulate them a lot faster, which improves overall performance. How fast would you be if you tried to calculate a tip of 15.187645 percent rather than 15 percent (or for you real cheapskates, 10 percent)?

The REGEN command does more than the REDRAW command. The REGEN command goes back to the DWG file and re-converts the high-precision numbers to the less precise integer numbers that are used for display purposes. In the process, REGEN detects what objects have changed and need to be displayed with their new positions, colors, or linetypes (normally, AutoCAD picks up on these changes automatically as you go, but in a few cases — again for performance reasons — it takes a REGEN to display them). AutoCAD then creates a new *display list* to control what shows up on-screen. The REGEN command also reorganizes the database that makes up the display for better performance and then redraws the current viewport from the new display list. REGEN regenerates the current viewport; REGENALL regenerates all views. (A *regen* is not, say, one of the wine-growing areas of France; in AutoCAD, it's a regeneration of your drawing's database, followed by an automatic redrawing of the on-screen image.)

Some changes introduced in AutoCAD 2000 of AutoCAD greatly reduce the need for redraws and regens. If you leave blips off, you may need to use the REDRAW and REGEN commands only rarely. The performance of these commands is still a big topic for AutoCAD aficionados, however, so you may hear about them more often than you would expect.

In AutoCAD 2000, REGENAUTO is set to On by default in new drawings. What does this mean? The system variable that tells AutoCAD whether to automatically do regens as needed, called REGENAUTO, is set to 1, or On. AutoCAD 2000 automatically regenerates your drawing as needed. If you're working in a large drawing and find performance to be slow, you may want to turn automatic regeneration off. This will speed performance but requires you to manually force a redraw or regen whenever you want to make sure the on-screen image is in full agreement with the underlying drawing database.

If you turn REGENAUTO off in a drawing, AutoCAD warns you when the on-screen image and the drawing database may not quite be in synch: it displays Regen queued on the command line. That's yet another good reason to look down at the command line regularly and find out what AutoCAD is mumbling about!

In AutoCAD 2000, you can force a redraw or regen in two quick ways. The first method is to use the REDRAW or REGEN command from the command line. The second way uses three commands on the View menu: Redraw (which runs the REDRAWALL command), Regen, and Regen All. The menu shortcuts for these commands are Alt+V, R, Alt+V, G and Alt+V, A. The keyboard shortcuts are Redraw, RedrawAll, REgen, and REgenAll.

Zooming: How to Zoom-Zoom-Zoom on Your Room-Room-Room

Moving your viewpoint in to get a closer view of your drawing data is called *zooming in;* moving your viewpoint back to get a more expansive view is called *zooming out*.

Zooming in and out of your drawing is one of the big advantages that AutoCAD offers over manual drawing. You can do detailed work on tiny little objects and then zoom out and move around rooms, houses, or neighborhoods from an Olympian perspective.

Panning is closely related to zooming. If you zoom in enough that some of your drawing no longer shows up on-screen, you're going to want to pan around — move left, right, up, and down in your drawing — without zooming in and out. AutoCAD makes panning easy with scroll bars, *realtime* panning, and the built-in aerial view.

Both panning and zooming change what is known as the *view*. The view is simply the current location and magnification of the AutoCAD depiction of your drawing. Each time you zoom or pan, you establish a new view. You can give a name to a specific view to make returning to that view easy.

Choosing the right-click to happiness

AutoCAD 2000 now enables right-click access to realtime panning and zooming, as well as Microsoft Intellimouse support for panning and zooming using the Intellimouse mouse wheel. Use these capabilities to make your work in AutoCAD more efficient.

Right-click based panning and zooming offers the easiest access to realtime zooming and panning, and realtime zooming and panning are the easiest, most interactive ways to get around in your drawings. In some situations, though, realtime panning and zooming are less efficient than the old-fashioned ZOOM command's options. If you are working in large or complex drawings and want to learn other, higher-efficiency ways to pan and zoom, read all parts of this chapter.

The easiest way to pan and zoom is by using the right-click menu. Although the contents of the right-click menu are *context-sensitive* — the menu changes depending on what you're doing — the right-click menu includes pan and zoom any time you don't have geometry selected.

In an existing or sample drawing, practice using the right-click menu to pan and zoom to the view of your drawing that you want.

Follow these steps to efficiently do realtime "freehand" panning and zooming on your drawing using the default right-click menu.

1. **In your drawing, with no geometry selected, right-click.**

   The default right-click menu appears, as shown in Figure 1.

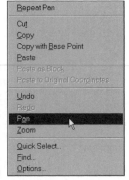

Figure 8-1:
The default right-click menu can be a "pan"acea.

2. **Choose Pan.**

   A hand appears in place of the regular cursor.

   Practice using the underlined characters in the right-click menu to quickly go to your command. For example, right-click and then quickly press the key you need (a for Pan, z for Zoom, or e for Exit).

3. **Move the hand to the spot you want to start panning from.**

   Think about where best to put the hand so that you can minimize the number of times you need to drag when panning a large distance relative to the current view.

4. **Click with the left mouse button and drag the hand in any direction to pan the drawing.**

   Repeat as needed to arrive at the view you want.

5. **To end the pan command without zooming, go to Step 9. To zoom, right-click again.**

   The Pan command is automatically ended and the default right-click menu appears.

6. **Choose Zoom.**

   A magnifying glass appears in place of the regular cursor.

7. **Move the magnifying glass to the appropriate part of the drawing window for your zoom: the top if you want to zoom in, the bottom if you want to zoom out, the center if you want the most flexibility in both directions.**

   Practice starting with the magnifying glass in the appropriate place to support what you want to do on the first try.

8. **Click with the left mouse button and drag the magnifying glass to zoom in (drag up) or out (drag down).**

   You'll zoom in or out as you drag the magnifying glass up or down, respectively.

9. **To end the command, right-click.**

   The default right-click menu appears.

10. **Choose Exit.**

    The command is ended.

Practice using the Exit option to end your final pan or zoom command. Otherwise, it's easy to forget to end the command, and AutoCAD may not respond as you expect when you try to start another command.

You can also pan and zoom using the mouse wheel on a Microsoft Intellimouse. To zoom in and out, roll the mouse wheel forward (in) or backward (out). Double-click the mouse wheel to zoom to the extents of your drawing. To pan, hold down the mouse wheel as you move the mouse.

The right and middle mouse button zoom and pan operations that we describe in this chapter depend on two AutoCAD 2000 configuration settings. The MBUTTONPAN system variable controls what happens when you click the middle button on a three-button mouse (or click the mouse wheel on a Microsoft Intellimouse). When MBUTTONPAN is set to 1 — the default value — you can use the middle button to pan and zoom, as we describe in the preceding tip. If you change MBUTTONPAN to 0, then clicking the middle mouse button displays a cursor object snap menu, as it did in previous AutoCAD versions. The Right-click Customization dialog box controls what happens when you click the right mouse button. You open this dialog box by choosing Tools⇨Options, clicking the User Preferences tab, and then choosing the Right-click Customization button. The standard settings for all three modes (Default, Edit, and Command) are available on a shortcut menu. Other settings provide backward compatibility with older AutoCAD versions. Use the Right-click Customization dialog box's help if you want to find out more.

Out of the frying pan...

In addition to right-click panning, there are several other ways to pan in AutoCAD. These other panning techniques can be complicated to keep separate until you're comfortable with them. Because panning is integral to the ZOOM DYNAMIC command, which is an important and fast way to get to the view you want, we introduce the details of panning first and then show you all the ways to zoom in the next section.

Knowing how to pan (and zoom) quickly and correctly can really set fire to your ability to be productive in AutoCAD. (Out of the frying pan — into the fire. Get it?) It's worth practicing moving quickly to specific points in complex drawings in order to become faster in your daily AutoCAD work.

Panning can be as simple or as powerful as you need it to be. The simpler approaches are very intuitive but may bog down with relatively slow performance in highly complex drawings. The more powerful approaches take more effort to master but work fast in almost any drawing.

After you practice using the right-click menu to pan, as we describe earlier, the next approach to panning in AutoCAD that you should get to know is simply using the *scroll bars*. If you're coming to AutoCAD 2000 from an early Windows version or a DOS version of AutoCAD, scrolling is a new capability for you. Even if you previously used a Windows version of AutoCAD with scroll bars, they're worth trying again, because the faster out-of-box display speed of AutoCAD 2000 makes the scroll bars more practical to use.

Scrolling is the same in AutoCAD as in any other Windows program; just click the arrows in the right and bottom borders of the drawing window to pan a step at a time, or click and drag on the little square "thumbs" in those borders to pan as little or as much as you want to.

If you haven't used scroll bars much before or haven't used them much in AutoCAD, take some time to experiment with scrolling. With practice, it may become your main method of panning, reducing the need to spend time getting used to some of the more complex methods.

Real realtime panning

Realtime panning is a relatively new approach to panning for AutoCAD. Introduced in AutoCAD Release 13, realtime panning mirrors panning in many other programs. Right-clicking in the drawing area, as we describe earlier in this chapter, is only one way to start a realtime pan:

1. **Start the PAN command, with the Realtime option, by using one of the following methods:**

   - Right-click in the drawing area with no geometry selected to get the default right-click menu. Then choose Pan, as described earlier in the chapter.

   - Type **Pan** at the command prompt and press Enter.

   - Click the Pan Realtime button (the one that looks like a hand) in the Standard toolbar.

   The cursor changes to a hand.

2. **Pan by clicking at any point on your drawing and dragging.**

   Clicking in the right spot can save you time. The farther to the left you click, for example, the farther to the right you can pan on a single drag of the mouse. Practice panning in your more complicated drawings until you are proficient.

3. **Repeat until you reach the part of your drawing that you want to reach.**

4. **To end the PAN command, use one of the following methods:**

   - Press Enter or the spacebar or the Escape key to terminate the command.

   - Right-click to activate a pop-up menu that enables you to switch to zooming.

Although realtime panning is relatively new in AutoCAD, it has replaced the less intuitive two-point method of panning in older versions of AutoCAD. If you want to see how Grandpa used to pan, enter **–Pan** (with the leading dash) at the command line.

Time to zoom

Zooming is easy using the right-click menu, as described earlier in this chapter. Zooming is simply a necessity for working in AutoCAD, so it's also worth your taking some time to find out all the different ways to zoom around, in, and out of your drawing.

The Zoom command has different options. The most important of these options are the following:

- ✔ **All and Extents.** ZOOM Extents zooms out just far enough to show all the objects in the current drawing. ZOOM All does the same thing, unless the drawings limits are larger than the extents, in which case ZOOM All zooms to show the entire rectangular area defined by the limits. If you've defined your limits properly (see Chapter 4), then ZOOM All is a good way to see your whole drawing area.

- ✔ **Dynamic.** This option supports both panning and zooming with a view box that you position. It's the next best thing to the aerial view (described later in this chapter), and it doesn't take up screen space, either.

- ✔ **Window.** Great for zooming in — zooms to a section of your drawing that you specify by placing a window around the area you want to look at. You can also use this option to zoom out, but then you have to enter the point coordinates at the command line.

- ✔ **Scale (X/XP).** Scales the drawing; values less than one cause you to zoom in, values greater than one cause you to zoom out. You can also think of the value as a scaling factor: 0.5X causes the screen image to shrink to half its apparent size, and 2X causes the screen image to double its apparent size. (Use XP after a number to scale relative to paper space; see Chapter 9 for information about paper space.)

- ✔ **Realtime.** Realtime zooming, the technique used when you start a zoom operation with the right-click menu as described previously, enables you to zoom in and out simply by starting a realtime zoom and then moving the cursor up to zoom in or down to zoom out. This method is natural and gives a great deal of control, but performance may be slow in complicated drawings.

- ✔ **Previous.** Undoes the last zoom and/or pan sequence. It's like going back in time but without the funny costumes!

The zoom options take some getting used to. Experiment with all the options and the aerial view to find the approach that works best for you. (Occasionally, too, your drawing may seem to disappear, in which case ZOOM All or ZOOM Extents will bring it back. Know how to use zoom, and you can always discover where it went!)

Unfortunately, zooming to extents doesn't leave a margin of white space around the objects in the drawing. Follow a ZOOM Extents command by typing **ZOOM 0.9X** at the command line (and pressing Enter) to get AutoCAD to zoom out just a little bit more.

Real realtime zooming

Just follow these steps to zoom realtime in AutoCAD 2000:

1. **Start the realtime ZOOM command by using one of the following methods:**

   - Right-click in the drawing area with no geometry selected to get the default right-click menu. Then choose Zoom, as described earlier in the chapter.

   - Type **Zoom** at the command prompt and press Enter; then press Enter again to select the Realtime option, which is the default.

   - Click the Zoom Realtime button that looks like a magnifying glass with a plus/minus symbol next to it near the right end of the Standard toolbar.

   The cursor changes to a magnifying glass.

2. **Zoom in or out by clicking at any point on your drawing and dragging up to zoom in, down to zoom out.**

   Clicking in the right spot initially can save you time. The farther up you click, for example, the farther in you can zoom on a single downward drag of the mouse.

3. **Repeat until you have zoomed as far as you want to.**

4. **To end the ZOOM command, use one of the following methods:**

   - Press Enter or the spacebar to terminate the command.

   - Right-click to activate a pop-up menu that enables you to switch to panning or other zooming methods.

Getting dynamic with your zooming

The following steps show you how to use dynamic zoom to handle both panning and zooming. Until you get used to it, however, ZOOM Dynamic is confusing to use. After you master this method, though, it's easy and fast, even in complex drawings. Consider also using realtime zooming, described in the preceding section, and the aerial view, described in the following section.

Follow these steps a few times in one of your own drawings until you become proficient:

1. **Start ZOOM Dynamic by using one of the following methods:**

   - Type **ZOOM** at the command prompt and press Enter. Type **D** followed by the Enter key in order to select the Dynamic option.

   - Choose <u>V</u>iew⇨<u>Z</u>oom⇨<u>D</u>ynamic from the menu bar.

The drawing window automatically zooms out beyond its limits or extents, whichever is larger, as indicated by a dashed blue box. A dashed green box indicates the original view; a movable box with an X in it indicates a view that you can pan and zoom; and a box around the edges of your drawing indicates its extents.

2. To pan the drawing, use the mouse to move the box around on-screen and click after you finish.

Clicking anchors the left edge of the box and starts the zoom part of the command. Figure 8-2 shows several overlapping rectangles during execution of the ZOOM Dynamic command.

3. To zoom, move the mouse left or right.

This action establishes the size of the new view.

4. To pan while zooming, move the mouse up or down.

You can also combine up/down and left/right motions to pan and zoom simultaneously.

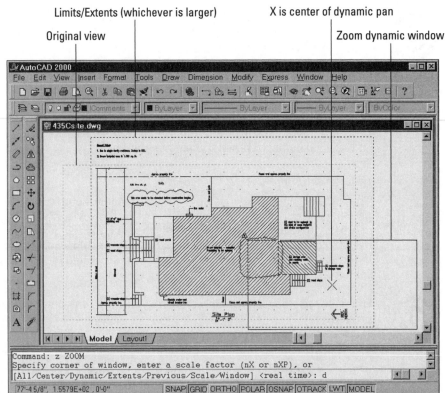

Figure 8-2:
The on-screen look during a ZOOM Dynamic operation.

This action establishes the up and down orientation of the new view. The left edge is anchored but the right edge changes as you move the mouse left or right.

5. **Click to return to pan mode.**

   Now that you've set the size of the view (by zooming), you get another chance to pan.

6. **Repeat Steps 3 through 6 until the new view is the right size and in the right location.**

   At first, this procedure takes several tries, moving between panning and zooming. With practice, you're able to do this sequence quickly.

7. **Press Enter, or click the right mouse button and then choose Enter from the cursor menu, to establish the new view.**

Seeing the View from Above: Aerial View

The aerial view feature offers a quick way to navigate around your drawing as well as a way to magnify parts of the drawing. Although the magnification part is occasionally useful, think of the aerial view primarily as a way to control zooming and panning around your drawing. Realtime pan and zoom should be all you need most of the time, but for complex drawings, the aerial view can be very useful.

Much of the "sizzle" of the aerial view is gone in AutoCAD 2000 due to the new realtime pan and zoom options; the aerial view is no longer always the easiest way to pan and zoom. However, it is still worth knowing for use in complex drawings with many levels of detail that otherwise might be slow to pan and zoom in.

Zooming and panning with aerial view requires a little bit of finesse, because the actual proportions of your drawing window are fixed. If you want to both pan and zoom, it's best to zoom first, to define how big an area you want to see, and then pan. Follow these steps to zoom and pan with aerial view:

1. **Choose View⇨Aerial View to open the Aerial View window.**

2. **Click in the Aerial View window to start panning; then move the mouse around to pan.**

3. **Click in the Aerial View window again to switch to zooming; move the mouse left to zoom in, right to zoom out.**

   Figure 8-3 shows the Aerial View window and the drawing area behind it during a zoom. The box with the X in it is the zoom window.

Zoom in aerial view

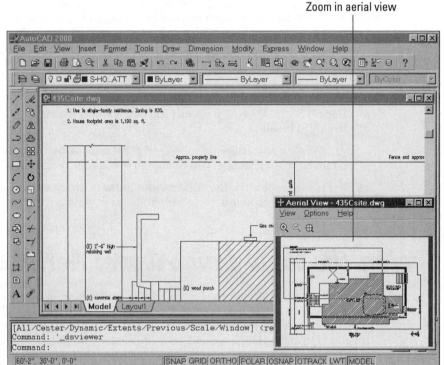

Figure 8-3:
Zooming
with the
aerial view.

Where you draw the zoom window determines where you pan the view as well. The left edge of the zoom window that you create by dragging becomes the left edge of the drawing window. If you drag correctly, you don't need to pan.

4. **Click again to switch back to panning and then move the panning window around.**

5. **Right-click to retain the new view in the drawing window.**

6. **Repeat Steps 2 through 5 until the drawing area has the correct view.**

7. **Click the X (the Close window icon) in the Aerial View window to close the Aerial View window.**

Part III
Make Your Drawing Beautiful

The 5th Wave   By Rich Tennant

WITH DAD'S AUTOCAD RENDERING OF FOREST TROLLS, HIS CAMPSIDE STORIES ACHIEVE A NEW HEIGHT IN REALISM.

In this part . . .

The most popular way to share your drawings with others is printing — or as CAD users call it, plotting. Plotting is totally revised and updated in AutoCAD 2000; this book tells you how to take advantage of the new features while still working smoothly with people using older setups. Text, dimensions, and hatch patterns — mysterious embellishments to the uninitiated — have long been important elements in drawing and drafting. In AutoCAD, these elements are flexible, and you can instantly edit and update them as you change the geometry beneath them. After you get everything working, AutoCAD is definitely much better for almost all drawing purposes than pencil and paper could ever be — and far more versatile in enabling you to create a drawing that's both accurate and good looking. In this part, you can pull all the pieces together and create a drawing you can be truly proud of.

Chapter 9

The Plot Thickens

Despite the increasing number of offices with a computer (or two) on every desk, many people still need to or want to work with printed drawings. Thus, sooner or later, you'll need to stop zooming around and start plotting. Depending on where you are in a project, plotting is the pop quiz, midterm, or final exam of your drawing-making semester. With some AutoCAD 2000 study and some preparation of each drawing, you can sail through the plotting experience and get back to working with virtual lines and sheets of paper. Without these preparations, you're likely to fail miserably at plotting and develop sweaty palms every time you think about trying to do it again.

Plotting originally meant creating hard-copy output on a device that was capable of printing on larger sheets, such as D size or E size, that measure several feet on a side. These "plotters" often used pens to draw, robot-fashion, on large sheets of vellum or mylar, which then could be run through *diazo blueline machines* — copying machines that create blueprints — in order to create inexpensive copies. *Printing* meant creating hard-copy output on ordinary printers — dot matrix or laser, in those days — that used ordinary sized paper, such as A size (letter size, 8½" x 11") or B size (ledger size, 11" by 17"). AutoCAD had different software drivers and different commands for plotting and printing. Nowadays, the distinction has disappeared. The PLOT and PRINT commands take you to the same dialog box, and AutoCAD 2000 makes no distinction between plotting and printing.

Unfortunately, plotting an AutoCAD drawing is considerably more complicated than printing a word processing document or spreadsheet. CAD has a larger range of different plotters and printers, drawing types, and output procedures than most other computer applications do. AutoCAD 2000 tries to help you tame the vast jungle of plotting permutations, but you'll probably find that it takes some time for you to get the lay of the land and clear a path to your desired hard-copy output. This chapter will help, and reading it is a lot less dangerous than swinging a machete around.

Plotting received a major facelift — and heart and brain transplant — in AutoCAD 2000. It's so different from AutoCAD Release 14 plotting that Autodesk saw fit to issue the Fast Track to Plotting Help message, shown in Figure 9-1, every time you plot.

Figure 9-1: Detour ahead: unfamiliar territory!

> **Fast Track to Plotting Help**
>
> (?) Plotting has been greatly enhanced. We STRONGLY encourage you to review the Plotting Help and video animations provided.
>
> Do you want to view the Fast Track to Plotting Help now?
>
> [Yes]   [No]
>
> ☐ Do not show this dialog again

Translated out of cheery marketing-speak, the message means: "Warning: We've changed plotting beyond recognition. If you're an experienced AutoCAD user from any release before this one, you will be completely disoriented and permanently confused unless you spend some time watching this video about the new plotting and layout procedures in AutoCAD 2000." At least your need to see the plotting video will help justify that new computer with the blazing video animation performance and great sound quality.

The Fast Track to Plotting Help is aimed especially at customers who are upgrading from a previous version of AutoCAD. Nonetheless, even if you're coming to AutoCAD 2000 without hauling around the baggage of old plotting methods, you'll need to study up. AutoCAD 2000 plotting is more flexible, powerful, and rational than plotting in previous versions. However, simple it is not.

If you work with grizzled old AutoCAD veterans who are used to the old-fashioned plotting methods, you'll probably notice that it takes some time for them to warm to the newfangled AutoCAD 2000 methods. At the end of this chapter, we give some advice to you new AutoCAD users for dealing with the plotting dinosaurs.

Plotting the Simple Way

OK, so you believe us. You know that you're not going to master AutoCAD 2000 plotting in five minutes. That doesn't change the fact that your boss, employee, wife, husband, construction foreman, or 11-year-old son is demanding a quick check plot of your drawing — and is sneering at you for not being able to do it.

Here's the quick, cut-to-the-chase procedure for plotting a simple drawing — a mere 17 steps! This procedure assumes that your drawing resides in model space (we cover paper space layouts later in this chapter). It doesn't deal with plotting to a specific scale, controlling plotted line widths, or any of the other weird and wonderful options that you'll eventually have to grapple with (see the rest of this chapter for details). It should, however, result in a piece of paper that bears some vague resemblance to what AutoCAD displays on your computer monitor.

1. **Open the drawing in AutoCAD.**

2. **Zoom to the drawing's current extents (choose View⇨Zoom⇨Extents or type** ZOOM Extents**) so that you can verify the area that you're going to plot.**

   Note whether your drawing is longer than it is tall or taller than it is long. See Chapter 8 if you need help with zooming to the drawing's extents.

3. **To display the Plot dialog box, do any of the following: choose File⇨Plot, click the Plot button on the Standard menu, type** PLOT **at the command prompt, or press CTRL+P.**

   The Plot dialog box appears.

4. **If the Fast Track to Plotting Help message appears, dismiss it by choosing No (you're in a hurry, remember?).**

   Now you can see the Plot dialog box, as shown in Figure 9-2.

5. **Make sure that the Plot Device tab is selected.**

6. **In the Plotter Configuration area, select a device that you're used to printing to from other Windows applications.**

   For example, choose the laser or inkjet printer that you customarily use to print word processing documents. Stick to printer names that display the little printer icon next to their names. Avoid for now any names with a little plotter icon next to their names. (These printer names always end in "pc3," and we talk about them a bit later.)

7. **Leave the remaining Plot Device settings set to their default values, as shown in Figure 9-2: Plot style table set to None, What to plot set to Current tab, and Plot to file left unchecked to set it to off.**

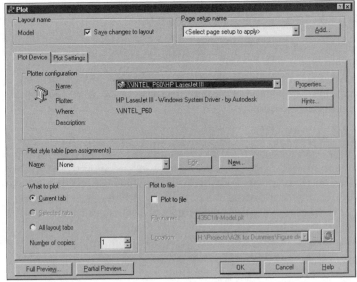

Figure 9-2:
The Plot
Device tab
on the Plot
dialog box.

8. **Choose the Plot Settings tab, as shown in Figure 9-3.**

9. **In the Paper size and paper units area, select a paper size that's loaded in your printer.**

10. **In the Plot area area (sponsored by the Department of Redundancy Department), choose Extents.**

11. **In the Drawing orientation area, choose either Portrait or Landscape, based upon the following rule: If your drawing is longer than it is tall, such as a side view of a typical ranch house, choose Landscape; if your drawing is taller than it is long, such as a side view of a typical skyscraper, choose Portrait.**

12. **In the Plot scale area, choose Scaled to Fit from the plot Scale list.**

13. **Leave the Plot offset and Plot options settings set to their default values, as shown previously in Figure 9-3.**

14. **Choose the Full Preview button and check that your entire drawing displays on the "paper," as shown in Figure 9-4; then, right-click and choose Exit to return to the Plot dialog box.**

15. **If you found any problems with the plot preview, adjust the Plot Settings (for example, Drawing orientation) and repeat the Full Preview until the plot looks right.**

16. **Make sure that Save changes to layout (in the Layout name area at the top of the Plot dialog box) is turned on.**

    This option saves the plot setting changes you made so that they become the default the next time you plot this drawing.

17. **Choose OK to create the plot.**

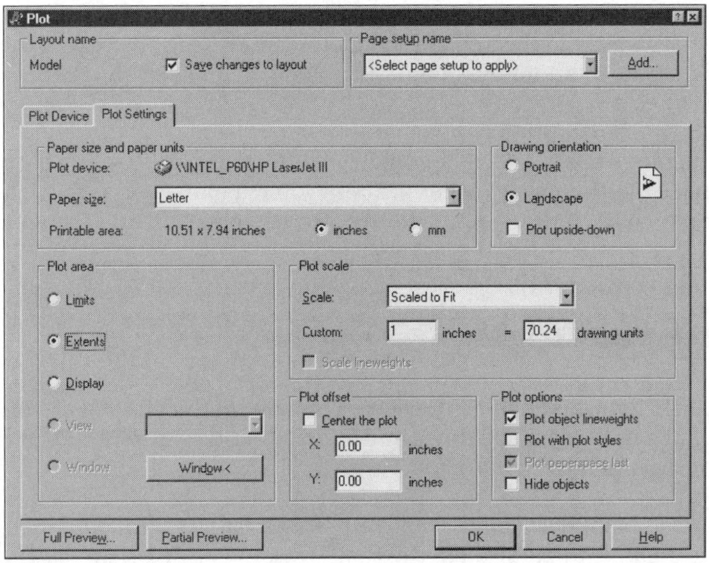

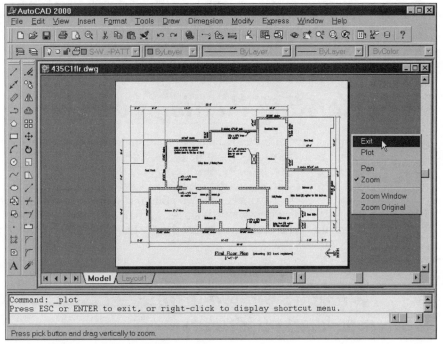

Figure 9-3:
The Plot
Settings tab
on the Plot
dialog box.

Figure 9-4:
The full
plot
preview.

If for some reason your plot didn't work, well, we warned you that AutoCAD plotting was complicated and temperamental! Read the rest of this chapter in order to learn about the numerous other plotting options that can cause plotting to go awry.

If the plot came out as you hoped it would and you're feeling cocky now, you can try plotting to any other printers you're connected to (such as a large-format inkjet plotter) or try plotting to a specific scale.

Plotting the Not-So-Simple Way

Now that you've enjoyed the almost-instant gratification of creating a simple plot, it's time to buckle down and learn about the AutoCAD 2000 range of plotting and layout options.

At some point early on in your AutoCAD-learning career, you really should take the time to go through the Fast Track to Plotting Help information offered by the message box shown in Figure 9-1. The plotting capabilities of AutoCAD 2000 are gratifyingly flexible, and along with that flexibility comes a certain amount of complexity. Read through this chapter first in order to get the basic plotting concepts and techniques down. Then spend a little bit of time with the documentation (online or printed) in order to extend your understanding.

Understanding Plotting Concepts

Before we dive into dialog boxes and commands — being careful not to bump our heads in the process — it helps to understand some basic AutoCAD 2000 plotting concepts. Most of these concepts are new in AutoCAD 2000, or at least so greatly changed that long-time users of older AutoCAD releases will be just as confused as you are. We point out some of the differences between AutoCAD 2000 and previous releases so that you'll be able to help the old-timers along and understand why they're having so much trouble plotting in AutoCAD 2000.

Windows system printer versus non-system drivers

Operating systems, and the programs that run in them, use a special piece of software called a *printer driver* in order to format data for printing and send it to the printer or plotter. When you configure Windows to recognize a new printer connected to your computer or your network, you're actually installing the printer's driver. ("Bring the Rolls around front, James. And bring me a gin and tonic and a D size plot while you're at it.") AutoCAD, like other Windows programs, works with the printers you've configured in Windows. AutoCAD calls these *system printers* because they're part of the Windows system.

But AutoCAD, unlike other Windows programs, can't leave well enough alone. It turns out that some output devices, especially larger plotters, aren't controlled very efficiently or very well by Windows system printer drivers. For that reason, AutoCAD comes with specialized *non-system drivers* (that is, not part of the Windows system) for plotters from companies such as Hewlett-Packard, Xerox, and Océ. These drivers are kind of like non-union workers. They ignore the nice, tidy rules for communicating with Windows printers in order to get things done a bit more quickly.

You use the AutoCAD 2000 Plotter Manager Add-A-Plotter wizard to create non-system driver configurations. When you complete the wizard steps, AutoCAD 2000 saves the information in a PC3 (Plot Configuration Version 3) file. The wizard can import some settings from older AutoCAD R14 PC2 (Version 2) and AutoCAD R12 PCP (Version 1) files.

Using already-configured Windows system printer drivers usually is easiest, and they work well with many devices — especially devices that print on smaller paper, such as laser and inkjet printers. If you have a large plotter, you may be able to get faster plotting, better plot quality, and more plot features by installing a non-system driver. Chapter 6 of the *AutoCAD 2000 Installation Guide* tells you how.

Paper space layouts

Layouts are an extension of the paper space concept that first appeared in AutoCAD R11. *Paper space* is a separate "space" for composing the printed version of your drawing. You create the drawing itself, called the *model,* in *model space.* (No, this is not the alternate universe in which the *Sports Illustrated* swimsuit issue is created.) Thus far in this book, all your work has been in model space, as you can tell by the Model tab that's active as you do your drawing. Some users of AutoCAD releases before AutoCAD 2000 embraced paper space for all their drawings, some used it selectively, and many ignored it completely.

With AutoCAD 2000, Autodesk hopes to make paper space layouts the standard operating procedure for all (or at least most) drawings. AutoCAD 2000 allows more than one paper space layout per drawing, and connects these layouts with plot settings. Figure 9-5 shows a drawing in model space, and Figure 9-6 shows a paper space layout for plotting the same drawing with a title block.

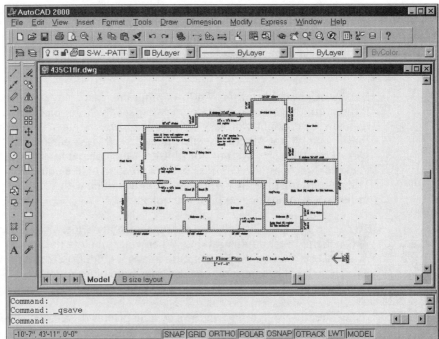

Figure 9-5:
Model
space.

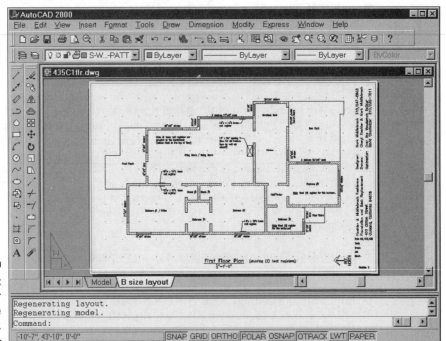

Figure 9-6:
A paper
space
layout.

A paper space layout begins as a blank sheet of paper but functions like an opaque screen laid over your model. You create one or more *viewports* — like carving an opening in the screen — to reveal the model "underneath." AutoCAD calls these openings *floating viewports* (to distinguish them from the old-fashioned tiled viewports that are allowed in model space).

In AutoCAD 2000, it's still possible to ignore paper space layouts entirely and do all your drawing *and* plotting in model space. But you owe it to yourself (and to the programmers who slaved over a hot keyboard cooking up all of those new layout features) to give layouts a try. We think you'll find that they make plotting more consistent and predictable. They'll certainly give you more plotting flexibility when the time comes that you need it.

You'll sometimes hear the word *tilemode* bandied about in discussions of paper space, including in the AutoCAD 2000 online help. In previous releases of AutoCAD, you used the TILEMODE command to switch between model space and paper space. (Previous releases had only one paper space layout and didn't display the convenient little tabs at the bottom of the drawing area.) TILEMODE 1 displayed model space and TILEMODE 0 displayed paper space. The insanely obscure name TILEMODE comes from the floating versus tiled viewport distinction, but the programmer who thought of that name still deserves to be sentenced to life behind a DOS prompt. In any case, you don't really need to worry about TILEMODE any more. Clicking the Model and Layout tabs takes care of everything for you.

Page setups

Page setups are brand new in AutoCAD 2000. They specify the plotter, paper size, and other plot settings that you use to plot a particular drawing. AutoCAD 2000 maintains separate page setups for model space and for each paper space model layout (that is, for each tab that you see in the drawing area). AutoCAD 2000 remembers the last page setup settings that you used to plot each tab, and it also lets you save page setups so that you can re-use them later. Page setups are stored with each drawing, but you can copy them from one drawing to another.

Controlling plotted lineweights

Because previous releases of AutoCAD didn't offer lineweight as an object or layer property, people used object display color to control the plotted lineweight and other plot characteristics of objects. AutoCAD provided a way of mapping each display color to a different printed thickness so that, for example, red lines were plotted thin, green lines were plotted thicker, and so on. This indirect approach sounds pretty strange now, but CAD drafters are an odd bunch, so everyone got used to it and considered it perfectly normal.

AutoCAD 2000 offers lineweight as an object and layer property (and also as a plot style property — see the next section), so object display color can revert to being used for — surprise! — color. You can use display colors to control plot colors, of course. But even if you make monochrome plots, you can use color to help you distinguish different kinds of objects when you view them on-screen, or to make compelling on-screen presentations of drawings for others.

It's still possible to control plotted lineweight by display color in AutoCAD 2000. Companies that have been using AutoCAD forever — at least, it seems like forever to some of us! — may choose to stick with their Old Ways for some time to come. If you work for one of those companies, you may find yourself forced to worship the color-mapped-to-lineweight idol, at least until the superstitious old-timers see the lineweight light.

Plot styles

Plot styles are another brand-new AutoCAD 2000 feature and come in two exciting flavors: color-based plot styles and named plot styles. Plot styles provide a way to override object properties with alternative plot properties. The properties include plotted lineweight, plotted color, and screening (plotting shades of gray). Figure 9-11, appearing later in this chapter, shows the full range of options.

The good news is that, in some cases, you won't need to bother with plot styles. If you've established your layer and object properties (especially lineweight) so that they reflect how you want objects to plot, then you can dispense with plot styles.

If you want objects in your drawing to plot with properties that are different from their display properties, then you need plot styles. For example, you might want to plot with different lineweights or colors than you're using for display purposes. Or you might want to map plotted lineweights to display colors, just like in the Good Ol' Days of AutoCAD Release 14 and before. AutoCAD 2000 groups plot styles into plot style tables, each of which is stored in a separate file.

Color-based plot style tables live in Color TaBle (CTB) files and they map the 255 AutoCAD display colors to 255 plot styles. AutoCAD 2000 automatically attaches the color-based plot styles to every object, based on — you guessed it — the object's color. (Are those AutoCAD programmers brilliant, or what?) Color-based plot style tables are especially handy for mimicking the old color-mapped-to-lineweight plotting approach of earlier AutoCAD releases.

Named plot style tables live in Style TaBle (STB) files. After you've created a named plot style table, you create one or more plot styles and give them any names you like. Then you can assign the named plot styles to layers or to individual objects.

"Named" refers to the plot styles, not to the tables. Both color-based plot style *tables* and named plot style *tables* have names, but color-based plot *styles* don't have names and named plot *styles* do have names.

To use a plot style table and its included plot styles (whether they're color-based or named), you must attach it to model space or a paper space layout. The plot style table then affects plotting only for that tab. This approach lets you plot the same drawing in different ways by attaching different plot styles to different tabs.

The Plotting tab on the Options dialog box contains a setting called "Default plot style behavior for new drawings." When you start a new drawing, the current value of this setting ("Use color dependent plot styles" or "Use named plot styles") determines whether you can choose CTB or STB files. Unfortunately, changing this setting does *not* change the current drawing. If you want to change from color-based plot styles to named plot styles (or vice versa), use the CONVERTPSTYLES command provided in the AutoCAD 2000 Migration Tools.

Drivers and layouts and styles, oh my!

Okay, enough theory; how do we use all this stuff? The shiny, new AutoCAD 2000 sequence goes as follows:

1. **Use the Windows Add Printer wizard (Start⇨Settings⇨Printers) to configure Windows printers, or use the AutoCAD 2000 Plotter Manager Add-A-Plotter wizard (File⇨Plotter Manager) to add a non-system printer, or AutoCAD-only, configuration.**

   Usually, you (or the Information Systems geek who sets up AutoCAD on your computer) perform printer configuration right after installing AutoCAD. But you'll need to revisit these wizards if you get a new printer or plotter, or if you forgot to configure one of your devices in the beginning.

   You also can use the AutoCAD 2000 Plotter Manager Add-A-Plotter wizard to create a special configuration for a Windows system printer (for example, a configuration that uses a special paper size or other weird settings that you don't want to inflict on your other Windows programs). Run the Add-A-Plotter wizard and choose System Printer during the step labeled Begin.

2. **Create your drawing in model space.**

   You can assign lineweights and colors to layers and objects and use these lineweights and colors for plotting. Alternatively, see Step 5.

3. **Create one or more paper space layouts for plotting (Tools⇨Wizards⇨Create Layout).**

   See the next section of this chapter for details.

4. **Define one or more page setups for each paper space layout — and for model space, if you want to plot from model space (File⇨Page Setup).**

   You can specify page setup settings during the Create Layout wizard (Step 3) or later.

5. **(Optional.) Create color-based plot or named plot style table(s) and attach them to one more tabs (the model tab and/or one or more of your paper space layouts).**

   You might not need to perform this step if you assigned your desired plot properties to layers and objects when you created the drawing geometry (Step 2).

6. **Plot one or more paper space layout and model space tab(s) (File⇨Plot).**

   The Plot dialog box is a superset of the Page Setup dialog box, so you'll have another chance to perform the Step 4 procedures.

Creating Layouts

Creating a simple paper space layout is straightforward, thanks to the new AutoCAD 2000 Create Layout wizard, shown in Figure 9-7. The command name is LAYOUTWIZARD (not to be confused with the WAYOUTLIZARD command for drawing geckos and iguanas), but you avoid a lot of typing with Tools⇨Wizards⇨Create Layout.

Although the Create Layout wizard guides you step by step through the process of creating a paper space layout from scratch, it doesn't eliminate the necessity of your coming up with a sensible set of layout parameters. The sheet size and plot scale that you choose provide a certain amount of space for showing your model (see Appendix A), and wizards aren't allowed to bend the laws of arithmetic in order to escape that fact. For example, a map of Texas at a scale of 1"=1' won't fit on an 8½" x 11" sheet, no way, no how. In other words, garbage in, garbage (lay)out. Fortunately, the Create Layout wizard lends itself to experimentation, and you can easily delete layouts that don't work.

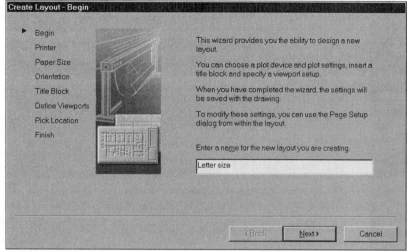

Figure 9-7:
The Create
Layout
wizard

Creating a layout

The following steps show you how to create a layout after you've drawn your model — in this example, an architectural floor plan of a house:

1. **Choose Tools⇨Wizards⇨Create Layout or type** LAYOUTWIZARD.

2. **Give the new layout a name (see Figure 9-7).**

   We recommend something more descriptive, such as "Letter size," than "Layout2," which is the default name.

3. **Choose a printer or plotter to use when plotting this layout.**

   Think of your choice as the *default* plotter for this layout. You can change to a different plotter later, or create page setups that plot the same layout on different plotters.

   Many of the names in the configured plotter list should look familiar because they're your Windows printers (*system printers* in AutoCAD lingo). Names with a PC3 extension represent non-system printer drivers.

4. **Choose a paper size and specify whether to use inches or millimeters in order to represent paper units.**

   The available paper sizes depend on the printer or plotter that you selected in Step 3.

5. **Specify the orientation of the drawing on the paper.**

   The icon showing the letter A on the piece of paper shows you which orientation is which.

6. **Choose a title block, or None (see Figure 9-8). If you choose a title block, specify whether AutoCAD should insert it as a Block — which is preferable in this case — or attach it as an Xref.**

Attaching a title block as an xref is a good practice if your title block DWG file is in the same folder as the current drawing that you're working on. The Create Layout wizard's title blocks live in the Template folder that's stored with the AutoCAD 2000 program files, which isn't — or shouldn't be — where you keep your project files. Thus, in this case Block is a safer choice.

Choose a title block that fits your paper size. If the title block is larger than the paper, the Create Layout wizard simply lets it run off the paper.

If you don't like any of the supplied title blocks, choose None. You can always draw, insert, or xref a title block later.

The list of available title blocks comes from all of the DWG files in the AutoCAD Template folder. You can add custom title block drawings to this directory.

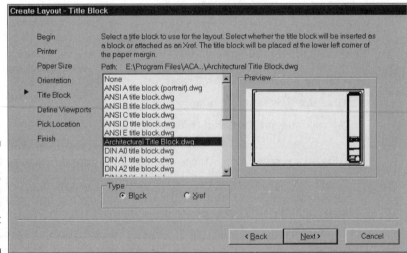

Figure 9-8:
Title block
options in
the Create
Layout
wizard.

7. **Define the arrangement of viewports that AutoCAD should create, and the paper space to model space scale for all viewports.**

A paper space layout viewport is a "window" into model space. You must create at least one viewport in order to display the model in your new layout. For most 2D drawings, a Single viewport is all you need. 3D models often benefit from multiple viewports, each showing the 3D model from a different perspective.

The default Viewport scale of Scaled to fit ensures that all of your model drawing displays in the viewport but results in an arbitrary scale factor. Most technical drawings require a specific scale, such as 1=10 or ⅛"=1'-0".

8. Specify the location of the viewport(s) on the paper by picking its corners.

After you choose the Select location button, the Create Layout wizard displays the preliminary layout with any title block that you've chosen. Pick two points to define a rectangle that falls within the drawing area of your title block (or within the plottable area of the sheet, if you chose no title block in Step 6).

AutoCAD represents the plottable area of the sheet with a dashed rectangle near the edge of the sheet. If you don't select a location for the viewport(s), the Create Layout wizard creates a viewport that fills the plottable area of the sheet.

9. Choose Finish.

AutoCAD creates the new layout, as shown in Figure 9-6 earlier in this chapter.

Working with layouts

After you've created a layout, you can delete, copy, rename, and otherwise manipulate it by right-clicking its tab. Figure 9-9 shows the right-click menu options.

The From template option refers to layout templates. You can save a layout to a template file (a DWT file) and then use it to create new layouts in other drawings. For details, see online help: Contents⇨How To⇨Plot Your Drawings⇨To use an existing layout template.

Many drawings require only one paper space layout. If you always plot the same view of the model, and always plot to the same device and on the same size paper, then a single paper space layout should suffice. If you want to plot your model in different ways (for example, at different scales, with different layers visible, with different areas visible, or with different plotted line characteristics), then you may want to create additional paper space layouts.

Some different ways of plotting the same model can be handled in a single paper space layout with different page setups. See the section "It's a setup!" later in this chapter.

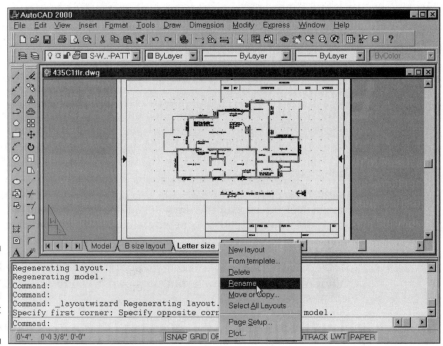

Figure 9-9:
The right-
click menu
for a layout
tab.

If you want to add another viewport to an existing layout, you'll need to grap-ple with the MVIEW command and the ZOOM command's mysterious XP option. See the MVIEW and ZOOM commands in the online help.

Working in layouts

After creating a paper space layout, you suddenly have two views of the same drawing geometry: the view on your original Model tab, and the new layout tab view (perhaps decorated with a handsome title block and other accou-trements of plotting nobility). It's important to realize that both views are of the *same* geometry. If you change the model geometry on one tab, you're changing it on all tabs, because all tabs display the same model space objects. It's like seeing double after downing a few too many drinks — the duplication is in your head, not in the real world (or in this case, in the CAD world).

When you make a paper space layout current by clicking its tab, you can move the cursor between paper space (that is, drawing and zooming on the sheet of paper) and model space (drawing and zooming on the model, inside the viewport) in several ways, including:

✔ Click the Paper / Model button on the status bar.

✔ In the drawing area, double-click over a viewport to move the cursor into model space in that viewport, or double-click outside of all viewports (for example, in the gray area outside the sheet) in order to move the cursor into paper space.

✔ Enter **MSpace** or **PSpace** at the command prompt.

When the cursor is in model space, anything you draw or edit changes the model (and thus appears on the Model tab and on all paper space layout tabs, assuming that they display that part of the model). When the cursor is in paper space, anything you draw appears only on that one paper space layout tab. It's as though you were drawing on an acetate sheet over the top of that sheet of plotter paper — the model beneath remains unaffected.

This distinction can be disorienting at first — even if you haven't had a few too many drinks. In order to avoid confusion, stick with the following approach (at least until you're more familiar with paper space):

✔ If you want to edit the model, switch to the Model tab first. (Don't try to edit the model in a paper space viewport.)

✔ If you want to edit a particular plot layout without affecting the model, switch to that layout's tab and make sure that the cursor is in paper space.

(Re-) Plotting

Now that you know how to create paper space layouts, you're ready to learn more about AutoCAD 2000 plotting. The concepts and techniques described in this section apply to plotting paper space layouts and model space, but they really shine in paper space.

Getting to know the plot dialog box

The Plot dialog box segregates the many plotting choices into four groups, as shown later in Figures 9-10 and 9-12:

✔ Choices that concern the device you're plotting to (Plot Device)

✔ Choices that concern the paper you want to plot on and how to transfer the drawing onto that piece of paper (Plot Settings)

✔ Two choices for previewing a plot before you take the final, fateful step of sending it to the printer

✔ Choices that allow you to save your other plot choices: Layout name for saving your choices as the default for the current layout, and Page setup name for saving your choices to a specific name that you can retrieve later

Next, we take you on a guided tour of these three groups. We don't cover every minute, obscure, useful-only-at-cocktail party-discussions detail. We point out what's important, steer you away from what's not important, and guide you over the bumpy spots.

Use the Plot dialog box's "question mark" help to find out more about any part of the dialog: Click the question mark at the upper right of the dialog box, then click the part of the dialog about which you're confused. If the pop-up help isn't enough, choose the Help button at the bottom of the dialog box.

Configuring the plotter

When you click the Plot Device tab in the Plot dialog, you see the options shown in Figure 9-10.

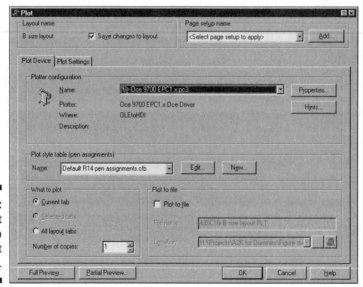

Figure 9-10:
The Plot Device tab on the Plot dialog box.

✔ **Plotter configuration.** Here you choose the Windows system printer or non-system driver configuration that you want to use for plotting. Windows system printer choices display a little printer icon next to their names (see Figure 9-2, appearing earlier in this chapter). Non-system (that is, AutoCAD-specific) plotter driver choices display a little plotter icon next to their names, which end in "pc3" (see Figure 9-10).

Use the Properties button to change media (paper) and other properties that are unique to the currently selected plotter or printer. In particular, you can define custom paper sizes.

✔ **Plot style table (pen assignments).** Choose a color-based (CBT) or named (SBT) plot style table if you want to override objects' display properties with other plot properties (see the "Plot styles" section earlier in this chapter for details). If you want to plot objects as they display in model space, set Plot style table to None.

You can use the New and Edit buttons to create and edit plot style tables. This procedure is not for the faint of heart, because of the numerous plot style options (see Figure 9-11). Color, Lineweight, and Screening are the options that you're most likely to want to configure.

✔ **What to plot.** Specify whether to plot only the currently selected tab (Model or a paper space layout) or all drawing editor tabs. Also specify the number of copies.

✔ **Plot to file.** If you need to plot to a file rather than directly to your plotter or network printer queue, turn on this option and specify the File name and folder (Location).

This option is especially useful when you want to use the ePlot feature to publish a DWF file on a Web site. (See Chapter 18 for details about using DWF files.)

Configuring the plot

When you click the Plot Settings tab in the Plot dialog, you see the options shown in Figure 9-12.

✔ **Paper size and paper units.** Specify a paper size, based on the choices provided by the device you selected on the Plot Device tab.

AutoCAD displays the Printable area, which is a bit smaller than the actual paper size because most plotters and printers can't plot all the way to the edge of the paper; they need a small margin.

✔ **Drawing orientation.** Specify whether AutoCAD should put the drawing on the paper in Portrait or Landscape orientation. Turn on Plot upside-down if you want to rotate the plot 180 degrees on the paper (a handy option for plotting in the southern hemisphere).

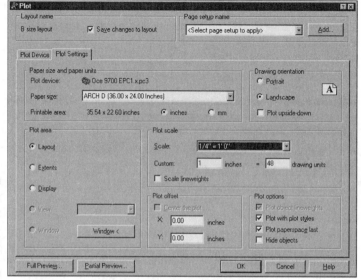

Figure 9-12:
The Plot
Settings tab
on the Plot
dialog box.

If you're confused about whether Portrait or Landscape is the right choice, a quick detour through Full Preview will un-confuse you fast.

✔ **Plot area.** Specify the area of the drawing to plot. Your choices include Extents, Display, View, and Window, regardless of whether you're plotting a paper space layout or the model space tab. In addition, your first choice is Layout for a paper space layout tab, or Limits for the model space tab.

Extents means an imaginary rectangle enclosing all the objects in the drawing. *Display* means the drawing as it's currently displayed in the drawing window (including any white space around the drawing objects). *View* means a named view, which you choose from the drop-down list. *Window* means a rectangular area that you specify by picking the Window button.

Usually, you'll choose to plot Layout in paper space. For model space, the choice depends on whether the drawing was set up properly and what you want to plot. If you set limits properly, as we suggest in Chapter 4, then plot Limits in order to get the whole drawing area. If you're trying to plot a drawing from some numbskull who didn't set limits properly — possibly the one you see in the mirror each morning — try Extents instead. Use Window or View if you want to plot just a portion of model space.

✔ **Plot scale.** Choose a plot scale from the drop-down list, or specify a Custom scale in the inches (or millimeters) = drawing units text boxes.

1:1 is the usual plot scale when plotting a paper space layout onto the paper size for which the layout was created. Use smaller scales to do check plots on smaller sheets of paper (for example, 1:2 to create a half-size plot). Scale to Fit is handy for squeezing a model space plot onto a piece of paper of any size. To plot model space at a specific scale, enter that scale in the Custom text boxes.

When you plot a paper space layout, you might want to turn on Scale lineweights if you're plotting at a scale other than 1:1. For example, if you do a half-size check plot (plot scale = 1:2), turning on Scale lineweights reduces the lineweights by 50 percent.

✔ **Plot offset.** A Plot offset of X=0 and Y=0 positions the plot at the lower-left corner of the plottable area. Enter nonzero numbers or turn on Center to plot if you want to move the plot from this default position on the paper.

✔ **Plot options.** These four options control whether lineweights applied to objects (directly or using the bylayer option) get plotted, whether plot style overrides get applied, whether paper space objects plot after model space geometry in viewports, and whether AutoCAD performs 3D hidden line removal on objects before plotting them.

When you plot a paper space layout, the Hide objects setting affects only objects in paper space. Use the object properties window to turn hidden line removal on or off for the objects in viewports (that is, click the PAPER/MODEL toggle button on the status bar until it says PAPER, select the viewport by clicking on its border, and run PROPERTIES).

Previewing the plot

AutoCAD improves on the full and partial previews from previous releases quite a bit. The full preview is now reasonably WYSIWYG (What You See Is What You Get), so there are fewer surprises between the preview and the plot. The partial preview is easier to understand and displays better warnings.

The partial preview is a quick reality check to make sure that your plot fits on the paper and is turned in the right direction. AutoCAD 2000 lists the Paper Size, Printable Area (that is, Paper Size minus a small margin), and Effective Area (that is, the amount of space that your plotted drawing takes up). The Paper Size appears as a white sheet, the Printable Area as a dashed rectangle, and the Effective Area as a blue box. AutoCAD 2000 displays warnings such as the one shown in Figure 9-13 when it detects that something is wrong.

The full preview takes a bit longer to generate but shows exactly how your drawing lays out on the paper and how the various lineweights, colors, and other object plot properties will appear. You can zoom and pan around the preview by using the right-click menu, as shown in Figure 9-14.

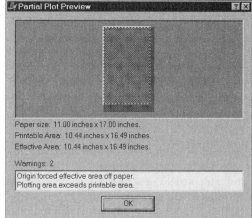

Figure 9-13:
A partial
preview.

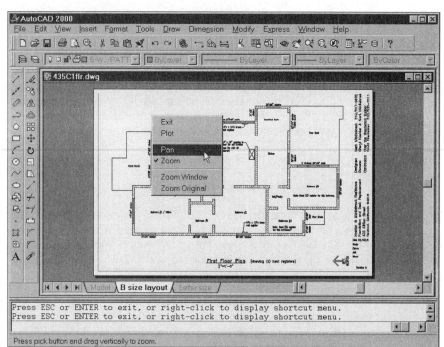

Figure 9-14:
A full
preview.

It's not a bad idea to do a partial preview and then a full preview before each plot (especially if you've made any changes to plot settings). The partial preview makes sure that you're in the ballpark, and helps you fix drawing orientation or scale problems quickly. The full preview makes sure that you're in the right seat in the ballpark, and gives you the best chance that the game turns out the way you hoped it would.

It's a setup!

As we mention in the "Page setups" section earlier in this chapter, AutoCAD 2000 saves the last group of plot settings for each tab with the drawing (assuming that you leave Save changes to layout, at the top of the Plot dialog box, turned on). If your plotting needs are simple, that should do it.

If you want to get fancier, you can create named page setups in order to plot the same layout (or the model tab) in different ways, or to copy plot settings from one drawing to another. Use the Add button to create a named page setup from the current plot settings.

You can use the PAGESETUP command to modify the current plot settings without plotting (see Figure 9-15). PAGESETUP opens the Page Setup dialog box, which is really just the Plot dialog in disguise (it just omits the What to plot and Plot to file areas on the Plot Device tab). Changes you make become the default plot settings for the current drawing tab.

The easiest way to run PAGESETUP is to right-click a paper space layout or model space tab and choose Page Setup.

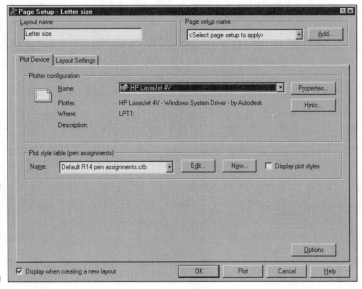

Figure 9-15:
The Page Setup dialog box: Plot in disguise.

The Page Setup dialog box, unlike the Plot dialog box, lets you save plot settings changes without plotting and without having to create a page setup name.

Reviewing plotting

Now that you've taken the in-depth tour of plotting, you should be able to understand all the steps in the Simple Plotting sequence at the beginning of the chapter. Review those steps and try them on a paper space layout with one of your drawings. The main difference when you plot a paper space layout is that you'll specify the Plot area to be Layout (see Step 10) and the Plot scale to be 1:1 (or 1:2 for a half-size check plot) (see Step 12).

Plotting with Plodders

If you're starting out fresh with AutoCAD 2000 and don't have the baggage of older plotting methods to carry around with you, consider yourself lucky. But many people will end up exchanging drawings with old AutoCAD geezers (such as the authors) who are inordinately fond of mapping colors to plotted lineweights and can't fathom why Autodesk would mess up the perfectly good AutoCAD Release 14 Plot dialog box by adding tabs and all those weird new choices. In fact, you may work in an office full of such people!

Here are a few suggestions for maintaining your sanity while straddling the old and new plotting worlds:

✔ Learn how to use color-based plot styles to mimic the old color-to-lineweight mapping scheme. Use the R14PENWIZARD command (Tools➪Wizards➪Add Color-Dependent Plot Style Table) to create plot style tables quickly from AutoCAD Release 14 PCP, PC2, or CFG files.

✔ Learn how to create and edit plot style tables so that you can create color-to-lineweight mappings in the absence of a PCP, PC2, or CFG file.

✔ Have your CAD-using friends and colleagues read this chapter so that they're as up-to-date on AutoCAD 2000 plotting as you are.

✔ Try not to sneer too much when you find "real" lineweights immediately obvious, while your CAD "expert" friends struggle with the New CAD World Order.

Chapter 10

Text with Character

*T*ext can be one of the most important parts of an AutoCAD drawing. Text can be an intrinsic part of the drawing, integrated with other drawing elements. Text in a drawing is most commonly used for brief descriptions and notes, but it can also consist of long paragraphs that describe, annotate, or otherwise add to the drawing.

Dimensions — text that displays the measurements of objects — is a kind of text that AutoCAD handles especially well (although with a staggering number of options). Dimensions also include leaders with text. You can find more about dimensions and the text that follows them around in Chapter 11.

The text improvements in Release 13 and Release 14, including TrueType font support, multiline text editing, and spell checking, have been nicely "finished" in AutoCAD 2000. AutoCAD 2000 text changes include improvements in fractions, the ability to specify capitalization within AutoCAD, and improved ability to control line spacing. Also, the Dtext command has been "folded into" the Text command.

If you're going to pass your drawings back and forth between AutoCAD 2000 and Release 13 or earlier versions, restrict yourself to the SHX fonts that come with AutoCAD; Release 13 sometimes has trouble finding TrueType fonts that have been installed on the user's system, and earlier versions of AutoCAD can't use TrueType fonts at all. Before using TrueType fonts, be sure that anyone else who will be working on your DWG file has or can get the same fonts you used. If you use TrueType fonts that are not available on another user's computer, either because they are using an earlier version of AutoCAD or because they don't have access to the fonts, your text will be preserved but the font information will be lost, causing the text in your drawing to look different than you intended.

Fine Redlining

An important part of the drafting process is *redlining*, which is marking up a drawing with comments and suggested changes. You can use AutoCAD's text capabilities to redline a drawing in a way that makes it easy to remove your comments after changes are made.

The basic idea is to create a new layer for comments and put your comments there. That makes it easy for the drafter or other person doing the actual work to see your comments; hide them while making corrections; make printouts with or without the comments; and delete them when the needed changes have been made. Follow these steps to quickly add a comments layer and redline a drawing with a single comment.

1. **Open a drawing.**

2. **To create a layer, choose Format⇨Layer, click the Layers button on the Object Properties toolbar, or type LAyer at the command prompt.**

   The Layer Properties Manager dialog box appears.

3. **Choose New (press the N key to do this quickly).**

   A new layer appears at the bottom of the layers list.

4. **Type the name of the layer, !Comments.**

   Preceding the name with an exclamation point makes this layer name float to the top when the list is alphabetized by layer name.

   If more than one person might make comments on this drawing (or you just want to make sure that you get credit for your brilliant insights), type a layer name that includes your initials, such as **!Comments-BS**.

5. **Click the new layer's color.**

   The Select Color dialog box appears.

6. **Choose a suitable color for a comment, such as red, and click OK.**

   The layer's color changes.

7. **Click the Plot icon for the layer to turn plotting off.**

   You can always turn plotting of comments on later, but it might be a good idea to start with plotting of them off.

8. **Click the Current button to make the layer current (or simply double-click the new layer's name).**

9. **Click OK to finish your layer-related changes.**

   Note that the !Comments layer is now shown as the current layer in the layer pull-down menu.

10. **Zoom and pan, as described in Chapter 8, to a spot in your drawing that requires a comment.**

   Notice that the text in the Object Properties toolbar appears grayed out when you're in the middle of a pan or zoom command; this alerts you that you need to press the Esc key to exit the command before starting to do anything else.

11. **Click the A icon in the Draw menu, choose Draw⇨Text⇨Multiline Text, or type MTEXT at the command line to start a multiline text paragraph.**

12. **Click twice to pick the corners of where your comment will go.**

   The Multiline Text Editor appears, as shown in Figure 10-1.

Figure 10-1:
Here's
Multiline
Text in
action.

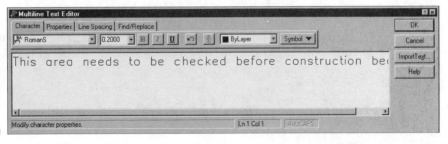

   (Having to pick the corners of the text box first is kind of annoying for those of us who don't know the exact size of what we're going to say until after we say it, but so it goes. You can always expand the text box later by grabbing a grip on the corner of the text box and stretching it.)

13. **Type in a comment, such as** This area needs to be checked before construction begins. **and click OK.**

   Your comment will appear in the Multiline Text Editor dialog box as you type it. When you click OK, it will appear on-screen in the box you specified.

   Your comment will appear using whatever text style is in effect for the current layer. Just accept the current style for now; you learn more about text styles later in this chapter.

14. **Experiment with the text: move it around, select it, then right-click and choose Mtext Edit to bring up the multi-line text editor again.**

15. **To delete the new layer, start by selecting and then erasing the text.**

16. **Now choose Format⊅Layer or type LAyer at the command prompt.**

    The Layer Properties Manager dialog box appears.

17. **Click another layer and click the Current button to make it current.**

    You have to make another layer current before you can delete the !Comments layer. You also must make sure that you've erased all objects on the layer. AutoCAD won't delete a layer if there are any objects on it.

18. **Click the !Comments layer to select it.**

19. **Click the Delete button to delete the layer.**

    You can click Cancel to undo the layer deletion or any and all other actions you've taken in the Layer Properties Manager dialog box.

You can call attention to your comment by drawing a rectangle around it (see Chapter 6), or by enclosing it in a revision cloud. Revision clouds are a groovy feature of the Express Tools (you did install them, didn't you!?). Choose Express⊅Draw⊅Revision Cloud and cloud away.

You can also use this approach of text on a separate layer for redlining a document using notes with *leaders*, a type of dimensioning described in the next chapter, and for annotations that describe to others a drawing you create.

Getting the Right Height

Both text and dimensions require that you specify a *height* for characters; text height is an important and difficult parameter to set correctly. Because it's a different kind of animal — and one that can bite you in an uncomfortable spot if you treat it badly — take a careful look at how to handle text height.

Text that looks good on-screen is no guarantee of text that looks good on your printout because the screen and the printout use text so differently. Most text in a drawing is not part of the drawing per se, but rather an attempt to communicate something about the drawing to the person using the printout. The text must be a height that the reader is used to. And physical and psychological factors have a big effect; for example, a reader tends to hold a small printout closer to his face than he does a large blueprint. Yet the larger blueprint may have more need for detail in text than the smaller drawing does.

Take note of the following tips for help in getting the height of your text right:

 ✔ Find out what the standard plotted text height is for your discipline, your office, or your current project. If several heights are standard, use the one that works best in your drawing.

 ✔ Multiply the plotted height by the drawing scale factor given in Appendix A and use this number for the text height in AutoCAD.

The drawing scale factor is the number you multiply the left side of a drawing scale by to equal the right side. For instance, if you are using a drawing scale of ⅛" = 1', the drawing scale factor is 96, because ⅛" x 96 = 1'.

If you don't have a figure for plotted text height handy, use ₃₂" or 0.1", about the same size as the height of the text in this book.

Using the Same Old Line

In AutoCAD 2000, the traditional AutoCAD TEXT and DTEXT commands have been combined into a single command, TEXT. (Entering DTEXT at the command line simply brings up the combined TEXT/DTEXT command.) The TEXT command is the simplest form of text entry and editing. This command enables you to enter single lines of text, one at a time; it's fast and easy to use for these single lines. Unlike more complex text-entry options, the text appears on-screen in the drawing area as you type it, not after you finish typing.

You can also use TEXT for multiple lines of text; just keep pressing Enter after each line of text, and TEXT puts the new line below the previous one. The problem is that, almost inevitably, you want to edit the text. If you cut a word or two in one line, the TEXT command doesn't automatically word-wrap the text. In other words, it doesn't "stitch up" the empty space so that all lines are approximately the same width. And it's even worse if you add words: The line just gets longer and longer until it runs off your sheet of paper. You must go in and move words from one line to another so that all lines remain approximately equal in width.

TEXT creates each line of text as a separate object, which is why it can't adjust line lengths in a paragraph as you make changes; TEXT "knows" about only one line of text at a time.

The TEXT command also doesn't let you choose fonts; for that option, use MTEXT, described in the next section. TEXT does enable you to select a previously created text style.

Despite its limitations, the TEXT command is useful. The following steps show you how to enter text by using the AutoCAD TEXT command:

1. **Start the TEXT command by using one of the following methods:**

   - Type **TEXT** at the command prompt and press Enter.

   - Choose Draw➪Text➪Single Line Text from the menu bar.

   The text icon on the Draw toolbar starts the multiline text command, MTEXT, and can't be used to start the TEXT command.

2. **Specify the insertion point for the first text character.**

   You can enter the point's coordinates from the command line, use the mouse to click a point on-screen, or press Enter to locate new text immediately following a previous text object.

3. **Specify the height for the text.**

   This prompt doesn't appear if you're using a text style that already has a defined height. You can find more details about text styles in the section "Creating text styles," later in this chapter.

4. **Specify the text rotation angle by entering the rotation angle from the command line and pressing Enter or by rotating the line on-screen by using the mouse.**

5. **Type the first line of text and press Enter.**

6. **Type additional lines of text, pressing Enter at the end of each line.**

   Figure 10-2 shows text appearing on-screen as you type it, following the TEXT command.

7. **To complete the command, press Enter at the start of a blank line.**

To align lines of text correctly, make sure that you type in all the lines just as you want them to appear, pressing Enter after each line to make the next line appear just after it. Otherwise, aligning different lines of text precisely is harder to do (unless you set your snap just right, or use a complicated combination of object snaps and point filters).

To edit text, enter the DDEDIT command, choose Modify➪Text from the menus, or simply select the text and then right-click and choose Text Edit. The Edit Text dialog appears, enabling you to edit the text.

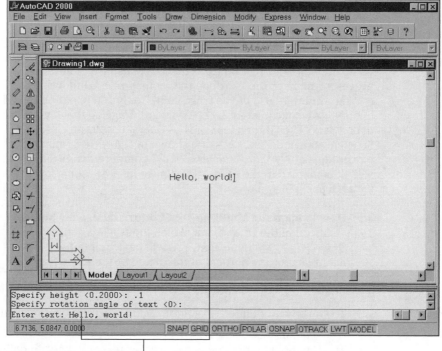

Figure 10-2:
The TEXT
command
puts the text
directly onto
the
AutoCAD
screen as
you type it.

Text appears in the drawing area as it's entered at the command line.

Entering and Editing Paragraph Text

AutoCAD 2000 adds additional improvements and fixes to the much-improved Multiline Text Editor that appeared in Release 14. AutoCAD finally has a text editor that can meet the needs of most of the users, most of the time. The text editor has a few unusual features in its interface, but it's easy to use after you master it.

In the next section, we describe the options of the Multiline Text Editor so that you can get acquainted with them, but you may just want to try the editor, especially if you have experience with other Windows word processing programs. Either read all about it here or try it in AutoCAD, and then work through the steps in the section "Using the paragraph editor," later in this chapter, to make sure that you really know how to use multiline text.

Learning multiline text characteristics

Using the Multiline Text Editor is much like using a mini-word processor, such as the WordPad that comes with Windows. (The editing window starts out as truly "mini," only 100 pixels or so high, but you can make it larger by clicking and dragging the edge of the dialog box.) The editor's four tabs — Character, Properties, Line Spacing, and Find/Replace — are shown in Figure 10-3. All the numerous options are already familiar to most computer users and well-documented in the AutoCAD Help, so here are some key highlights of using the editor:

- ✔ **How to open the Multiline Text Editor:** Choose the Multiline Text icon in the Draw menu, which looks like a capital A, or use Draw⇨Text⇨Multiline Text. You will be prompted at the command line for the corners of the dialog box; choose the corners. The Multiline Text Editor dialog box appears, with the Character tab at the front.

  To start the Multiline Text Editor dialog box from the command line, enter **mText**.

- ✔ **The text box:** Before you can type your text, you have to define a box to hold it. Don't worry about the height of the box; the text goes as far down the screen as it needs to. The important thing to get right is the width, which stays the same regardless of how much or how little text you enter (though you can change the width later).

- ✔ **Create text styles first:** Unlike Microsoft Word, the Multiline Text Editor doesn't enable you to make changes to your text and then name the changed text as a style. You have to create the style and define it completely before you can use it. Use the Text Style dialog box to create a style.

- ✔ **How to create text styles:** Use Format⇨Text Style to open the Text Style dialog box, shown in Figure 10-4. You can specify the text style's font name, style (bold, italic, and so on), and effects, such as upside down, backward, and vertical text. Use the detailed instructions later in this chapter on how to create a text style or experiment to find out how to create text styles that work well for you.

  To start the Text Style dialog box from the command line, enter **STyle**.

Stack/Unstack

Font height   Undo   Text color

Character
formats

Font   Insert symbol   Import text

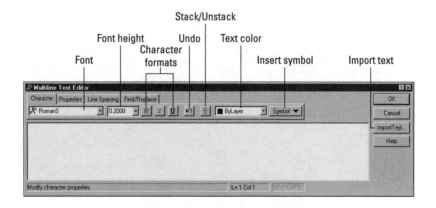

Character width

Text style   Justification   Text rotation

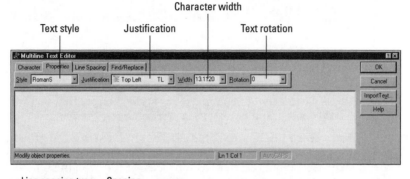

Line spacing type   Spacing

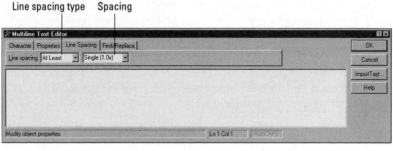

Match case yes/no

Find   Replace

Text to find   Text to replace   Whole word yes/no

Figure 10-3:
The
Multiline
Text Editor's
options.

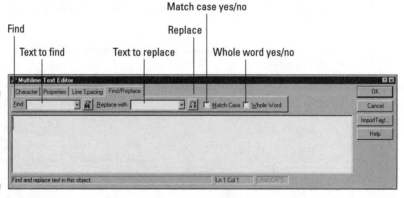

✔ **Specify style before character:** When you start the Multiline Text Editor, the Character tab comes up first. But if you use text styles, start by clicking the Properties tab and choosing the style you want to use. Then go to the Character tab and make any style changes that you want to make for this paragraph of text; then start entering the text.

✔ **Use a word processor:** For large blocks of text, a word processor is still the best bet; it has more functions and you're likely to already know how to use it. Create text in a word processor (or even the built-in WordPad editor in Windows), save it as RTF (Rich Text Format) text, and then use the Import Text button in the Multiline Text Editor to bring in the text. Do be aware, though, that some advanced formatting — such as hanging indents — will be lost when you bring the text into AutoCAD.

In AutoCAD 2000, you can resize the Multiline Text Editor dialog box so that it can display more than a few lines of text at a time. This makes using the Multiline Text Editor for larger blocks of text easier.

✔ **How to edit text:** To edit existing text, choose Modify➪Text. Then choose a multiline text object. The Multiline Text Editor appears, with the selected object ready to be edited. Alternatively, you can click a multiline text object, right-click, and choose Mtext Edit from the cursor menu.

To start the Multiline Text Editor for existing text from the command line, enter **ddEDit**.

✔ **Cheat on width:** You can get more text into a limited space by reducing the text width by 20 percent or so, without changing legibility much.

✔ **Don't overdo it:** You can spend a great deal of time improving the content or the look of the text in your AutoCAD drawing, but the text is almost always secondary to the drawing geometry — and has to be changed anytime the geometry is changed. In other words, text is the tail and the drawing is the dog, so don't put too much work into making text pretty.

✔ **Have someone else do it:** It's probably not a good idea for everyone on a project to be mastering the fine points of text styles and font choices. Have one person on the project be responsible for deciding what fonts to use and managing text styles for that project.

Unlike Release 13 and Release 14, AutoCAD 2000 handles stacked fractions well. Experiment with the stacking button in the Character tab of the Multiline Text Editor. The following characters work when placed between two numbers to make them a fraction:

✔ **^:** The caret character, a shifted 6 on most keyboards, specifies that the numbers before and after it appear as stacked, left-justified values, without any horizontal or diagonal fraction sign between them.

✔ **/:** The forward slash character, the one next to the period (*not* the DOS backslash character higher on the keyboard), specifies that the numbers before and after it appear as center-justified numbers above and below a horizontal fraction bar.

✔ **#:** The pound sign, a shifted 3 on most keyboards, specifies that the numbers before and after it appear as numbers aligned with a diagonal fraction bar.

Enter the numbers in question, separated by the caret, slash, or pound sign. Then select the two numbers and the character and click the Stack/Unstack button. The numbers will reformat as indicated by the character.

The caret character also works other magic when placed next to a single number:

✔ **^2 (or other number):** Specifies that the number is placed as a subscript next to the character before the caret.

✔ **2^ (or other number):** Specifies that the number is placed as a superscript next to the character before the caret.

Enter the caret symbol before or after a number; then select the caret and the number. Click the Stack/Unstack button. The number will reformat as indicated by the position of the caret.

Using the paragraph editor

Here's a brief how-to on using the Multiline Text Editor. Use this section to get acquainted with the basic functions for editing blocks of text in AutoCAD. The following steps show you how to enter and edit text by using the Multiline Text Editor dialog box:

1. **Start the Multiline Text Editor by using one of the following methods:**

   - Type **mText** at the command prompt and press Enter.
   - Click the Text icon on the Draw toolbar or choose <u>D</u>raw⇨Te<u>x</u>t⇨<u>M</u>ultiline Text.

2. **Specify the insertion point for the first character.**

   You can either enter the coordinates of the point on the command line or use the mouse to select a point on-screen.

3. **Specify the other corner of the text box.**

   Enter the coordinates of the point on the command line or use the mouse to select a point on-screen.

   Ignore the other options that appear after you start the command; you can access all of them more easily in the paragraph editor.

   You aren't really specifying a box here, because the text just keeps spilling out of the bottom of the box if you type too much. You're really specifying the width of the text.

   After you specify the other corner, the Multiline Text Editor dialog box appears (refer back to Figure 10-1).

4. **Type the text you need in the Multiline Text Editor's text box.**

5. **Modify the text's properties by using the dialog box's options.**

   The Multiline Text Editor dialog box includes a number of options, which are described in the following section. You can probably figure most of them out by experimentation.

6. **To complete the text, click OK.**

Another way to get text into your AutoCAD 2000 drawing is to create an OLE (Object Linking and Embedding) link to text in an external word processing document. For more on this, look up OLE in the AutoCAD online help system. Be careful, though — using OLE to place objects in AutoCAD drawings is fraught with potential pitfalls, especially when you plot or send your draw-ings to other people. Experiment with this feature before you commit to using it.

Fonts and performance

A *text font* actually consists of dozens, hundreds, or thousands of tiny lines. Drawing these lines is not a fast process, especially with the many characters that may exist in a really complicated font.

Imagine a drawing of an entire floor of a large building, with labels for each of the major parts of the floor. If you work on the whole drawing at one time, AutoCAD may need to update thousands of characters each time you pan or zoom. The complexity of the task and the time you must wait to complete the task are greatly affected by the simplicity or complexity of the font you use.

AutoCAD includes a number of fonts. For the most effective performance, consider using the simpler fonts, such as TXT or ROMANS. ROMANS is a good compromise between appearance and performance.

You can also manage performance/attractiveness tradeoffs using AutoCAD features such as

layers. By isolating each kind of text — annotations, dimensions, comments — on its own separate layer, you get maximum control over what is getting updated on-screen by unfreezing only the layers that you need at any one time.

You can also use more elaborate and attractive TrueType fonts for the very best appearance, but you'll pay a performance penalty. And performance is not the only concern in using these fonts: if a font is not one of the standard Windows or AutoCAD TrueType fonts, you must also be sure to load the fonts on each machine on which you intend to view or print the drawing. In order to load TrueType fonts on a computer, you (or better yet, the guy or gal your office pays to take care of this stuff) must use the Fonts applet in the Windows Control Panel. Choose Start⇨Settings⇨Control Panel to open the Fonts window. Then choose File⇨Install New Font.

Creating text styles

A text style is a description of the properties used in creating text. A text style gives you a running start on getting all the various text settings right and helps maintain consistency of text appearance within and across drawings.

When you use the Multiline Text Editor, you can change anything in the style; however, the change is not then embedded in a style for re-use by yourself or others in other drawings. Also, the single-line text entry command, TEXT, uses only existing styles; the only way to change text options for TEXT is to set up a style with the options set as you want them.

By default, new AutoCAD drawings come with only a single text style: *STANDARD*. To create a new text style or to modify an existing one, follow these steps:

1. **To start the STYLE command, type** STyle **at the command prompt and press Enter (or choose F**o**rmat⇨Text** S**tyle).**

   The Text Style dialog box appears.

2. **To modify an existing style, choose it from the pull-down menu; to create a new style, click the New button, and enter the style's name.**

3. **Select the font name from the pull-down menu.**

   The Preview box shows what the font looks like and is updated as you specify other text style options. Click Preview to make sure that the pre-view is up-to-date.

   AutoCAD 2000 can use two different kinds of fonts: native AutoCAD SHX (compiled SHape) fonts and Windows TTF (TrueType) fonts. SHX fonts usually provide better performance, because they're optimized for AutoCAD's use. TTF fonts give you more and fancier font options, but they slow down AutoCAD when you zoom, pan, and select and snap to objects. To have SHX fonts available, you must choose the Install Fonts option when you install AutoCAD. If you do not have the SHX fonts avail-able, you can rerun the AutoCAD installation process and install them.

4. **Select the font style from the pull-down menu.**

   For TrueType fonts that have multiple styles, such as bold, italic, and so on, choose the style that you want from the pull-down menu.

5. **Enter the text height in the text entry box and then press Enter.**

   If you enter 0, the style definition does not determine the height of text; instead, AutoCAD prompts you for a text height each time you use this style. If you enter a value for the text height, that value is used each time you use the style.

   You may want to create several versions of each style — one style for each of the fixed heights you expect to need, and one with no fixed height for flexibility.

6. **Specify whether to use a Big Font.**

   To use a Big Font with an SHX font, just check the Use Big Font check box. This option is grayed out if you choose a non-SHX font.

   Big Fonts are used for fonts that require additional storage space for each character. Big Fonts are used for Asian-language character sets, specialized drafting symbols, and other characters. Before AutoCAD included decent support for fractions, some people used special Big Fonts in order to display fractions.

7. **Specify effects: Upside down, Backward, Vertical, Width Factor, Oblique Angle.**

   Check the check boxes and enter values as needed.

For the Oblique Angle option, the angle range you can enter is from −80 degrees (tilted backward, almost horizontal) to 80 degrees (tilted forward, like normal italics, but also almost horizontal). An angle between 15 and 30 degrees looks like normal italics. The Oblique Angle option is primarily for SHX fonts; with many TTF fonts, you can choose Italic from the Font Style drop-down list instead.

8. **Click Apply when you're finished.**

    The new style is created.

It's easy to spend a great deal of time experimenting with text style options; set a time limit for yourself or choose a time when you're not under deadline pressure.

Checking It Out

Although the spell checker may seem like a small deal, given that most drawings contain relatively few words, even one misspelling in a drawing for a $10 million proposal can be a major problem. So the spell checker, first seen in Release 13, is a welcome addition to AutoCAD. Use it!

Because most computer users are, by now, pretty familiar with the general concept of a spell checker and because the one in AutoCAD is relatively simple, the following steps should be enough to get you started on checking your spelling in AutoCAD:

1. **Start the spell checker by using one of the following methods:**

    • Type **SPell** at the command prompt and press Enter.

    • Choose Tools⇨Spelling from the menu bar.

2. **Select the objects you want to check by clicking them in the drawing area.**

    Entering ALL in the command line selects all text objects. Press Enter to initiate the check.

    If AutoCAD finds no misspellings, it displays an alert box and the command terminates. If the program finds a misspelling, the Check Spelling dialog box appears with the misspelled or unrecognized word. See Figure 10-5 for an example.

3. **Use the following options to tell AutoCAD how to handle a misspelling:**

    • **Suggestions:** AutoCAD puts its #1 suggestion here. Click another suggestion in the list to use that suggestion instead, or type the correct spelling yourself.

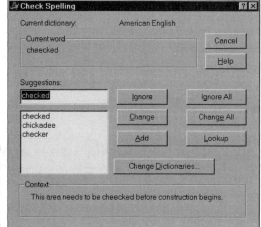

Figure 10-5:
Cheecking
your
spelling.

• **Ignore/Ignore All:** Ignores the current word and continues check-ing, or ignores the current word and any future instances of it as well.

• **Change/Change All:** Changes the current word to the highlighted word and continues checking, or changes the current word and all other instances of it as well.

• **Add:** Adds the misspelled word to the custom dictionary.

• **Lookup:** Checks the spelling of the new word entered in the text-entry area under Suggestions.

• **Change Dictionaries:** Changes to a different dictionary (for exam-ple, a dictionary for a different language).

• **Context:** Displays the words among which AutoCAD found the mis-spelled word.

AutoCAD continues with spell checking until it has checked all the selected text objects. If it finds no more misspellings, the dialog box dis-appears and the "all clear" alert appears.

When you use the Add button to dadd a new word, AutoCAD appends the word to the end of your *custom dictionary* file — \Program Files\ACAD2000\ Support\Sample.cus by default. You can view the current custom dictionary's filename or change to different custom dictionary file by clicking the Change Dictionaries button. If you do go to the trouble of adding your industry's and office's special lingo to your custom dictionary, you can share this file with othes in the office. It's an ordinary ASCII text file, so you can edit it with a text editor such as Windows NotPad.

Chapter 11

Entering New Dimensions

• •

• •

*F*irst, let us assure you that you have not actually entered the Twilight Zone in this chapter (although sometimes when you work with dimensions in AutoCAD, it may *seem* as though you have). *Dimensions* are labels that you put on an object to show the object's length, width, diameter, angles, and other important numbers. AutoCAD dimensions automatically update themselves as you change the dimensioning points associated with the dimensioned object. If you have a dimension that shows the length of a gun barrel, for example, and you drag the barrel to lengthen it, AutoCAD automatically updates the dimension that shows the barrel length. Sounds easy, right? Often, it is.

At other times, dimensioning is one of the most complicated features of AutoCAD. Marking dimensions with pencil and paper is so flexible that drafters have developed an enormous number of ways to show dimensions. And with the cramped nature of most drawings, both traditional and CAD drafters want many ways to force dimensions into small spaces in the drawing. Myriad ways exist to depict dimensions, therefore, and AutoCAD offers dozens of dimensioning variables to support as many dimension styles as possible.

Dimensioning hasn't changed much in AutoCAD 2000, but the dialog for creating and controlling dimension styles received a major facelift and is now easier to use. Also, a new QDIM (quick dimension) command — promoted from the AutoCAD R14 Bonus Tools to full citizenship in AutoCAD 2000 — speeds some dimensioning tasks.

AutoCAD groups dimension variable settings into dialog boxes, reorganized in AutoCAD 2000. AutoCAD 2000 also includes a dimensions preview that makes it easier to see the effect of your changes before applying them, and a quick dimensioning command for drawing a series of dimensions at one time. Dialog boxes remind you what your options are and show you how related variables may affect each other. Dimension styles enable you to group options together and apply them as a group, and dimension substyles make handling minor variations within a style easier than the task would otherwise be.

But even with all these changes, complexity abounds. Dimensioning in AutoCAD is just so powerful — and flexible, in order to serve lots of different industries — that getting to know it all takes time. To avoid being overwhelming (and very lengthy), this chapter covers only the basics of dimensioning. The chapter is very useful to the novice who wants to get a feel for dimensioning, as well as to the more advanced user who wants a quick look at the dimension preview and quick dimensioning features introduced in AutoCAD 2000. For more information on the advanced features of dimensioning, however, you need to go to the AutoCAD documentation — and be ready to do a great deal of experimenting as well.

Among the important concerns in dimensioning is getting the size of all the dimension elements right. Set the Scale for Dimension Features in the Fit tab of the Modify Dimension Style dialog box to the drawing scale factor, which is explained in Chapter 4 and Appendix A. See the section on the Fit tab later in this chapter for more information.

Discovering New Dimensions of Sight, Sound, and CAD

(Okay, so maybe we *have* entered the Twilight Zone. Rod Serling, where are you?) Although you may have drawn or at least have seen dimensions in your past work, you may not realize that a dimension actually consists of many parts. Figure 11-1 displays the following important parts of a dimension:

- **Dimension text:** Dimension text is the set of numbers that indicate the actual dimension. In AutoCAD, you can specify a prefix to appear before the dimension text, a suffix to appear after it, and the tolerance to use in indicating the precision of the measurement.

- **Dimension line and arrowhead:** The dimension line goes from the dimension text outward, to indicate the extent of the dimensioned length. The arrowhead shows where the dimension line terminates. You can also use another kind of line ending, such as a tick mark, to indicate the end of the line. (AutoCAD calls the line ending an *arrowhead* even when, as in the case of a tick mark, it doesn't look like an arrow.)

✔ **Extension line:** The extension line extends outward from the object being measured beyond the dimension text and dimension line.

You can see these same basic elements — the dimension text, dimension line, arrowhead, and extension line — in the preview within the Modify Dimension Style dialog box, described later in this chapter.

Imagine that you have to specify to a very young child — who is, of course, excellent at drafting — every aspect of every part of a dimension and how it fits into a drawing; only then can you start to realize the potential complexity of dimensioning in AutoCAD. To get the most out of the limited attention span that most people have for dimensions — to stop everyone's inner child from getting upset at us — this section explains dimensions in general via the Dimension Style Manager dialog box, and then describes specific types of dimensions only to the extent that they differ from linear dimensions.

Setting up dimensions

To create even a simple dimension, you must do some setup work and then make an informed choice from many different options. This section includes what you need to know to start using dimensions.

The fastest way to access dimensioning commands is from the Dimension toolbar. The only trouble is that you want to put this toolbar away much of the time because it takes up so much screen space. So train yourself to bring the toolbar up and put it away quickly; for extra productivity, memorize the command line commands for the dimensioning that you use most.

The following steps show you how to make the Dimension toolbar appear and disappear on-screen:

1. **Right click any AutoCAD toolbar icon and choose Dimension from the cursor menu to turn on the Dimension toolbar, as shown in Figure 11-2.**

   The Dimension toolbar appears on-screen.

2. **Use the mouse to click and drag the Dimension toolbar to where you want it on-screen.**

   You can dock the toolbar on any side of the screen or leave it floating.

3. **After you finish using the Dimension toolbar, close it by right-clicking any toolbar and choosing the Dimension toolbar to deselect it from the displayed toolbars; or click the Close box in the upper right of the toolbar (if the toolbar's docked against an edge, drag it out into the open first, so the Close box will appear).**

   The Dimension toolbar vanishes from your screen — poof! (Almost as though it disappeared into . . . another dimension!)

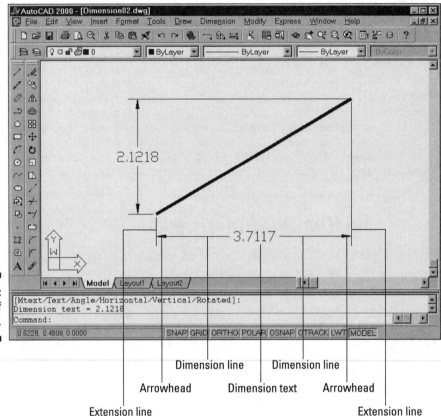

Figure 11-1:
The parts of
a dimension.

Dimension line   Dimension line

Arrowhead   Dimension text   Arrowhead

Extension line   Extension line

What all these crazy dimensions mean

Take a few seconds to start the Dimension toolbar when you need it and hide it when you don't; the productivity improvement over using the menu is likely to be worthwhile.

Several different types of dimensions are available from the Dimension tool-bar. Not all the options are equally important to everyone, but knowing in general what these options are certainly helps you get to the actual work of creating a dimension sooner rather than later. (The Dimension menu is similar to the Dimension toolbar; only some of the last few items on the menu are different.) The following options are represented by the icons, from left to right or top to bottom, on the Dimension Toolbar:

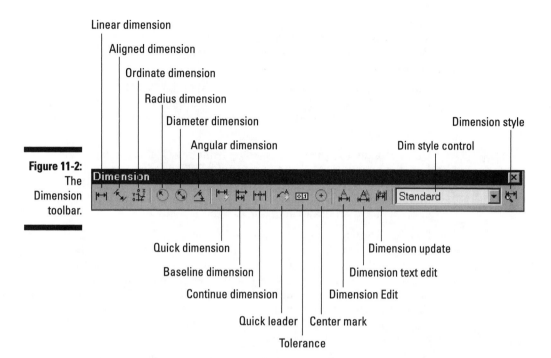

Figure 11-2:
The
Dimension
toolbar.

Linear dimension

Aligned dimension

Ordinate dimension

Radius dimension

Diameter dimension

Angular dimension

Dim style control

Dimension style

Quick dimension

Baseline dimension

Continue dimension

Quick leader

Tolerance

Center mark

Dimension Edit

Dimension text edit

Dimension update

✔ **Linear Dimension** (also accessed by using the DIMLINEAR command, keyboard shortcut DLI): A *linear dimension* is a horizontal or vertical dimension with extension lines going vertically (for a horizontal linear dimension) or horizontally (for a vertical linear dimension) to the origins of the extension lines, which define the endpoint of the dimension. You also can draw linear dimensions that are rotated a specific angle, but those are less common than horizontal or vertical dimensions.

✔ **Aligned Dimension** (also accessed by using the DIMALIGNED command, keyboard shortcut DAL): An *aligned dimension* is a linear dimension tilted to the same angle as a line drawn through the endpoints of its extension lines.

✔ **Ordinate Dimension** (also accessed by using the DIMORDINATE command, keyboard shortcut DOR): An *ordinate dimension* is a leader (defined later in this section), followed by the X or Y coordinate of the point.

✔ **Radius Dimension** (also accessed by using the DIMRADIUS command, keyboard shortcut DRA): A *radius dimension* is a dimension from the center of an arc or circle, with one end of the dimension line at the center and an arrowhead at the curve.

- ✔ **Diameter Dimension** (also accessed by using the DIMDIAMETER command, keyboard shortcut DDI): A *diameter dimension* is a dimension through the center of an arc or circle, with each end of the dimension line at an opposite point on the curve.

- ✔ **Angular Dimension** (also accessed by using the DIMANGULAR command, keyboard shortcut DAN): An *angular dimension* is a dimension drawn inside an angle; the dimension line curves along an arc inside the measured angle.

- ✔ **Quick Dimension** (also accessed by using the QDIM command, keyboard shortcut QDIM): The new AutoCAD 2000 quick dimensioning capability is at the top of the Dimension menu and in the middle of the Dimension toolbar. QDIM allows you to quickly generate a set of dimensions rather than draw them one at a time.

- ✔ **Baseline Dimension** (also accessed by using the DIMBASELINE command, keyboard shortcut DBA): A *baseline dimension* is actually a series of related dimensions drawn from a single baseline. Each dimension is incremented from the previous one by a value that you enter. Baseline dimensions can be angular, linear, or ordinate, depending on the type of the previous dimension. If the previous dimension isn't one of these three types, AutoCAD prompts you for a dimension of one of the types to use as the baseline dimension.

- ✔ **Continue** (also accessed by using the DIMCONTINUE command, keyboard shortcut DCO): This option *continues* a dimension from the previous dimension's second extension line.

- ✔ **Leader** (also accessed by using the LEADER command; the keyboard shortcut LE runs a quicker version called QLEADER): A *leader* is a pointer that connects an annotation to a drawing feature. (So if you're asked by a spacey-looking stranger to "take me to your leader," just turn on AutoCAD. . . .)

- ✔ **Tolerance** (also accessed by using the TOLERANCE command, keyboard shortcut TOL): A *tolerance* is a specifically formatted description of the maximum allowable variation in a measurement. The TOLERANCE command enables you to specify the symbol and other aspects of the tolerance.

- ✔ **Center Mark** (also accessed by using the DIMCENTER command, keyboard shortcut DCE): The *center mark* indicates the central point of a circle or arc. You can control whether the center mark displays only a little plus sign, or the plus sign plus longer lines that run through the circle or arc. You can combine a center mark with a radial or diameter dimension if you really want to pin that sucker down.

- ✔ **Dimension Edit** (also accessed by using the DIMEDIT command, keyboard shortcut DED): This icon lets you edit dimension characteristics, one or several dimensions at a time.

✔ **Dimension Text Edit** (also accessed by using the DIMTEDIT command): This icon gives you direct access to text location and rotation angle.

✔ **Dimension Update** (also accessed by using the -DIMSTYLE Apply command): Runs the equivalent of the old DIM Update subcommand, which applies the current dimension style, plus any style overrides that are currently in effect, to the dimension or dimensions you select.

✔ **Dim Style Control** (also accessed by using the -DIMSTYLE Restore command, but you have to type rather than select the style name): Allows you to make a different dimension style current by selecting its name from a drop-down list.

✔ **Dimension Style** (also accessed by using the DIMSTYLE or old Release 14 DDIM command, keyboard shortcut D): This icon enables you to specify the *dimension style,* a set of dimension options that are grouped together and given a name, and modify the style's characteristics by using the Dimension Style Manager dialog box.

The three-letter keyboard shortcuts for most dimensioning commands start with D, skip the I and the M, and use the next two letters of the command name. For example, the keyboard shortcuts for DIMLINEAR, DIMALIGNED, and DIMRADIUS are DLI, DAL, and DRA, respectively.

AutoCAD does not require you to specify objects to dimension; it draws a dimension between any points you specify. Usually, however, the points for which you want to indicate a dimension are part of an object. To keep things general, though, the points that you attach the dimension to are referred to as the *origins* of the dimension's extension lines, and they can be any points that you want to create a dimension between.

Creating dimensions

Although many types of dimensions exist, most dimensioning concerns the three most common types you encounter: *linear dimensions, radial dimensions,* and *angular dimensions*. This section describes how to create linear dimensions, the most common type. Look for more about the detailed options for different kinds of dimensions in the section "Doing Dimensions with Style(s)," later in this chapter.

The following steps show you how to create linear dimensions that indicate the horizontal and vertical projected distance of a line, as shown in Figure 11-1, earlier in this chapter:

1. **Use the LINE command to draw a non-orthogonal line — that is, a line segment that's not horizontal or vertical.**

   An angle of about 30 degrees works well for this exercise.

If you want to apply dimensioning to an object rather than a line, use these steps as a general guideline, filling in the appropriate commands and data as applicable to your drawing.

2. **Start the DIMLINEAR command by using one of the following methods:**

    • Type **DimLInear** at the command prompt and press Enter.

    • Choose Dimension⇨Linear.

    • Click the Linear Dimension button (the leftmost or topmost button) on the Dimension toolbar.

3. **To specify the origin of the first extension line, snap to the lower-left endpoint of the line by using endpoint object snap.**

    If you don't have endpoint as one of your current running object snaps, specify a single endpoint object snap by holding down the Shift key, right-clicking, and choosing Endpoint from the cursor menu. See Chapter 7 for more about object snaps.

4. **To specify the origin of the second extension line, snap to the other endpoint of the line by using endpoint object snap again.**

    AutoCAD draws a *horizontal* dimension — the length of the displace-ment in the left-to-right direction — if you move the cursor above or below the line. It draws a *vertical* dimension — the length of the dis-placement in the up-and-down direction — if you move the cursor to the left or right of the line. If you move the cursor near the line, the type of dimension displayed is determined by where the cursor was the last time it was outside of an imaginary rectangle that just encloses the line.

5. **Move the mouse to generate the type of dimension you want, horizon-tal or vertical, and then click wherever you want to place it, or type a location for the dimension on the command line and press Enter.**

6. **Repeat Steps 2 through 5 to create another linear dimension of the opposite orientation (vertical or horizontal).**

Now that you have the hang of ordinary linear dimensions, you should be able to master other common dimension types quickly. Draw some lines, arcs, and circles, and try the DIMALIGNED, DIMANGULAR, DIMRADIUS, and DIMDIAMETER commands. You can choose these commands from the Dimension toolbar or type them at the command line.

After you're comfortable picking dimension points, you can graduate to let-ting AutoCAD find the points for you. When you start the DIMLINEAR or DIMALIGNED command, the default option if you press Enter is <select object>. If you do press Enter and select a line, polyline segment, circle, or arc, AutoCAD automatically selects the endpoints of the object (or the diame-ter points, if the object is a circle). Then all you have to do is pick where you want the dimension line to sit (Step 5 in the previous example.) This tech-nique reduces the amount of picking you have to do and objects snaps you have to use.

Quick dimensions

The QDIM, or Quick DIMension, command started life in AutoCAD Release 14 as a Bonus Tool extra. In AutoCAD 2000, it has been promoted to first position on the Dimension pull-down menu. QDIM is designed to draw a whole series of dimensions in one fell swoop. It makes for a spectacular AutoCAD demo ("look how AutoCAD just drew 57 dimensions with a single command!"), but whether you find it useful will depend on the kinds of objects you dimension.

When you run QDIM, you select a bunch of objects that you want to dimension, specify the type of dimensions you want at the command line — Continuous, Staggered, Baseline, Ordinate, Radius, or Diameter — and then hope that QDIM makes the right choices about what to dimension. QDIM works well for certain kinds of dimensioning tasks on certain kinds of objects, as long as you select objects carefully. There are additional options for adding and removing dimension points. On other kinds of objects, QDIM probably isn't worth the trouble. In any case, you should master the ordinary dimensioning commands, which provide maximum flexibility, before you rely too heavily on QDIM. For more information, look up QDIM in the AutoCAD on-line help system.

Doing Dimensions with Style (s)

Using the Dimension Style Manager dialog box is the best way to begin to understand dimensions thoroughly. The Dimension Style Manager dialog box enables you to change just about any dimension variable and almost automatically groups the variables into a style you can use later. It also displays a continuously updated preview showing how the choices you make will affect the look of the actual dimensions for your drawing.

The Dimension Style Manager dialog box and its subdialog boxes are significantly modified and rearranged from earlier releases of AutoCAD. To get to know it, take the time to read this section carefully and experiment.

Figure 11-3 shows the Dimension Style Manager dialog box, which is really the doorway to a number of related dialog boxes. The following sections explain the parts of this initial dialog box; descriptions of other, related dialog boxes follow. Type **Dimstyle** at the command line and press Enter to open the Dimension Style Manager dialog box.

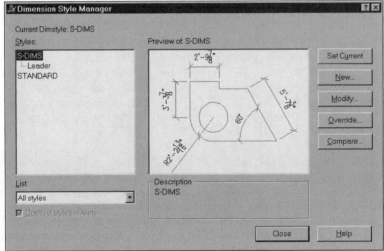

Figure 11-3:
The
Dimension
Style
Manager
dialog box.

The New and Modify buttons

Use the New button in the Dimension Style Manager to create a new style, then the Modify button to modify either the Standard style or the new style you create. We suggest that you leave the Standard style as is and create your own dimension style(s) for the settings that you'll actually use. This approach ensures that you can use the default Standard style as a reference. More important, it avoids the naming conflict that can change the way your dimensions look if the current drawing gets inserted into another drawing.

When you click New, you can specify the style name, its parent style, and what kind of dimensions to use the new style settings for — for All dimensions, for Linear, Angular, Radius, Diameter, or Ordinate dimensions, or for Leaders and Tolerances. Make the choice that fits what you're trying to accomplish.

In AutoCAD 2000, dimensions have "real" parents — if you change the dimension options for a given style, all the styles based on it change as well. This can either give you a great feeling of control or a terrible, sinking feeling as a change in one style propagates in an unintended way through all the dimensions that are substyles of that "parent" dimension. There is a certain art to creating one or more overall styles that apply to all dimensions, plus specific dimension styles based on the overall styles for linear dimensions, angular dimensions, and so on. There is an even greater art to modifying the style family in an effective and predictable way. You will probably need some practice with dimension styles before you become entirely comfortable with, and competent at, the process.

If you use several dimensioning standards within a drawing, consider creating a naming standard to indicate which dimension styles are related and unrelated to others so that you and others can quickly predict the effect of changes. Also consider writing a brief description of each style, its heritage, and its purpose. (Of course, watch out that one of your dimension styles doesn't slap you for questioning its heritage!)

After you've created one or more dimension styles, click the Modify button to bring up the Modify Dimension Style dialog box, which is where you actually change dimensioning parameters.

One or more system variables control each aspect of dimensions. In general, memorizing which of the dozens of dimensioning-related system variables control which aspect isn't worth your valuable time; just use the Dimension Style Manager dialog box to control each parameter. If you simply can't live without knowing more about the dimension variable names and how they relate to the choices in the dialog box, look in the Command Reference (under the Contents tab in the AutoCAD 2000 Help dialog). There you'll find a Dimension Variables Quick Reference.

Following Lines and Arrows

Figure 11-4 shows the Lines and Arrows tab of the Modify Dimension Style dialog box. The Lines and Arrows tab enables you to specify several options that relate to the look of the parts of the dimension other than text.

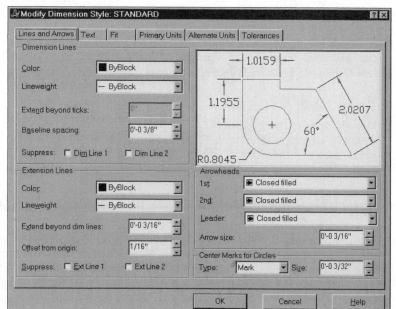

Figure 11-4:
The Lines and Arrows tab of Dimension Style.

Dimension Lines

Color and Lineweight, usually set to ByBlock but sometimes specified directly, allow you to control the look of dimension lines. Extend beyond ticks specifies the length that the dimension line gets extended outside of the extension lines; it is available only for certain kinds of arrowheads, such as tick marks. You can also set the Baseline spacing between consecutive baseline dimension and Suppress Dim Line 1, or Dim Line 2, or both. (Dim Line 1 and Dim Line 2 refer to the pieces of the dimension line to the left and to the right of the text, respectively — assuming that you picked the left dimension point first and the right dimension point second.)

Extension Lines

The Extension Lines area enables you to set the Color and Lineweight of extension lines. You can also specify the length extension lines should Extend beyond the dimension line and the distance they are Offset from the origin (that is, from the dimension points that you pick). You can Suppress either Ext Line 1, Ext Line 2, or both. (Ext Line 1 and Ext Line 2 refer to the left and the right extension lines, respectively — assuming that you picked the left dimension point first and the right dimension point second.)

You might want to suppress one of the extension lines if, for example, one of the dimension arrows points to a center line with a dash-dot pattern, and you don't want the dimension's continuous extension line to obliterate the gaps in the center line's dash-dot pattern.

Arrowheads

You can specify the look of 1st and 2nd arrowheads, of a Leader, and the arrowhead Size in this area.

Being able to specifically set the arrowhead for a leader as opposed to other types of arrowheads is a new feature in AutoCAD 2000. It can eliminate the need to create a separate leader substyle.

Center Marks for Circles

You can specify the Type of the Center Mark used in a radial dimension — as a small cross inside the circle (Mark), a small cross plus cross hairs (Line), or no mark at all (None) — as well as the center mark's Size.

Tabbing to Text

Figure 11-5 shows the Text tab of the Modify Dimension Style dialog box. This tab allows you to control the appearance and placement of the dimension text that's automatically generated by AutoCAD as part of the dimension.

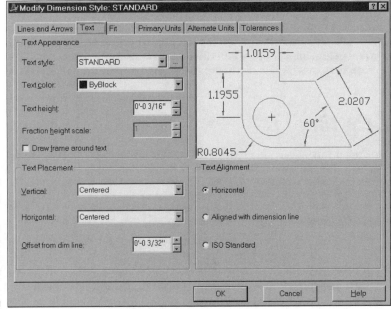

Figure 11-5:
AutoCAD
generates
the number;
you control
its
appearance.

As with other dimension options, to better understand what the choices mean, you should try different choices on the Text tab and then watch the Preview area change.

Text Appearance

You can specify in this area a Text style, Text color, and plotted Text height (which takes effect only if the style's text height is 0). The Fraction height scale specifies the height of fractions relative to the text; for instance, a value of 1.25 will make the fraction 25 percent taller than other text. Check the Draw frame around text check box to put your dimension text in a box.

Text Placement

These choices help position the text relative to the rest of the dimension. The Vertical choices are Centered in the middle of the dimension line, Above the dimension line, Outside the dimension line, or in the position specified by a Japanese Industrial Standards (JIS) representation. Horizontal options are centered horizontally, aligned next to the 1st Extension Line (think left-justified), positioned next to the 2nd Extension Line (think right-justified), or rotated to align with an extension line and positioned Over 1st Extension Line or Over 2nd Extension Line. The Offset from dimension line is the amount of space AutoCAD will generate between the dimension text and the dimension line that surrounds it.

Text Alignment

Use the radio buttons here to specify whether dimension text is aligned horizontally, in line with the dimension line, or to ISO standard: aligned with the dimension line except when the dimensioned area is too small for the dimension text, in which case the text is aligned horizontally.

Getting Fit

The Fit tab, shown in Figure 11-6, allows you to tell AutoCAD what to do in exceptional cases — when the text doesn't fit inside the dimension lines.

Fit Options

If there isn't room to fit both dimension text and the dimension lines and arrowheads between the extension lines, what is AutoCAD to do? Should it put the text out, the arrows out, or both? Use the radio buttons to let AutoCAD choose to move arrows out first, text out first, move them both out together, or always keep text between the extension lines. Use the check box to suppress arrows if they don't fit, which neatly solves that part of the problem.

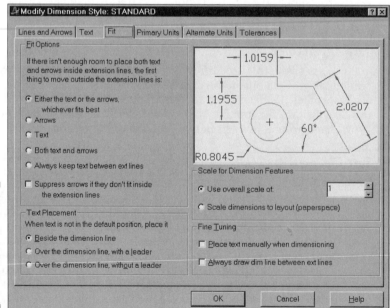

Figure 11-6: AutoCAD generates the number; you control its appearance.

This is an important option that takes practice to get right. Experiment with different Fit options to see how each affects the way dimensions work.

Text Placement

Okay, so the dimension text has been kicked out of its nice, cozy spot between the extension lines; now it's up to you to tell it where to go and what to do when it gets there. Use the radio buttons to choose the following options for text placement: Beside the dimension line, Over the dimension line with a leader, or Over the dimension line without a leader.

Scale for Dimension Features

Use the radio buttons to select the option Use overall scale of a number that you specify, which makes all the dimension features such as text and lines larger or smaller together; or Scale dimensions to layout (paperspace), which allows AutoCAD to figure out an appropriate scaling factor based on the scaling between model space and paper space. (See Chapter 9 for more on layouts.) Usually, you'll want to specify a Use overall scale of a number that's equal to your drawing scale factor.

Fine-tuning

You thought all of the above was fine-tuning already! Now you have super-fine tuning options. Use the first check box to specify the option Place text manually when dimensioning, rather than let AutoCAD place the text automatically. Use the second check box to select Always draw the dimension line between the extension lines, even if the arrowheads are placed outside.

After you've drawn a dimension, you can always adjust the text position (and many other aspects of the dimension) by grip editing it.

Using Primary Units

The Primary Units tab, shown in Figure 11-7, and the Alternate Units tab, described shortly, are very similar. Primary units choices are important for everyone doing dimensions; alternate units options matter only if you want to display a second set of dimensions on the same drawing that give the same measurements in different units. Adding alternate units is inescapably necessary sometimes, but with luck it is avoidable for most of the people, most of the time.

Linear Dimensions

There are a lot of choices here, but they're likely to be pretty familiar to you from choosing similar choices in setting up your AutoCAD drawing, as described in Chapter 4. Choose the Unit Format — Scientific, Decimal, Engineering, Architectural, Fractional, or Windows Desktop — and the Precision of display.

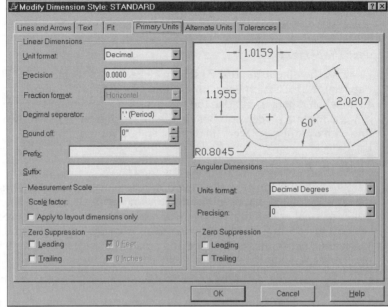

Figure 11-7:
Win the
primary,
then worry
about the
alternate.

If fractions are used in the unit format you've chosen, specify a Fraction format of Horizontal, Diagonal, or Not Stacked alignment. If decimals are used instead, specify a Decimal separator of a period, comma, or space.

Choose a Round off value to specify what to round your values to, and a Prefix and/or Suffix for dimension text and tolerances, if any.

For the Measurement Scale, set a Scale factor if you want to change the actual dimension text values by a set amount. You can check the check box to have the scaling factor Apply to layout dimensions only.

Finally, you can specify Zero Suppression. (No, this isn't Orwell's *1984*, just a cleanup matter.) You can suppress leading, trailing zeroes, or both; doing this can really clean up the appearance of your dimensions if you're using high precision of dimension display. If your units include feet and inches, you can suppress zeros in the display of feet or in the display of inches.

Different industries have different standards for which zeroes to suppress and when. If you're not sure how it's done in your industry, ask others in your office or profession. (If you're not sure how it's done in your industry, then maybe you should be working in a different industry, but who are we to say?)

Angular Dimensions

Angular dimensions are not affected by the choices in Linear Dimensions. The choices that exist work the same way, though; choose your Units format, the Precision of display, and Zero Suppression for Leading or Trailing zeros.

Choosing alternate units

The choices for alternate units, as shown in Figure 11-8, are very similar to those for Primary Units, described in the preceding section. Here we describe only those choices unique to alternate units.

Display alternate units

This check box turns the display of alternate units on or off.

If you need alternate units, your drawing is likely to be quite crowded with the extra set of dimensions. Revisit all your dimensioning choices, and even consider putting less geometry in each plotted sheet or using a larger plot scale so that the information content and visual appearance of each sheet are not overwhelming.

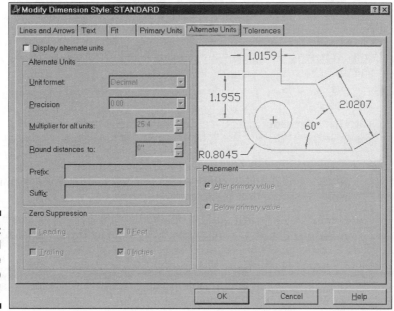

Figure 11-8:
If you need alternate units, do them right!

Alternate units and Zero Suppression

The choices for Unit format, Precision, Round distances to, Prefix, and Suffix are described under the Primary Units tab description, above. Consider using a suffix for both primary and alternate units to indicate which units are which. The Multiplier for alternate units is the conversion factor between the primary and alternate units. The Zero Suppression check boxes — Leading, Trailing, 0 Feet, and 0 Inches — work the same way here as they do for Primary Units, described previously.

Placement

Placement options are After primary value and Below primary value. Try both to see how they look in the preview area to help you decide which to use in your drawing.

Checking your tolerances

AutoCAD can calculate and display tolerances for you, potentially saving you a great deal of time and effort. You may have even avoided using tolerances before because they were hard to draft; now you can do them relatively easily. Study the options on the Tolerances tab, shown in Figure 11-9, so that you can use the options to their best advantage.

As with alternate units, displaying tolerances will make your drawing more crowded. If you use tolerances, revisit your other dimensioning and layout choices to make sure that your drawing is not too crowded to be easily usable.

Tolerance format

The Method pull-down lets you choose what the tolerances look like overall. You have five choices:

- ✔ **None.** No tolerance in this drawing! Alternatively, you can take the time to set up tolerances using one of the other methods and then use the None choice to turn them off temporarily.

- ✔ **Symmetrical.** This is what most people think of for tolerances — the measured dimension and then a +/- symbol followed by the amount of tolerance in either the positive or negative direction.

- ✔ **Deviation.** Gives the measured dimension and then separately lists the plus value on top and the minus value below so that you can specify different upper and lower bounds.

- ✔ **Limits.** Does not display the measured dimension, just the upper bound over the lower bound.

- ✔ **Basic.** This is just a box around the measured dimension, not really a tolerance in the usual sense.

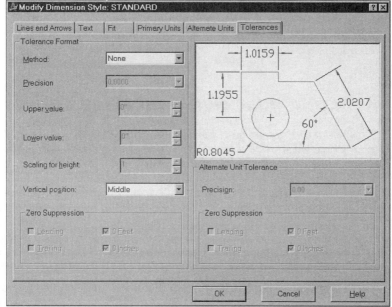

In mechanical drafting, a box around a dimension indicates that it's a *nominal* or *reference* dimension — one that's referenced in another tolerance note.

The Precision tells how many digits (or how small a fractional unit) to display. Upper value is the only value used for Symmetrical tolerances; the Lower value is used for the Deviation and Limits methods but ignored for Symmetrical tolerances.

Scaling for Height affects the look of the tolerance text. This affects the height of each tolerance value, *not* the total height of stacked tolerance values. So if you use a height scale of .75, for instance, your stacked tolerance heights (for the Deviation or Limits methods) will be 1.5 times as high as the dimension text.

Zero Suppression is the same as for Primary Units, described previously; you can suppress Leading zeros, Trailing zeros, 0 Feet, or 0 Inches.

Alternate unit tolerance

For alternate unit tolerance, you specify the Precision of display and Zero Suppression of Leading zeros, Trailing zeros, 0 Feet, or 0 Inches.

If you're using alternate units *and* tolerances for primary units, alternate units, or both, your drawing will get pretty crowded. Carefully consider your dimensioning choices and your drawing layout to make sure the drawing is comprehensible.

Creating your own dimension styles

Now that we've given you the scenic tour of the Dimension Style Manager dialog box, we show you how to create your own dimension style(s) so that you can experiment with various settings:

1. **Choose Format⇨Dimension Style from the menu bar or enter** Dimstyle **at the command line.**

   The Dimension Style Manager dialog box appears.

2. **In the Styles list, choose the existing dimension style whose settings you want to use as the starting point for the settings of your new style.**

   For example, choose the default dimension style named Standard.

   Although you can use and modify the default Standard style, we suggest that you leave the Standard style as is and create your own dimension style(s) for the settings that you'll actually use.

3. **Choose the New button to create a new dimension style that's a copy of the existing style.**

   The Create New Dimension Style dialog box appears.

4. **Enter a New Style Name and click Continue.**

   The New Dimension Style dialog box appears.

5. **Modify dimension settings on any of the six tabs of the New Dimension Style dialog box.**

   See the descriptions of these settings earlier in this chapter.

6. **Click OK to close the New Dimension Style dialog box.**

   The Dimension Style Manager dialog box reappears.

7. **Choose your new dimension style from the Styles list and then click the Set Current button.**

   Your new dimension style becomes the current dimension style that AutoCAD uses for future dimensions.

8. **Click the Close button.**

   The Dimension Style Manager dialog box closes.

9. **Draw some dimensions to test your new dimension style.**

You should spend some time setting up at least one dimension style with settings that work for the dimensioning conventions in your industry and office. After you have the settings the way you want them, copy the dimension style to your template drawings so that it's available in all new drawings. See Chapter 4 for information about template drawings and Chapter 14 for instructions on copying dimension styles using AutoCAD DesignCenter.

When you set up a new drawing, make sure that you change the "Use overall scale of" setting on the Fit tab so that it matches the drawing scale factor. See Chapter 4 for detailed instructions.

Following Pointy-Headed Leaders

We close out the dimensioning chapter with something short and sweet: a look at leaders. At this point, you might be scratching your head and wondering what leaders have to do with dimensioning. We did the same thing when we started learning AutoCAD — as our growing bald spots demonstrate — but now we're used to it. Although leaders aren't exactly dimensions, they share a few characteristics with dimensions, including arrowheads and text that's associated with lines. In addition, leaders in AutoCAD include a number of fancy options for attaching special annotations such as blocks and tolerance frames (another AutoCAD dimensioning feature). When Autodesk first developed AutoCAD, it decided to treat leaders as part of the AutoCAD dimensioning subsystem, and that's the way it's been ever since.

The most important consequence of leaders being part of dimensioning in AutoCAD is that their appearance is controlled by dimension variables. Several of the dimension settings on the first three tabs of the Modify Dimension Style dialog box — Lines and Arrows, Text, and Fit — affect how leaders get drawn. See the Doing Dimensions with Style(s) section earlier in this chapter for more information about the settings in this dialog box.

Drawing a basic leader in AutoCAD is straightforward. What can complicate things is the large number of options for drawing leaders differently. The following steps show you how to create leaders and experiment with the options:

1. **Create a new dimension style for leaders.**

   See the preceding section of this chapter for details. Give the new style a descriptive name such as Leader. Check the dimension settings on the Lines and Arrows, Text, and Fit tabs and modify them as necessary. You may need to experiment some in order to discover your preferred settings.

Depending on your leader-drawing and dimensioning conventions, it might be possible to use the same dimension style for both leaders and ordinary dimensions. In that case, you can skip Step 1. In any event, you can skip this step if you already have a suitable dimension style in the current drawing.

2. **Run the DIMSTYLE command to open the Dimension Style Manager dialog box, choose your leader dimension style from the Styles list, click the Set Current button, and then click the Close button.**

Your leader dimension style becomes the current dimension style that AutoCAD uses for future leaders (and dimensions).

3. **Start the QLEADER command by using one of the following methods:**

   • Type **qLEader** at the command prompt and press Enter.

   • Choose Dimension⇨Leader.

   • Click the Quick Leader button (the one with the leader, letter A, and tiny yellow lightning bolt on it) on the Dimension toolbar.

4. **Press Enter to view or change the quick leader settings,**

The Leader Settings dialog box appears, as shown in Figure 11-10. Take a look at each of the three tabs so that you're familiar with what kinds of settings you can change. Use the dialog box help to learn more about any particular setting.

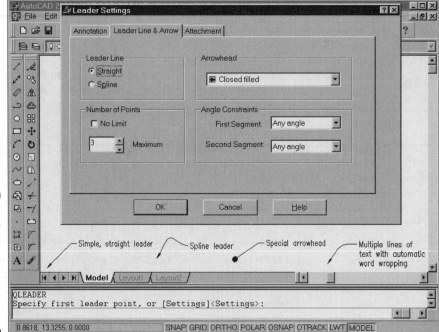

Figure 11-10:
The Leader Settings dialog box, with leaders in the background.

5. **Click OK to exit the Leader Settings dialog box.**

6. **Pick a point where you want to place the arrowhead of the leader.**

7. **Pick additional points to trace out the leader line.**

   You can draw a single leader "shaft" or multiple segments.

8. **Press Enter to finish specifying leader points.**

9. **Specify a width for the text that's connected with the leader.**

   The default width of zero tells AutoCAD not to perform automatic word wrap on the text — in other words, your leader text will be a single line, no matter how long it gets. You can specify a text width on the screen or type a width on the command line if you want AutoCAD to wrap longer leader text automatically.

10. **Enter the text that you want to have associated with this leader and press Enter.**

    If you want more text formatting options, press Enter to open the Multiline Text Editor dialog box before you type any text. (See Chapter 10 for information about using this dialog box.)

11. **Enter additional lines of text, pressing Enter after each line, and then press Enter once more to complete the leader and text.**

    If you opened the Multiline Text Editor dialog box in Step 10, click OK instead.

12. **Repeat Steps 3 through 11 to draw additional leaders.**

Figure 11-10, which appeared previously, shows some of the leader possibilities in AutoCAD.

The dimension style that you set current in Step 2 affects all leaders *and* dimensions that you draw from that point forward. After you finish drawing leaders and before you start drawing dimensions, repeat Step 2, but this time select your preferred dimension style for ordinary dimensions and make it the current style.

After you've drawn a leader with text, if you move the text, AutoCAD also moves the tail end of the leader. Alas, the reverse isn't true — if you move the tail end of the leader, the text doesn't follow. Bad dog!

The QLEADER command is both more efficient and easier to use than the un-quick LEADER command, so you shouldn't need to bother with LEADER.

Chapter 12

Hatch . . . Hatch . . . Hatchoo!

● ●

In This Chapter

▶ Defining a hatch

▶ Creating a simple hatch

▶ Using the Boundary Hatch dialog box

▶ Setting hatch boundaries

▶ Using hatch patterns

▶ Moving up to advanced hatching options

● ●

A *hatch* is a pattern that fills in an area of a drawing that's within a closed boundary. Hatching is often used to convey the type of material represented by an object, such as insulation, metal, and so on. A hatch is similar to a linetype in that it conveys information about part of the drawing. But unlike a linetype, a hatch isn't connected to a single line. Instead, you use a hatch to fill a space, which is surrounded by objects such as lines, polylines, or arcs. (In many fields, delineating particular spaces is important, such as when an architect depicts a grassy open space or an engineer shows a cutout.)

These details help explain why *hatch* is actually a short name for a longer idea. A hatch is a pattern that fills an area that you define either by selecting objects that define a closed boundary or by picking a point inside a closed area and letting AutoCAD try to find a closed boundary that surrounds it. Thus, *hatch* is shorthand for *boundary hatch* — that is, a hatch pattern filling an area within an existing boundary in your drawing. (A hatch *boundary* acts like a fence to keep the hatch pattern from sneaking out and trampling the rest of the drawing.) If you use the second option just described — ask AutoCAD to try to find a closed hatch boundary that surrounds a point you pick — AutoCAD must engage in some guesswork about the exact nature of the boundary. If there are other objects inside the boundary, AutoCAD may also have to guess which areas within the boundary you do and don't want hatched. If AutoCAD guesses wrong, you must tell it what to do.

Even *boundary hatch* is short for a longer term. The default type of boundary hatch is called an *associative boundary hatch*. This kind of hatch was introduced in Release 13. An associative boundary hatch remains associated — clever, huh? — with the objects that make up its boundary. If you modify the objects that make up the boundary, AutoCAD tries to adjust the hatch to fit. Of course, if the changes open up a hole in the boundary, AutoCAD may just have a hard time adjusting the hatch correctly.

If you use only simple hatches, you may not need to worry about modifying the objects defining the boundary of the hatch or whether AutoCAD can make the correct adjustments. You should, however, at least know what to do if you run into a situation that requires modification or adjustment. With this knowledge, you can avoid problems with the hatch and have some idea of how to go about making the hatch right if you do experience problems.

It's tempting to start adding hatches early in your drawings, but they're actually a "prettification" step that you may want to defer until you get the basic geometry of the drawing right. Creating hatches near the end of your project benefits your productivity and redraw and plotting performance during the drafting process, and can even help you avoid the need to rework your drawing.

Not much about hatching has changed in AutoCAD 2000, except for a redesign of the Boundary Hatch dialog box and the availability of a right-click menu for hatching. If you are an experienced Release 13 or Release 14 user, you need only look at the dialog box figures in this chapter and try using the right-click menu during the hatch process; you'll quickly discover what's new.

If you're experienced with early releases of AutoCAD, you can continue to use the HATCH command, which prompts you on the command line rather than from a dialog box. Figure 12-1 shows a simple hatch created with the HATCH command so that you can see what the options are. The BHATCH command, which opens the Boundary Hatch dialog box, is much easier to use for most purposes, but HATCH does include a *direct hatch* option, whereby you can draw a hatch boundary on the fly.

Using the Boundary Hatch Dialog Box

If you want a flexible hatch that's defined by its boundaries — that is, a hatch that updates if you update its boundaries — use the Boundary Hatch dialog box (see Figure 12-2), which you access by any of the following methods:

- Choose Draw➪Hatch from the menus.
- Click the Hatch button (the one with a little red hatch pattern) on the Draw toolbar.
- Type **BHatch** at the command prompt and press Enter.

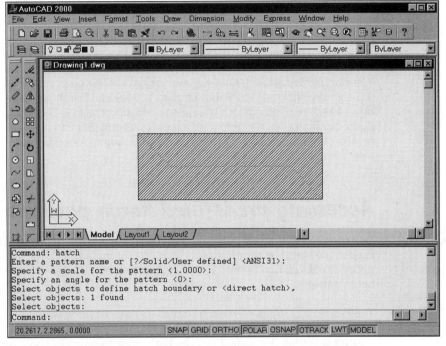

Figure 12-1:
A simple hatch created with the HATCH command.

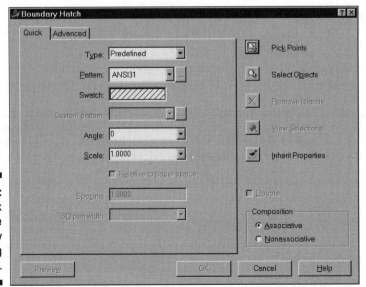

Figure 12-2:
The Quick tab of the Boundary Hatch dialog box.

Either H or BH will work as a shortcut for the BHATCH command, but you might as well learn the shorter one. Use H as the keyboard shortcut for the BHATCH command.

The Boundary Hatch dialog box enables you to do two main tasks: specify the hatch pattern to use, and define the boundary of the hatch area. Just about every option in the dialog box relates to one of these two tasks.

You can use predefined, user-defined, or custom hatch patterns. Most of the time, you're likely to find yourself using predefined hatch patterns, but the other hatch pattern options are nice to have. The next three sections describe the basics of specifying a hatch pattern. You can find out how to create a boundary hatch in the section "Creating a boundary hatch," later in this chapter.

Accessing predefined hatch patterns

To use *predefined* hatch patterns that exist in all copies of AutoCAD, select Predefined from the drop-down list box at the top of the Quick tab of the Boundary Hatch dialog box. This selection sets the stage for choosing the hatch pattern.

You can scan through the hatch patterns in one of three ways:

- ✔ By selecting the name from the Pattern drop-down list box; this action changes the hatch pattern shown in the Swatch area.

- ✔ By clicking the Pattern button (the tiny button with the ellipsis [three dots] to the right of the Pattern prompt and pattern name); this button brings up the Hatch Pattern Palette with pattern previews.

- ✔ By clicking the Swatch that's displayed; this action also brings up the Hatch Pattern palette.

AutoCAD has about 70 predefined hatch patterns from which to choose, which is quite a long list. The list includes ANSI (American National Standards Institute) and ISO (International Standards Organization) standard hatch patterns. Figure 12-3 shows the ANSI hatch patterns to give you an idea of the kinds of hatch patterns available.

A good idea is to print a small cheat sheet of hatch patterns that you commonly use (whether predefined, user-defined, or custom) and then share them with others in your organization. You may also want a larger cheat sheet of all the standard AutoCAD hatch patterns, which is available in AutoCAD's online help (search for "standard libraries, hatch patterns"). These cheat sheets can save time and help you choose the right hatch pattern for all your drawings instead of settling for one of the first hatch patterns you stumble on while clicking through the hatch patterns list.

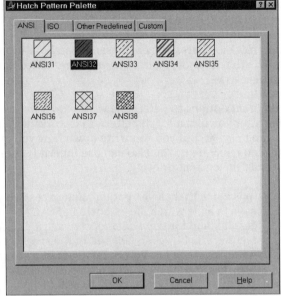

Figure 12-3:
The eight
ANSI hatch
patterns
available in
AutoCAD
2000.

For a cheat sheet of hatch patterns, include the hatch scale and angle that you prefer for each pattern. Suggestions for how to figure out these numbers appear later in this chapter.

Using user-defined and custom hatch patterns

You can use, in addition to the predefined hatch patterns, *user-defined* hatch patterns and *custom* hatch patterns. These two kinds of hatch patterns meet two different needs.

A *user-defined* hatch pattern makes a hatch pattern out of simple parallel lines, drawn in the currently selected linetype. (All hatch patterns use the currently selected linetype, but for user-defined hatch patterns this can be an important element in designing the hatch.) Start by specifying the linetype you want to use, by choosing a linetype or layer from the Object Properties toolbar. Then open the Boundary Hatch dialog box and specify User defined hatch pattern in the Pattern Type area. You can specify the Angle and Spacing of the lines in the Pattern Properties area, and you can turn on Double in order to achieve a crosshatching effect (two perpendicular sets of hatching lines). The top row of squares in Figure 12-4 shows four user-defined hatch patterns with spacing increasing from one to four units and angles increasing from 20 degrees through 80 degrees. All the shapes are squares, aligned at right angles; the apparent tilt in the third and fourth squares is an optical illusion. Use it to confuse any nearby children! (If no kids are handy, a boss will suffice.) The second row of squares shows the same hatch patterns with Double turned on. The third row of squares shows user-defined hatch patterns with a dashed linetype.

Experiment with different options to determine what works well for you. Unfortunately, even after you find a hatch pattern that works well for a particular purpose, you can't save it. But you can write down how you created that pattern so that you can re-create it. You also can use Inherit Properties to copy a hatch pattern in the current drawing.

A *custom* hatch pattern is a one that clever, patient, and excessively nerdy users can define and save in a file with a file extension of PAT. (No, football fans, I'm sorry. PAT doesn't stand for *point after touchdown*; it stands for *pattern*.) This type of hatch pattern, however, falls out of the scope of a book such as *AutoCAD 2000 For Dummies,* but you can find out more about creating custom hatch patterns by looking up "hatch patterns, defining" in the AutoCAD online help.

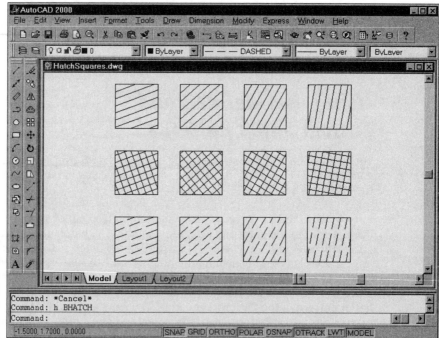

Figure 12-4:
User-
defined
hatch
patterns.

Specifying hatch angle and scale

All predefined and custom hatch patterns require that you enter the Angle and Scale for AutoCAD to use when generating the hatching. You usually won't have any trouble deciding on an appropriate angle, but figuring out a suitable scale can be tricky.

The hatch scale usually should be a multiplier times the drawing scale factor, as described in Chapter 4. For example, the EARTH pattern (in the Other Predefined tab of the Hatch Pattern Palette dialog box) looks pretty good in a full scale (1=1) drawing with a hatch scale of 0.75. If you are adding hatching in the EARTH pattern to a 1"=1'-0" detail (drawing scale factor equals 12), try using a hatch scale of 0.75 x 12, or 9.0. This multiplier and drawing scale factor approach ensures that hatching looks consistent (that is, the spaces between the lines are the same) at all scales when you plot.

So, assuming that you know your drawing's scale factor, the only complication is figuring out what the multiplier should be for a particular hatch pattern. In a more rational world, the multiplier would always be something sensible like 1.0. Unfortunately that's not the case for all hatch pattern definitions. Even worse, there's no way to predict before you use a hatch pattern for the first time what an appropriate multiplier might be. You have to use trial and error the first time, and then make a note of the hatch pattern and multiplier for future use.

The first time you use a hatch pattern definition, try 1.0 as the multiplier — in other words, assume that we live in a rational world and that 1.0 will work. Don't forget to multiply by the drawing scale factor. Preview the hatch and then adjust the hatch scale iteratively, previewing after each change. After you settle upon a suitable scale for the current drawing, you can calculate the corresponding multiplier (for future use) by dividing the hatch scale by the current drawing's scale factor.

User-defined patterns require that you enter an Angle and Spacing, rather than Angle and Scale. Spacing is expressed in drawing units, so if you set up your drawing for architectural units and you want user-defined hatch lines that are three inches apart, specify a spacing of 3.

Defining basic boundaries

After you specify the hatch pattern, angle, and scale you want to use, you define the boundary (or boundaries) into which you want to "pour" that hatch pattern in one of two ways: by picking points within the area(s) you want hatched, or by selecting objects that surround those areas. The actual operation involved in using either of these options is confusing to most people, and you'll probably need a little practice before you get used to it. (Not that you're simply "most people" — after all, you *did* buy our book. . . .)

The idea behind either definition option is simple, if applied to simple areas — that is, closed objects with no additional objects inside them. To hatch such a simple area, you enter the BHATCH command on the command line and then either pick a point on the inside of the object or select the object or objects surrounding the area. AutoCAD then applies the hatch for you within the boundary — and you're done.

This simple hatching gets a little more complicated if you have one closed object inside another. If you pick points inside the *enclosing* (outermost) object but outside the *enclosed* (inner) object, AutoCAD hatches only the area between the boundaries of the two objects. If you pick some points inside each object, AutoCAD hatches the entire area within the outermost surrounding boundary, including the area within the inner boundary.

The results are somewhat reversed if you select objects instead of picking points. If you pick the outermost enclosing object(s) as well as the enclosed one(s), AutoCAD uses both boundaries and hatches only the area between them. Pick only the outermost object to hatch everything within it. In any event, after you finish picking or selecting, press Enter to return to the dialog box.

Fortunately, the AutoCAD hatch preview and a bit of experimentation can clarify all of these confusing permutations.

Creating a boundary hatch

To demonstrate the workings of boundary hatches, the following steps show you how to hatch an object, such as the wheels of a (very) simple drawing of a car, by using the "picking-points" method of selecting the hatch area:

1. **Draw any object for use in creating a boundary hatch (or use an existing object that you want hatched).**

   You can, for example, draw an object such as a car. If you want to hatch an existing object in a drawing, you can do so, too, using these steps as a guideline.

2. **Open the Boundary Hatch dialog box by using one of the following methods:**

   • Type **BHatch** at the command prompt and press Enter.

   • Click the Hatch button on the Draw toolbar.

   • Choose <u>D</u>raw⇨<u>H</u>atch from the menu bar.

   The Boundary Hatch dialog box appears.

3. **Choose any predefined hatch by clicking a swatch to bring up the Hatch Pattern Palette dialog box and then selecting a hatch from the dialog box.**

You can scan through the 68 available predefined hatch patterns, plus any custom ones you've created, by clicking each tab — ANSI, ISO, Other Predefined, or Custom in the dialog box.

The Solid hatch pattern is the first option among the Other Predefined hatch patterns. Like any other object, a solid hatch takes on the current color — or the current layer's color if you leave color set to ByLayer.

4. **Click the Pick Points button.**

The Boundary Hatch dialog box (temporarily) disappears and your drawing reappears.

5. **Select a point inside the object you want to hatch by clicking it with the mouse.**

On a simple drawing of a car, for example, you might select a point inside the left tire — that is, between the outermost and innermost circles and below the side of the car.

AutoCAD analyzes the drawing and decides what boundaries to use. In a complex drawing, this analysis can take a few seconds.

To preview the effect of the hatch, right-click; then choose Preview from the right-click menu.

6. **Press Enter (or right-click and select Enter from the right-click menu) to indicate that you have no more points you want to select.**

The Boundary Hatch dialog box reappears.

If you forgot to preview the hatch in Step 5, choose the Preview button now. After previewing, you can return to the Boundary Hatch dialog, adjust any of the settings, and preview again.

7. **Click the OK button.**

AutoCAD hatches the part of the object you selected. (If you're using the tire example, it hatches only the part of the tire below the car; the hubcap area and the part of the tire behind the car body are not hatched.) If you want to hatch another object in the drawing with the same hatch pattern (such as the other tire in the car example), you can continue on with Step 8. If you have only one object to hatch, you're finished.

8. **Press Enter to open the Boundary Hatch dialog box again if you want to hatch another object by using the same hatch pattern, and repeat Steps 3 through 7.**

In the car wheels example, you repeat these steps for the second tire. Figure 12-5 shows how this drawing appears midway through the hatching process for the second tire.

Inheriting properties

A neat option that can change the entire way you hatch objects is the Inherit Properties button on the Boundary Hatch dialog box. Despite its position in the Boundary Hatch dialog box (underneath the buttons used to establish the hatching boundary), this feature works only with the Pattern Type and Pattern Properties areas and doesn't affect how boundaries are handled.

Inherit Properties simply updates the pattern characteristics in the dialog box to make them the same as a hatch pattern you pick from the screen, so you can clone an existing hatch pattern simply by clicking Inherit Properties and then choosing the existing hatch pattern from the screen. You can use the copied hatch pattern specifications as is or modify them by making changes in the Boundary Hatch dialog box.

Exploring Advanced Hatching Options

AutoCAD has a number of advanced options for hatching, most of which you can ignore. This section covers two options that occasionally are worthwhile, however: defining boundary sets and styling. Figure 12-6 shows the Advanced Options tab of the Boundary Hatch dialog box. The Advanced Options tab contains the Define Boundary Set and Style areas that the following two sections describe.

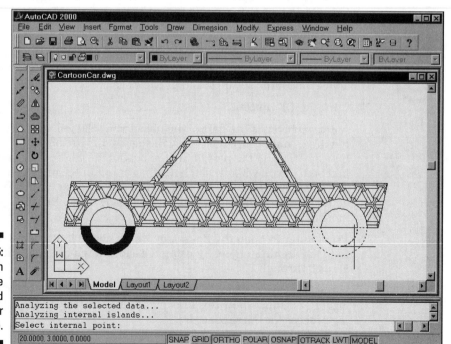

Figure 12-5: A car with one tire hatched and the other about to be.

Boundary sets

If an area is bounded by several different objects and is part of a complex drawing, for AutoCAD to determine the boundaries of the area to hatch can be "computationally expensive" — that is, it can take a *long* time! A complicated drawing area containing many objects also increases the odds that AutoCAD won't guess right when it's looking for boundaries. A *boundary set* limits the area that AutoCAD considers when it determines where to hatch, thus saving you time. If you choose the New button on the Advanced tab, you temporarily return to your drawing, where you select objects using any of the methods described in Chapter 7. AutoCAD then considers only the objects you selected as it decides what to hatch.

To return to using the entire screen, choose Current Viewport from the pull-down menu in the dialog box. All objects in the current viewport (which is the entire visible drawing area if you're in model space and have just one viewport) are again available for boundary selection.

You often can get the same effect as a boundary set simply by zooming in tighter onto the area you're hatching. The edges of the current view serve as an ad hoc boundary.

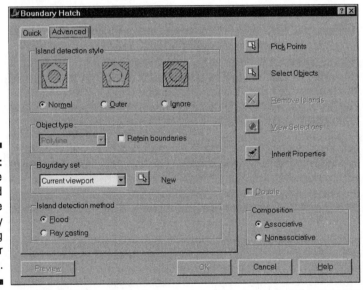

Figure 12-6:
The
Advanced
tab of the
Boundary
Hatch dialog
box for
hatching.

Styling

If you have several objects enclosing each other, knowing exactly which objects you hatch and which ones you don't can be very important. AutoCAD offers three style options in the Island detection style area of the Advanced tab to help you determine the hatch option: Normal, Outer, and Ignore. Each is described briefly in the following list.

- ✔ **Normal:** This option may seem strange to users with no AutoCAD experience. The Normal option hatches the outermost ring between boundaries, skips the next ring in, hatches the next one, and so on, until alternating enclosed areas are hatched. This style is the default.

- ✔ **Outer:** This easy-to-understand option simply hatches the outermost enclosed area of an object and ignores all other enclosed objects.

- ✔ **Ignore:** This option is also easy to understand. It ignores the boundaries of enclosed objects and hatches everything within the outermost boundary of the object.

After you design your hatch and pick points or select objects to hatch, click the OK button to close the Boundary Hatch dialog box and reveal your newly hatched drawing.

Part IV
Having It Your Way

The 5th Wave — By Rich Tennant

©RICHTENNANT

"Is this what they mean when they say AutoCAD uses the third dimension?"

In this part . . .

After you get the lines and text right, you might be justified in thinking that your work in AutoCAD is done. But AutoCAD enables you to do so much more! Blocks and external references help you manage data within drawings, between drawings, and even across a network. AutoCAD 2000 adds the AutoCAD DesignCenter, a new capability for getting the most out of existing drawings for use in your new drawings. 3D commands enable you to do a whole new kind of work in AutoCAD without buying any add-on packages or a different program. Together, these options extend the capabilities of AutoCAD beyond anything possible without a computer — and even beyond those of just about any other drawing/drafting program in existence.

Chapter 13

Playing Blocks and Rasteroids

• •

In This Chapter

▶ Introducing blocks and external references

▶ Creating blocks

▶ Inserting blocks

▶ Exploding blocks

▶ Creating external references

▶ Removing external references

▶ Attaching raster images

▶ Managing raster images

• •

A thing of beauty is a joy forever, as the old saying goes. But if you work and work on a drawing until it's a thing of beauty, you must be able to reuse it to make it a joy forever. Reusability is also a huge advantage of CAD over paper drafting. That's where the AutoCAD blocks and external references come in.

A *block* is a collection of objects grouped together to form a single object. A block can live within a specific drawing, or you can export a block so that multiple drawings can share access to it. At any time, you can *explode* the block — that is, divide it back into the objects that make it up — and edit the objects.

An *external reference* is like an industrial-strength block. An external reference is a pointer to a separate drawing outside the drawing you're working on. The referenced drawing then appears on-screen and in printouts as part of the original drawing, but continues to "live" as a separate document on your hard disk. This arrangement lets you include a whole separate drawing without increasing the size of the drawing you're working on. But you can't explode the external reference; you can only change its appearance by editing the externally referenced drawing. If you do actually edit the externally referenced drawing, the appearance of the drawing changes in all the other drawings that reference it, too.

When should you use a block versus an external reference? Start with blocks; using blocks is what you do most often for individual work. Blocks save storage space within a drawing and make work more convenient. Writing out a block to a separate file by using the WBLOCK command is an intermediate step and makes the block more easily accessible to multiple drawings while preserving the capability to explode the block. An external reference is for truly serious data sharing, especially in a networked environment with multiple users sharing data files. Your own preferences and work style, however, as well as the standards in your organization, ultimately determine how you use blocks and external references.

Raster image importing is a crucial AutoCAD feature added in Release 14. Each *raster,* or bit-mapped, image is referenced as a separate object, similar to an external reference. Raster images matter a great deal to some AutoCAD users and little to others. (Even those who use raster images only a little will like being able to include a scanned-in image of their company logo in their drawings.) Read about raster features here to help you decide how much you need them.

This chapter describes how to use blocks, external references, and raster image importing. (What a coincidence, considering that's what we were just talking about! Wonder of wonders. . . .) Try these features out and then use each as often as makes sense for your work.

Blocks and external references demand extra thought and care compared to other geometry that you create in AutoCAD. They can save you a lot of work, help standardize and improve your drawings, and make the work of large groups of people better and more consistent. They can also cause a lot of problems if, for example, a widely used external reference file is changed in a way that doesn't work well for all the drawings that it's used in. Think about how to get the most mileage out of blocks and external references within your working environment as you create and use them. For instance, take advantage of the opportunity to attach detailed descriptions to blocks, as described in this chapter.

Rocking with Blocks

First, a little more block theory and then you can rock right into those blocks.

In order to use a block in a drawing, you need two things: a block *definition* and one or more block *inserts*. AutoCAD doesn't always make the distinction between these two things very clear, but you need to understand the difference to avoid terminal confusion about blocks. (Maybe we should call this syndrome *blockheadedness*?)

A block definition lives in an invisible area of your drawing file called the *block table*. Think of it as a table of graphical recipes for making different kinds of blocks. Thus each block definition is like a recipe for making one kind of block. When you insert a block, as we describe later in this chapter, AutoCAD creates a special object called a *block insert*. The insert simply "points to" the recipe and tells AutoCAD, "Hey, draw me according to the instructions in this recipe!"

Thus, although a block looks at first like a collection of objects stored together and given a name, it's really a graphical recipe (the block definition), together with one or more pointers to that recipe (one or more block inserts). Each time you insert a particular block, you create another pointer to the same recipe.

The advantages of blocks include:

- ✔ **Grouping objects together when they belong together logically.** For instance, you can draw a screw using lines, polylines, and arcs, and then make a block definition out of all these objects. When you insert the screw block, AutoCAD treats it as a single object for purposes of copying, moving, and so on.

- ✔ **Efficiency of storage when you re-use the same block repeatedly.** For instance, if you insert the same screw block 15 times in a drawing, AutoCAD stores the detailed block definition only once. The 15 block inserts that point to the block definition are very compact, so they take up less disk space than 15 copies of all the lines, polylines, and arcs would.

- ✔ **The ability to edit all instances of a symbol in a drawing simply by modifying a single block definition.** For instance, if you decide that your design requires a different kind of screw, you simply redefine the screw's block definition. With this new recipe, AutoCAD then replaces all 15 screws automatically (don't you wish you could've done that in your last home improvement project?)

Blocks are great for convenience and storage savings within a drawing. Blocks *aren't* great for drawing elements used in multiple drawings, however, especially in a multiuser environment. That's because blocks, after they get into multiple drawings, stay in each drawing; a later modification to a block definition in one drawing does not automatically modify all the other drawings that use that block. So if you use a block with your company's name in a number of drawings and then you decide to use fancier lettering on the name, you must make the change within each drawing that uses the block.

External references, however, do enable you to modify multiple drawings from the original referenced drawing. You can find out more about external references in the section "Going External," later in this chapter.

Though not quite as flexible as external references, blocks are important and convenient; they save file space and organize your drawing better. They are also an important step on the way to using external references. So take the time to explore blocks and then use them as much as possible.

If all you need to do is make some objects into a group so that you can more easily select them for copying, moving, and so on, use the GROUP command. Enter **Group** at the command line to open the Object Grouping dialog box. Enter a Group Name (or turn on Unnamed if you don't care about being able to refer to the group by name later) and choose the New button to create a new group of objects. Use CTRL+A to toggle "group-ness" on or off. If you've toggled "group-ness" on, picking any object in a group selects all objects in the group. If you've toggled it off, picking an object selects only that object, even if it happens to be a member of a group.

Creating block definitions

To create a block definition from objects in the current drawing, you use the BLOCK command. Alternatively, you can create a block definition by inserting another AutoCAD DWG file into your current drawing (see the next section for details). The following steps show you how:

1. **Start the BLOCK command by using one of the following methods:**

    • Type **Block** at the command prompt and press Enter.

    • Choose Draw⇨Block⇨Make from the menu bar.

    • Choose the Make Block button (the yellow circle and square) from the Draw toolbar.

    The Block Definition dialog box appears (see Figure 13-1).

Whenever you create objects that you'll later include in a block definition, pay attention to what AutoCAD layers those objects are on. In AutoCAD, layer 0 functions as a special construction layer for blocks. If you create geometry on layer 0 and include it in a block definition, when you insert the block, the geometry takes on the layer characteristics, such as color and linetype, of the layer on which the block is inserted. If you create a block from geometry drawn on any other layer, it always retains the color and linetype in effect when it was created. Think of block definition geometry created on layer 0 as a chameleon. (If you don't know what a chameleon is, ask a zoology teacher, or search for the word on the Internet.)

2. **Type the block definition's name in the text entry box.**

    You must name the block definition before you create it, so have a good name thought up in advance. (Hmmm — how about *Godzilla*? Oh, been used before? . . . .)

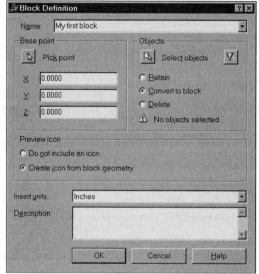

Figure 13-1:
The Block
Definition
dialog box.

If you use the name of an existing block definition, AutoCAD replaces that block definition with the new group of objects you select. AutoCAD first warns you and then updates all instances of the block in the current drawing to match the changed block definition.

The AutoCAD capability to replace instantly all occurrences of a block with the new block that you create with the same name is a good reason to be careful with blocks. Pay attention when AutoCAD displays the prompt "Overwrite block definition?." Think twice before answering yes.

To see a list of the names of all the current blocks in your drawing, drop down the Name list.

3. **Specify the base point, also known as the insertion point, of the block, using either of the following methods:**

   • Enter the coordinates of the insertion point at the *X, Y,* and *Z* prompts.

   • Click the Pick point button and then select a point on the screen.

   The *base point* is the point on the block by which you insert it later, as we describe in the next section.

   Try to use a consistent point on the group of objects for the base point, such as the upper-left corner, so that you always know what to expect when you insert the block.

   Some people mark the base point with a tiny cross or circle.

4. **Click the Select Objects button and then select the objects that you want as part of the block.**

AutoCAD will use the selected objects to create a block definition. Figure 13-2 shows the base point and group of selected objects during the process of creating a new block definition.

Click the Quick Select button to assist in making complex, rule-based selections. See Chapter 7 for details.

5. **Click a radio button to tell AutoCAD what to do with the objects used to define the block: Retain them in place, Convert them into a block instance, or Delete them.**

6. **Click a radio button to choose either Do not include an icon or Create icon from block geometry.**

Go ahead and create the icon; it will help you and others find the right block to use later.

7. **Specify the Insert units to which the block will be scaled.**

When the block is dragged from one drawing into another via the AutoCAD DesignCenter, the units you specify here will specify its units.

8. **Enter the block Description.**

Now's the time to think like a database manager and enter a useful description that will identify the block to yourself and others.

9. **Click OK to complete the block definition process.**

If you don't choose the Convert to block or the Retain radio button, your objects disappear! AutoCAD has stored the block definition in the current drawing's block table, however, and the block is ready to use. If you choose the Convert to block radio button (the default), AutoCAD creates a block insert pointing to the new block definition — the objects look the same on the screen, but now they're part of a block insert rather than existing as separate objects. If you choose the Retain radio button, the objects remain in place but aren't converted into a block insert — they stay individual objects with no connection to the new block definition.

The Make Block command is great for use within a drawing, but what if you want to use the block definition in multiple drawings?

The easiest method is to use the new AutoCAD DesignCenter to copy a block definition from one drawing to another (see Chapter 14 for details). Another method involves the WBLOCK and INSERT commands. You first use the oddly-named WBLOCK command to create a separate DWG file out of the objects that you want to include in the block definition. You then open the target drawing (the one to which you want to transfer the block definition) and use the INSERT command to create a block definition and block insert from the new DWG file in one fell swoop. (We cover the INSERT command in the next section.) This procedure is less intuitive than using AutoCAD DesignCenter, but it allows the block definition to live as an independent DWG file, available for use in multiple drawings. You don't have to haul around a huge drawing file just in order to pick puny little blocks out of it.

Base point

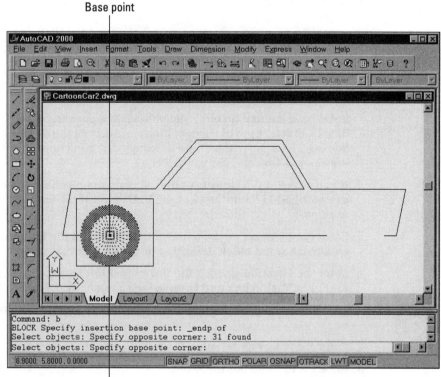

Figure 13-2:
Creating a
wheely cool
block
definition.

Selected objects

There is nothing inherently "blocky" about the results of the WBLOCK (Write BLOCK) command — WBLOCK creates an ordinary DWG file, just as though you had created a new drawing, drawn some objects, and saved the new drawing. Maybe the command should be called "WDWG" (Write DWG file) — but then nobody could figure out how to pronounce it. In any case, there are two reasons why the WBLOCK name isn't completely crazy:

✔ The WBLOCK command gives you the option of creating a separate DWG file by selecting objects in the current drawing, or by specifying the name of a block definition in the current drawing.

✔ The WBLOCK command is often used with the INSERT command in order to transfer block definitions from one drawing to another.

The following steps show you how to use the WBLOCK command to create a new DWG file from an existing block definition or from objects in the current drawing:

1. **Optional: Create a block definition as described in the previous set of steps.**

2. **Type** Wblock **at the command prompt and press Enter to start the WBLOCK command.**

   The Write Block dialog box appears.

3. **Choose the source of the block definition.**

   If you have an existing block definition in the current drawing, choose Block and select the block definition's name from the drop-down list. You can also specify the Entire drawing (that is, all objects in the current drawing) or Objects that you select.

4. **If you selected the Objects option, specify the block's characteristics as described in Steps 3 to 5 of the BLOCK example in the previous set of steps.**

5. **Enter the filename — the name of the new DWG file that AutoCAD will create out of the block definition or the objects that you selected.**

6. **Enter the Location or click the Browse button to bring up the Browse for Folder dialog box and browse your system for a folder.**

   You can browse your way right on out to an intranet or the Internet if you want.

7. **Enter the Insert units, using the pull-down menu if needed.**

8. **Click OK to write out the block.**

In summary, the BLOCK command creates a block definition from objects in the current drawing. The WBLOCK command creates a new DWG file from objects in the current drawing, or from a block definition in the current drawing.

If you know in advance that you want to use a block definition in the current drawing and also write it out to a separate DWG file, you can use two possible sequences:

✔ Use BLOCK to create the block definition from objects in the current drawing and then WBLOCK to write the block definition to a separate DWG file.

✔ Use WBLOCK to create the block definition from objects in the current drawing.

Both sequences work equally well.

Be careful when inserting one drawing into another. If the parent drawing (the drawing into which you're inserting) and the child drawing (the drawing being inserted) have different definitions for the same layers, then the objects in the child drawing will take on the layer characteristics of the parent drawing. For example, if you insert a drawing with lines on a layer called Walls that's blue and dashed into a drawing with a layer called Walls that's red and continuous, the inserted lines on the wall layer will turn red and continuous after they're inserted. The same rules apply to all *named objects*, including linetypes and text and dimension styles. (See Chapter 14 for more information about named objects).

You may want to develop a "block library" containing symbols that you use frequently. You can create a separate DWG file for each symbol (using WBLOCK, or simply by drawing each one in a new drawing). Alternatively, you can store a bunch of symbols as block definitions in one drawing and use AutoCAD DesignCenter to import block definitions from this drawing when you need them. In either case, it's a good idea to keep your common symbol drawings in one or more specific folders that you set aside just for that purpose.

Inserting blocks

AutoCAD provides a number of ways to insert a block, but the most common and most flexible is the INSERT command, which displays the Insert dialog box. Here's how it works:

1. **Open the Insert dialog box by using one of the following methods:**

   • Type **Insert** at the command prompt and press Enter.

   • Choose Insert⇨Block from the menu bar.

   • Choose the Insert Block button from the Draw toolbar.

   The Insert dialog box appears, as shown in Figure 13-3.

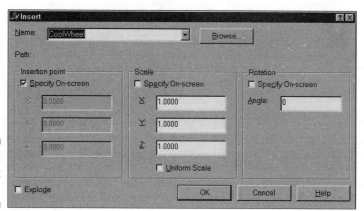

Figure 13-3:
The Insert
dialog box.

2. **Enter the block definition name or external filename by using one of the following methods:**

   - Enter the name of the block defined in your current drawing in the Block text box.

   - Use the pull-down menu to select from a list of block definitions in the current drawing.

   - Click the Browse button to select an external DWG file and have AutoCAD create a block definition from it.

   If you click the Browse button, you can modify the name in the Name text entry box so that the name of the block in your drawing is different from the external DWG file's name. You might want to do this to make the block name more descriptive of the way the block is used in your drawing.

   If you use the Browse button and enter the name of a block that's already in your drawing, AutoCAD warns you and then updates the block definition in your drawing with the current contents of the file.

3. **Enter the insertion point, scale, and rotation angle of the block.**

   You can either click the Specify On-Screen check box in each area, to specify the parameters on-screen at the command prompt, or type the values you want in the Insertion Point, Scale, and Rotation text boxes.

   Check the Uniform Scale check box to constrain the X, Y, and Z scaling parameters to the same value.

4. **(Optional) Click the Explode check box if you want AutoCAD to create individual objects rather than a block insert that points to the block definition.**

5. **Click OK.**

6. **If you checked Specify On-Screen for the insertion point, scale, or rotation angle, answer the prompts on the command line to specify these parameters.**

Another way to insert a block is to drag a DWG file's name from Windows Explorer and drop it anywhere in the current drawing window. AutoCAD then provides a prompt that lets you choose an insertion point and optionally change the default scale factor and rotation angle.

Similarly, you can drag a block definition's name from the Blocks section of AutoCAD DesignCenter and drop it into the current drawing window. Type **ADCenter** on the command line or click the AutoCAD DesignCenter button (the one fourth from the right on the Standard toolbar that looks like a six-button calculator.) If you left-click and drag, AutoCAD puts the block where you drop it. If you right-click and drag, an Insert Block cursor menu choice allows you to specify the insertion point and other insertion parameters. See Chapter 14 for more information about AutoCAD DesignCenter.

After you've inserted a block, all the objects displayed in the block insert behave like a single object. When you pick on any object in the block insert, AutoCAD highlights all the objects in it.

The GRIPBLOCK system variable controls the number of grips shown on each block insert. Normally, you should set GRIPBLOCK to 0, indicating that one grip appears on the block, at its insertion point (a setting of 0 = 1 grip; got that?). If you set GRIPBLOCK to 1, grips appear on every object in the block insert (a setting of 1 = 2 or more grips; got that?). Drawing all those grips on each block insert can slow down performance slightly. But if you use grips to snap to objects and you want to snap to different points on block geometry, set GRIPBLOCK to 1 when needed.

Exploding a block

This feature is easy but important. Simply type the **eXplode** command at the command prompt and press Enter, choose Modify⇨Explode from the menu bar, or choose Explode (the firecracker button) from the Edit toolbar. Then select the block insert.

AutoCAD breaks down, or explodes, the block into its component objects. In fact, what AutoCAD really does is replace the block insert with all the objects — lines, polylines, arcs, and so on — specified in the block definition. You can then edit the objects and, if you wish, use them to make more block definitions.

Going External

In AutoCAD, an *xref*, or external reference, is not someone who used to be an official in a sporting contest. (Ex-ref — get it?) An xref is a reference to another, *external* file — one outside the current drawing — that you can make act as though it's part of your drawing. Technically, a reference is simply a pointer from one file to another. The xref is the actual pointer, but the combination of the pointer and the external file is often called the xref. Drawings that you include in other drawings by means of an external reference are "xref-ed in."

The big advantage of xrefs over blocks is that if you change an original file, AutoCAD automatically copies the change into your drawing when you reload the xref — that is, force an update — or when you save or reopen the drawing. This feature is both good and bad news.

If you improve the hatching on the screw drawing that you've xrefed in so that it looks more realistic — voilà, your drawing also looks better. But if you lengthen that same screw ¼ inch and then find that the change helps in one of your drawings but hurts in another, you have problems. And you might not mind fixing those problems for your own set of drawings; but when multiple people departments are sharing drawings within an organization or project team, minor nightmares can result.

To avoid any other problems, AutoCAD creates new layers in your current drawing that correspond to the layers that are xrefed in. The new layers have names in the form drawing name│layer name; for instance, if you xref in layers from the drawing MYSCREW.DWG that have the names GEOMETRY, TEXT, and so on, the xrefed layers will be named MYSCREW│GEOMETRY, MYSCREW│TEXT, and so on. By creating separate layers corresponding to each layer in the xref-ed file, AutoCAD eliminates the potential problem we warn you about with blocks when layers have the same name but different color or linetype in the two drawings.

AutoCAD also creates new linetypes, text styles, and dimension styles for each of these items in the xref-ed file — for example, MYSCREW│DASHED, MYSCREW│NOTES, and MYSCREW│A-DIMS.

Using the xref

So, you need a certain amount of trust within an organization to use xrefs. If you don't have that feeling of trust — or even if you just don't want the hassle of remembering or tracking how you've used xrefs across an ever-growing set of drawings — don't use xrefs.

The other major advantage of xrefs over blocks is that they aren't stored in your drawing even once. The disk storage space taken up by the original drawing you're xrefing in isn't duplicated, no matter how many people refer to that file. This makes xrefs much more efficient than blocks for larger drawings that are reused several times.

But you can always buy more hard disk space, so the storage issue is not crucial. The key reason xrefs are good is that they enable you to leverage your own or someone else's work easily and transparently, thereby increasing both consistency and productivity.

How you use xrefs, or whether you use them at all, varies greatly, depending on your own tastes and needs and those of the organization you work in, if any. So this book doesn't go into great depth on how best to use and manage xrefs. If you're in an organization that uses them, find out from colleagues how they use xrefs, and imitate them. If you want to initiate greater use of xrefs on your own, use the AutoCAD documentation, other in-depth AutoCAD resources, and your knowledge of how your own department or organization works to develop constructive ways to use them. (No pun intended for all you architects out there.)

Creating an external reference file

To create a file that you can use as an external reference, just create a drawing and save it (or use WBLOCK to create a new DWG from geometry in the current drawing). That's it. You can then start up a new drawing and create an external reference to the previous one. The xrefed drawing opens into your drawing as a visible but untouchable part of your drawing. You can measure or object snap to the xrefed geometry, but you can't modify or delete xrefed geometry until you "own" it. (See the following paragraph for more information.) This arrangement is so simple that it takes a while to figure out all the opportunities that xrefs provide. But don't worry; if you've been setting up your files carefully and following some of the other suggestions in this book, such as using blocks whenever possible, you're at least mostly ready to use xrefs.

In AutoCAD 2000, you can edit blocks and xrefs *in place* — that is, without finding the original, opening it, editing it, saving it, and then re-opening the parent drawing that references it. This feature is good because it improves ease of use, but it can also make it easier for a person working on one drawing to make changes that have negative impacts on other drawings. Use this new capability with care. If you want more information about it, look for "xrefs (external references), editing" in the AutoCAD online help.

Attaching an xref

Attaching an external reference is easy. Just use the following steps:

1. **To start the XREF command, use either of these methods:**

   • Type **XRef** at the command prompt.

   • Choose Insert⇨Xref Manager from the menu bar.

   The Xref Manager dialog box appears (see Figure 13-4).

2. **Click the Attach button.**

   The Select Reference File dialog box appears.

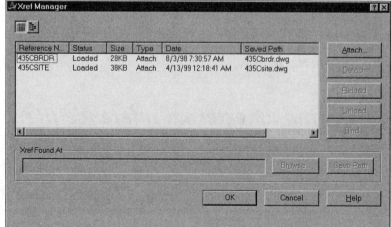

3. Browse to find the file you want to attach, select it, and then click Open.

The External Reference dialog box appears.

If you choose a file that is already being used as an xref in your document, it is re-referenced with the new parameters you specify.

4. Specify the parameters for the xref in the dialog box.

Parameters include the insertion point, scaling factors, and rotation angle. You can set these parameters in the dialog box or specify them on-screen, just as you can do with blocks, as described earlier in this chapter.

You can choose the Attachment or Overlay radio button to tell AutoCAD how to handle the xref. The choice matters only if you create a drawing that uses xrefs, and then your drawing is in turn used as an xref. Attachment is the default choice, and it means that the xrefed file will always be included with your drawing when someone else uses it as an xref. Overlay, the other choice, means that you see the xrefed drawing, but someone who xrefs your drawing won't see the overlaid file. By choosing Overlay, you can xref in a map, for instance, to your drawing of a house, but not have the map show up when someone else xrefs your house drawing. (That person can xref the map him- or herself, if need be.)

5. Click OK.

The externally referenced file appears in your drawing. Layers from that file also appear as layers in your file, with the name of the xrefed drawing included before the layer name.

To drive the process of attaching external references from the command line, type **-XRef** at the command line and follow the prompts.

Managing xrefs and more

The Xref Manager dialog box includes many more options for managing xrefs after you attach them. To bring up the Xref Manager, enter XRef at the command line or choose Insert➪Xref Manager. Important dialog box options include:

- ✔ **List of external references:** You can change between a List and a Tree view of your drawing's external references just by clicking the appropriate button at the top of the dialog box. You can also resize the columns by dragging the column dividers or re-sort the list by clicking the column header names, just as in other Windows dialog boxes.
- ✔ **Detach:** Completely separates the xref from your drawing.
- ✔ **Unload/Reload:** Temporarily separates the xref from your drawing and then renews the attachment. The Reload button causes AutoCAD to update your drawing with the latest version of the xref.
- ✔ **Bind:** Imports the xref into your drawing as a block.

None of these options affects the xrefed drawing itself; it continues to exist as a separate file. If you need to delete it or move it, do so as a separate operation (quickly, before you forget!).

The fact that the xrefed drawing is a separate file is a potential source of problems when you send your drawing to someone else; that someone else needs *all* the files that your drawing depends on, or it will be useless to the receiving party. Make sure to include xrefed files in the "package" with your drawing. Experiment with the Express tool Pack 'n Go to see whether it meets your needs for packaging up your drawing.

You can do quite a bit more with xrefs. You can edit the externally referenced file in place. You can clip an externally referenced file so that only part of it is used in your drawing; use the XCLIP command or choose Modify➪ Clip➪Xref from the menu bar. You also need to watch out for people who may move your xrefed files out from under you or change them without telling you. (This sort of situation can have very embarrassing results if you make a presentation to a client and are surprised by something you see in your own drawings!)

If you work with very large xrefs that take a long time to load, you might be able to improve performance with AutoCAD's xref *demand loading* feature, which uses layer and spatial geometry indexes to load parts of an xref more quickly. Look up "indexing objects in xrefs" in the AutoCAD online help for more information.

You also need to watch out for circular references, in which two or more files refer to one another in an overly intimate, though no doubt enjoyable, fashion. If you really have time on your hands between projects, you can even enable and monitor an Xref Log File and then use it to track your xref history. Look up "xref" in the index of the on-line AutoCAD documentation if you need to know more about xrefs.

Also beyond the scope of this chapter and this book are other xref concerns to think about: standard ways of maintaining xrefed files, specifying who is in charge of changing them, and more. The information in this chapter, however, is enough to get you started and maybe enough to get you finished, too. If you start to use xrefs extensively, find out what standards exist for their use in your organization; if none exist, create some and then publish and distribute them. The people who should have done it in the first place will (with any luck) be appropriately grateful.

Mastering the Raster

AutoCAD Release 14 was the first version of AutoCAD to fully support *bit-mapped,* or *raster,* images. A raster image is an image that's defined by storing each of the points that make it up. For example, a TV screen displays a raster image. If you capture an image of your computer screen, that's a raster image, too.

Most AutoCAD drawings, by contrast, are *vector* images. A vector image is an image that's defined by storing geometrical definitions of a bunch of objects. Typical objects include a line, defined by its two endpoints, and a circle, defined by its center point and radius. Every time the object is displayed or printed, the pixels to create an image of it are recalculated from the image's description. Vector-based images are typically smaller (in terms of the disk space they occupy) and more flexible than raster images, but are also less rich in visual detail and, if sufficiently complex, can be slower to display or print.

Raster images normally come into the computer from some kind of scanner that imports a blueprint, photograph, or other image. Raster images, such as company logos, can also be created in programs such as Photoshop. You may end up outsourcing your scanning work or buying your own scanner — but be warned, a good scanner that can handle large-format images such as blueprints and capture the full-color depth of a photograph well is expensive.

Whether you're doing your scanning yourself or having a service bureau do it for you, you need to know that AutoCAD handles most of the popular image file formats including the Windows BMP format, the popular Web graphics formats GIF and JPEG, the popular PCX and TIFF formats, as well as DIB, FLC, FLI, GP4, MIL, PNG, RLE, RST, and TGA.

If you don't already have a scanner set up in your workplace, then consider outsourcing scanning work or doing it at a copy and computer self-service shop such as Kinko's until you're sure that you need a scanner of your own and have a firm grasp on what features you need. (Yes, you can start by getting a cheap scanner, but that will be a waste of time and money if you then find out you really needed an expensive one.)

An AutoCAD drawing that incorporates a raster image is called a *hybrid* drawing, because it uses both the vector object support built into AutoCAD and the recently added support of raster images in AutoCAD.

Why does AutoCAD, the market-leading vector graphics program, also support raster images? Because a large subset of AutoCAD users need to incorporate raster images in their drawings. Here are three scenarios in which raster images are important:

- ✔ **Small stuff:** With the AutoCAD raster support, you don't have to sweat the small stuff — things like logos, special symbols, and so on that you need to place in your drawing.

- ✔ **Vectorization:** Imagine that you want to convert a raster image into a vector image by tracing lines in the raster image. What simpler way to do so than by importing the raster image into AutoCAD, tracing the needed lines using AutoCAD tools, and then disposing of the raster image? (This procedure works okay for a simple raster image; add-on software is available, from Autodesk and others, to support vectorization of more complex images.)

- ✔ **Design visualization:** Imagine that you want to show how a new building will look in an existing location. What more effective way to do so than by importing a photograph of the location into AutoCAD and then drawing the new building *in situ* (that's "in place," if you skipped Latin), surrounded by its future environment?

Using raster images is much like using external references. The raster image isn't actually stored with your drawing file; instead, a reference to the raster image file is established from within your drawing, like an xref. You can clip the image and control its size, brightness, contrast, fade, and transparency. These controls enable you to fine-tune the appearance of the raster image both on-screen and on a printout or plot.

Don't save drawings that use raster images to Release 12 format; they lose the connection to the external image file, and you have to reestablish the connection when you bring the image back into AutoCAD 2000.

Attaching an image

Follow these steps to bring a raster image into AutoCAD:

1. **Choose Insert⇨ Image Manager from the menu bar or type** IMage **at the command line to start the IMAGE command.**

   The Image Manager dialog box appears (see Figure 13-5).

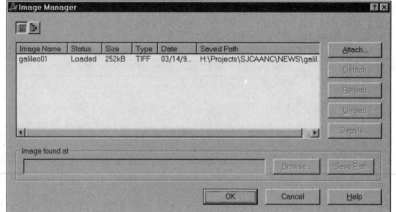

Figure 13-5:
The Image
Manager
dialog box.

2. **Click the Attach button.**

   The Select Image File dialog box appears.

3. **Browse to find the file you want to attach, select it, and then click Open.**

   The Image dialog box appears.

   Get in the habit of clicking the Details button in the Image dialog box to see more information about the resolution and image size of the image you're attaching.

4. **Specify the parameters for the attached image in the dialog box.**

   Parameters include the insertion point, scale factor, and rotation angle. You can set these parameters in the dialog box or specify them on-screen, similar to what you can do with blocks and external references, as described earlier in this chapter. Use the quick dialog box help (click the question mark in the dialog box's title bar and then click the area in the dialog box for which you want help) or click the dialog box's Help button to find out more about specific options.

5. **Click OK.**

The image appears in your drawing. Figure 13-6 shows a drawing with a raster image attached to it, with the Select Image File dialog box in the foreground.

6. **If you need to ensure that the raster image is drawn first, last, or in some other specific order relative to other geometry in your drawing that it overlaps with, set the drawing order; start the command from the menu bar or from the keyboard:**

- From the command line, type **DRaworder** and press Enter; select the raster image and then press Enter to select the default choice, which puts the selected object at the bottom of the drawing order.

  The command ends.

- From the menu bar, start by selecting the raster image and then choose Tools➪Display Order➪Send to Back.

  The raster image is put at the bottom of the drawing order.

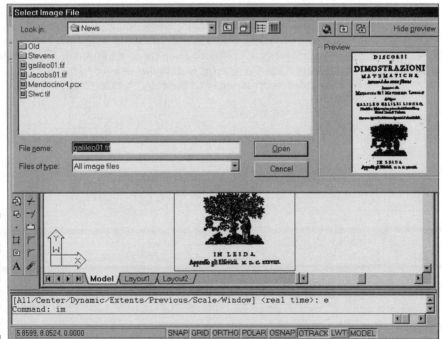

Figure 13-6:
The Select Image File dialog box with an image in the background.

To drive the process of attaching images from the command line, type **–IMage** at the command line and follow the prompts.

Managing images

Images in your drawing can be managed from the Image dialog box, which includes virtually the same options as the External References dialog box. Important dialog box options include a list of image references, the capability to detach (remove) image references, and the capability to unload images to save memory and then to reload them when needed. You can't bind an image to your drawing; it always remains an external file.

As with xrefs, you can clip images so that only part of the image is displayed in your drawing. Use either of the following methods:

  ✔ Choose Modify➪Clip➪Image.
  ✔ Enter **ImageCLip** on the command line.

Follow the prompts to clip the image. You can have multiple overlapping or distinct "pieces" of any number of images in your drawing, and only the parts you need are loaded into memory when you have your drawing open.

The raster image capabilities in AutoCAD were defined by Autodesk in consultation with a consortium of companies that make plotters, scanners, and other imaging products. If you need to do more with raster images, look for hardware and software products, from these and related companies, that can greatly extend what you can do with raster images in AutoCAD. Start your search for more information with the resources in Chapter 17.

Chapter 14

Data-Based Drawing

In This Chapter

▶ Transferring objects and properties with MDE

▶ Viewing and changing properties

▶ Using AutoCAD DesignCenter to "mine" drawings

*W*hen you hear the word *database*, you probably think of rows of alphanumerical information (unless you're a near-sighted baseball player from Brooklyn, in which case you might ask the coach "is dat a base?"). You probably have several such databases on your computer, such as a list of contacts or a record of the hours that you've spent on tasks for various projects.

At first glance, your CAD drawings don't seem to have much to do with databases. Each drawing is just a random collection — well, not totally random, we hope — of lines, circles, and other geometrical stuff, right? Wrong! When you dig deeper, you discover that underneath that mild-mannered line-and-circle exterior, every AutoCAD drawing is in fact a highly organized database of objects and properties.

Unlike the features described in previous chapters, the more advanced features described in this chapter for working with your AutoCAD drawings as databases aren't absolutely necessary for getting your work done. However, you'll work more confidently and quickly and have better control over the objects in your drawing if you do become adept with these features.

This chapter describes how your drawings are organized as databases and demonstrates several ways you can take advantage of the data that they contain. You see how to copy objects and properties between drawings with MDE, the Multiple Design Environment, view and modify the properties of existing objects using the Properties window, and work with blocks, layers, and other kinds of named objects in the AutoCAD DesignCenter. All these features are brand new in AutoCAD 2000.

Don't confuse the treatment of AutoCAD drawings as databases, which we cover in this chapter, with the capability of AutoCAD to link drawing objects to external nongraphical databases, which we don't cover. The latter capability, called dbConnect in AutoCAD 2000, is an advanced feature that we don't address in this book.

Understanding Types of Data

Each AutoCAD drawing file is a database that contains the following types of data:

- ✔ Graphical objects (lines, circles, text, and so on) with properties (defining points, layer, linetype, lineweight, color, and so on)
- ✔ Named objects (layers, text and dimension styles, block definitions, and so on)
- ✔ System variable settings (for example, grid, snap, and limits settings)

The graphical objects are normally what you care about most, but they're dependent on the properties and named objects. The system variable settings control how AutoCAD behaves as you work on a drawing.

AutoCAD 2000 has more than 350 *system variables*, settings that control how AutoCAD works. Most computer applications have internal settings that control their operations; for instance, a word processor can either be in "normal" mode or "page view" mode, and you can change the setting with a menu choice. The difference with AutoCAD is that it not only lets you change these internal settings with a menu choice or a dialog box option but also gives each such setting a name that users can access it by, and change the setting directly from the command line. Together, these user-accessible settings are called system variables.

Look up "system variables, listed" in the AutoCAD online help if you want to see the entire list. Some of the system variable settings are stored in each drawing file, which means that those variables can have different settings in each drawing. Other system variable settings are global and are stored in the Windows registry. If you change one of the global settings, the change applies to all drawings. When you change a system variable setting in an AutoCAD 2000 dialog box, AutoCAD helps you distinguish the kind of setting that you're changing. AutoCAD 2000 displays a little red drawing icon next to drawing-specific settings.

MDE for You and Me

One of the most useful improvements in AutoCAD 2000 is the new Multiple Design Environment, or *MDE*. MDE is the AutoCAD version of what other Windows programs call Multiple Document Interface (MDI). MDI is a fancy way of saying "you can open more than one file at a time within this application." MDE is a fancier — some might even say pretentious! — way of saying the same thing. Before AutoCAD 2000, AutoCAD could open only one drawing at a time. If you wanted to open more than one drawing, you had to launch a new AutoCAD session, which ate up lots of memory and used another slot on the Windows taskbar.

MDE makes possible all kinds of useful things, such as looking at one drawing for reference while you're working on another. (Unfortunately, the screen gets crowded very quickly as you do this; the people who sell big monitors can expect a wave of AutoCAD users at their doorsteps as AutoCAD 2000 becomes popular.) MDE also allows you to copy objects and properties between drawings, as we demonstrate in this section.

If you're unable to open more than one drawing, then MDE somehow got turned off on your system. To turn it back on, open the Options dialog box, choose the System tab, and turn off the "Single-drawing compatibility mode" setting. Autodesk included this setting because some older, third-party applications — and maybe some older CAD users, too — get confused when more than one drawing is open.

The alternative way to turn on MDE is to enter the system variable name SDI at the command line and set it to 0. SDI is short for Single Document Interface — the opposite of MDI. (Shouldn't that be MDE and SDE? Apparently, even Autodesk can't keep its acronyms straight!) An SDI setting of 0 means that Single Document Interface is off, or in other words, Multiple Design Environment is on. An SDI setting of 1 means the opposite.

Scissors, paper, clipboard: transferring objects between drawings

In Chapter 7 we cover how to edit objects, including copying and moving objects within a drawing using the AutoCAD COPY and MOVE commands. What if you want to copy or move objects between two drawings? It's the Windows Clipboard to the rescue! The procedure probably is familiar to you from using other Windows programs, but AutoCAD has a few interesting and unique twists. You can use the familiar toolbar buttons found in most Windows programs — the scissors, twin pieces of paper, and Clipboard buttons — on the AutoCAD Standard toolbar, but the right-click cursor menu, shown in Figure 14-1, provides more options, as we explain later.

Figure 14-1:
The cursor
menu's cut,
copy, and
paste
options.

In the example that follows, we demonstrate how to copy objects and point out the one difference if you want to move objects instead.

1. **Create a new drawing and draw some geometry (or open a drawing containing geometry that you want to copy).**

2. **Create a second new drawing (or open a second drawing) that will receive a copy of the geometry.**

3. **Arrange the two drawings so that you can see both of them, as shown in Figure 14-2.**

If you don't have enough screen real estate to arrange the two drawings side by side, you can leave them overlapped and change between the two drawing windows by using the Window menu, the CTRL+TAB keyboard shortcut, or the CTRL+F6 keyboard shortcut.

4. **In the first drawing, right-click and choose Copy from the cursor menu.**

Choose Cut if you want to move rather than copy the objects to the other drawing. Choose Copy with Base Point if you want to choose a specific base point rather than let AutoCAD choose a base point.

The base point that AutoCAD chooses is the lower-left corner of an imaginary rectangle that just barely encloses all the objects you've selected.

5. **If you chose Copy with Base Point in Step 4, pick a base point to use for the copy operation.**

The base point is like a base point for a block definition, as described in Chapter 13. Choose a useful point such as the endpoint of a line, lower-left corner of a rectangle, or center of a circle.

6. **Select the objects that you want to copy and then press Enter to end object selection.**

You can use any of the object selection methods described in Chapter 7. You also can reverse Steps 4 and 6 if you prefer selection-first editing, but then you won't have quite as many object selection methods available to you — see Chapter 7 for details.

7. **Click in the second drawing's window to make it current.**

8. **Right-click in the second drawing's window and choose Paste from the cursor menu.**

   Choose Paste to Original Coordinates if you want to copy the objects so that they land at the same point (with respect to 0,0) in the second drawing as they were located in the first drawing. Choose Paste as Block if you want AutoCAD to group the objects in a block with a goofy name like A$C71FE2E0D.

   If you do choose Paste as Block, you can change the block definition's name to something more sensible by running the BLOCK command.

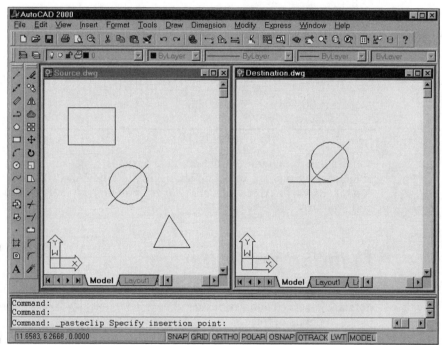

Figure 14-2:
Copying
objects
between
drawings.

The right-click cursor menu is the easiest way to use the various copy, cut, and paste commands, but you can type the corresponding command names for any of them at the command line, or click the Cut, Copy, or Paste buttons on the Standard toolbar for those options. Table 14-1 shows the relationship among cursor menu choices, command names, and toolbar buttons.

Table 14-1	The AutoCAD 2000 Clipboard Commands		
Cursor Menu Choice	*Command Name*	*Toolbar Button Name*	*Comment*
Cut	CUTCLIP	Cut to Clipboard	
Copy	COPYCLIP	Copy to Clipboard	
Copy with Base Point	COPYBASE	(none)	New in AutoCAD 2000
Paste	PASTECLIP	Paste from Clipboard	
Paste as Block	PASTEBLOCK	(none)	New in AutoCAD 2000
Paste to Original Coordinates	PASTEORIG	(none)	New in AutoCAD 2000

You can use the Windows Clipboard cut and paste method to copy or move objects within a single drawing, but using the AutoCAD COPY and MOVE commands via the right-click menu or the command line usually gives you better control and precision.

Painting properties

Every object in an AutoCAD drawing has, besides its geometrical defining points, the set of basic properties shown in Figure 14-3. These properties are part and parcel of the object — wherever the object goes, the properties go with it.

Chapter 4 introduces you to most of these properties and discusses how to set the current layer, color, linetype, and so on before drawing objects. Occasionally, though, people forget to change settings before drawing objects, or change their minds later about existing objects (not that *you* would ever do anything like that). For those absent-minded, flaky people, AutoCAD provides several ways to change the properties of existing objects. One of the simplest — and most fun — ways is the MATCHPROP (Match Properties) command, which resembles the Format Painter in Microsoft Word.

You use MATCHPROP to "paint" properties from one object (the *source*) onto one or more other objects (the *destination*). The source and destination objects can reside in the same drawing or in different drawings, as shown in the following example:

1. **Open or create a drawing containing an object with the properties you want to copy.**

   Skip the next two steps if the source and destination objects are in the same drawing.

2. **Open or create a second drawing containing one or more objects to which you want to copy the properties.**

3. **Arrange the two drawings so that you can see both of them.**

4. **Start the MATCHPROP command by using one of the following methods:**

   • Choose the Match Properties button (the one showing a paintbrush) on the Standard toolbar.

   • Type **MAtchprop** at the command prompt and press Enter.

   • Choose Modify⇨Match Properties from the menu bar.

5. **In the first drawing, choose the source object (the object whose properties you want to copy).**

   On the command line, AutoCAD displays the properties that will get copied (Color, Layer, Ltype, and so on) — see the command line in Figure 14-3.

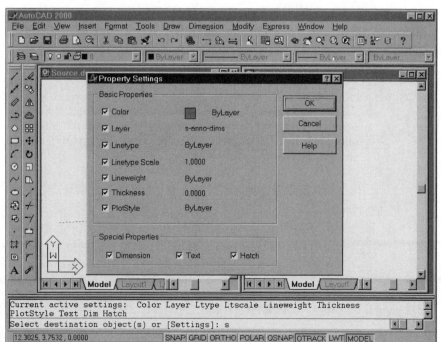

Figure 14-3:
The
Property
Settings
dialog box.

6. **If you want to change the properties that will get copied, type Settings and press Enter.**

   AutoCAD displays the Property Settings dialog box, as shown in Figure 14-3. Turn on the properties that you want to copy and turn off the properties that you don't want to copy. Choose OK when you're finished adjusting the settings.

   Note that you can copy, besides basic properties, the special properties Dimension style, Text style, and Hatch parameters. Of course, in order to copy these special properties, you need to select dimensions, text, or hatching as both the source object and the destination object.

7. **In the second drawing, choose the destination object(s) (the object(s) to which you want to copy the properties) and press Enter to end object selection.**

   AutoCAD copies the properties to the destination objects.

   If the destination objects are in a different drawing from the source object, the destination drawing may not contain a layer, dimension style, or other named object to which the source object's properties refer. In that case, AutoCAD creates the named object (layer, dimension style, and so on) in the destination drawing. Thus a side benefit of MATCHPROP is that it can copy named objects between drawings automatically. See the section on AutoCAD DesignCenter later in this chapter for more information about named objects.

Peeking in the Properties Window

Another great tool for changing — and viewing — objects' properties is the new Properties window, shown in Figure 14-4. Whereas MATCHPROP is the quick and simple, slap-on-the-paint-with-a-big-brush technique, the Properties window gives you complete, surgical control over every aspect of object properties.

You can use any of these methods to display the Properties window:

- Choose the Properties button on the Standard toolbar — the one on the right end with an A and a hand — to toggle the Properties window on and off.
- Press CTRL+1 to toggle the Properties window on and off.
- Select objects, right-click, and choose Properties.
- Enter **PROPERTIES** at the command line.

The left column of the Properties window lists property names and the right column lists the corresponding property values. The Properties window is a nonmodal window, rather than a modal dialog box. In plain English, that means that when you display the Properties window, it just sits there politely displaying properties, without interrupting whatever other commands you happen to be running. Unfortunately, you can't put it in the background and then bring it back to the front from the Windows taskbar, as you can with the Help menu; it always floats over the AutoCAD drawing area. If you have your monitor set to 800 x 600 resolution, it covers almost one-third of the screen, including the command line and big chunks of the Standard toolbar and Object Properties toolbar, not to mention a big part of your drawing. Even in higher-resolution modes, the Properties window covers up more of the screen than you can really afford to give up. Yet another reason to get a big screen. . . .

The Properties window has two tabs — Categorized and Alphabetic — that display the same property information sorted in different orders. You'll probably find the Categorized view easier to use, unless you're looking for a specifically named property in a long list.

If you haven't selected any objects, the Properties window displays "No selection" at the top, and displays and lets you change the current properties for the drawing, as shown in Figure 14-4. AutoCAD applies the current properties to the objects that you draw from that point on.

When you select one object using selection-first editing (see Chapter 7 for details), the Properties Window changes to display the properties of that object, as shown in Figure 14-5.

When you select more than one object using selection-first editing, the Properties Window displays the properties that are common to all those objects. You can use the drop-down list at the top of the window to change from viewing properties for all selected objects to viewing properties for specific types of objects in the selection set (for example, just the selected line objects or just the selected multiline text objects). These subsets of objects usually let you view and change more properties, because specific types of objects have more in common. For example, all multiline text objects have a text style property.

List of selecting subject of objects

Property names

Quick Select button

Property values

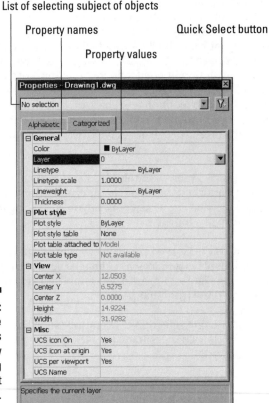

Figure 14-4:
The
Properties
window
showing
current
properties.

You can use the Quick Select button at the upper right of the window to select objects based on their properties.

Whether you're viewing current properties, properties for one object, or properties for more than one object, you can change properties by clicking in the values column on the right. In many cases, you'll find a drop-down list containing valid choices (for example, layer names). In other cases, you'll be able to enter a number or a text string or pick a point.

The Properties window makes it ridiculously easy to mess up a large number of objects quickly. Before you change any properties, look at the drop-down list at the top of the window and verify that you're changing the objects that you want to change. If you do accidentally commit "property damage," use Undo to restore the original properties.

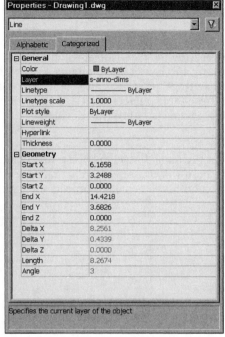

Figure 14-5:
The
Properties
window
showing the
properties
of a single
line.

You can let the Properties window float outside the AutoCAD program window or dock it like a toolbar. You can also resize it and use the scrollbar to make the properties you're most interested in display where you want them to. The Properties button on the AutoCAD Standard toolbar and the CTRL+1 keyboard shortcut provide efficient ways to toggle the Properties window on when you need it and off when you don't.

Using AutoCAD DesignCenter

Despite the fact that "DesignCenter" sounds like a booth set up in Home Depot to help you remodel your kitchen, the new AutoCAD DesignCenter window is handy for mining data from all kinds of drawings. Whereas the Properties window is concerned with object properties, the DesignCenter window deals primarily with *named objects*: layers, block definitions, text styles, and other organizational objects in your drawings.

Named objects

Every drawing includes a set of *symbol tables* that contain *named objects*. For example, in Chapter 13, we describe the *block table*, which contains objects called *block definitions*. Similarly, the layer table contains a list of the layers in your drawing, along with the settings for each layer (color, linetype, on/off setting, and so on). Each of these table objects, be it a block definition, a layer, or some other type, has a name, so Autodesk decided to call them "named objects" (duh!).

Neither the symbol tables nor the named objects appear as graphical objects in your drawing. They're like hard-working stagehands that stay hidden while they keep the show running smoothly. The named objects include:

- ✔ Layers
- ✔ Linetypes
- ✔ Text styles
- ✔ Dimension styles
- ✔ Block definitions
- ✔ Xrefs
- ✔ Layouts

When you use commands such as BLOCK, DIMSTYLE, and LAYER, you are creating and editing named objects. After you've created named objects in one drawing, AutoCAD DesignCenter gives you the tools to copy them to other drawings.

We realize that no one says "We've got to get this building up in six months; let's fire up AutoCAD 2000 and create some named objects!" However, becoming aware of the hidden personality of AutoCAD as a drawing database manager, not just a drawing program, will help you do better work, faster and with fewer mistakes.

 In case there are any customization nerds — or customization nerd wannabes — reading this book, we should mention that layouts aren't stored in a symbol table. Also, xrefs are stored in the block table, rather than in a separate xref table. Nonetheless, for the purposes of using DesignCenter, you can treat layouts and xrefs as two other types of named objects.

Getting (Design)Centered

You can use any of these methods to display the DesignCenter window:

✔ Choose the AutoCAD DesignCenter button on the Standard toolbar — the one just to the left of the Properties icon that looks like a white calculator — to toggle the DesignCenter on and off.

✔ Press CTRL+2 to toggle the DesignCenter window on and off.

✔ Enter **ADCenter** at the command line.

Like the Properties window, the DesignCenter window is nonmodal — it doesn't interrupt other AutoCAD commands, but waits like a patient butler for you to request something of it. It initially appears docked on the left side of the drawing window, but you can move it around as a floating window or even re-dock it on the right side of the drawing window. When the DesignCenter window is docked, you can drag its inside edge to make it narrower or wider. When it's floating, you can grab an edge or a corner to resize it.

The window consists of a toolbar at the top, a navigation pane on the left, and a content pane on the right (see Figure 14-6). The navigation pane displays a tree view with drawing files and the symbol tables contained in each drawing. The content pane, or *palette*, usually displays the contents of the drawing or symbol table.

The relationships among the various toolbar buttons and how you should use them aren't obvious at first. The callouts in Figure 14-6 organize them into six groups:

✔ **Tree view options:** The first three buttons — Desktop, Open Drawings, and History — change what's displayed in the tree view navigation pane. *Desktop* displays a part of your local or network disks, as though you were viewing folders in Windows Explorer. *Open Drawings* displays the drawings that you currently have open in AutoCAD — note that "open" is an adjective here, not a command! *History* displays drawings that you've recently browsed in DesignCenter.

You might wonder why parts of DesignCenter — and windows or dialog boxes in other programs — bear such a striking resemblance to Windows Explorer (not to be confused with the Internet Explorer browser program or, for that matter, with the Ford Explorer you might have in your driveway). Windows software development tools offers programmers a set of high-level programming components, such as tree view panes. Microsoft used these same programming components to develop Windows Explorer. They make programming easier and help ensure a fairly consistent interface in the various Windows programs that you use.

Toolbar

Tree view options

Tree view pane toggle

Desktop options

Move up a level

Preview a description toggles

Content pane views

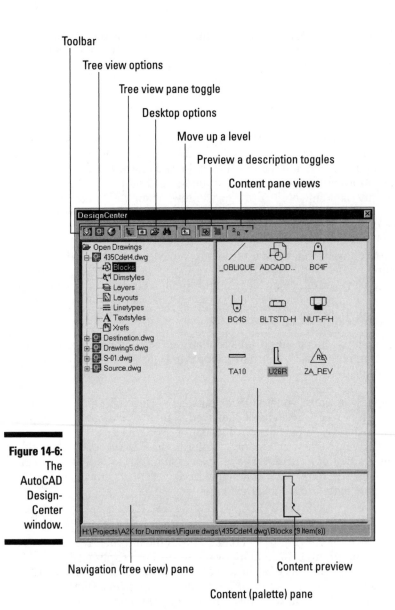

Figure 14-6:
The
AutoCAD
Design-
Center
window.

Navigation (tree view) pane

Content preview

Content (palette) pane

✔ **Tree view pane toggle:** The fourth button toggles the entire tree view navigational panel off and on. You can toggle it off temporarily in order to give the content pane more room.

✔ **Desktop options:** The next three buttons — Favorites, Load, and Find — provide different ways of locating drawings to display in Desktop view in the navigation panel. *Favorites* displays your personal DesignCenter favorites folder, which contains shortcuts to drawings or other folders that you've added to DesignCenter (see "Playing favorites," later in this chapter, for details). *Load* displays a standard Windows file open dialog box, in which you can select a drawing whose content you want to view or use. Find opens a search dialog box containing lots of options for locating drawings that match criteria you specify (see "Searching for drawings," later in this chapter, for details).

Rather than use Load, you can drag a drawing file from Windows Explorer into the DesignCenter window. Be careful, though — the Desktop view must be displayed in the tree view pane and you must drop the DWG filename in the palette or tree view pane. If these conditions aren't met, AutoCAD opens the drawing in the drawing editor rather than in DesignCenter.

✔ **Move up a level:** Moves the cursor in the navigation pane up one level in the hierarchy — for example, from a symbol table to the drawing that contains it, or from a drawing to the folder that contains it.

✔ **Preview and description toggles:** These two buttons toggle the display of two areas at the bottom of the content panel. The Preview area shows graphical previews of blocks and xrefs, and the Description area shows descriptions of blocks.

Unfortunately, DesignCenter doesn't display previews or descriptions of other kinds of named objects. Can you spell "unfinished feature"?

In addition, block previews and descriptions display only if you added them at the time that you created the block definition in AutoCAD 2000 — see Chapter 13 for details. Block icons display only if the block was created in AutoCAD 2000, or if you've deliberately added an icon to a block from an earlier version of AutoCAD. You can use the BLOCKICON command to generate preview icons for block definitions in drawings from earlier AutoCAD versions.

✔ **Content pane views:** This drop-down list changes the content pane display style among Large icons, Small icons, List, and Detail, just like in Windows Explorer.

All the DesignCenter toolbar options are available as well from the cursor menu that appears when you right-click in a blank area of the content pane, as shown in Figure 14-7. You may find that the grouping of items in this menu makes their relationships clearer.

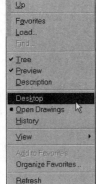

Figure 14-7:
The Design
Center
right-click
menu.

The usual sequence for using DesignCenter follows:

1. **Load the drawing(s) whose content you want to view or use into the navigation pane on the left.**

2. **Navigate through the various symbol tables (blocks, dimstyles, layers, and so on), viewing their individual named objects in the content pane on the right.**

3. **(Optional) Drag — or copy and paste — individual named objects from the content pane into any drawings that you have open in AutoCAD.**

DesignCenter can display, besides drawing files and their named objects, raster images and "custom content" defined by third-party applications.

Copying layers, linetypes, dimension styles, and more

The following example demonstrates how to copy layers from one drawing to another using DesignCenter. You can use the same technique to copy dimension styles, layouts, linetypes, and text styles.

1. **Toggle the DesignCenter window on by choosing the AutoCAD DesignCenter button on the Standard toolbar, pressing CTRL+2, or entering** ADCenter **at the command line.**

   If the DesignCenter window steals too much space from your drawing area, either make the DesignCenter window smaller, make the AutoCAD window larger, or, if you don't have the AutoCAD program window maximized, undock the DesignCenter window and float it off to the side.

2. **Open or create a drawing containing named objects you want to copy.**

   Alternatively, you can use the Desktop, Load, or Find button to load a drawing into DesignCenter without opening it in AutoCAD.

3. **Open or create a second drawing to which you want to copy the named objects.**

4. **Click the Open Drawings button to display your two currently opened drawings in DesignCenter's navigation pane on the left.**

   If you used Desktop, Load, or Find in Step 2, skip this step — DesignCenter already displays the drawing you selected in Desktop view.

5. **If DesignCenter doesn't display the symbol tables indented underneath the source drawing (the one you opened in Step 2) as shown in Figure 14-8, click the plus sign next to the drawing's name to display them.**

6. **Click the Layers table to display the source drawing's layers in the content pane.**

7. **Choose one or more layers in the content pane.**

8. **Right-click in the content pane and choose Copy from the cursor menu to copy the layer(s) to the Windows clipboard.**

9. **Click in the AutoCAD destination drawing's window (the drawing that you opened in Step 3).**

10. **Right-click and choose Paste from the cursor menu.**

    AutoCAD copies the layers into the current drawing, using the colors, linetypes, and other settings from the source drawing.

If the current drawing contains a layer whose name matches the name of one of the layers you're copying, AutoCAD leaves that layer defined as is — named objects from DesignCenter never overwrite objects with the same name in the destination drawing. AutoCAD always displays "Duplicate definitions will be ignored" even if there aren't any duplicates.

There are two other ways to copy layers from DesignCenter. You can drag layers from the content pane to a drawing window. You also can right-click in the content pane and choose Add Layer(s) from the cursor menu, which adds layers to the current drawing. The copy-and-paste method in our example requires the least amount of manual dexterity and less guesswork about which drawing the layers get added to.

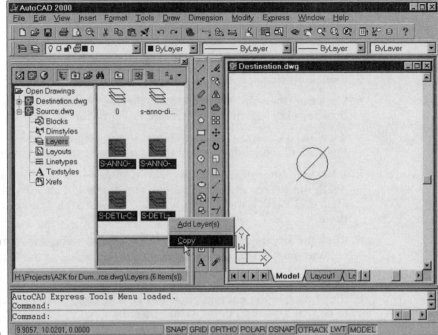

Figure 14-8:
Copying
layers with
Design
Center.

Inserting blocks

The following example demonstrates how to insert blocks from one drawing into another using DesignCenter. You can use the same technique to attach xrefs or raster images.

1. **Make sure that you performed Steps 1 through 5 from the previous example ("Copying layers") to open a source and a destination drawing in DesignCenter.**

   The source drawing from Step 2 needs to contain one or more block definitions.

2. **Click the Blocks table to display the source drawing's block definitions in the content pane.**

3. **Choose a block definition in the content pane.**

   DesignCenter displays a preview and description at the bottom of the content pane if these items are available and if the Preview and Description subpanes are turned on.

4. **Right-click in the content pane and choose Copy from the cursor menu to copy the block definition to the Windows clipboard.**

5. **Click in the AutoCAD destination drawing's window.**

6. **Right-click and choose Paste from the cursor menu, as shown in Figure 14-9.**

The other two paste options — Paste as Block and Paste to Original Coordinates — are misleading in this instance. Paste as Block does the same thing as Paste. Paste to Original Coordinates inserts the block into your drawing with its insertion point at 0,0, *not* at the original coordinates at which the block was first drawn in the source drawing.

7. **Specify an insertion point for the block insert.**

AutoCAD copies the block definition into the current drawing's block table and inserts the block at the point you pick.

There are several other ways to insert blocks from DesignCenter. You can drag a block definition with either the left or right mouse button from the content pane and drop it in a drawing window. You also can right-click a block definition in the content pane and choose Insert Block from the cursor menu to insert it into the current drawing. The copy-and-paste method in our example is the most reliable for most people, but it doesn't let you change the insertion scale factor. Use the right-click drag-and-drop method if you need to control the insertion scale factor.

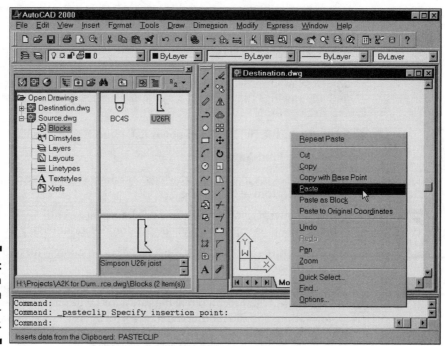

Figure 14-9:
Inserting a block with Design-Center.

Searching for drawings

The DesignCenter's Find button opens a dialog box that's similar to the Find dialog in Windows Explorer. You can use DesignCenter's Find dialog box to search for drawings based on myriad criteria. (If your drawings don't contain any myriads, you can search for lots of other stuff, too.) After you've found one or more matching drawings you can load them into DesignCenter, open them in AutoCAD, insert them as blocks, or attach them as xrefs by right-clicking on each drawing's name.

The most straightforward kind of search is one based on the drawing's file-name. To accomplish this kind of search, perform the following steps:

1. **From the Loo̲k for drop-down list, choose Drawings.**

2. **From the I̲n drop-down list, choose a drive to search; if you want to search a specific folder, use the B̲rowse button to choose it.**

    Turn on Search subdirectories if you want Find to look in all subfolders of the drive or folder you've specified in I̲n.

3. **Make sure the Drawings tab is current and type part or all of the name of the file(s) you're looking for.**

    Unlike Find in Windows Explorer, AutoCAD DesignCenter's Find doesn't automatically act as though you'd put asterisk wildcards around your search string. For example, if you search for files using the string "foo", Windows Explorer will find any filename that contains "foo" (Foo.dwg, Oldfoo.dwg, Fool.dwg, Youngfool.dwg, Foobar.doc, Kungfoo.txt, and so on). DesignCenter will find only Foo.dwg. If you want DesignCenter to find all drawings that contain a particular string, enclose the string in asterisks: "*foo*".

4. **From the In the f̲ield(s) drop-down list, choose File Name.**

5. **Choose the Find N̲ow button.**

    Find searches for matching drawings and displays any matches in the list at the bottom of the dialog box.

    As in Windows Explorer, you can sort the list differently by clicking the column headings (for example, File Size or File Modified).

6. **Right-click any drawing file name and choose any of the options from the cursor menu.**

There are many other search criteria you can use, including the names of named objects (for example, a block definition or layer name), drawing prop-erties information, and file modified dates. If you spend a minute looking at the drop-down lists and tabs in the Find dialog box, you'll quickly develop a good idea of the kinds of search options it provides.

You can search for drawings based on Title, Subject, Author, and Keywords information that's stored with each drawing file and displayed in the Drawing Properties dialog box (see Figure 14-10). Of course, the usefulness of this kind of search depends on whether you had the foresight to enter any of the information in the Drawing Properties dialog box when you were working on the drawings. You may want to get in the habit of using File⇨Drawing Properties (or DWGPROPS at the command line) in each drawing to enter searchable information.

Opening drawings

If you have a folder open in DesignCenter's navigation pane Desktop view, you can use drag and drop to open a drawing contained in the folder. This feature is handy because DesignCenter displays previews — albeit tiny ones — of all the drawings in the folder. Thus you can do a visual search for the drawing that you're after.

To open or insert a drawing from DesignCenter you must drag the drawing from the content pane on the right, not the navigation pane on the left. If you try to drag from the left pane, nothing happens.

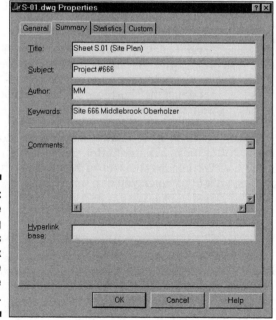

Figure 14-10:
Use the
Drawing
Properties
dialog box
to store
searchable
information.

When you use drag and drop to open a drawing from DesignCenter, you must drop it in the gray area *behind* any open drawings' windows. If you drop the drawing name from DesignCenter into another drawing's window, AutoCAD inserts it as a block. You may need to minimize any open drawings in order to expose the gray area before performing this drag and drop operation.

Playing favorites

The Load and Find buttons provide two ways to locate folders and files that you want to load into DesignCenter's navigation pane. If you find that you're repeatedly returning to the same folders or drawings, you'll probably want to add them to your list of DesignCenter favorites. Accessing your favorites requires a bit of dancing back and forth between the left and right panes. Click the Favorites button to display a list of shortcuts in the content pane and then double-click one of the shortcuts to load what it points to into the navigation pane.

AutoCAD 2000 comes with one DesignCenter favorites shortcut, which points to the folder \Program Files\Acad2000\Sample\DesignCenter. This folder contains some sample drawings, most of which contain blocks for a variety of different disciplines (for example, fasteners, kitchen appliances, and weld symbols). These samples demonstrate how you can build drawings that serve as block libraries and then "search the shelves" with DesignCenter.

When you come upon a file or folder that you want to add to your DesignCenter favorites, simply right-click on it and choose Add to Favorites from the cursor menu. This procedure adds another shortcut to your list of favorites. Another right-click menu choice — Organize favorites — opens a Windows Explorer window containing the shortcuts so that you can delete or add shortcuts in your Favorites folder.

The DesignCenter window, like the Properties window, takes up a lot of screen space. Use the AutoCAD DesignCenter button on the AutoCAD Standard toolbar or the Ctrl+2 keyboard shortcut to toggle the DesignCenter window on when you need it and off when you don't.

Chapter 15

3D for Me, See?

· ·

· ·

*T*hree-dimensional (3D) drafting and design capabilities — that is, adding height as well as length and width to your drawing — were once a high-end, extra-cost add-on to AutoCAD. Users who wanted to tackle 3D bought high-end machines and underwent additional training to be able to work in this new environment. Now 3D is part of the base AutoCAD package, but it has not suddenly become fast, easy-to-use, or trouble-free. This chapter offers a gentle introduction to the power and promise of 3D work in AutoCAD.

The most important visible change to the 3D graphics of AutoCAD 2000 is the new 3D Orbit command that lets you easily rotate rendered 3D models in real time, as described later in this chapter. You can also now zoom on rendered 3D models.

OpenGL is an industry-standard language for describing 3D graphics that is supported by AutoCAD 2000. This is good news for Autodesk because the company can take advantage of code libraries, trained programmers, and other resources available for OpenGL. It's good news for you because the growing number of powerful and relatively affordable OpenGL graphics accelerators becoming available on the market can now be used to support high-performance 3D in AutoCAD. If you use AutoCAD 2000 3D frequently, look into an OpenGL accelerator for your computer. Check the AutoCAD resources described in Chapter 16 to find sources for reviews of OpenGL accelerators that describe which models work best with AutoCAD.

3D thumbs up

Using 3D takes time to learn, creates additional work, and slows down your computer, so why bother using it? Here are four key reasons why anyone in his or her right mind would bother with 3D:

Wave of the future. As CAD pursues greater and greater realism, 3D becomes important in more and more areas. So any CAD user who wants to be competent a few years down the road needs to become familiar with 3D now.

Sometimes it's nice. Drawing in 3D is useful for a number of tasks, including creating shaded renderings to help sell a design to a client, and fit-and-finish testing to find potential problems before a design is actually put into construction or manufacturing.

Sometimes it's needed. Drawing in 3D is required for a small but growing number of tasks. Many mechanical designs are done in 3D or converted into 3D at some point in the design process. 3D perspective views make drawings easier to understand. And the shaded renderings used for both designing and selling are becoming a practical necessity in some fields.

Sometimes it's faster. The fastest way to create a single view of something is to draw it in the needed size and perspective in 2D. But if you need multiple views, it may be faster to create a 3D model and then slice and render it as needed for the views you want to create.

3D for Me? . . .

The concept of 3D hardly seems to need introduction. We live in a three-dimensional world, and all the objects you model in your 2D AutoCAD drawings are actually three-dimensional.

But at a basic level, the way in which people see things is actually a two-dimensional (2D) representation of the three-dimensional world. The image that your eyes project onto the inside rear of your eyeballs is, after all, just as two-dimensional as a TV picture. (The image on the back of your eyeballs is upside-down, too, but that's another problem; your brain automatically flips it right-side up.)

Your mind uses a number of clues to generate a moving, three-dimensional model from the two-dimensional images it receives from your eyes. These clues include depth cues from combining left-eye and right-eye images and inferences from the motion of objects, sounds, and previous experience. The mind puts all this information together to help you perceive the world in 3D.

3D thumbs down

Why not use 3D all the time? For several reasons, which you should take into account before you decide how much to use 3D on any given project:

2D input and editing. The mouse, keyboard, and drawing tablet are all 2D devices; the more complex the 3D object you're trying to model, the more complicated you'll find it is to construct it with these devices. In addition, the AutoCAD 2000 3D editing tools are fairly limited in scope. For most real-world 3D editing work, you need a third-party application or discipline-specific version of AutoCAD such as Mechanical Desktop (see Chapter 1 for details).

2D output. Almost all the output methods available to you, notably paper and the computer screen, are 2D; the full beauty of your 3D model may only be known to you!

Performance. Today's personal computers are adequate for the task of storing moderately complex 2D models and displaying them on-screen and on the plotter; if the model is 3D, the difficulty increases geometrically, and performance seems to slow geometrically as well. You may need to add 3D acceleration to your computer system to get adequate performance — or even upgrade to a faster computer.

Similarly, drafting provides clues to help the mind construct a 3D model from the 2D image on paper. The use of multiple views and the experience of the viewer are probably the two most important clues to making 3D sense of 2D drawings. Design and drafting have succeeded pretty well for a long time by using 2D representations as the guide to creating 3D objects. But at some point, nothing can replace a true 3D model, such as in helping someone understand how a building will look when constructed or how two parts fit together.

So what does using 3D in CAD mean? Basically, it means creating models instead of views. Rather than create cross-sections of objects, or views of objects from certain perspectives, the designer or draftsperson creates a complete, accurate, 3D model of each object. This description or depiction of each object includes all the necessary information for AutoCAD to create a view from any perspective. With a properly constructed 3D model, AutoCAD can even output commands to machines to create actual 3D objects, whether plastic prototypes carved from a tank of jelly by lasers, or an actual bolt, valve, or piston created by numerically controlled machine tools.

In AutoCAD, 3D means three different things — no, *3D* doesn't really mean *three different*, it means *three-dimensional*. The three different kinds of 3D objects in AutoCAD are

✔ **Wireframes.** A wireframe model is like a skeleton of a 3D object; a wireframe model shows the edges of the object, not any of its surfaces. Wireframes are simple to create but tedious to build; you create a set of 2D objects that represent an outline of each part of the object and then connect them three-dimensionally to make the wireframe. It's like building a model out of wire coat-hangers. One of the biggest limitations of wireframe models is that you can't shade them because there aren't any surfaces "inside" the wire edges to catch the light — imagine shining a flashlight on a coat-hanger.

✔ **Surfaces.** A surface model represents the "skin" of an object, but not the solid mass of what's inside. AutoCAD uses objects called *meshes* to create surfaces. A mesh is a faceted surface that you use to represent the edges and surfaces of a 3D object. Creating a 3D mesh is like building a house out of cards. You also can build up parts of a surface mesh model by sweeping a 2D object such as a polyline around an axis. A surface model is one step up from a wireframe model, because you can apply material properties and shading to its surfaces. Surface meshes are just the thing for some 3D modeling tasks, but other kinds of 3D objects are awkward to build by pasting surfaces together.

✔ **Solids.** A solid model is as close to true 3D as you can get without whipping out some Play-Do and building a real-world model yourself. Solid models are built by constructing basic 3D shapes and then combining them — adding, subtracting, or finding their intersections — and modifying them. Learning to build up real-world objects out of basic 3D shapes is a skill that takes time and practice to acquire — like, for instance, wine-tasting. (The two disciplines are also similar in that doing either one for too long can make your head spin!)

In this chapter we briefly introduce 3D solids. You can experiment with all three types of 3D models, but start by asking around among colleagues to find out what they use — no sense in spending a whole lot of time on 3D solids, for instance, if wireframes are the preferred method of 3D expression in your discipline or office.

You can do some experimentation with 3D on any computer system that can run AutoCAD. But if you want to pursue serious work in 3D AutoCAD, pay attention to the following prerequisites:

✔ **Know AutoCAD well.** You need to know the ins and outs of AutoCAD as a 2D tool thoroughly before doing much with 3D. Otherwise, the time you waste may be your own! If you're making avoidable errors at the 2D level at the same time that you're trying to get to know and use 3D, accomplishing anything is slow going.

✔ **Get a fast computer.** For beginning 3D work, any AutoCAD-adequate system will do the job; but for serious work with 3D models, you need the fastest computer you can get. One or two Pentium III microprocessors running Windows NT with 128 MB of RAM and a two-gigabyte hard disk is in the ballpark. The additional processor won't help AutoCAD directly, but it will help some 3D programs you may run along with AutoCAD, and will also help you multitask with AutoCAD and another program simultaneously. (Now you know why "real" 3D work is done on high-end workstations!)

✔ **Get and master additional software.** In addition to AutoCAD, you need other programs — either AutoCAD add-ons or separate packages — to do work that AutoCAD isn't as good at. Illustration packages, for example, can really help jazz up the appearance of your drawing.

✔ **Do a real project.** Real work is the best motivation of all for discovering 3D. If you don't have an actual work assignment, create a task for yourself. Something as "simple" as creating a 3D model of your living room and its furniture can make the difference between really finding out something useful about 3D and just reading about it in the manuals.

The Mechanical Desktop product from Autodesk has advanced 3D features, including specialized geometry construction and editing tools, libraries of standard 3D parts, and a fast display driver specifically for 3D. Contact Autodesk or your AutoCAD dealer for more information.

Starting with 3D

The best way to get started with 3D is to create several 3D solids and combine them into an interesting model. Not only is this fun and educational, it's also a quick and dirty version of something that you may need to do in the real world: a "massing study" in which you take rough approximations of real objects, such as buildings, and arrange them to get a rough idea of what the finished product will look like *in situ* (which means "in place" in Latin, a language that was invented before situation comedies became popular.) So you can quickly experiment with 3D by taking a photo of a city skyline, creating some shapes that roughly mimic the buildings, and arranging them in something like their real-world order. (Extra points for you if the resulting skyline is recognizable by your colleagues. Double bonus points if you include Godzilla climbing the tallest building!)

Don't let this easy approach give you a false sense of security, though. To use 3D effectively, you basically must relearn how to enter coordinates, create and manipulate objects, and more. The rest of this chapter skips all that relearning in favor of getting a quick 3D bang for your buck with AutoCAD features most users already know. For a more thorough approach to using 3D

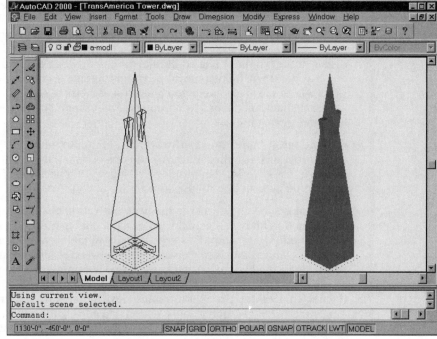

Figure 15-1:
A simple
model of the
TransAmeri-
ca tower,
rendered on
the right.

with AutoCAD, see Chapters 17–19 in the AutoCAD 2000 *User's Guide*. Also check out the "Working in Three Dimensions" tutorials on the AutoCAD 2000 Learning Assistance CD and the reliable AutoCAD resources listed in Chapter 17 of this book.

To demonstrate 3D, this chapter uses a simple model resembling the TransAmerica tower in San Francisco, an architecturally interesting building. We show you later in this chapter how to create a similar drawing yourself as the base for your experiments with 3D.

Exploring viewports in model space

Chapter 9 discusses viewports in paper space, which are useful for creating layouts for use in printouts and presentations in both 2D and 3D. *Model space viewports,* cousins of paper viewports, are less powerful but simpler, and they impose less of a performance hit on AutoCAD.

Unlike paper space viewports, model space viewports divide the screen into separate rectangles with no gap between them, and you can't move or stretch them. You can't plot multiple model space viewports; that's what paper space is for. And, unlike in layouts, a layer that's visible in one model space viewport always is visible in all of them.

Model space viewports enable you to see several views of your model at one time, each from a different angle. Although the different views subdivide the screen, using them can have performance advantages. Rendering a small viewport, for example, is quicker than rendering a full-screen image. After you get everything the way you really want it, you can change your drawing back to full-screen and render the whole thing. Model space viewports are also very helpful when working in 3D. If you have different viewpoints in three or four viewports, creating 3D models is easier. An object that looks correct in one viewport can be "double-checked" in another viewport for accuracy.

To set up model space viewports, use the Tiled Viewport Layout dialog box. Start it by choosing View⇨Viewports⇨4 Viewports, or another number of viewports, from the menu bar. Figure 15-2 shows the menu choice and the result, which makes choosing the viewport setup you want very easy.

AutoCAD displays a UCS (User Coordinate System) icon in the lower-left corner of each viewport — the little X-Y icon that you usually see in the same position in the drawing area. This icon defines the working construction plane — the plane in which AutoCAD places 2D objects when you draw them.

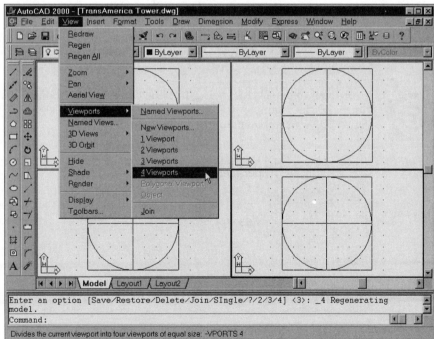

Figure 15-2:
The Tiled Viewport Layout dialog box makes setting up viewports easy.

Start your viewport explorations with the menus, as described previously. For speed, you can set up model space viewports from the command line by using the -VPORTS command, which enables you to create, save, and restore viewport layouts. To use -VPORTS, you tell AutoCAD how many viewports to create and then specify the style. Experiment to find out how it works.

Watch out; AutoCAD continues to subdivide the screen each time you use the -VPORTS command. You can have up to 16 viewports open at a time. Of course, at that point they're too small to see much of anything in them.

Expect delays when you first start using 3D as AutoCAD loads into memory the needed code to support different 3D operations. (Not loading this code every time is how AutoCAD stays "lean and mean" while you work with 2D drawings.) Of course, loading this code uses up RAM that you would just as soon have for your 3D model. Gotten more RAM yet?

Changing the viewpoint in your viewports

AutoCAD initializes all your viewports with the same point of view. You can change the viewpoints of your various viewports so that they all have different points of view — or else, what good are they?

To change the viewpoint in a viewport, choose View➪3D Views➪Viewpoint Presets (DDVPOINT from the command line). Figure 15-3 shows the Viewpoint Presets dialog box.

If you want to bypass the dialog box, you can instead choose a standard viewpoint (for example, Top, Bottom, Left, Right, or SW Isometric) from the View➪3D Views submenu or the View toolbar.

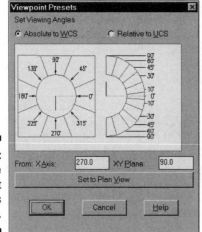

Figure 15-3:
The
Viewpoint
Presets
dialog box.

To set viewpoint options with the keyboard, type **VPOINT** at the command prompt and press Enter. Prompts and even simple on-screen animations appear to take you through the steps to set viewpoint options. However, we recommend using the menu choices and dialog box, at least until you gain expertise.

To help you make sense of 3D viewing options in general, and the Viewpoint Presets dialog box in particular, review this description of the parts of the dialog box:

- ✔ **Set Viewing Angles.** This option tells the dialog box whether to set the viewing angle Absolute to WCS, in relation to the World Coordinate System (WCS), or Relative to UCS, in relation to the current User Coordinate System. (***Note:*** The WCS is the default XYZ coordinate system when you start a new drawing. X is horizontal on the screen, Y is vertical on the screen, and Z extends toward the viewer in the third dimension. A UCS is a different coordinate system that you, the all-powerful user, define in order to make certain 3D construction tasks easier.)

  Look up UCS in AutoCAD's online help to learn more about UCSs and how to work with them.

- ✔ **From X Axis.** This text box and the square area above it set the viewing angle relative to the horizontal, or X, axis.

  Changing this angle on a typical house plan, for example, is similar to strolling around the house to look at the house from different horizontal vantage points. To set the exact angle to within a fraction of a degree, enter the value in the text entry box or click a spot on the circumference of the circle. To set the angle to a 45-degree increment, click inside the square but outside the circle, near to the angle that you want.

- ✔ **XY Plane.** This text box and the curved area above it set the viewing angle relative to the flat, 2D XY plane — the "floor" of the living room for a model of a house.

  Changing this angle from 90 degrees to –90 degrees on a typical house plan, for example, is similar to floating directly above a house, and then around and down to one side of it, and then around and down into the ground until you're looking up at the house from directly beneath. You can consider the half circle shown in the dialog box to be an arched, semicircular catwalk, with its endpoints directly above and directly under the house. As with the X Axis choice, you can set the exact viewing angle by entering a value in the text entry box or by clicking a spot on the circumference of the inner semicircle. You can set the viewing angle in larger increments by clicking one of the numbers at various increments around the semicircle.

- ✔ **Set to Plan View.** This option resets the X axis and XY plane views to 270 degrees from the X axis and 90 degrees from the XY plane, which is the AutoCAD default, top-down plan view.

By using the Viewpoint Presets dialog box, you can change the viewpoint in a viewport. (Say "viewpoint in a viewport" three times fast and notice the funny looks you get.) This dialog box even works in a single 2D viewport (that is, the default model space view that you see when you start a new drawing).

The results of using the Viewpoint Presets dialog box can be surprising at first. Carefully compare the current settings indicated in the dialog box to the new settings — you want to make sure that you're doing the right thing. Accidentally changing the XY plane angle so that you're looking at your plan from underground, for example, is all too easy to do. You may not even notice what you've done until you use a HIDE, SHADE, or RENDER command; get in the habit of checking yourself by using the HIDE command whenever you use 3D objects.

Going to the Third Dimension

Working in 3D can be fun, especially when you're not trying to do anything difficult such as make shapes connect exactly or do complicated work that runs slowly. A massing study, as mentioned earlier in this chapter, is a good place to start.

A massing study has nothing to do with what people do on Sunday morning. Instead, it's a rough 3D view of what an area looks like — or what it *will* look like when certain changes, such as bulldozing 10 historically unique buildings and replacing them with a parking structure, are made. (You can also bulldoze 10 parking structures and replace them with historically unique buildings, if the mood strikes you.) You can do similar studies when planning how mechanical parts will fit together or in other disciplines as well.

There are a surprising number of existing 3D models of city skylines, some of them quite good. If you have to do a real massing study — or any other serious 3D work — start by checking to see what pre-existing work you can borrow — with permission, of course — and use as a starting point.

In the next few steps, we show you how to create and then render a simple 3D model suitable for use in a massing study.

Starting on solids

Remember when you were just a little baby and you were starting on solid foods? Probably not. But here's your chance to start on solids all over again.

In this section, we introduce you to creating and rendering a simple solid model. Try it yourself!

When working in 2D, it's useful to start by roughing out your drawing using rectangles and circles to get an idea of how to arrange items on the printed sheet. This trick of doing a very rough draft in advance is an even better idea for 3D work, in which errors can mean dozens of hours of difficult reworking. No matter how intricate your final product will be, consider starting with a massing study like the one described here.

1. **Choose a solid, such as a rectangular prism, and choose <u>D</u>raw⇨ Sol<u>i</u>ds⇨Box to start.**

   AutoCAD 2000 will prompt you for the location of the box from the command line.

2. **Specify the location of the box.**

   If you're experimenting, make the box shape simple so that you can easily attach other items to it.

3. **Choose another solid, such as a cone, and choose <u>D</u>raw⇨Sol<u>i</u>ds⇨<u>C</u>one.**

   The CONE command will be entered on the command line and AutoCAD will prompt you for the location of the cone.

4. **Specify the location of the cone, such as atop the box.**

   So far, your 3D model looks more like a far-out dunce cap than the TransAmerica tower. Creating a 3D model that more accurately represents the building will require additional 3D modeling commands, including editing commands.

5. **To see your shape in progress, choose <u>V</u>iew⇨3D Or<u>b</u>it (3D Orbit is new in AutoCAD 2000).**

   The 3D Orbit "ring" and an XYZ coordinate indicator will appear on-screen, as shown in Figure 15-4.

6. **Rotate the object to view it from different angles.**

   To rotate the top of the object toward you or away from you, grab the top or bottom circle and drag it down or up, respectively. To rotate the front of the object left or right, grab either the left or right circle and drag it in the direction that you want the front of the object to move.

   The object and the XYZ coordinate indicator will rotate. Feeling seasick yet?

7. **Press Esc to exit 3D Orbit.**

   You will be returned to a fixed 2D view of your object.

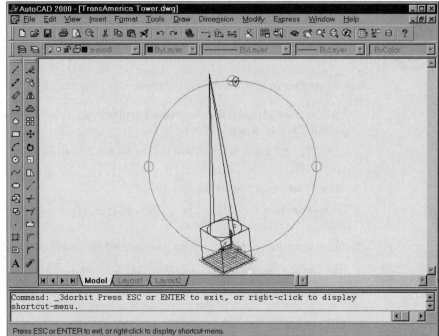

Figure 15-4:
Using 3D
Orbit to
rotate your
shapes.

3D Orbit is an alternative to working with multiple views on-screen simultane-ously, because you can easily check how the object looks from different angles. 3D Orbit allows you to see your model in a larger size; multiple views give you an instant blow-by-blow view of the changes in your model from multiple directions as you edit it. You can trade off between one way of look-ing at your model and the other, based on your needs and preferences.

Ending with rendering

Rendering is what you do to fat to make it into lard, correct? Not in the world of CAD. In CAD, rendering is the process of illuminating a 3D object with one or more imaginary lights and then drawing the resulting shape. The objects that you see in a movie such as *Toy Story* or *A Bug's Life* are first created as 3D models and then rendered frame by frame — a process that can take dozens of hours of computer time per frame — to produce the beautifully well-rendered images you see.

AutoCAD creates still renderings — that is, a single picture rather than a series of frames for an animation. If you want to create animations, you need to use other software programs such as Autodesk's 3D Studio. Even if you use animation programs, AutoCAD can be useful for developing the initial 3D models.

Rendering has steadily improved in speed and usability as PCs have become faster and rendering algorithms have been improved. Rendering of simple scenes is now practical on a mainstream PC, and a built-up personal computer can create some pretty impressive images in a reasonable amount of time. Rendered images are very useful for previewing how your models will work in real life, and are also powerful tools for sales and marketing communications for your company. A (rendered) picture can be worth quite a bit more than a thousand words.

To see how rendering works using the default options in AutoCAD 2000, use the steps that follow. Then experiment on your own and read Chapter 19 in the AutoCAD 2000 *User's Guide* to discover more.

To read about 3D in detail in the extensive AutoCAD 2000 Help files, press the F1 key to bring up Help. Then choose the Contents tab, double-click on the User's Guide topic, and read Chapter 17, "Working in Three-Dimensional Space," Chapter 18, "Creating Three-Dimensional Objects," and Chapter 19, "Rendering and Imaging." A printed version of the *User's Guide* comes with AutoCAD 2000, so you can read this chapters away from the computer if that's more convenient for you.

1. **Create a 3D object.**

   Use the steps in the previous section or create a 3D object on your own.

2. **Choose View⇨Render⇨Render.**

   The Render dialog box will appear, as shown in Figure 15-5.

3. **Ignore all the options and click OK.**

   You can get okay results without changing the options. When you click OK, the 3D object will be rendered. See Figure 15-5 for an example.

To quickly render the contents of a viewport using the current rendering settings, type **RENDER** at the command line and then press Enter once to start the command, and press Enter again to render with the current options.

You might find yourself getting frustrated if you try to use 3D Orbit, as described earlier in this chapter, on a rendered object — and watching the object instantly switch back to a wireframe as soon as you try it. The problem is that a rendering is, by definition, a view of an object as it appears from a specific point of view, with lighting from one or more other specific places.

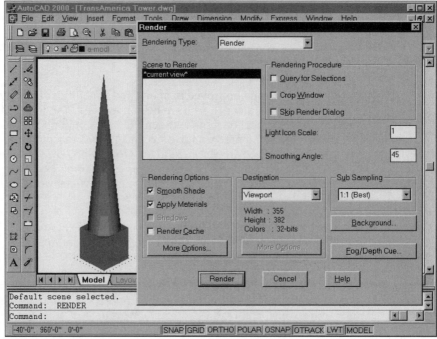

Figure 15-5:
The Render
dialog box
and a ren-
dered
object.

Any movement of the object requires re-rendering to produce an accurate result. An alternative is to run the SHADE command before using 3D Orbit. SHADE is a simplified form of rendering, and the 3D Orbit command preserves shading as you move around the model.

To quickly see two or more rendered views of an object from different angles, open multiple viewports on an object, rotate the object into a different perspective in each viewport, and then render each viewport in turn.

Finding More 3D Stuff

This chapter only touches on what 3D can do — and on what you need to find out to use it effectively. Rendering is faster and better in AutoCAD 2000. But these topics are worth a book of their own.

If you want to continue to experiment with 3D, take a course or two and buy one or more books on the topic. Your reading and training time will be quickly repaid in fewer mistakes and re-renderings — and better results.

Part V
The Part of Tens

The 5th Wave   By Rich Tennant

"What is it, Lassie? Is it Gramps? Is it his hard disk? Is he stuck somewhere, girl? Is there trouble with his system variables? What, girl, what?"

In this part . . .

"**T**ens" sounds a lot like "tense," and tense is how AutoCAD may make you feel sometimes. But never fear— help is on the way! Checklists are always a big help in getting things right and fixing things that are wrong. And a Top Ten list is a good way to quickly spot the best — or the worst — of almost anything, AutoCAD included. This Part of Tens features several lists — not all of which have exactly ten items (but, hey, who's counting?) — designed to help you get right into AutoCAD, get right out of trouble, and maybe have a chuckle or two in the meantime.

Chapter 16

Ten Ways to Do No Harm

- -

In This Chapter

▶ Working from copies of drawings

▶ Not cramming your geometry

▶ Planning not to plot

▶ Getting your system working right

▶ Getting a bigger monitor

▶ Getting third-party apps

▶ Using industry standards

▶ Using office standards

▶ Reusing like crazy

▶ Investing in training and support

- -

The Hippocratic Oath sworn by doctors begins, "First, do no harm."

Follow these steps to avoid doing harm to the hard work of others and the productive potential of yourself.

Working from Copies of Drawings

Be quick to make a copy of a drawing before or during your work session. Make copies before editing someone else's drawing; before trying a new idea; at the end of the day; or any other time you think of it. Be sure to save your copy someplace "out of the way" so that you don't confuse it with the latest and greatest version of your drawing.

Not Cramming Your Geometry

Leave some white space in your drawing! Better three drawings that people can understand and use — perhaps a main drawing, a page of details, and a page of notes — than one crammed so full of stuff, no one can see what's going on.

Plotting Not to Plot

You're better off to "plan not to print" — that is, work in a way that reduces the number of times you have to print your drawing, and that reduces the amount of time it actually takes your drawing to print. If you're suggesting changes to others' drawings, take the time to think of all the changes you can at one time; this approach reduces rework and the need for check plots. Look at xrefs first, then blocks, then similar pieces across various drawings so that changes can be propagated through all drawings before a final check. Use simple hatch patterns sparingly rather than complex hatch patterns lavishly, because hatches take time to print.

Getting Your System Working Right

Don't hurt your own productivity by skimping on hardware. It's crucial to have a hardware and software setup that supports you in getting things done right. Those of you who are new to AutoCAD may not realize this, but it used to take a high-end PC — say, a system in the $4,000 range — to run AutoCAD well. Now you can get good performance from a system that costs half as much. Given that hardware prices are dropping and that the value of your time is not, it may well be worth getting a new system just so that you can have a known, stable hardware and software base from which you can run AutoCAD 2000. If you're spending time troubleshooting problems with your Windows 3.1-compatible printer drivers or waiting for your system's 100 MHz processor to regenerate drawings, it's definitely time to move up.

Getting a Bigger Monitor

Remember when Spock did the Vulcan mind meld with a variety of alien creatures (which, to him, included Dr. McCoy) on "Star Trek"? Well, when you do a mind meld with your computer system, the size and resolution of your computer monitor determine the bandwidth of your human/computer communications. A 17" monitor is the minimum practical size for doing CAD. A 19" monitor is better, and a 21" monitor is better still. Keep in mind that a large, high-quality monitor is a good investment because it normally will last through two or three computers.

Getting Add-On Apps

As the AutoCAD world expands, the world of add-on utilities and tools increases in importance. You can even get discipline-specific versions of AutoCAD, with programs that were formerly third-party applications integrated into AutoCAD, from Autodesk itself, as described in Chapter 1. Take the time to research, try, buy, learn, and use one or more third-party applications. You will increase your productivity and reduce the number of mistakes you make.

Using Industry Standards

Using third-party applications is just one way to make sure you take advantage of resources and approaches that are standard in the discipline you're working in. Become knowledgeable about industry standards for how work is done and how drawings are put together in your discipline. Follow these standards throughout your office and ask other companies that you work with to follow them as well. Following standards consistently allows you to apply your creativity, expertise, and energy to the interesting and novel parts of the task at hand rather than to arguing about which hatching patterns to use.

Using Office Standards

Though industry standards may save you time and money, office standards help even more. That's because you can standardize a great many more things, from layer names (which may be partly covered already by industry standards in your discipline) right down to processes such as deciding what scale to use and how and when to use color in your company's drawings. Every time you make a big decision on a drawing, consider whether that decision can contribute to setting a standard for some or all of the drawings created in your company.

Recycling: Don't Refuse to Re-Use

Aretha Franklin once sang, "Thank you, I'll do it myself." This is a typical and very human attitude, but one you should try to avoid in your CAD work. The more work you can re-use, the better. Using an existing drawing as a starting point is one form of re-use. Blocks and xrefs, described in Chapter 13, are another. The AutoCAD DesignCenter, described in Chapter 14, makes it easy to raid many existing drawings for pieces you can put into your own "new" drawing.

Investing in Training and Support

You get a gold star on this last recommendation in advance just for buying and reading this book. Taking the time for formal and informal training and support is an investment in better, faster work. Joining online and real-world user groups, taking classes, and reading books are all forms of training and support. The classic form of training — instructor-led classes taken by all the people in a group or company — helps set a least common denominator of knowledge and lets you "synch up" with your colleagues on a shared knowledge base you can leverage for years to come.

Speaking of leverage for years to come, pay particular attention to studying new features in new or upgraded software that you have purchased. Decide how to change your in-house processes to accommodate the most useful of the new features. AutoCAD 2000 still allows you to work almost entirely the same way as you did 10 years ago in Release 11; it's up to you to decide how to take advantage of new features.

Chapter 17

Ten Great AutoCAD Resources (Plus One)

*H*ere, in no particular order, are ten great AutoCAD resources for you to use.

Online Help

The most-overlooked resource for help with your AutoCAD questions is the online help and documentation. Hundreds and hundreds of pages of AutoCAD help and information are right on the AutoCAD CD-ROM. More is on the Learning Assistance CD-ROM that comes free with AutoCAD. Look in the online help first!

The World Wide Web

The World Wide Web is a hot topic of conversation, well, worldwide, and it's becoming a great resource for CAD use (and has now overtaken CompuServe, which had long been the top stop online for AutoCAD users). You really need Web access to be an effective CAD user — you'll miss out on too many support and information resources if you don't have it. If you get CompuServe, you get both Web access and access to the CompuServe ACAD forum. See Chapter 18 for detailed info.

GO ACAD

CompuServe was, for many years, the #1 hangout on the Information Superhighway for AutoCAD users. After you're on CompuServe, GO ACAD is the command you use to get to the AutoCAD forum. Use CompuServe together with the Web to get quick answers to technical questions from experts.

Introductory CompuServe memberships are included with many hardware and software purchases, and you can purchase a CompuServe starter kit in many stores. You can also order a kit by calling CompuServe's customer service at 800–848–8990. Or download the software from CompuServe's Web page at `www.compuserve.com`. You can also call this number to find out about membership fees, log-in numbers, and more.

CADALYST and CADENCE Magazines

Although AutoCAD is no doubt responsible for billions of dollars in sales of PC hardware and related software, most of the computer press tends to ignore AutoCAD. *CADALYST* and *CADENCE* are the leading magazines devoted exclusively to AutoCAD. Both magazines provide tips and tricks, tutorials, technical columns, and hardware and software reviews, all specifically for CAD users.

To subscribe to *CADALYST,* call 800–949–6525. To subscribe to *CADENCE,* call 800–486–4995.

AutoCAD Resource Guide

This handy little manual includes an overview of the different AutoCAD versions and supporting computer platforms, third-party add-on applications and their developers, peripheral devices, books and training products, a directory of users' groups, and a directory of Autodesk Training Centers (ATCs). The book also contains a CD-ROM version with additional product information, device drivers, and more. (The information is also available on the Autodesk Web site, but having the printed version handy when you need it is nice.) To get the AutoCAD Resource Guide, go to the Autodesk Web site at www.autodesk.com and look for the AutoCAD Resource Guide link, or call Autodesk customer information at 800–964–6432.

Local Users' Groups

Local users' groups are the heart and soul of the AutoCAD community. One of the authors has been co-chairman of the San Francisco AutoCAD Users Group; the other has attended several and remembers a meeting of the Silicon Valley AutoCAD Power Users group, in San Jose, California, as the biggest and best-organized user's group meeting he's ever attended. Find out where the users' group nearest you meets and go to a few meetings. Call Autodesk at 800–964–6432 or look in the AutoCAD Resource Guide to locate the group nearest you.

AUGI

No, "AUGI" isn't what you yell after a basketball hits you in the wrong spot. The Autodesk User Group International is administered by Autodesk, but it's a real users' group made up of real users, dealers, and other concerned individuals. AUGI sponsors an annual learning conference (Autodesk University), a newsletter, software, and more. To join, see its Web site at www.augi.com or call the User Group Hotline at 415–507–6565.

AutoCAD Training Centers

AutoCAD Training Centers, or ATCs, are the only authorized deliverers of AutoCAD training. Courses are expensive, so make sure to clear your schedule and give the class your full attention when you do go. Check the AutoCAD Resource Guide, call Autodesk, or check out the Autodesk home page on the Web for the number of the ATC nearest you. Training from AutoCAD dealers, consultants, or local community colleges are other options.

Autodesk

In our experience, Autodesk is more accessible than most big companies. Its main numbers are 415–507–6000 and 800–964–6432. Call and tell someone there what you're looking for; you're pretty likely to reach a friendly and helpful reception person who connects you to another friendly and helpful person who gives you the information you need or tells you where to find it.

The big exception to Autodesk's accessibility is technical support. AutoCAD depends on its dealers to provide technical support, so don't call Autodesk with technical questions; call your dealer instead. And use Autodesk's Web site for online technical support, FAQs (Frequently Asked Questions documents), and downloadable software patches and tools.

Your Dealer

The first and foremost line of support for AutoCAD users is the dealer from whom you bought AutoCAD. Dealer support policies and areas of expertise differ, but the dealer is your starting point for AutoCAD support and information.

If you're using AutoCAD within a multiuser, networked setup, though, find out whether someone in your company has been designated as the first line of defense for technical support and other information. Contact that person first with your questions.

Plus One: Express Tools

Number 11 in your list of ten great AutoCAD resources is the set of Express tools on the AutoCAD CD-ROM. You can have literally hours of fun exploring the tools for layer management, text, dimensioning, and more in the Express tools menu. And you can have the AutoCAD installer include them in your AutoCAD 2000 setup by choosing the Complete installation, or by selecting Custom installation and choosing to include Express tools.

Chapter 18

Ten Ways to Use the Web with AutoCAD

The World Wide Web is the biggest thing to hit computing since possibly the PC itself. AutoCAD 2000 includes enough Web features to let you go as far as you'd like in integrating the Web into your daily work.

Getting on the Web

Though it seems as though the Web must be everywhere from all the discussion about it, that's not entirely true. Only a bit more than half the PCs in North America are connected to the Internet, and the percentage is even lower elsewhere. If you're not, now is the time to get connected — even if you use your PC only to run AutoCAD and think that Microsoft Word, for instance, is a frivolous distraction. The Internet is now so widely used that you're just left out of the loop too much if you're not online. Not only is extensive technical support available online, but your colleagues and friends are going to want to send you e-mail and AutoCAD drawing files over the Internet.

Getting online can be a pretty complicated topic when you consider that, as an AutoCAD user, you are likely to have big files to send; and if you have big files to send, you may want a fast connection such as Digital Subscriber Line (DSL), a cable modem, or, for a multi-person office, a dedicated phone line such as a T-1 line. To get connected quickly, establish a dial-up Internet account that you connect to with a modem — it should cost about $20 per month whether you choose an ordinary Internet Service Provider (ISP) or CompuServe (see Chapter 17 for more about CompuServe.). But if you have larger concerns, such as getting an office wired quickly, consider hiring a consultant to handle the messy details for you.

Getting the Right System

Any computer system capable of running AutoCAD 2000 is capable of running Web access software; as an AutoCAD 2000 user, you have the right kind of computer (100 MHz Pentium or better), the right amount of RAM (32 MB or more), the right amount of hard disk space free for swap and cache files (50 MB or more), and the right-size screen (800 x 600 resolution or better). To run a Web browser at the same time as AutoCAD, add 32 MB more RAM — and don't be surprised if your system crashes more often while doing this.

Surfing Defensively

A quick but vital tip: Save your drawings before you start running any Internet access program or Web browser, including CompuServe. The race between Microsoft and Netscape to lead Web browser development, and the simultaneous race among online services to provide fast access and the latest and greatest features, mean that plenty of buggy and crash-prone Internet software is getting sent out there right now. So save early and often if you're going to be running AutoCAD and any kind of Internet connection at the same time.

Opening Your Web Browser from AutoCAD

Like Release 14, AutoCAD 2000 includes the BROWSER command for opening your browser from within AutoCAD. Although doing so is something of a stupid pet trick — there's no reason you can't take an extra step and launch your browser from Windows — it does underscore Autodesk's desire to bring the World Wide Web into its programs. AutoCAD 2000 also includes a new Search the Web button on most file dialog boxes so that you can open drawings and other CAD content over the Internet or an intranet.

Putting URLs in Your Drawings

You can now more easily put URLs — Uniform Resource Locators, that is, Web addresses such as `www.dummies.com` — in your AutoCAD drawings. Just use the Insert⇨Hyperlink command to create and manage the Web links, which are stored as object properties. (See Chapter 14 for more on properties.)

We encourage you to put URLs in drawings that are published on the Internet or an intranet. We are conservative enough, though, to discourage you from putting URLs in ordinary drawings that are viewed and modified by using AutoCAD. Why? Not everyone has a reliable connection to the Web at all times. Drawings stored on your company intranet become inaccessible when a document goes outside your organization; drawings stored on a public Web site may be moved without your being notified. There is nothing more frustrating than for you or others to be unable to print, sell, or build using your drawing file because a piece of it has become inaccessible. Be careful before putting URLs in your drawings.

Looking for the HyperLink Cursor

If you pass the AutoCAD cursor over an object with an attached hyperlink, a little globe icon shows up next to the cursor. This icon tells you that the object has a hyperlink property, and if you pause the cursor for a moment, a yellow ToolTip displays the URL. If you right-click the object, the cursor menu displays a Hyperlink submenu with choices for opening the link in your Web browser, editing the URL, or copying the link to other objects.

Sharing AutoCAD Drawings on the Web with ePlot

The AutoCAD DWG format works well for storing drawing information on local and network disks, but the high precision and large number of object properties that AutoCAD uses make for comparatively large files.

In order to overcome this size problem and encourage people to publish drawings on the Web, Autodesk developed an alternative format for representing AutoCAD drawings: DWF (Drawing Web Format). A DWF file is a more compact representation of a DWG file. DWF uses less space — and less transfer time over the Web — because it's less accurate and doesn't have all of the information in the DWG file. It can also be viewed by people who don't have AutoCAD; see the next section for details.

AutoCAD Release 14 included a simple command called DWFOUT for writing a representation of the current drawing to a DWF file. AutoCAD 2000 does away with the DWFOUT command and instead incorporates DWF file creation into the new Plot dialog box. AutoCAD 2000 treats DWF files like "electronic plots," or ePlots. You create a DWF file from the current drawing just as if you were plotting it to a piece of paper. The only difference is that, on the Plot dialog box's Plot Device tab, you choose the plotter configuration named "DWF ePlot.pc3." When you do so, AutoCAD automatically turns on the Plot to file setting, and you can specify a filename and location for the DWF file that gets created. The location can be a folder on a hard disk or a Web site. See Chapter 9 for more information on using the Plot dialog box. Look up "ePlot" in the AutoCAD online help and "Concept: ePlot" in the Concepts section of the Learning Assistance CD to find out more about creating and using DWF files.

DWF files open up all kinds of interesting possibilities for sharing your drawings — or electronically plotted representations of them, anyway — with others. For example, you can present your work to prospective clients, post a current set of drawings on the Web for review by clients and subcontractors, or create a drawing library that co-workers can browse over the office intranet.

Only a minority of Web users are going to have the WHIP! ActiveX control or plug-in installed. Only a few of the most popular plug-ins have been installed by more than a tiny percentage of Web users. However, a pretty good percentage of AutoCAD users may well take the plunge. If you do publish a DWF file on the Web, include detailed instructions on how the user can get and install the WHIP! plug-in (see the section "Getting AutoCAD Information on the Web," later in this chapter, for the URL).

Installing the WHIP! Plug-In or ActiveX Control

To see AutoCAD DWF files from within your browser, you need the WHIP! plug-in (for Netscape Navigator) or ActiveX control (for Microsoft Internet Explorer).

If you use Internet Explorer, you're in luck; the needed version of the ActiveX control is automatically downloaded to and installed on your machine the first time you access a page with a DWF file in it. If you're a Microsoft hater, or you just prefer to use Netscape Navigator, point your Web browser to the WHIP! area of Autodesk's Web site — listed in the next section — and download and install the current version of the WHIP! plug-in.

At the time of this writing, WHIP! is expected to be replaced, for AutoCAD 2000 users, by Volo View Express!; check the Volo Web site at www.autodesk.com/products/index.htm for details.

Getting AutoCAD Information on the Web

The Web is a great source for information about AutoCAD, having recently moved ahead of CompuServe and getting better every day. Here are a few URLs to get you started:

- ✔ www.autodesk.com/products/whip/ Learn about and download the WHIP! plug-in

- ✔ www.cadonline.com/sv.htm *CADALYST* magazine Solution Columns, including several columns by one of the authors of this book on CAD standards and drawing exchange

- ✔ www.power.org/ The Silicon Valley AutoCAD Power User's Web site with AutoCAD resources, including SVAPU's latest newsletters

- ✔ www.autodesk.com/support/discsgrp The Autodesk on-line discussion groups for AutoCAD and other Autodesk products

- ✔ www.gsfeng.com/ Graphic Solutions for Engineers, the site of this book's technical editor, Ron Morin. Ron's site has cool tools and pointers to useful information for CAD users in general and AutoCAD-using engineers specifically

- ✔ users.uniserve.com/~ralphg/ upFront.eZine, a shareware weekly e-mail newsletter by Ralph Grabowski describing what's going on in the CAD world

- ✔ The Autodesk locator for your nearby *ATC* (AutoCAD Training Center)

Web site URLs change frequently. If any of these URLs doesn't work, try going to the home page of the company or organization (for example, www.autodesk.com) and then look for an appropriate link or use the Web site's search function to find what you're looking for.

Chatting about AutoCAD on the Web (Autodesk's Site)

At the Autodesk Web site (www.autodesk.com/support/discsrp), you can find pointers to Web-based online newsgroups about AutoCAD 2000 and other topics. If you want to chat about AutoCAD, this is the place! You may feel a touch inhibited, knowing that Autodesk not only reads the forums but also runs them, but don't worry; Autodesk just uses these forums as input to help create better versions of AutoCAD, and the folks there really won't "forget" to send you your next AutoCAD upgrade on time if you criticize them too much.

Creating Your Own Web Pages

The biggest single reason for the Web's popularity is that anyone, and that does mean anyone, can put a Web page or a Web site up. Here comes some self-serving self-promotion: As the co-author of *Creating Web Pages For Dummies,* 4th Edition, one of the authors of this book has discovered many free and easy ways to get a Web site up and running on the Web. If you want to try the most popular self-publishing sites on the Web on your own, go to www.geocities.com and follow the instructions; you can probably get a simple, free Web site up and running within a couple of hours. For detailed instructions and descriptions of the best Web publishing options and tools, buy the book!

Part VI

Appendixes

The 5th Wave — By Rich Tennant

@RICHTENNANT

"That reminds me - I installed AutoCAD 2000 on my 386 last week."

In this part . . .

In your body, an appendix is something that's unnecessary at best and hazardous to your health at worst. The appendixes in this book, however, are meant to be more helpful — and certainly less harmful — than that other kind. As you soon discover, getting your drawing to print at just the right size and scale is tricky; ah, but the tables in Appendix A make setting everything up for optimal printing . . . well, a snap. You find, too, as you get into the program that AutoCAD has a vocabulary all its own. The glossary in Appendix B should help you cross the bridge from English to the language of CAD.

Appendix A

Paper Size and Scale

· ·

*T*he standard American paper sizes are called A, B, C, D, and E. The measurements of the sizes for ANSI (American National Standards Institute) standards are described in the following list:

- ✔ ANSI *A* = 8 ½ x 11". Standard letter size in the U.S.
- ✔ ANSI *B* = 11 x 17". Double the length of *A* paper.
- ✔ ANSI *C* = 17 x 22". Double the length and width of *A* paper.
- ✔ ANSI *D* = 22 x 34". Double the length and width of *B* paper.
- ✔ ANSI *E* = 34 x 44". Double the length and width of *C* paper.

Note that each ANSI size folded in half has the same dimensions as the next smaller size.

Not all industries use ANSI paper sizes, even in the United States. The building industry, including architectural and structural engineering companies, often use so-called "architectural sheet sizes" which — confusingly — have the same letter names as the ANSI sheet sizes, but slightly larger dimensions, as shown in the following list:

- ✔ Architectural *A* = 9 x 12"
- ✔ Architectural *B* = 12 x 18"
- ✔ Architectural *C* = 18 x 24"
- ✔ Architectural *D* = 24 x 36"
- ✔ Architectural *E* = 36 x 48"

Outside the United States, the most common paper sizes are designated by ISO (the International Standards Organization) as shown in the following list:

- ✔ *A4* = 210 x 297 mm
- ✔ *A3* = 297 x 420 mm
- ✔ *A2* = 420 x 594 mm
- ✔ *A1* = 594 x 841 mm
- ✔ *A0* = 841 x 1189 mm

If you're called upon to use metric sheet sizes on a project and, like most Americans, you still have trouble "thinking metric," you can convert the ISO sizes to inches by dividing the millimeter sizes by 25.4.

Figure A-1 shows how the various standard paper sizes relate to one another.

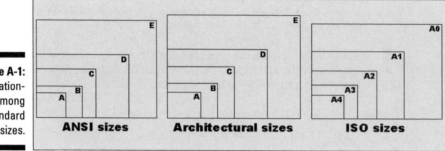

Figure A-1: Relationships among standard paper sizes.

Use the ANSI size relationships among the various paper sizes to your advantage in doing small check prints of large drawings. You can, for example, perform a check print with correct proportions and layout for either *C* or *E* paper on plain old letter-sized *A* paper on a standard laser printer. (Your check print, of course, lacks the color and detail that appears on the full-sized plot.)

For a *C* final plot, your *A* check print has measurements half the size of the final; for an *E* plot, the *A* check print has measurements a quarter the size of the final version. (But don't do a check print to take down to the bank and try to cash!)

Unfortunately, the architectural sheet sizes don't exhibit a correspondingly tidy relationship. Thus, when you're doing smaller check plots on architectural sheets, you often have to plot to fit and live with the fact that the plot scale isn't an easy-to-use number.

The paper size and the real-world size of the objects you want to represent in your drawing are the determining factors in setting up the parameters for your drawing. Another limitation is the use of certain standard drawing scales. You generally can't pick an unusual drawing scale such as ⅟₃₂" = 1' or 35 mm = 1 m just because it makes the drawing fit on the paper nicely. If you're using architectural units, you usually want to use a 1 in the drawing scale's numerator, or upper part of the fraction, and an even multiple of two in the drawing scale denominator, or lower part of the fraction. Examples of drawing scales that fit these rules are ½", ¼", ⅛", ⅟₁₆", ⅟₃₂", ⅟₆₄", and so on, to 1'.

(Hope this stuff doesn't become "2" confusing.) After you know the real-world sizes of the objects, the paper size, and the drawing scale, you can choose the limits you want to use.

Of course, in real life, you may have some flexibility in the paper size and drawing scale, depending on what lets you fit a given set of objects conveniently. So knowing all the possibilities is very helpful, and that's what the tables in this chapter are for.

The tables show you many of the combinations of paper size, drawing scale, and limits that you're likely to want to use with ANSI sheet sizes. You can review the tables and discover what works for your drawing. Table A-1 is for units in feet and inches; Table A-2 is for any unit of measurement that works by powers of ten.

In addition to columns for paper size, drawing scale, and limits, the tables include columns for grid distance, snap distance, and linetype and dimension scale. These columns can help you set up your drawing so that everything works together. The grid distance and snap distance aren't too important, because you can easily change them as your needs change during the drawing process. But linetype and dimension scale do matter. Getting these settings correct from the start can greatly ease the process of printing a usable drawing. Use the values listed in these tables as a handy guide.

The number in the Linetype and Dimension Scale column is the *drawing scale factor:* the number that you multiply the left side of the drawing scale by to get the right side. Depending on which linetypes you're using and how they look when you print them out, you may want to use a value that's half the drawing scale factor for linetypes.

If you don't find the exact combination you're looking for in this table, it's not too difficult to calculate your own limits or required drawing scale factors. If you know the sheet size and drawing scale factor, multiply the sheet's dimensions (X and Y) by the drawing scale factor in order to calculate the drawing limits. Conversely, if you know the sheet size and real-world size of what you're going to draw, divide the needed real-world drawing area dimensions (X and Y) by the sheet's dimensions (X and Y). Take the larger number (X or Y will control) and round up to the nearest "real" drawing scale factor (that is, one that's commonly used in your industry). See Chapter 4 of this book for example calculations.

In most cases, the plottable area for your drawing will be slightly smaller than the physical sheet size because of the small margin required by most plotters and printers. For example, a Hewlett-Packard LaserJet III has a printable area of about 7.9" x 10.5" on an 8.5" x 11" ANSI A size (letter size) sheet.

Table A-1 Picking Limits — Architectural Units, Horizontal Orientation

Paper Size	*Drawing Scale*	*Limits*	*Grid*	*Snap*	*Linetype & Dimension Scale*
8 ½" x 11"	1/64" = 1'	704 x 544'	64'	10'	768
8 ½" x 11"	1/32" = 1'	352 x 272'	32'	10'	384
8 ½" x 11"	1/16" = 1'	176 x 136'	16'	5'	192
8 ½" x 11"	⅛" = 1'	88 x 68'	8'	5'	96
8 ½" x 11"	¼" = 1'	44 x 34'	4'	1'	48
8 ½" x 11"	½" = 1'	22 x 17'	2'	1'	24
8 ½" x 11"	1" = 1'	11 x 8 ½'	1'	6"	12
11" x 17"	1/64" = 1'	704 x 1088'	64'	100'	768
11" x 17"	1/32" = 1'	352 x 544'	32'	10'	384
11" x 17"	1/16" = 1'	176 x 272'	16'	5'	192
11" x 17"	⅛" = 1'	88 x 136'	8'	5'	96
11" x 17"	¼" = 1'	44 x 68'	4'	1'	48
11" x 17"	½" = 1'	22 x 34'	2'	1'	24
11" x 17"	1" = 1'	11 x 17'	1'	6"	12
17" x 22"	1/64" = 1'	1408 x 1088'	64'	10'	768
17" x 22"	1/32" = 1'	704 x 544'	32'	10'	384
17" x 22"	1/16" = 1'	352 x 272'	16'	5'	192
17" x 22"	⅛" = 1'	176 x 136'	2'	5'	96
17" x 22"	¼" = 1'	88 x 68'	4'	1'	48
17" x 22"	½" = 1'	44 x 34'	2'	1'	24
17" x 22"	1" = 1'	22 x 17'	1'	6"	12
22" x 34"	1/64" = 1'	1408 x 2176'	64'	10'	768
22" x 34"	1/32" = 1'	704 x 1088'	32'	10'	384
22" x 34"	1/16" = 1'	352 x 544'	16'	5'	192
22" x 34"	⅛" = 1'	176 x 272'	8'	5'	96
22" x 34"	¼" = 1'	88 x 136'	4'	1'	48

Paper Size	*Drawing Scale*	*Limits*	*Grid*	*Snap*	*Linetype & Dimension Scale*
22″ x 34″	1/2″ = 1′	44 x 68′	2′	1′	24
22″ x 34″	1″ = 1′	22 x 34′	1′	6″	12
34″ x 44″	1/64″ = 1′	2816 x 2176′	64′	10′	768
34″ x 44″	1/32″ = 1′	1408 x 1088′	32′	10′	384
34″ x 44″	1/16″ = 1′	704 x 544′	16′	5′	192
34″ x 44″	1/8″ = 1′	352 x 272′	8′	5′	96
34″ x 44″	1/14″ = 1′	176 x 136′	4′	1′	48
34″ x 44″	1/2″ = 1′	88 x 68′	2′	1′	24
34″ x 44″	1″ = 1′	44 x 34′	1′	6″	12

Table A-2 Picking Limits — Mechanical and Other Units, Horizontal Orientation

Paper Size	*Drawing Scale*	*Limits*	*Grid*	*Snap*	*Linetype & Dimension Scale*
8 1/2″ x 11″	1/1000 = 1	11000 x 8500	1000	100	1000
8 1/2″ x 11″	1/500 = 1	5500 x 4250	500	50	500
8 1/2″ x 11″	1/100 = 1	1100 x 850	100	10	100
8 1/2″ x 11″	1/50 = 1	550 x 425	50	5	50
8 1/2″ x 11″	1/10 = 1	110 x 85	10	1	10
8 1/2″ x 11″	1/5 = 1	55 x 42.5	5	0.5	5
11″ x 17″	1/1000 = 1	17000 x 11000	1000	100	1000
11″ x 17″	1/500 = 1	8500 x 5500	500	50	500
11″ x 17″	1/100 = 1	1700 x 1100	100	10	100
11″ x 17″	1/50 = 1	850 x 550	50	5	50
11″ x 17″	1/10 = 1	170 x 110	10	1	10
11″ x 17″	1/5 = 1	85 x 55	5	0.5	5

Table A-2 *(Continued)*

Paper Size	Drawing Scale	Limits	Grid	Snap	Linetype & Dimension Scale
17" x 22"	$\frac{1}{1000} = 1$	22000 x 17000	1000	100	1000
17" x 22"	$\frac{1}{500} = 1$	11000 x 8500	500	50	500
17" x 22"	$\frac{1}{100} = 1$	2200 x 1700	100	10	100
17" x 22"	$\frac{1}{50} = 1$	1100 x 850	50	5	50
17" x 22"	$\frac{1}{10} = 1$	220 x 170	10	1	10
17" x 22"	$\frac{1}{5} = 1$	110 x 85	5	0.5	5
22" x 34"	$\frac{1}{1000} = 1$	34000 x 22000	1000	100	1000
22" x 34"	$\frac{1}{500} = 1$	17000 x 11000	500	50	500
22" x 34"	$\frac{1}{100} = 1$	3400 x 2200	100	10	100
22" x 34"	$\frac{1}{50} = 1$	1700 x 1100	50	5	50
22" x 34"	$\frac{1}{10} = 1$	340 x 220	10	1	10
22" x 34"	$\frac{1}{5} = 1$	170 x 110	5	0.5	5
34" x 44"	$\frac{1}{1000} = 1$	44000 x 34000	1000	100	1000
34" x 44"	$\frac{1}{500} = 1$	22000 x 17000	500	50	500
34" x 44"	$\frac{1}{100} = 1$	4400 x 3400	100	10	100
34" x 44"	$\frac{1}{50} = 1$	2200 x 1700	50	5	50
34" x 44"	$\frac{1}{10} = 1$	440 x 340	10	1	10
34" x 44"	$\frac{1}{5} = 1$	220 x 170	5	0.5	5

Appendix B

Glossary of AutoCAD Terms

• •

*T*he definitions that appear in this appendix are informal and describe each term in the way that this book uses it. For more complete and general definitions, see the AutoCAD on-line or printed documentation — especially the glossary at the end of the AutoCAD 2000 *User's Guide*.

3DOrbit: A new feature in AutoCAD 2000 that allows you to easily rotate shaded objects to view them from different angles.

aerial view: A separate window that displays a "navigational window" for moving around in your drawing. As you pan and zoom within the Aerial View window, the main drawing area also pans and zooms.

Angle 0 Direction: Specifies the direction that AutoCAD regards as 0 degrees within a 360-degree circle. The default Angle 0 Direction is east, or toward the right. You can tell AutoCAD to use a different direction as 0 degrees.

ANSI: American National Standards Institute, a leading standards body.

AUGI: Autodesk User Group International, the worldwide user group for AutoCAD and other programs from Autodesk.

AutoCAD DesignCenter: That's not a typo; Autodesk really has munged "Design" and "Center," two perfectly respectable words that do plenty of heavy lifting in English, into a single made-up word. (Possibly so that Autodesk can trademark it.) AutoCAD DesignCenter lists components within a drawing, such as blocks, xrefs, linetypes, text styles, and layers, so that you can import them into other drawings.

There may be a special circle of linguistic Hell reserved for the inventor and the users of intercaps, capital letters stuck in the middle of words such as DesignCenter. For some reason, the generally sensible computer industry has made a habit of using intercaps in various names. Use them at your own risk.

AutoLISP: A programming language for AutoCAD based on LISP, a computer language used mostly in artificial intelligence programming.

AutoSnap: A new feature in Release 14 that makes connecting objects to specific spots on other objects — such as the endpoint of a line or the center of a circle — much easier.

AutoTracking: A new feature in Release 2000 that reduces the need for temporary construction lines by making it easier to pick points that have specific relationships to existing geometry, such as points that are horizontal or vertical from the endpoint of an existing line.

batch plotting: The capability, new in AutoCAD Release 14, to plot several drawings at one time instead of having to send each plot to the printer or plotter separately.

blips: Little marks that show spots you've "picked" on-screen with the cursor. Turn the BLIPMODE system variable ON if you want the screen to show blips, OFF if you want to get rid of them.

bounding rectangle, bounding window: A rectangle surrounding objects. When you select objects with a bounding window, AutoCAD includes only objects that are fully enclosed within the window. See also *crossing window.*

CAD: Computer-Aided Drafting or Design. Also known as CADD, or Computer-Aided Design and Drafting. The term CAD is now used to describe activities that include computer-aided design, computer-aided drafting, or both.

chamfer: A straight line that connects two other lines short of the point where they would intersect.

command line: A specific area of the AutoCAD screen, usually at the bottom, in which AutoCAD prompts you for the information it needs, and you enter commands and options. Many menu choices in AutoCAD also cause commands to appear on the command line.

command-first editing: Modifying the current drawing by entering a command and then selecting the objects that the command affects. The opposite of *selection-first editing.* See also *Noun/Verb Selection.*

coordinate entry: Locating a point in the drawing by entering numbers on the command line that represent the point's coordinates. See also *cursor coordinates.*

crossing window: A selection window that includes objects that are enclosed within it or that cross the window's boundaries. See also *bounding window.*

cursor coordinates: The location of the cursor as represented by its horizontal, or *X,* coordinate and its vertical, or *Y,* coordinate.

dialog box: A set of related options that are displayed on-screen in a rectangular window, or box, for you to specify or change.

digitizer: A drawing tablet. The name comes from the fact that the tablet converts lines and curves that are entered by drawing, into a series of numbers (or digits).

dimension: A set of drawn objects including lines, numbers, and additional symbols and text to indicate the distance between two points.

dimension line: The line that shows the extent of a dimension.

dimension scale factor: The number by which the size of the text and arrowheads in a dimension are scaled in order for them to appear correctly in the final printout of a drawing.

dimension text: The text that denotes the actual measurement of a dimension (for example, length or angle).

direct distance entry: An efficient way of picking a point that lies a particular direction and distance from the previous point. You simply point the cursor in the desired direction (usually with ortho mode turned on), type a distance at the command line, and press Enter.

direct manipulation: Entering or modifying data by using the mouse to move or change an on-screen representation. Dragging a file icon into a trash can icon to discard it, for example, is direct manipulation.

displacement: Fancy word for the X and Y distance between two points.

display list: A set of directions that AutoCAD uses for displaying the current open drawing and viewport on-screen.

docked: Embedded in the program's interface. A docked toolbar is a toolbar that has been dragged to any edge of the program window until it "connects" itself to that window. A docked toolbar has no title, and the area around the title has no color, so it takes up less space. See also *toolbar*.

Draw toolbar: A toolbar that enables you to start commonly used drawing commands quickly. Usually found on the far left side of the drawing area.

drawing area: The part of the AutoCAD screen that you can actually draw on. It's an all-too-small area wedged between the menus, toolbars, and command line.

endpoint: One of the two terminating points of a line or polyline.

extension line: In dimensioning, a line connecting one end of the dimension line to one end of the object being dimensioned.

fill: The pattern used in filling (placing a pattern in the interior of an object). See also *hatch, boundary hatch, associative boundary hatch*.

floating toolbars: Groups of icons that you can drag around on-screen and that always appear — or float — over the drawing. Each icon represents an AutoCAD command.

geometry: The drawn objects that make up a drawing, not including additional elements such as dimensions and text.

grid interval: The distance between grid points. See also *grid, grid mode*.

grid, grid mode: A grid is a visible array of dots used to indicate distances on-screen. The grid is intended to serve as a kind of flexible graph paper in which the user can, at any time, redefine the size of the grid. Grid mode is either on (that is, grid dots displayed) or off (grid dots not displayed). AutoCAD never plots the grid — it's for display purposes only.

grip editing: Editing an object by dragging one of the "handles," or grips, that appear on an object after you select it. See also *grips — hot, warm, cold*.

grips — hot, warm, cold: A hot grip is the grip that you can directly manipulate; it appears on-screen in red. A warm grip is any other grip on a currently selected object. A cold grip is a grip on an unselected object.

hatch, boundary hatch, associative boundary hatch: A hatch is a pattern placed in the interior of an area enclosed by objects. A boundary hatch is a hatch that is begun by calculating the boundary from among the objects surrounding an empty space. An associative boundary hatch is a hatch that updates automatically if one or more of the objects that make up its boundary is modified.

Internet: A worldwide computer network that connects (via modem) universities, government bodies, companies, and individuals.

ISO: International Standards Organization, a leading standards body.

layer: A group of objects that are associated for purposes of displaying, plotting, editing, and controlling properties (color, linetype, lineweight, and plot style).

leader: A pointer that connects a dimension or note to an object.

linetype: The pattern of dashes, dots, and spaces used to display objects.

menu bar: The list of menu names displayed across the top of the AutoCAD screen.

model space: The mode in which most AutoCAD work takes place; where you create and edit most of objects in your drawing. See also *paper space*.

Modify toolbar: A toolbar that enables you to start commonly used editing commands quickly. Usually found on the left side of the drawing area, just inside the Draw toolbar.

multiline: A group of two or more parallel lines that behave as a single object. You must use special commands to create and edit multilines.

Multiple Design Environment (MDE): A somewhat grandiose name for the ability of AutoCAD to let you work on several open drawings simultaneously.

named objects: Nongraphical elements such as layers, block definitions, linetypes, text styles, and dimension styles that live in each drawing and provide properties and other characteristics of graphical objects.

Noun/Verb Selection: An option that allows most commands to operate on an existing selection set. With Noun/Verb Selection turned off, the commands that you enter ignore any existing selection set, and you must select one or more objects after entering the command.

object: A single item that you can select and edit separately. In older versions of AutoCAD, objects were called *entities*.

Object Grouping: An option that enables you to place objects into named groups. The group of objects then behaves as a single object for the purposes of copying, moving, and erasing.

Object Properties toolbar: A toolbar that enables you to view and specify object properties, such as layer and linetype, with little or no keyboard entry.

object snap: Makes certain points on an object act like magnets so that clicking near a point is the same as clicking the point itself.

ortho, ortho mode: A setting that forces lines to be drawn horizontally or vertically only.

pan: Panning is moving the drawing around (without changing the zoom factor) so that a different part of the drawing appears on-screen in the current viewport.

paper space: A different mode for working with your drawing that enables you to compose a particular plotted view of your drawing, complete with title block. Paper space also can present different views and plotting styles of the same drawing. See also *model space*.

polygon: What your 3-year-old says when your parrot dies. (Groan!) Seriously, any closed shape made up of three or more line segments. Triangles, rectangles, pentagons, hexagons, and other multisided shapes are examples of polygons. The AutoCAD POLYGON command draws closed polyline objects.

polyline: A single object made up of multiple line or arc segments.

Press and Drag: Specifies that you can create a selection rectangle by pressing the left mouse button at one point, holding the button down while moving the mouse, and then releasing the button at a second point. (Moving the mouse with the button held down is called dragging.)

RAM: Random-Access Memory. The memory that your computer can access quickly and use as a "scratch pad" while working. AutoCAD 2000 requires at least 32 MB (MB is for *megabytes,* or million characters) of RAM, but 64 MB (or more) is better.

raster image: An image made up of a bunch of dots, as opposed to the typical CAD *vector* image, which is made up of a bunch of lines. A scanned photograph is an example of a raster image.

real-time pan and zoom: The capability, added to the ZOOM command in Release 14, to pan and zoom smoothly by dragging the mouse.

redraw: Clears the screen and redraws the drawing by using the current display list. See also *display list.*

regeneration (REGEN): Clears the screen and uses the drawing database to create a new display list and then redraws the drawing with the new display list. A *regen,* as it is referred to, can take from a fraction of a second on simple drawings to many minutes on complex drawings.

SCSI: Small Computer System Interface. Affectionately known as "scuzzy," a method for connecting peripheral devices, such as hard disks and tape drives, to the computer.

selection set: A set, or group, of objects that you have selected.

selection settings: Options that affect how selections are made and treated, such as Press and Drag and Noun/Verb Selection.

selection window: A window used to create a selection. See also *bounding window* and *crossing window.*

selection-first editing: Editing by first creating a selection and then entering a command that affects the selected objects. Opposite of *command-first editing.*

side-screen menu: A menu of options that appears on-screen, usually in a strip down the right side of the screen. All but obsolete now.

snap grid: If snap mode is on, the snap grid is the array of imaginary points that the cursor jumps to, based on the *snap interval.*

snap interval: The distance between snap points if snap mode is on.

snap, snap mode: A mode that causes the cursor to be attracted to points on-screen that are a specified distance apart.

solid fill: Your trustworthy friend Philip. Also, a type of hatch pattern added in Release 14 that fills an area with a color.

spline: A flexible type of curve that has a shape defined by control points.

Standard toolbar: A toolbar with icons for commonly used functions such as opening a file. Usually found near the top of the screen, between the menu bar and the Object Properties toolbar.

Startup dialog box: The dialog box that appears when you start a new AutoCAD session by double-clicking on the AutoCAD icon, rather than by double-clicking on a drawing. The Startup dialog box gives you several choices for creating a drawing, including using a wizard to help with setup or creating a drawing from a template.

status bar: A "toolbar," always positioned at the bottom of the screen, that displays information about the current AutoCAD session, such as the current coordinates of the cursor and whether ortho mode is in effect. You can change many options by clicking or right-clicking the status bar's icons.

system variable: A setting that controls the way that a particular aspect of AutoCAD works. You can change system variables by typing their names at the command line, or, less obtusely, by choosing various dialog box options that are linked to the system variables.

tangent: A tangent point on a circle is the only point at which a line at a specific angle to and direction from the circle can touch the circle.

template: An AutoCAD drawing that serves as a starting point for new drawings. When you create a new drawing from a template drawing, AutoCAD creates a new drawing using the contents and settings of the template file.

text height: The height of text, in the same units that are currently in effect for the drawing.

third-party application: A program that works with or within AutoCAD.

title bar: The strip across the top of the program window that displays the name of the program and the currently active drawing if it is maximized.

title block: An area on a drawing that is set aside for descriptive information about the drawing, such as the company name, project name, drafter's name, and so on.

ToolTip or tooltip: A descriptive word or phrase that appears on-screen if you hold the cursor over an icon for a brief period of time.

TrueType fonts: A kind of font that is standard within Microsoft Windows. TrueType fonts first appeared in Release 13 and are also supported, with better performance, in AutoCAD 2000.

UCS: User Coordinate System. The current coordinate system used to describe the location of objects.

UCS icon: The "X-Y" icon that appears in the lower-left corner of the drawing area to indicate the angle of the User Coordinate System.

Use Shift to Add: An option that determines what happens if a selection is already made when you click an object. If Use Shift to Add is turned on, you must press and hold the Shift key to add an additional item to the selection set; if this option is turned off, you must hold down the Shift key to remove a currently selected item from the selection set.

viewport: A window that displays part of a drawing.

Web, World Wide Web: A network of interconnected servers that support access to integrated text, graphics, and multimedia content.

Wizard: A form of online help in which you are taken through a series of steps to accomplish a goal, such as setting up a new drawing.

zoom: Zooming is moving the viewpoint closer to or farther from the drawing so that more or less of the drawing appears on-screen.

Index

YOUR ONLINE RESOURCE

WWW.DUMMIES.COM

Discover Dummies™ Online!

The *Dummies* Web Site is your fun and friendly online resource for the latest information about *...For Dummies*® books on all your favorite topics. From cars to computers, wine to Windows, and investing to the Internet, we've got a shelf full of *...For Dummies* books waiting for you!

Ten Fun and Useful Things You Can Do at www.dummies.com

1. Register this book and win!
2. Find and buy the *...For Dummies* books you want online.
3. Get ten great *Dummies Tips*™ every week.
4. Chat with your favorite *...For Dummies* authors.
5. Subscribe free to *The Dummies Dispatch*™ newsletter.
6. Enter our sweepstakes and win cool stuff.
7. Send a free cartoon postcard to a friend.
8. Download free software.
9. Sample a book before you buy.
10. Talk to us. Make comments, ask questions, and get answers!

Jump online to these ten
fun and useful things at
http://www.dummies.com/10useful

SURF THE NET

WWW.DUMMIES.COM

For other technology titles from IDG Books Worldwide, go to
www.idgbooks.com

Not online yet? It's easy to get started with *The Internet For Dummies*® 5th Edition, or *Dummies 101*®: *The Internet For Windows*® 98, available at local retailers everywhere.

IDG BOOKS WORLDWIDE

Find other *...For Dummies* books on these topics:
Business • Careers • Databases • Food & Beverages • Games • Gardening • Graphics
Hardware • Health & Fitness • Internet and the World Wide Web • Networking • Office Suites
Operating Systems • Personal Finance • Pets • Programming • Recreation • Sports
Spreadsheets • Teacher Resources • Test Prep • Word Processing

IDG BOOKS WORLDWIDE BOOK REGISTRATION

Register This Book and Win!

We want to hear from you!

Visit **http://my2cents.dummies.com** to register this book and tell us how you liked it!

- ✔ Get entered in our monthly prize giveaway.

- ✔ Give us feedback about this book — tell us what you like best, what you like least, or maybe what you'd like to ask the author and us to change!

- ✔ Let us know any other ...*For Dummies*® topics that interest you.

Your feedback helps us determine what books to publish, tells us what coverage to add as we revise our books, and lets us know whether we're meeting your needs as a ...*For Dummies* reader. You're our most valuable resource, and what you have to say is important to us!

Not on the Web yet? It's easy to get started with *Dummies 101*®: *The Internet For Windows*® *98* or *The Internet For Dummies*®, 5th Edition, at local retailers everywhere.

Or let us know what you think by sending us a letter at the following address:

...*For Dummies* Book Registration
Dummies Press
7260 Shadeland Station, Suite 100
Indianapolis, IN 46256-3917
Fax 317-596-5498

BESTSELLING BOOK SERIES